The Great Arizona
Orphan Abduction

The Great Arizona Orphan Abduction

LINDA GORDON

HARVARD UNIVERSITY PRESS

Cambridge, Massachusetts

Printed in the United States of America

Fifth printing, 2001

First Harvard University Press paperback edition, 2001

Library of Congress Cataloging-in-Publication Data
Gordon, Linda.
  The great Arizona orphan abduction / Linda Gordon.
    p. cm.
  Includes bibliographical references and index.
  ISBN 0-674-36041-9 (cloth : alk. paper)
  ISBN 0-674-00535-X (pbk.)
  1. Clifton (Ariz.)–Race relations. 2. Orphans–Arizona–
Clifton–History–20th century. 3. Kidnapping–Arizona–
Clifton–History–20th century. 4. Catholic Church–
Arizona–Clifton–History–20th century. 5. Mexican
Americans–Arizona–Clifton–History–20th century.
6. Whites–Arizona–Clifton–History–20th century.
7. Vigilantes–Arizona–Clifton–History–20th century.
I. Title.
F819.C55G67   1999
305.8′009791′51–dc21   99-30984

To see a World in a grain of sand . . .

–William Blake,
  "Auguries of Innocence"

Contents

Illustrations follow page 200.

Preface

The stories that stay with us, often the simplest in their narrative line, can also be the most complex in their multiple meanings. I think of children's tales like Hansel and Gretel or *Where the Wild Things Are,* which tell us about persecution and triumph, order and disorder, cowardice and bravery, and the strongest of passions, including particularly those between parents and children.

In the story that follows, the protagonists are not renowned or heroic. The small town they lived in is rarely mentioned in history books. But the issues about which these people fought remain with us today, unresolved. And although their story is virtually unremembered outside the town itself, yet it is packed with timeless and placeless meaning. It offers simultaneously universal and local knowledge. Just as all politics is ultimately local, so all rich narratives take on their meanings from the way in which universal motives interact with local contexts. This century-old conflict, small by most measures of historical importance, possesses great powers of revelation.

The dramatic events occurring in an Arizona mining boomtown in the year 1904 focused my imagination like a crystal whose facets each reflect light differently. It sent me on research paths I could not have previously imagined. As this narrative is rigorously a work of nonfiction, I could not make it fuller or embellish it beyond the evidence I had. I interpreted the evidence to explore its many meanings, but invented nothing.

I used this tale of the wild west to illuminate many aspects of the history of the U.S. southwest. The book spotlights Mexican-Anglo* relations at a moment when they intersected that most powerful of emotions, parental feeling for children. But to record that intersection fully, I had to focus my camera wide, to a panorama setting. To understand the participants' motivations it was necessary to show the expansive southwestern industrial frontier in which they lived: mining, company towns, Mexican immigration, class structure, labor conflict, racial conflict in the labor movement, and violence, particularly vigilantism. The narrative connects these typically male phenomena with the daily domestic and public lives of women, and by doing so shows how gender and family concerns contributed to racial boundaries.

This story contains a great deal that is saddening and infuriating, but it also contains some good news. It reveals how racial, ethnic, or nationalist fervor, furious as it may be, can also be transient and changeable.

---

*Throughout this book I use the term "Mexican" for people of Mexican ethnic origin, because that is what they were called in this place at the time, both in Spanish and in English. I use the terms "Anglo" and "white" interchangeably, for the same reason.

Cast of Principal Characters

From the New York Foundling Hospital:
  Sister Anna Michaella, assistant secretary
  G. Whitney Swayne, western placement agent
  Sister Teresa Vincent, head sister

From the Arizona Catholic Church:
  Henri Granjon, bishop of Tucson
  Constant Mandin, Clifton-Morenci parish priest

Law Enforcement Officials:
  James Parks, Graham County sheriff, Solomonville
  Johnnie Parks (his brother), deputy sheriff, Clifton
  Jeff Dunagan, deputy sheriff, Clifton
  Gus Hobbs, deputy sheriff, Morenci
  P. C. Little, probate judge, Solomonville

Clifton-Morenci Mexicans:
  Cornelio Chacón, smelter worker
  Margarita Chacón, teacher and foster mother
  Francisco Alvidrez, smelter worker
  Trancita Alvidrez, foster mother
  Rafael Holguín, smelter worker
  Josefa Holguín, seamstress and foster mother

Ramón Balles, shopkeeper
Baleria Balles, foster mother
Lee Windham, smelter worker
Refugia Windham, foster mother
Juan Esquivel, mill worker
Angela Flores, foster mother

Clifton-Morenci Anglos:
  Charles E. Mills, superintendent, Detroit Copper Company,
    Morenci
  James Colquhoun, superintendent, Arizona Copper Company,
    Clifton
  John Gatti, rancher and butcher, Clifton
  Louisa Gatti
  Jake Abraham, Clifton Hotel manager
  Mrs. Jake Abraham
  Sam Abraham, Clifton Hotel owner
  Laura (Mrs. Sam) Abraham
  George Frazer, smelter superintendent, Arizona Copper
    Company, Clifton
  Mrs. Frazer
  Neville Leggatt, deliveryman, Arizona Copper company store
  Tom Simpson, locomotive engineer, Clifton
  May (Mrs. Tom) Simpson
  Harry Wright, saloon owner, Clifton
  Muriel (Mrs. Harry) Wright
  A. M. Tuthill, M.D., Detroit Copper Company physician and state
    legislator, Morenci

Lawyers:
  Charles E. Miller, New York City, for the Foundling Hospital
  Eugene Semme Ives, Tucson, for the Foundling Hospital
  Thomas D. Bennett, Bisbee, for the Foundling Hospital
  Walter Bennett, Phoenix, for John Gatti et al.
  W. C. McFarland, Solomonville, for John Gatti et al.

The Great Arizona
Orphan Abduction

ARIZONA

NEW MEXICO

Phoenix
Gila R.
Globe/Miami
Metcalf
San Francisco R.
Morenci
Clifton
Solomonville
Silver City
Southern Pacific R.R.
Northern R.R.
Rio Grande R.

Tucson
S.P.R.R.
Lordsburg
N.M. & Ariz. R.R.
El Paso

N.M. &
Ariz. R.R.
Southwestern R.R.

Nogales
Bisbee
Douglas
Ciudad Juarez

MEXICO
Nogales
Cananea
Aqua
Prieta

NORTH
Nacozari
CHIHUAHUA

SONORA

Sonora R.R.

SONORAN HIGHLANDS
MINING REGION IN 1903
++++++++   Railroads
—··—··—   International Boundary
— — —   State Boundary
⚒   Mine   0   30
●   Town   Miles
[shaded]   Indian Reservations

Hermosillo

Guaymas

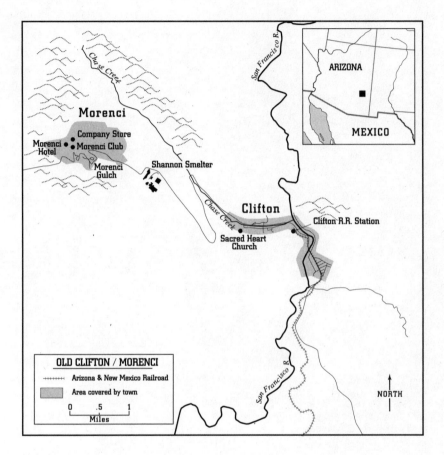

Chase Creek

San Francisco R.

Morenci

Company Store

Morenci
Hotel

Morenci Club

Morenci
Gulch

Shannon Smelter

Chase Creek

Clifton

Clifton R.R. Station

Sacred Heart
Church

San Francisco R

ARIZONA

MEXICO

OLD CLIFTON / MORENCI

+++++++ Arizona & New Mexico Railroad

Area covered by town

0   .5   1
Miles

NORTH

October 2, 1904, Night

North Clifton, Arizona

WHEN THE POSSE ARRIVED at Margarita Chacón's house at 11 P.M. on this rainy night, George Frazer, superintendent of the copper smelter, banged on the door with the butt of his Winchester. Neville Leggatt, the only member of the posse who actually knew Margarita, cringed; when she opened the door he kept his hand away from his revolver and hoped the others would do likewise. Leggatt knew exactly where to go because, he said, he knew every Mexican in North Clifton since he was delivery man for the company store. He didn't think there would be any trouble from Margarita. She was familiar to most of Clifton: a schoolteacher who taught the Mexican kids in her own home, a devout woman who went to church every day, dressed entirely in black, her face hidden under her shawl. Her husband, Cornelio, was a skimmer for the copper smelter, earning top wages for a Mexican. Frazer naturally did the talking for the posse. He said that she was to hand over the white orphans the priest had given her. She asked "if I had an order from the padre to take the child; but I said, No . . . the citizens of the town demand the children back."[1] The children were four-year-old Jerome Shanley and three-year-old Katherine Fitzpatrick, Irish Catholic orphans from New York City; they had been shipped out to Arizona on an orphan train to their new home with Señora Chacón as arranged by the padre. Frazer testified (later, at the trial) that she was "very obliging and accommodating" to the four armed men. But by that time Frazer was trying to avoid the impression that the men had taken the children by force. It is true that, after she kept them waiting in the wind and rain a while, she invited them in, seeing that they were already carrying three kids they had picked up from Francisco Alvidrez and from Lee Windham's Mexican wife whose name they didn't know. But Leggatt admitted that Margarita was not so obliging and pointed out that she took forty-five minutes to confer with her family and dress the two orphans before handing them over. In fact, he said she was the only one who did not want to give up the children. But then he also said that she was the only one who could speak English, and since his Spanish was extremely limited, it remains unclear how much resistance the posse encountered. From the Chacóns' the vigilantes went to take another child from the home of José Bonillas, so by the time they made their way back to the hotel the four men were carrying and pulling along six kids through the rain.

None of these people in a remote Arizona copper-mining camp could have anticipated that their actions would create front-page stories and editorials in newspapers throughout the United States or lead, eventually, to the U.S. Supreme Court. But even had they known, the possemen would not have hesitated because they believed so strongly that their cause was just: they could not have lived with themselves had they not rescued these toddlers from what they believed were foster homes so terrible as to constitute child abuse.

September 25, 1904

Grand Central Station, New York City

FIFTY-SEVEN EXCITED TODDLERS, or "run-arounds" as the nuns called them, aged two to six, squeezed three to a seat in a special tourist sleeping car as the westbound Pennsylvania Railroad pulled out.[1] With them were seven staff members from their Catholic institutional home, the New York Foundling Hospital: three members of the Sisters of Charity, who ran the home; four nurses; and one male child-placement agent. Waving from the platform were a few other sisters who had helped bring the children to the station in taxis. There each sister had kissed each of the children good-bye. One of the nuns cried, for she had grown attached to several whom she knew she would never see again, and this sister was a novice at these partings. The children did not cry because they did not understand the permanence of their departure from the only home they knew, but they were agitated. They had never been in a taxi or a train, of course, and they knew something momentous was happening because they had sensed the preparations for about a week.

These farewells happened several times a year. Only about a third of the approximately 35,000 children who had been in "the Foundling," as it was called, were placed out in this manner. The lucky children chosen for a western destiny, accustomed to hand-me-downs, got new and special clothing. A sister embroidered each child's name onto a collar, skirt hem, or coat lining. She then sewed a ribbon onto the collar, color-coded (pink, white, blue, yellow, brown) according to destination, since the orphan train would make several stops, and stitched onto it a number which corresponded to a number that had been mailed to a foster family.[2] When the children arrived at their new home, each foster family was to present this numbered card in order to collect its child. Along with each child went a letter:

> Dear Friends,
>   Within a week after the reception of the little one, will you please fill out the enclosed slip and forward it to us.
>   Please also to write us yearly about May 1st, how the little child is progressing, with any items of interest.
>   Wishing you many blessings for your kindness to the orphan, I am, in our dear Lord,
>   Yours respectfully,
>   Sr. Teresa Vincent[3]

On the appointed day, a great bell sounded in the main hall of the Foundling building and the various sisters led the deportees in neat lines to the center of the hall. The rest of the kids circled around them to offer a formal good-bye. An occasional journalist came to the Foundling to write about these well-publicized departures and even rode in a taxi with the children in the hopes of obtaining a touching quotation for a human-interest story. On September 25, 1904, several journalists, mainly from the Catholic press, gathered at the station. Head Sister Teresa Vincent made an upbeat send-off speech, right on the Grand Central departure platform, about the families and op-portunities the children would find in the West, followed by admoni-tions about virtue. The ceremony—for it was Sunday—concluded with prayers and a hymn, which also served the purpose of distracting the children from the sisters' emotional good-byes.

Sister Teresa Vincent never went west herself, but she supervised every detail of the foundling shipments; she knew every child's prove-nance and retained for herself the responsibility of final approval of the list of those to be sent. She was also careful to prepare a successor, and her heir was apparent: Sister Anna Michaella Bowen, assistant secre-tary of the Foundling, took charge on the trips, and her ambition and energy were beginning to be recognized and deferred to. The difficul-ties she was to encounter on this trip did not slow her ascent, perhaps even accelerated it. In just a few months she would become treasurer and assistant administrator of the Foundling, in which job she traveled throughout the Midwest and the South visiting foster homes, deter-

mined to maintain quality control over these placements. (She succeeded Sister Teresa Vincent as head administrator in 1917.) She dickered and parried confidently with bishops and lay charity officials,
maintaining the Foundling's autonomy as a female Catholic institution
and its power and resources as a premier child-saving institution of
New York. The first head of the Sisters of Charity to be born in the
United States, she had been educated in public school and normal
(teacher-training) school before taking her vows as a novice at age
twenty-two. Now forty-one, she was already a veteran of two decades
at the Foundling and worked with confidence and decisiveness.
Because of her managerial ability she had risen to outrank her two
older accompanying sisters. Ann Corsini Cross was a fifty-four-year-
old Irish immigrant who taught the kindergarten classes at the Foundling. Francis Liguori Keller, a French-born woman in her sixties, had
been with the Foundling since its establishment thirty-four years earlier, first as housekeeper, then sacristan. Much praised for her humility,
she was the perfect deputy to Anna Michaella and a favorite of the
children.[4]

By contrast, the Foundling's agent, George Whitney Swayne, was by
no means a good complement to the sister in charge.[5] He took care of
important details on the trips, arranging transportation and food, and
some of the sisters might have agreed that these negotiations were best
handled by a man. But his work was not always meticulous, and he
could be a nuisance because of his very presence and his personality.
Although he was an employee of the Sisters of Charity, subordinate to
Sister Anna Michaella on the placement trips, many people they dealt
with on the road—priests as well as parent applicants—treated him as
the boss. Their behavior sometimes demeaned Sister Anna and required her to signal her authority conspicuously. What's more, Swayne
was cocky in demeanor and ineffective as a negotiator when disagreements arose over the children's placements. In 1904, however, it would
not have been respectable for these women to travel without a male
escort.

The children to be exported were chosen for their promise, their
hardiness, and the unlikelihood that anyone in New York might try to
reclaim them. The sisters' usual practice was to place out foundlings
only after they reached the age of three. The mothers were required to
relinquish their legal rights upon placing children at the Foundling—a
rule meant especially to discourage married mothers from using the

home as a temporary placement for a child they could not afford—but the three years gave the mothers a long period of time in which to reclaim their children.[6] Although these Foundling children were often called orphans, most of them were not orphans in today's meaning of that term; rather, most were children turned over to the institution by poor lone mothers who could not afford to keep them. Such was Jerome Shanley, born on July 14, 1900, at a home for unwed mothers. His mother simply disappeared, and on August 21 a nurse from the home brought the one-month-old to the Foundling. Katherine Fitzpatrick had a different story: born September 9, 1901, in the charity wards of the Sloane Maternity Hospital in New York City, she stayed with her mother for six months until her mother personally surrendered her to the Foundling on March 25, 1902.[7] For these two children, the Foundling's records lack even the mothers' names. But we can make educated guesses about the mothers because of what is known about New York's dependent children in general: Irish immigrant or Irish American destitute mothers, most likely young in years if not in appearance, left alone with child because of out-of-wedlock birth or father's desertion, unable to support the child or to withstand the opprobrium of single motherhood.

A mother surrendering her baby could do so by placing him or her in a cradle in the reception area and, if she wished, could leave with no questions asked; or she could volunteer name, birth date, and health information. Some mothers wrote notes, such as:

> This is little Augusta, born January 30, 1870. O Crule Poverty.

> Dear Sister Irene, It gives me much pain to part with my boy, but circumstances oblige me to do so . . . I wish you would keep him in this home where you can look after him until I come to claim him. I wish you would put in the Herald Personals on Friday how he is getting along. . . I should like to have him called Charles.

> This child was born February 3, but has not been christened . . . The medicine the doctor left to give him when he is worrisome or has a stomach ache.[8]

Or a desperate woman could come in while pregnant: she was allowed to deliver with the help of the Foundling's nurses and leave her baby there if she agreed to remain and nurse her child for three months.[9] A new baby, whether just born or just left, was measured and weighed, its temperature taken, its general health examined, a diphtheria immunization administered. The sisters rated its condition on something like today's Apgar scale, a score of one meaning very poor and ten meaning excellent. The most sickly babies, too weak to be breast-fed, were spoon-fed a formula; others were put out to a wet nurse. Over a thousand wet nurses served the Foundling. The first Wednesday of each month, every wet nurse was required to bring in the child for an examination and to collect her ten-dollar monthly wage if the baby was in good condition.[10]

One can only wonder what these young poor mothers felt in surrendering their babies. Had they already given up previous children? Were they glad to be rid of a stigmatizing burden or ashamed of that relief or both? Were they conducting triage, surrendering one child in order to save others? Many, perhaps the majority, hoped that they would be able to reclaim their children when they found a living wage or a husband with a living wage. They left notes like

> Please do not give him up as I shall claim him some day with the help of God. If I call for it and pay for it, surely you will give it to me.[11]

But they usually found that they could not reclaim their children, because they could never get out of poverty, or because a new male partner was not willing to take the children, or because their young children died in the institutions—the most common outcome for those under three—or because they could not regain custody from the orphanages. Searching through the Foundling's records ninety years later, I could find only five mothers' names for this shipment of fifty-seven children.

One also wonders what the children felt and how they comforted themselves. The sisters told the children nothing about their birth mothers, wanting to spare them the shame of illegitimacy; when placed out, the foundlings were told that they were going "home," encouraged to believe that the families had been long awaiting them. Most of the babies were too young when their mothers left to have felt acute anxiety about the parting, but afterward, were they cuddled, sung to, talked to? Or were the other kids, the sisters' authority, and a consistent routine their only sources of security?

At the age of two the children were weaned from wet nurses and returned to the Foundling. There they attended kindergarten and elementary school, played on a rooftop playground and in Central

Park. The sisters worked hard to teach them "truth, virtue and obedience . . . order, neatness, and industry."[12] Above all the sisters taught them to be Catholics, because saving souls for the religion was an objective second only to saving their lives.

Not all New York's "orphans" were lucky enough to be in the Foundling. Many hung out on the streets. Gangs of urchins with dirty bodies and clothes, ragged, unkempt, unkept, possibly infectious, formed a kind of youthful underclass, the older children bold, vulgar, even threatening. In all the late-nineteenth-century "orphanages," not just the Foundling, the majority of children had one if not two living parents. Many of their parents were doing their best, but low wages, unemployment, discrimination, housing shortages and high rents, lack of a welfare system, drunkenness, depression, and despair made even their best often inadequate. Many kids were on the streets to earn—through work, scavenging, prostitution, or theft. For many, street life offered the only available community.

The largest group of these "orphans" were the children of living single mothers (a group that, even then, constituted 9–10 percent of all children in the United States).[13] The low wages and harsh working conditions of the jobs that were available to women—domestic service and sewing most commonly—often made it impossible for lone mothers simultaneously to care for their children and earn enough to support them. Single mothers accounted for almost 55 percent of child-neglect cases in a city where only 10–15 percent of households with children had single mothers at their heads. The child neglect of which they were accused was often difficult to distinguish from, simply, poverty: the children were malnourished, poorly clad, without medical care, or living in unheated flats; they were left unsupervised or with slightly older siblings while mothers worked.[14] So it is not surprising to read estimates that 150 children were abandoned every month in New York in the 1870s.

Earlier in the century poor and neglected children had been dumped into almshouses of unspeakable filth and brutality, institutions that held adults, children and the aged, the poor, the insane and the handicapped indiscriminately together. From midcentury a growing current among child-welfare experts condemned institutional care as a cause of obsequiousness and abuse. New York City slowly developed alternatives for children, and Yale-educated Protestant minister Charles Loring Brace, founder of the Children's Aid Society in the 1850s, is usually presented

as the undisputed hero and villain of the story. He was a man possessed
by a messianic sense of his power to uplift the poor by molding their
children into something better, higher than the slums from which they
came. He saw the children as polluted, the flotsam and jetsam of the
urban ships, nearly ruined by their unparented, undisciplined life on
the streets. Yet he believed they could be cleansed and reclaimed, and
his moralism and disrespect for those whose "family values" were
constrained by poverty only strengthened his commitment to child
welfare. His passion and charisma helped stimulate a great deal of
charitable activity for child welfare.

Brace is best known as the initiator of the "orphan trains." Express-
ing a quintessentially new-world romance about rural life, he inaugurated a massive program of placing out children in the rural West.
Listen to him explain in 1880 why even the poorest rural home was
better than the best institution:

> The demand here for children's labor is practically unlimited. A child's
> place at the table of the farmer is always open; his food and cost to the
> family are of little account . . . The chances, too, of ill treatment in a new
> country, where children are petted and favored, and every man's affairs
> are known to all his neighbors, are far less than in an old. The very
> constitution, too, of an agricultural and democratic community favors the
> probability of a poor child's succeeding. When placed in a farmer's
> family, he grows up as one of their number . . . The peculiar temptations
> to which he has been subject—such, for instance, as stealing and va-
> grancy—are reduced to a minimum; his self-respect is raised, and the
> chances of success held out to a laborer in this country . . . soon raise him
> far above the class from which he sprang.[15]

It was not inconvenient to Brace's ideology that placing out, mainly
regarded by the receiving parents as a modern form of apprenticeship,
was far, far cheaper than institutional care. Nor was it inconvenient that
in the countryside and small towns there was a demand for children,
while in the cities it was easier for those who were infertile or needed
more help to supply themselves with children locally. Brace commanded financial support from contributors whose pity for the orphans did not exclude revulsion for—and even fear of—these dirty street
kids. Then as now some of the wealthy preferred to deal with the poor
and homeless by expelling them. "Ulcers of society," the *New York
Times* called the street children in 1859.[16]

By 1864 Brace's "Emigration Department" was sending out over

1,000 "orphans" a year; by 1875 over 4,000 a year; by 1910 over 110,000 had been placed.[17] Children would be shipped en masse to western towns where newspaper ads advised interested parents to look over the available children at the station; one ad in Chicago offered children on a ninety-day trial basis.[18] The children's experiences as they were set up for inspection offends the late-twentieth-century sensibility: "At Savannah they took us to the courthouse and lined us up, you know, like they was going to mow us down with a machine gun . . . My brothers were all picked the first day, but I wasn't taken till the second. People came up and felt our arms and legs, and mine were kind of spindly. I was hoping that whoever picked me would have plenty to eat, that was my main goal."[19] The demand for children's labor that made these placements so popular simultaneously yielded abuse and violated even nineteenth-century standards, judging from the mounting complaints: children were beaten and overworked and sexually assaulted. These placements were not accompanied by any legal bonds between child and parents (legal adoption became customary only in the twentieth century and was rarely practiced previously), and foster parents often returned children they found unsatisfactory. Some reformers claimed that Brace was merely dumping New York's troublesome street kids onto other states. Several midwestern states— Illinois, Indiana, Michigan, and Minnesota—prohibited mass placements of children starting around the turn of the century.[20]

At the New York end there were complaints about how Brace and his agents obtained the "orphans." Creating an institution that could offer not only care but the promise of upward mobility for the children was, no doubt, a great gift to mothers racked by conflict, guilt, and loss. But the Children's Aid Society's method was overzealous at best. Society members combed the "lower quarters" of the city looking for street kids and hauled them in, often making only perfunctory efforts to locate their parents. Poor parents and children were sometimes terrified that these agents would snatch their children.[21] The child savers, as these agents styled themselves, imagined proper child raising in norms specific to their class and ethnic culture, as we all do. They were mainly elite, prosperous white Protestants dealing with the children of poor immigrants—often Irish and later Slavic or Italian. The child savers' standards of proper parenting were not only antagonistic to the practices of many of these immigrants but also often inimical to the economic necessities of their lives. Children who appeared to child savers as uncared-for strays were often contributing to their families' incomes by begging, peddling, gathering castoffs for use or resale, selling their services, or stealing. The Children's Aid Society agents thought that proper children should stay clean, remain in school, speak modestly, and never—at least not in the cities—play outside unattended. When agents found the parents of street children, or when parents themselves delivered children to the Children's Aid Society, there were often "misunderstandings" about the extent to which parents wished to renounce permanently their rights to the children. Many parents were pressured to surrender their children, and later evaluations found that half of all placed-out children had been removed from parents only because of poverty. To many of the poor, the child savers were actually child stealers.[22]

These children, stolen or rescued, depending on one's point of view, were mostly Catholic, while the major child-saving organizations and their foster homes were Protestant. New York at that time was 40 to 50 percent Catholic, its poor population even more heavily Catholic, and its poor and orphaned children more Catholic yet.[23] Brace claimed that he offered a nonsectarian Christianity, but "nonsectarian" really meant, encompassing several Protestant denominations; it did not include Catholicism, which he considered an inferior, superstitious, servile religion.[24] So did most of New York City's elite. Brace's society emphasized religious training for the orphans to correct whatever unwholesome childhood indoctrination they had received. Coinciding as the placing-out system did with major Protestant attempts to convert Catholics, it is not surprising that the policy appeared genocidal to many Catholics, many of whom also shared a general working-class hostility to elite child savers. Catholic rumors reported that their children were being sold as slaves, with Brace's agents enriching themselves from the proceeds; that the children's names were changed with the result that brothers and sisters might marry each other; and that the purpose of the emigration was to destroy the Catholic faith by stealing and converting its children. The Protestant child savers explicitly preached that poor neighborhoods bred delinquency and immorality and should be broken up: "Disintegration is the true watchword for mission work among the destitute."[25]

The poor orphans were not only religiously unenlightened, from the point of view of Brace and company, but equally benighted racially. Largely Irish with increasing numbers from Italy and Poland, they came from crowded immigrant neighborhoods so foreign that one could walk for blocks without hearing English spoken. The racial system in New York in these years was complex and changing rapidly. The idea of race was becoming sharper and more stable—what varied were the meanings, numbers, and labels of these "races." Rival academic taxonomies competed in dividing the world's people into three, four, and five basic races, typically, Caucasian, Ethiopian, Mongolian, Malay, and American (meaning, to the European authors of these categorizations, American Indian), often colloquially called white, black, yellow, brown, and red. But at the same time "race" was used to refer to humanity in general, as the "human race," and to refer to ill-defined "peoples" or "ethnical" groups. The U.S. Immigration Commission's *Dictionary of Races of Peoples,* published in 1911, recognized forty-five races among immigrants to the United States, including such races as the Hebrews, Germans, Greeks, Irish, Italians, Persians, Poles, Great Russians, White Russians and Little Russians (Ukrainians), and Serbs (who were considered identical to Croatians).[26]

Given such variety among expert usage, it is understandable that the New York City racial vernacular was inconsistent in the number of races it recognized. Race had not been reduced here to a black-white binary, as in the southern states. Neither Brace's society nor the New York Foundling Hospital categorized any of their inmates as white, and both claimed they had no "color line" (although the African American children they accepted were not likely to have been treated equally). Instead they talked about black, Irish, and Polish as comparable categories.[27] New Yorkers—indeed, even one individual New Yorker—might in quick succession refer to blacks, Africans, whites, and Irishmen as races. Elite talk about the Irish was saturated with notions of Irish wildness, primitivism, lack of discipline. This did not mean that African Americans and the Irish seemed equally nonwhite but rather that the prominent, operative identifications used in New York required more specificity to do the work of the concept of "race"— that is, to classify status. These were not physical or cultural descriptions of innocuous "difference," but social and economic markings of rank. For example, elites typically labeled upscale German Jews as Germans, and Russian Jews as Hebrews.

For Catholic leadership in New York, overwhelmingly Irish, these social categories seemed less important than the critical distinction between Catholics and non-Catholics. Brace's society was placing out orphans it saw as religiously and racially inferior. The Catholic charity establishment, defending its faith and its people, could only respond by expanding its own child-saving operation. Catholic child-welfare institutions emerged as part of a general post–Civil War campaign in which Irish Catholics asserted their right to citizenship and participation in national and especially New York City municipal political processes. They challenged the teaching of the Protestant Bible in public schools while simultaneously building and defending their parochial schools. They ran openly Catholic candidates, sometimes successfully, to political office. They asked to have Catholic chaplains alongside Protestant ones in prisons. They contested the claims of the Protestant-dominated charities to being nonsectarian. And by arguing successfully that Catholic institutions could be just as nonsectarian, they got public funding for their institutions.

Catholic charities in New York were fundamentally Irish and developed along with Irish political power in the city. In 1890 eighty percent of New Yorkers were of foreign parentage and one-third of these were Irish. They controlled the Democratic Party, a large parochial school system, and most of the nation's Roman Catholic Church. Indeed, the Irish built their church at the cost of great sacrifice, to some degree giving up personal upward mobility to strengthen and secure their religious institutions. But notwithstanding this substantial and growing political power, New York's Irish were by no means well represented among the social elite. Despite their numbers in the population, the Irish accounted for only 10 percent of white-collar workers in 1900; even the richest among them were not to be found in the exclusive social clubs.[28] The Irish remained disproportionately working class and poor, disproportionately given to drink (though nowhere near as much so as the stereotypes pictured them), and the orphans at the Foundling were regarded by Irish and non-Irish alike as base, children of the underclass.

Those who did the actual work of Catholic charities in New York were disproportionately female. By 1900, 50,000 religious women staffed Catholic institutions throughout the United States.[29] Several groups of nuns initiated welfare programs but none more successfully than the Sisters of Charity, who began in the 1860s to challenge the Protestant dominance of the field both institutionally and ideologically, bringing a distinct approach to the problem of dependent children. They had inherited a European Catholic tradition whereby mothers of unwanted newborns could leave them at convents, which often provided a special depository for the purpose. Opening a new home for foundlings at 17 East Twelfth Street in 1870, the Sisters of Charity created a "crib" where mothers could leave babies without being seen. In this initiative the nuns fused religious and maternal emotion:

> On the evening of their first day in the new house, in a steady drizzle of rain, they heard a faint cry that seemed to come from just outside . . . Opening the door, they saw on the stoop a newborn infant, their first foundling . . . Laying the child in Sister Irene's arms, Sister Mary Frances said, "Remember that you are to be a mother to all the foundlings in New York." . . . Meanwhile her companions were gazing upon the child with awe and compassion. "What shall we call him?" . . . and the answer came without hesitation . . . Joseph . . . [But] having made this decision, the Sisters unpinned the baby's blanket and found a note attached to its clothing: "The child's name is Sara."[30]

Growing Catholic political power won them a regular state subsidy by 1873 as well as a grant for a new building, which the Sisters of Charity put up between Sixty-seventh and Sixty-eighth Streets and Lexington and Third Avenues.[31] Their undertaking quickly grew into a major operation: the building complex occupied an entire square block, housing apartments for staff, dormitories for the children, and a maternity and a children's hospital. Soon they opened a country branch at Sputen Duyvil, where up to 250 sick children could convalesce in country surroundings. The Foundling ran with the free labor of many sisters, their effective fund-raising and appropriation of volunteers. By 1894 they had admitted 26,000 children and placed out 10,000, about 39 percent. The Foundling used 250 pounds of meat, 270 loaves of bread, 30 dozen eggs, and a barrel of sugar daily. Mothers who delivered at the Foundling were each required to breast-feed not only their own but also another baby, and an additional 1,000 wet nurses were employed. The Foundling established New York's first system of paid foster care: it took the thirty-eight cents per day per child allotted to the Foundling by the city and gave it directly to mothers who were usually caring for their own as well as the Foundling's children. Their boarding system reduced the mortality from epidemic disease, which haunted all children's institutions at the time. But the numbers of their children quickly outstripped the New York homes they could find and required a wider search for homes; as foster homes became harder to get, their placements moved further west. By 1879, 1,000 had been "emigrated," by 1919, almost 25,000. In 1904 the Foundling Hospital was handling 1,900 children a year and emigrating 450–475.[32]

In this work the Sisters of Charity not only competed with Protestants to guarantee Catholic homes for children but also resisted some of the dominant Protestant ideologies and policies regarding care for orphans, substituting some distinctively Catholic female ideas. The sisters enacted and symbolized a gender system that did not place women's highest aspirations into the frame of marriage, motherhood, and family. Their sense of the superiority of their own dedication, their marriage to Christ flowed into the sensibility of the Catholic laity as well. If wife- and motherhood was the acme of women's achievement for Protestants and Jews, it was otherwise for Irish Catholics. Some of their values seem feminist a century later: for example, they indulged far less than the Protestants in characterizing single mothers as "fallen." Instead the sisters dedicated themselves to rescuing poor mothers, by providing opportunities for them to shed the burden of a baby with relatively little humiliation, and by offering a chance to surrender a child only temporarily. (The poor mother who lost her children to the Protestant child savers was a prominent figure in Catholic funding appeals.)

Nor did they indulge in moralistic condemnations of the poor through preaching about work, discipline, and self-help as the Protestant Charity Organization Society and its affiliates did. The sisters did not label New York's street children or orphans as urban waste. Although they had no critique of racism, their own personal and collective history as an Irish sisterhood made them skeptical of social Darwinist or evolutionary hierarchies of peoples. They did not join in the Protestant-led scientific-charity campaign to prevent the poor from becoming lazy and dependent by reducing public welfare expenditures. Their very absolutism and authoritarianism, their own submission to the authority of their church, made them confident that all, including the poorest single mothers, could become good Catholics.

Since the nuns did not share the romance with nuclear-family domesticity characteristic of the Protestant reformers, they did not assume that children must be raised in families in order to grow up properly. They believed that institutional care could be nurturant. As the Protestants emphasized the evils and cruelties of institutional care, so the Catholics emphasized the potential for exploitation and callousness in the inevitably undersupervised conditions of placing out. They also had a religious bias against placing out: nurturing the faith required a kind of education and inculcation more easily done in institutions; and they opposed dispersing Catholics from their New York power base, which they believed to be one of the Protestant child savers' goals. Throughout the 1880s the Protestant child-welfare establishment tried to force the sisters to place out more of the children in their charge, in part through limiting the public funding that the Catholic homes received, and the sisters resisted.

But the sisters could not, and did not wish to, abjure placing out entirely, because of the huge volume of children they cared for. Furthermore, after 1880 there developed a stream of thought within the church, a faction known as the American or assimilationist tendency, that promoted Catholic expansion westward.[33] The sisters developed their own orphan trains to the West, to place Catholic children in Catholic homes. Although their homes were preselected, in publicizing departures like that from Grand Central on September 25, 1904, their need for donations led them to use the same rhetoric of children as goods that Protestants employed. "One hundred Christmas presents, gifts in curls and pinafores, will be despatched from this city to-morrow . . . The hundred kiddies are the gift of the New York Foundling Asylum to a hundred homes in the West." And occasionally they resorted to characterizations of the children as waste: "These waifs, human driftwood thrown up by a great city in the ebb tide of misfortune . . ."[34]

This young driftwood was predominantly Irish, with Polish, Italian, German, and other European-origin Catholic children making up the second largest group. Of the group that departed New York on September 25, 1904, nineteen ended up staying in Clifton and Morenci, Arizona, and they may have been even more heavily Irish than usual: besides Jerome Shanley and Katherine Fitzpatrick there were Elizabeth and Hannah Kane, Violet Lanovick (or Lanwick), Gabriella Welsh, Josephine Corcoran, Anna Louise Doherty, Pearl Kendricks, Agnes Mullen, George Weber, Edward Cummiskey, William Norton, Sadie Green, Joseph Ryan, Raymond Spencer, Marie Mack, Ambrose Lamb, and Edward Gibson. The mothers who left their names were Agnes, Katie, Mary, Nora, and Sarah.[35] Three were younger than was the rule: Elizabeth Kane was only two, but she had her big sister with her; perhaps Josephine Corcoran and Gabriella Welsh, also under three, were true orphans, having no one who would ever claim them. These poor children, commonly classified as immigrants whether or not they were born in the United States, did not possess the status or future of elite children. They could expect no careful supervision, education, upward mobility, social respect. In New York they might have political weight as the constituents of Irish politicians, and some might become politicians or the wives of politicians themselves, but most of them would stay at the bottom, or such was the expectation of their parents and guardians.

Thus to the pressure to defend the faith and to empty their asylum a bit was added the sisters' understanding that the children might have a brighter future out West—and in this respect, they saw, Brace and his lieutenants were right. The procedure, if all went well, worked like this: The sisters sent out announcements to parishes, requiring that parents be Catholics in good standing, and priests then appealed for homes at masses. The pastors helped those interested fill out application forms. Parishioners often made specific requests: for curly hair, or red hair, or merely "one that can be the sunshine of our home."[36]

> Your agent has promised me a nice red-haired boy. I have a red-haired wife and five red-haired girls and we want a boy to match.
>
> We would like a little girl between three and five years, with dark, auburn or brown hair and blue eyes—Must have a pretty nose.[37]

Requests for girls widely outnumbered those for boys. (This is still true: apparently adoptive parents believe that girls will be more tractable.)

The sisters believed that three was the optimal age for placing a child—"the age when they can begin a new life, as the memory of the past doesn't amount to much."[38] So when they received babies, the nuns preferred to keep them for a time. Luckily they also occasionally got requests for older children as these were harder to place: "There are two of us here that want a child apiece," someone wrote from Texas, "a bright boy about twelve years of age and a girl from ten to twelve. I want a girl able to read and write some."[39]

Local agents of the sisters visited prospective homes and made recommendations to the sisters who made assignments of children.[40] Unlike the Protestant agencies, the Foundling Hospital matched each child with a foster parent before she or he left New York. When necessary, several of the Foundling's staff would remain in the town of placement in order to review the home situations a week or so later.

The Clifton-Morenci parish priest, Constant Mandin, had responded to the Foundling Hospital's request with "a list of forty families that wished to adopt little ones; stated that they were not wealthy people, but all had work at good wages, had comfortable homes, were mostly childless and could well take care of the little ones, that they were all good, practicing Catholics, that eighteen more parties wished children, but as they were widows having to work for their living, he thought it would be imposing on good nature and refused them."[41] The Foundling Hospital agreed to send the forty children, adding that Sisters Francis Liguori and Ann Corsini would remain in Clifton two to three weeks to make sure the foster homes were acceptable.[42]

Mandin's requested forty were among the fifty-seven that were watching from train windows that Sunday in 1904. Their itinerary routed them via the Pennsylvania Railroad to St. Louis, where a few children were dropped off and the rest of the group changed to the Missouri, Kansas, and Texas Railroad; they stopped again in Arkansas, where a few more orphans were left with foster parents, and then continued to Houston; from here they took the Southern Pacific to Lordsburg, New Mexico, and finally a spur line to Clifton.[43] The trip took seven days. They all knew that the promise of a family, a mother and a father, was something of great value; even these run-arounds with no memories of family life or mother could understand this from the emotional valence of the sisters' and nurses' talk. The older children, like four-year-old Jerome or six-year-old Marie Mack, knew what a family was. But in the most important sense all were entering the unknown.

The children had been changed into older clothing soon after their departure so that their days of exposure to dust and soot, without bathing, would not soil their new outfits. Just before arriving every child was redressed in his or her best so as to make as good as possible a first appearance. They looked picture perfect when the train pulled into the Clifton, Arizona, station on Saturday, October 1, at about 6:30 P.M.

Every orphan train's arrival at a railroad station created a sensation, attracting hundreds of spectators, the arrivals usually having been reported in advance by local newspapers and posters. The very idea of the orphans stimulated women's interest in particular. On one shipment to Texas, people at Houston, the first stop, had nearly "confiscated" a quota reserved for San Antonio. A *New York Times* article reported that "it is believed that the . . . demand for babies . . . was stimulated by intermaternal gossip and boasting over last week's cargo of infantile sunshine and squalls."[44] A similarly talkative crowd had gathered in Clifton when the train pulled in.

The children were quieter, awed and anxious. Seven days on a train had left them restless and cranky, but the nuns' dressing them in their finest communicated to them the solemnity of the occasion awaiting. Their long train ride had transported them from orphanhood to son- and daughterhood, though they lacked, of course, any visceral sense of what this might mean. They did not grasp that this trip was to offer them not only parents but also upward mobility. Even less did they know that that mobility took the form of a racial transformation unique to the American Southwest, that the same train ride had transformed them from Irish to white.

1

King Copper

THE SCENE AT THE CHACÓN HOUSE, the drama that was to envelop Clifton and Morenci, to put the Sisters of Charity and the local padre at the risk of their lives, and to make some New York Irish orphans into "Anglos"—all this was created by copper. Copper shook these parts like a slow, protracted earthquake, transforming not only people but the very earth itself. Today in Morenci, where there were once valleys there are now peaks, built up by millions of tons of slag. Where there were hills and gulches there are now approximately twelve square miles of flat yellow areas paved by tailings.[1] Where there were once peaks and a town of five thousand there is now a giant hole in the ground, a man-made Grand Canyon, created over a few decades rather than a few centuries by Phelps Dodge Copper dynamiting the mountain it had been mining underground and turning it into an open-pit mine. Three thousand feet separate the pit floor from the highest point of its rim. One looks down into a red, orange, gray, and brown crater, fuchsia tinting the edges of the terraced levels as the sun sinks, giant earth-moving trucks and tractors moving like tiny ants along these plateaus in giant spirals upward and downward. Up close the 240-ton trucks dwarf the workers' pickups, and they carry 1.6 billion pounds of rock out of the pit every day. It is the largest open-pit mine in North America, producing 35 percent of the copper for the largest mining company in the United States.[2]

In 1904 the lavender and gray mountains of the Gila and Peloncillo ranges still hid their wealth, and men had to dig through hard rock to get to the gold, silver, zinc, manganese, tungsten, lead, iron, uranium, and copper of this Sonoran highlands region. Precious metals had been mined in these mountains for centuries, and the Americans who first exploited the copper on a large scale had originally been looking for gold. But the fortunes they made from that base metal, copper, its dark burnished amber peeking out as "beautiful blue and green croppings" from the brown and gray earth,[3] far exceeded those from its glowing precious cousin. Phelps Dodge's gleaming brochure tells us that the development of copper around 8700 B.C. inaugurated "western civilization": the Sumerians alloyed it with tin to produce bronze, the Egyptians then used bronze tools to build the pyramids, the Phoenicians mined it in what are today Spain and Cornwall and then created a mercantile empire by selling it throughout their world. From their time until the mid-nineteenth century, copper was used mainly for luxuries: high-quality pots and pans, roofs of large buildings, sculpture. The new industrial technologies that took off after the Civil War escalated copper requirements geometrically: for the first transcontinental telegraph line in 1861, for the spread of indoor plumbing, and above all for the transmission of electricity. Copper was as much the symbol of the new industrial world as steel; the Statue of Liberty, for example, is clad with 100 tons of copper one-tenth of an inch thick. In 1929 the world used twenty-one times more copper than it had in 1860. Today 1,750 pounds of copper are used for every person in the United States; the average car contains 50 pounds; an average single-family house contains 439 pounds.[4]

The mines that had supplied the world's copper requirements for ten thousand years—in the Sinai peninsula, Cyprus, Cornwall, Spain, Mexico, and a few other places—were completely inadequate to the post–Civil War industrial demand.[5] This demand coincided with rapid European expansion westward through the North American continent and led to the discovery of orebodies first along the shores of Lake Superior, then in the intermountain West. Between 1850 and 1875 the average price of copper rose from twenty to fifty cents a pound, threatening to inhibit the growth of electricity and industry. Butte's copper riches in Montana brought the price down to fifteen cents but still could not meet the demand. It was then that early venture capitalists found ways to exploit the great deposits of the Arizona-Sonora desert mountains. These huge individual orebodies, sometimes containing hundreds of thousands of tons each, grouped together in areas two to three miles square. Here surface water had circulated through the porous desert rocks to a greater depth than was usual elsewhere, oxidizing and dissolving the copper from the upper levels to settle below in rich concentrations. These were, along with Butte's, the largest high-grade copper deposits ever found.[6] British and American capital began to speed around the world, their communications jetting along the copper wires, investing in six new areas—Clifton-Morenci, Globe, Bisbee, and Jerome in Arizona, Cananea and Nacozari in Sonora.

Almost every resident of Clifton-Morenci and its adjacent mining camp, Metcalf, was there because of the copper. The "original" owners of the land were the Chiricahua Apaches and some Mexican farmers and ranchers. By 1904 every resident served the copper industry directly or indirectly, except for the Chiricahuas, who had been imprisoned on the San Carlos Reservation. This region had little good farmland. Some low-density farming took place along the Gila River a millennium ago but never developed the substantial peasant communities and irrigated agriculture found along the Rio Grande. When the mines first opened there were no roads at all, just an Indian trail leading to the Gila River and to the Apache reservation.[7] The cattle ranches that expanded so vigorously in the late nineteenth century survived at first by feeding the miners and later by taking advantage of the railroads to bring their beef out.

The hidden lodes knew nothing of provincial, state, or national borders: a single geologically and climatically unified region, the Sonoran highlands includes the southeastern part of today's Arizona, the southwestern part of New Mexico, and most of today's Mexican states of Chihuahua and Sonora. Between 1848 and 1854 half of Mexico, including most of this highlands region, was annexed to the United States, yet because annexation took place before the Americans comprehended the size of the deposits and the demand for copper, the international boundary they drew bisected this mineral-rich strip. But the border made little social or economic difference during the next half-century anyway. There were no guards at the borders, no checking of papers, and indeed no one had papers; few residents knew exactly where the border was. Americans and Europeans invested in and managed mines on both sides of the border.[8]

Although the Sonoran desert and mountains formed one of the least populated regions of North America, small-scale mining was known there since ancient times. Archaeologists have been able to infer, from artifacts, the mining methods of old Michoacán, where pyrite copper ore was crushed by hand, concentrated by multiple washings with water, roasted with wood and charcoal, and then smelted with hand-driven bellows. The conquistadors, despite their lust for mineral wealth, were not at first interested in copper.[9] Some prescient Europeans grasped the potential of these deposits, as for example the explorer and engineer Alexander von Humboldt, who predicted early in the nineteenth century "that the mineral wealth of the world would be developed in Sonora . . . and the territory of Arizona."[10]

Tucson was historically the northern capital of this Sonoran region, the end of a prosperous north-south trade route traveled from the days of the ancient Indians through the Spanish and Mexican periods and the first thirty years of U.S. control.[11] Commerce throughout the area used the Mexican peso, often called by Anglos the "doby dollar" ("adobe dollar").[12] Until the east-west Southern Pacific Railroad reached these areas in the 1880s, the closest port and transhipment point was Guaymas, directly south from Tucson on the Gulf of California.

The population of southern Arizona and northern Mexico had become thinner than ever by the 1840s, because of the deadly guerrilla war with which the Western and Chiricahua Apaches tried to drive outsiders from their lands.[13] The takeoff of commercial copper production, and the ultimate U.S. Army suppression of the Apaches, were driven by the California gold rush. There the first prospectors were Californios, long-term ethnically Mexican residents of the California territory. They were soon outnumbered by a large influx of Mexican miners, primarily from Sonora; five to six thousand headed to California at first news of the strikes in 1848. Hundreds of others came from as far as Chile and other South American mining communities. "Americans," also attracted by the gold, soon poured in from the east, but no group could compete with the Mexicans and Chileans who brought mining skills and experience. The Sonorans were notoriously enterprising and competitive. The "Yankees of Mexico," they were "not only everywhere, but doing everything: mining, freighting, selling goods and supplies, and generally offering very real competition in both trading and mining." Some wealthy Americans took advantage of the Sonorans by hiring them, collecting 50 percent of their takings in return for protecting them against violent harassment from other Americans. (These employers included future presidential candidate General John Frémont.)[14]

As a British observer saw the gold-rush relationships, "Americans resorted . . . in the first instance, to the Chileans and Mexicans for instruction and information, which they gave them with cheerful alacrity; but as soon as Jonathan got an inkling of the system, with peculiar bad taste and ungenerous feeling, he organized a crusade against these obliging strangers."[15] Nativist hostility against the Mexicans grew. To weaken or eliminate this competition, Anglos pushed through the California legislature the Foreign Miners' Tax Law of 1850, levying a prohibitive twenty-dollar monthly assessment on foreign miners, a tax generally enforced only against Mexicans. Some Mexicans resisted, there were open armed battles, and lynching of Mexicans became common in the third quarter of the century in the California gold districts.[16]

By the end of the 1850s the majority of the Sonorans had been driven out and returned home. Some headed east but stayed in the United States, and throughout the 1860s Mexicans provided skilled labor for many hard-rock mines.[17] Other thousands of disappointed American and European immigrant gold-rush prospectors also discovered new opportunities as they headed east: what had previously been nothing but difficult terrain to get through was now examined.

Most of them began by prospecting for placer deposits, that is, looking for ores on the earth's surface. The gradual transition from placer mining to underground hard-rock mining transformed not only the economy and labor process but the culture and politics of the region, a metamorphosis that reached down and changed the lives of everyone involved in the foundling events. Placer mining was quintessentially an individual man's enterprise. It gripped the male imagination with such muscular force not only because it fed on a lust for wealth but also because it satisfied a longing for the ultimate adventure that pitted man alone against nature and other men, with a minimum of tools. And that romance became unusually violent, as prospectors fought to control or steal strikes. Hard-rock mining, by contrast, became cost-effective only when hugely capitalized with heavy equipment, modern transportation systems, hundreds of laborers, and soon, as the demand for copper led to the exploitation of thinner orebodies, the production of new technological processes for concentrating and then smelting out the metal from the raw ore.

The story of Clifton-Morenci copper and the Clifton orphans is a story of a mythical western individualism joined unstably to mass industrial labor–capital relations. A story of a "wild west" different from that in the traditional cowboy and prospector lore: a "wageworkers' frontier," as one historian called it, or a "corporate frontier," as another put it.[18] A story of adventurous, stouthearted prospectors and investors forced to sell out because they were unable, despite their best efforts, to find the capital or the technological means to make copper-mining profitable. A story of Jewish mercantile and venture capitalists overtaken and incorporated by Anglo-Saxons. A story of remote mountain mines scouted and developed by frontiersmen ending in the portfolios of the world's largest corporations run from New York and Edinburgh and, today, Phoenix.

CHARLES E. MILLS WAS THE FIRST American mining boss to make a fortune from Clifton-Morenci, a quintessential western mining capitalist. His handling of the orphan conflict illustrated both his authority and its limits, for 1904 was but early times in the development of his own and his corporation's power in Arizona. But in Mills's style with his men and his town one could already see the future.

Mills first appeared in Arizona in 1885, employed as an engineer on the construction of the Santa Fe Railroad into Bisbee from Guaymas. Then hired by the Copper Queen mine as an engineer, he soon moved up into the general office, where James Douglas of Phelps Dodge discovered him. (Douglas was unquestionably the chief honcho of all copper mining in Arizona. The true "father of Arizona," one historian called him.)[19] Douglas sent Mills to Yavapai County, north of Tucson, to supervise the Big Bug and Senator mines, then to Morenci in 1896. By this time he had become Douglas's second in command. A taciturn bachelor, he climbed up through skill, hard work, a hard way with his workers, and some sharp financial dealing. To the Morenci townspeople he was simply the boss; *patrón* or *mayordomo* to the Mexicans, depending on the context, perhaps even *cacique* to those who wanted to emphasize the reach of his fiefdom.

This quiet man of calculation and ambition had a passionate, adventurous side, one the Mexicans would admiringly call macho. His lust for the strenuous life was such that not even the wilds of Arizona Territory were sufficient challenge, and he resigned his job to enlist in the Rough Riders, Company A.[20] Serving in Cuba he fell to the fever that knocked out so many American troops and, after convalescing, returned to Morenci. Perhaps needless to say, neither this expedition nor his pull with Theodore Roosevelt hindered his corporate rise, and a tough reputation hurt no man in Arizona. Still, war exerted a pull on him that he couldn't resist and two decades later, at nearly forty, he took up a commission as a major in World War I; he was in New York set to sail for France when the Armistice was signed.

As soon as he arrived in Morenci, Mills seemed more like an owner than a manager. Combining vision with a gift for making do, he was able both to turn a handsome profit when the Morenci mines were just a "rawhide" operation, men living in boxes and tents and digging with picks, and to build the country's first modern company town. He invested in his mines and used his profits to become a leading Arizona banker. In 1902 Mills brought the Gila Valley Bank to Morenci, with 61 percent of the shares owned by Jewish prospector and merchant Isadore Solomon and his relatives. Within the Arizona banking world Mills spearheaded an aggressive copper faction that used copper profits to produce a second fortune through banking, and then used banking capital to build the copper industry. Soon Mills and his allies squeezed out the Solomon group, which represented ranching and mercantile capital. By 1914 the bank was Arizona's largest, and at his death Mills had amassed a private fortune of $2.3 million. Yet this finance capitalist was still a miner in 1904: he supervised everything personally, his boots dirty like other men's, and he missed nothing. The orphan problem must have seemed to him like many other breaks to repair or conflicts to resolve—hard choices that required his powers of decisiveness.

When Mills first saw Arizona copper mining, it was primitive, not much advanced beyond traditional Mexican mining techniques. This was "plain diggings," which could turn out only small amounts of copper.[21] Add to the lack of technology the continuing Apache attacks, and it is understandable why Arizona mining did not take off until approximately twenty years after the Rocky Mountain mines of Nevada, Montana, Idaho, and Colorado. The "Indian problem" became a violent spiral: as miners encroached on Apache lands, the Apaches fought back more fiercely.[22] Mine owners hired guards against Apache raids but these could not protect miners once they dispersed to their homes; stable industrial mining required political or military control over the Apaches. Better transportation was required not only to get the copper out but equally to get supplies in—everything from food and water and fuel to timbers for the mines and coke for the smelters. The annexation of Mexican land had not provided Arizona with a seaport, as originally hoped, and the east-west railroads remained several hundred miles to the north. Winter snows and summer rains and floods sometimes brought animal-powered freight teams to a stop. Most of all, the costs–of transporting ore out and supplies in–reduced copper profits to the vanishing point, even with high-grade ore containing 50–70 percent copper. Expensive transportation also doubled the price of coke.[23] The Indian and transportation problems connected in a vicious circle: The federal government was unlikely to invest heavily in repression of the Apaches without a larger population to justify doing so, but Indian attacks deterred European-American as well as Mexican settlement.

Copper demand, increasing exponentially, particularly in telegraphy and electricity, changed the direction of the spiral. Satisfying that demand produced an upwardly circular effect: mining interests stimulated railroad building, which stimulated further prospecting and mineral discoveries, which produced more railroad building, and so on. In this process, government initiatives and contracts reduced some of the risk for these early venture capitalists. The 1848 Treaty of Guadalupe Hidalgo had provided the land needed to complete a northern railroad route to the West Coast, but such a route promised continued commercial domination to the northern states. The Treaty of La Mesilla, which followed in 1854 (known in the United States as the Gadsden Purchase), was a project largely of southern interests: In 1853 Jefferson Davis as secretary of war inaugurated a survey for a southern railroad route, concluding that the best course included land in Mexico. The annexation of the La Mesilla region also expanded U.S. holdings of the richest mineral-bearing lands. Immediately afterward the U.S. Topographical Engineers surveyed the area, sending back information (and rumors) about the location of mineral deposits. The occupation of Tucson by U.S. troops in 1856 provided a political capital for development. Men interested in mineral development energized petitions to Congress to organize the Arizona Territory, and the first Territorial Legislature of 1864–in which mining entrepreneurs constituted 44 percent of the members–believed that the new Arizona was to be mainly a mineral empire. As the territory developed, political and mining ambition fused in support of venture capital. These investment interests formed a powerful pressure group for anti-Indian military activity, and, inversely, mining schemes were "the rage" among army officers at the forts established in the Indian battles. Indeed, because of the power of these interests, "the government . . . arrived before the people in Arizona," as historian Howard Lamar put it.[24]

In fact Arizona miners predated government impact, but the government changed everything. The first mines and mining camps of Arizona were built and supplied mainly by Mexicans—not only by the miners but also by the *barrateros y arrieros,* the pick and crowbar men who built the railroads and "the teamsters who fought with reins and rifle to glaze the course of the silver stream soon to issue from this hostile and isolated zone." Mexican freighting was Arizona's second largest industry by the mid-1870s. Not only was ore shipped out from Guaymas, but heavy equipment was imported through Guaymas, and food came mainly from Sonora. But the U.S. government furnished the capital needed for profitable mining in the region. The government provided funding for roads and military engineers to build them, telegraph lines, and a dozen army posts that in turn provided a major source of income to entrepreneurs. William Zeckendorf, typical of Arizona's early mercantile capitalists, contracted to supply the military bases with sugar, grain, and hay purchased in Sonora and hauled by Mexican freighters. For a time the Mexican merchants who had dominated Tucson before the Gadsden Purchase were able to hang on to their dominion, but by the 1870s these contracts elevated Anglos such as Michael Goldwater to mercantile supremacy. The first significant investor in Clifton-Morenci copper derived his capital from federal contracts to supply the military.[25]

As the mining speculators and developers began to encroach on Indian lands, the Western and Chiricahua Apaches responded with ever greater violence, so that in the first three decades of these developments the mining-camp populations remained small, confined to the hardy, the desperate, and the most ambitious. Without better transportation, none of the early mining entrepreneurs, not even the talented and driving Charles Mills, could have broken out of a mercantile economy with an unfavorable balance of trade. The railroads changed that. Their development at first recapitulated the traditional north-south orientation of Sonoran trade: the first plan was for a Denver to Mexico City route, the second to run from Kansas to Guaymas. But these plans were permanently altered as the Southern Pacific made its way eastward from Los Angeles to Tucson and then El Paso. Less wealthy investors were then able to build many smaller lines connecting mining areas to the Southern Pacific. Moreover, the greater freight capacity of the trains allowed a shift from precious metals to high-volume copper.[26]

THE HALF-LEGENDARY, HALF-HISTORICAL story of the Clifton-Morenci mines not only tells us what Charles Mills inherited but also provides a microcosmic illustration of the whole copper story: the insignificance of international borders at the time, the transformation from individual to big-capital mining, the role of the federal government in giving birth to that capital, the centrality of railroad construction. Mexican prospectors had found copper ore along the San Francisco River by the beginning of the century. Federal surveyor Henry Clifton rediscovered the ore in 1864 but thought it was too remote to file a claim and, besides, he was looking for precious metals.[27] The first investor was Henry Lesinsky, a dynamic Jew from Central Europe who had initially sought his fortune in Australian gold mines, then in New Mexico. In Las Cruces he prospered by purchasing grain from the Rio Grande Mexican farmers and selling it to the federal government, developing a supply firm with his uncle Julius Freudenthal. After the Civil War they added mail delivery to the services they provided for the government and their capital grew to $300,000. When silver was discovered in Silver City, Lesinsky opened a store there and supplied the miners. It was at this store that he heard news of the copper at Clifton and bought a controlling interest for $10,000.[28]

When Lesinsky first found copper ore, it was in an old Mexican mine, three thousand feet above the river, accessible only by an Indian trail. The impediments were formidable: there was no iron or steel, no firebricks, no machinery, no coke or coal, the railroad was twelve hundred miles away, and the land belonged to the Apaches. The last problem Lesinsky solved adeptly: He petitioned to have the mine "segregated" from the reservation; the Arizona Territory attorney general, in consultation with a U.S. Indian agent, sought a bribe of $5,000 from Lesinsky for his "trouble, responsibility, expense"; Lesinsky exposed him to the U.S. Indian commissioner and the *Arizona Citizen* and got the "segregation" he wanted as well as the dismissal of the attorney general without having to pay the money.[29] The other problems were more intransigent. Lesinsky had observed that Mexican workers knew how to smelt copper ore.[30] So he went to El Paso del Norte (the Mexican side of El Paso, Texas, renamed Ciudad Juárez in 1888) and hired Mexicans, packed in to the site, and left it to them to devise a method.[31] They improvised, or "rawhided" as they called it. To smelt they made charcoal, which produces twice the heat of wood, from mesquite and scrub oak trees.[32] With the charcoal they wielded hand (or foot) bellows of cowhide to raise the heat. They built a smelting furnace along Chase Creek out of quartzite rock and adobe. It could smelt a ton a day, but the heat tended to melt the adobe, and the time required to rebuild the furnaces cut into production. They next built a stone furnace, but the heat expanded the stone and split the rock, so they returned to adobe. Then Lesinsky brought in a German metallurgist who spent eight months building a $20,000 furnace, which burned up within twenty-four hours. Finally another German workman devised a workable furnace, adobe with a copper water-jacket inside the walls.[33]

The first ore they mined was so rich it needed no milling—they were able to put the ore right in the smelting furnace. The copper matte bullion or ingots went by Mexican pack train overland to the closest railroad—then at Kansas City.[34] Other Mexicans were hired to build an adobe store and houses for the Lesinskys and their managers. Soon the Lesinskys built a "baby gauge," twenty-inch, railway and bought a tiny, light locomotive—called "Baby," the first locomotive in Arizona—to haul ore down to the smelter, a four-mile trip.[35] To get the ore from the mine to the railroad, they installed wire ropes and track the length of the 2,000- to 3,000-foot, 40–50 percent grade inclines; gravity sent the cable cars down and mules pulled them up. As long as productive capacity remained below two tons of ore per day this transportation system seemed adequate.

But transportation, supply, security, and labor problems continually threatened the profitability of the enterprise. The teamsters would frequently stop at their farms on the Rio Grande to plow or harvest. Their twelve-hundred-mile route to Kansas City took them through Apache and Comanche lands, and several groups were waylaid and killed by these Indians. The charcoal made from mesquite was inferior and spoiled batches of the unmilled ore. The camps were ridden with typhus and smallpox. The operation was just moving into the black by the late 1870s when a new round of Apache raids sent many of the Mexican workers back home. In 1877 the Lesinskys contracted with a San Francisco firm for 150 Chinese laborers, whose arrival elicited other workers' fury.[36] And in 1880 the Clifton settlement experienced the first of what was to be many floods: already deforestation had bared the soil and the spring melt sent such a volume of water into the Frisco River that it swept out the bridge and cut an entirely new channel, leaving the workers' houses literally on an island.[37] Apaches, under the leadership of Victoria in 1880 and then Geronimo in 1882, terrorized the mining camps for six years. Geronimo, who was born in present-day Clifton, conducted raids over a five-hundred-square-mile area, including Bisbee, where Mills was then stationed, and led direct attacks on the Clifton mines and smelters, killing hundreds of soldiers, American settlers, Mexicans, and other Apaches, until he was finally captured in 1886–a feat accomplished because the U.S. Army was able to recruit enough Apache soldiers to do the job.[38]

Meanwhile William Church, another experienced prospector, staked out four nearby claims and got financial backing from a Detroit capitalist; in 1882 he named his new company Detroit Copper and his camp Morenci, after his hometown, a copper camp in Michigan.[39] In addition to his mines, he built two smelters and Arizona's first concentrating plant to handle the lower-grade ores he was exploiting.[40] Here the transportation obstacles were even greater, as Morenci was almost a mile high, fifteen hundred feet above Clifton. Church used Mexican vendors to pack in wood and all other mining and living supplies. Despite these difficulties the Clifton-Morenci mines hobbled along and by 1880 were jointly smelting sixty to eighty tons a day of 20 percent ore, producing four thousand tons of copper a year, and turning a profit despite the long haul to the railroad.

But Morenci had a bigger problem: water. While Clifton had the Frisco River, Morenci had nothing. Church figured out that the best solution was a six-mile-long pipeline west to Eagle Creek, lifting the water fifteen hundred feet across an intervening mountain ridge, at a rate sufficient to supply 100,000 gallons a day. The cost and engineering of such an undertaking were beyond Church's capacity. Enter Phelps Dodge, which invested $30,000 in Detroit Copper in 1881 and loaned out its Bisbee manager, James Douglas, to help design two twenty-ton smelters and a water-pumping system. An old import-export firm established in 1834, Phelps Dodge (PD, pronounced "peedy" by everyone in Clifton-Morenci) had begun to manufacture copper items and by the 1840s was the largest manufacturer of copper and tin plate and wire in the United States. Douglas could see that with the right engineering and management, Morenci could be profitable, so he sent Mills there and PD bought out Church.[41]

Thus absentee ownership and dynamic management entered Morenci, and soon came to Clifton too. Henry Lesinsky fell ill and withdrew, and his brother sold out to a speculator who in turn sold the operation to a group of Scottish investors for $2 million.[42] The Scottish, calling themselves the Arizona Copper Company Ltd., were doing what the British were then practicing all over the world—investing in extractive industries in the colonies. From Edinburgh James Colquhoun was sent to Arizona in 1883 and remained to head the Clifton operation until 1907.[43]

Like Douglas in Bisbee and Mills in Morenci, Colquhoun was a gifted, inventive manager, although less ambitious and more remote, a man who built a luxurious home for his family where he spent many long hours and entertained lavishly. He was much less likely than Mills to appear unannounced at the mine head. Nevertheless, he superintended some massive developments. He built a one-hundred-mile private railway through formidable terrain—sometimes blasting through solid rock—to connect with the Southern Pacific at Lordsburg, New Mexico. He developed a milling and smelting system that could process the new leaner oxide and porphyry ores after the sulfide ores petered out.[44] He began using still leaner ore by dissolving it in sulfuric acid and precipitating it on iron. And he returned to the tailings deposits left from previous smeltings, re-leaching them with sulfuric acid to produce yet more copper. Reaping substantial profits—$20 million in dividends paid out—Colquhoun's Scottish company prospered, although not on the magnitude of Mills's operation in Morenci. Eventually Arizona Copper, too, sold out to Phelps Dodge, a merger completed by 1921.[45]

By 1904 the two absentee companies with their on-site managers—Colquhoun with his smelter superintendent George Frazer in Clifton, and Phelps Dodge run by Mills in Morenci—had created boomtowns.[46] They lobbied to win tax exemptions, and in 1901 the Territorial Legislature again defeated a bill to impose taxation upon them.[47] The population of Clifton and Morenci doubled, at least, between 1900 and 1910. For capitalists in mining, Clifton and Morenci were on the map.

Outsiders considered Clifton-Morenci one "camp," a "Mexican camp" as distinguished from other copper-mining centers that were "white camps," such as Jerome, Bisbee, and Globe-Miami.[48] Residents knew that Clifton and Morenci were towns of distinct personalities. Clifton was more civilized, with more stores, professionals, culture, women, and families, and was 55–60 percent Mexican. The hub of several stage lines and the Arizona and New Mexico Railroad connecting to the Southern Pacific, it was the obvious choice to be county seat when the new Greenlee County was created in 1909. Morenci was just as big but less a town, more a bunk for workers at the mines, mill, and smelter. About 70 percent Mexican, it had more familyless men living as lodgers and was more violent and more sharply divided between its mass of workers and their supervisors. Except for saloons its small-business sector was less developed. It remained less accessible, as the railroad connection to Clifton built by Phelps Dodge lacked passenger service. In 1903 Arizona Copper in Clifton employed about two thousand men, owned four thousand acres of mining property, produced 27 million pounds of refined copper a year, and paid large dividends–£352,000 from mining and £175,000 from the railroad line. Detroit Copper in Morenci employed about one thousand and produced 17 million pounds of refined copper. (The whole district, including several smaller companies, produced 60 million pounds a year.) The operations were massive and modern. Arizona Copper, considered in the industry to be one of the world's leading mines, operated a railway, five concentrators, an acid plant reclaiming fourteen tons of sulfuric acid daily from the fumes of the roasters, and five smelter furnaces, not to mention a foundry, sawmill, ice plant, charcoal briquette plant, machine shops, carpenter shops, smithy, car shops, roundhouses, and many other buildings and pieces of large equipment.[49]

No wonder Cornelio Chacón was proud to be employed in Arizona Copper's smelter. His job required both toughness and delicacy: he skimmed the iron oxide slag off the final "blister" copper emerging from the last stage of smelting, the converters. It was particularly hard to bear during the summer, when stepping outside brought no cooling wind. He could become indignant about being paid less than whites, many of whom he knew to be less skilled, but still his $2.25 a day was reliable and significantly more than he could get in Mexico, his wife took in a little more from her catechism classes, and he had never run from hard work. There was a future here and he had been proud also to be able to provide a home for two poor orphans.

October 1, 1904, 6:30 P.M.

Clifton Railroad Station

THE THREE SISTERS and four nurses accompanying the orphans had traveled to many towns in America, but no arrival had been more wondrous and dramatic than this. After dropping off seventeen children in Missouri and Arkansas, they traveled smoothly until a flooded-out section of track in New Mexico Territory delayed them for a whole day.[1] As they left El Paso they headed northwest for many hours through a desert mesa thirty-five hundred feet high (if they knew they were that high, it was only from a slight shortness of breath) sprinkled with occasional small mesas and clumps of sharp mountains, rising abruptly, without foothills. The women were repelled by a land so unpeopled, unworked, unfruitful. The colors of the sparse vegetation at the end of September–nothing higher than a few feet–were limited to straw, brown, and the faintest tinges of blue green. By Deming, on the Mimbres River fifty miles west of Las Cruces, they had reached forty-three hundred feet and welcomed the cooler temperature. Peddlers at the station tried to sell them some of the ancient Mimbres Indians' pottery, not yet discovered by the Bohemians and artists who made old southwestern ceramics priceless. From here the vista softened but remained cold and lonely, and as they gradually descended they found themselves encircled by a distant ring of mountains all around, vivid blue, with a few scattered gray-brown closer ones.

Although Clifton was the oldest and biggest copper camp in Arizona, it was not on a main east-west railroad line so the railroad car had to be transferred at Lordsburg (scene of the final shoot-out between Ringo Kid and the Plummers thirty-five years later in the movie *Stagecoach*), from the Southern Pacific to the small Arizona and New Mexico Railroad, owned by the Arizona Copper Company, which ran a once-daily passenger service into Clifton. But nothing changed in their window views until they reached Duncan, where suddenly the panorama shrank and turned green. Here they saw the first "verdure" since the Rio Grande; from the depot they could see grain and alfalfa fields, cottonwood trees and mistletoe, because the Gila River watered the land and permitted high-yield farming.[2] This kinder environment raised their hopes that the children would find comfort here, but not for long. As they approached Clifton, they entered the mountains that had once been in the distance; up close they became less blue and more gray and brown, frightening in their barrenness. Nothing green was visible. As they climbed, deep chasms moved ever closer to the edges of the track.

Then rather suddenly, at about 6 P.M., they spied dark smoke, darker and denser than the engine's, and saw first the Shannon and then the Clifton smelter, state-of-the-art huge industrial plants, puffing thick smoke trails and clouds, their hulks resting in thousand-foot-deep gulches, with steep cliffs and hills alongside. In the distance were 4,600-foot Clifton Peak immediately ahead and 5,600-foot Mulligan Peak off to the right. Huge heaps and ridges seemed to be built of pure coal, but they were slag, residue from the smelter, and in the dark one could see the molten red slag oozing down the hill. Not only the New Yorkers but perhaps even newly arrived cowboys, businessmen, ranchers, and miners were taken aback at the spectacle: "the Dantesque image obtained—sulphur, slag, glaring heat, perpetual subterranean fires, roasted landscape . . . seems to fulfill the abomination of desolation of scripture."[3] But some saw only its economic promise.

The station, like the whole small town of about forty-five hundred, rests in a deep canyon walled in by rock and chalk bluffs 200–300 feet. The hills are today austere—red, gray, and white—because they are treeless; once they had been gray green from the mesquite and scrub oak. At about 6:30 P.M., when the train pulled to a stop, the sun was already behind the peaks, deepening the haze created by the smoke and fumes.

There was a big crowd at the station but these sisters—so much more worldly than many other nuns because they often traveled far to deliver orphans—were not surprised by that. There were always crowds greeting the orphan trains, and in a town of this size people would hear about all the new arrivals on the daily train, not just celebrities like these. The event had been anticipated in Clifton for months previous. Clifton-Morenci's priest, Father Mandin, had received the New York Foundling Hospital's letter soon after he arrived at this mission the previous February. A young neophyte immigrant priest, just off the boat from France, he knew that his bishop in Tucson would be watching his performance. He knew nothing of orphan trains or of the Irish Sisters of Charity; and he knew that his bishop answered to St. Louis, not to the Irish New York church. But as a foreign "missioner" who had been transported thousands of miles precisely because the church was universal, this offer of foundlings still struck him as an opportunity to organize a dramatic action that might help unite his new community around him. Drawing his parishioners into providing homes for motherless foundlings promised a wonderful beginning to his stewardship. So when he had the letter translated and read aloud, he made a special pitch for the motherless waifs.

He could tell that the women were talking and taking the request seriously, and he was not surprised when several dozen women in both Clifton and Morenci wanted to sign up immediately. He followed the New York instructions closely, checking to make sure these were respectable Catholic women, communicants, and the more demands he made, the more committed they became. He learned that numerous of his parishioners had not been married in the church, and he insisted on their doing so as the price of his approving their applications for children. Finally forty children had been assigned to Clifton-Morenci, so almost forty families (a few volunteered to take two orphans) were directly involved. These families and their relatives, friends, and neighbors as well as other curious parishioners came to the station to watch. And it was Saturday night. The crowd was, of course, mainly female because men were more likely to be in saloons on this payday evening and less likely to be interested in orphans, but the crowd also included some of the Chinese men who worked as laundrymen and cooks.

The New York sisters, accustomed to coping with curious onlookers, had closed the curtains in the railroad car so the children would not be visible from the outside, and as a result the crowd concentrated at the car door. Father Mandin had ordered horse-drawn wagons to take the children to the Sacred Heart Church, where their assigned families would come to get them. There are stories about orphan-train orphans being displayed like animals or slaves, potential parents looking them over, checking their teeth and muscles before choosing them, but the Sisters of Charity took pride in the fact that they never operated that way. The Foundling Hospital arranged careful, professional advance assignments of the orphans to families vetted by the priests. Father Mandin maintained, later, that sixty families had applied for orphans, of which he selected thirty-three and rejected twenty-seven. (That Mandin claimed to have selected thirty-three families and the sisters claimed he had asked for forty is one of the unresolvable inconsistencies among different testimonies about these events.) He had checked out not only their homes but their jobs and wages.[4] Children were never distributed without the proper paperwork. But since the sisters had never placed children as far away as Arizona before, they had not been able to send their agent, George Swayne, to investigate the potential homes beforehand. The sisters planned to look over the volunteer parents and warn them that the placements were only probationary until all the homes could be checked out. At least this is what the sisters claimed afterward.

One of the prospective mothers had helped the padre organize the paperwork and arrangements, because she had become his trusted assistant in just about everything and because she was fluent in Spanish and English: Margarita Chacón. She was one of the first parishioners Mandin met, although she had not made a unique first impression because, like some of the other women, she always dressed in black with a black shawl shadowing her face. Her dress and demeanor and, just possibly, her eyeglasses led many to think that she was older than her actual years, which were somewhere between twenty-four and twenty-seven. He might also have assumed that she was a Mexican, since she had light brown skin and wore Mexican style dress, and she was a Mexican as far as everyone in town was concerned, but she was born Margaret Miller in New Mexico of German and Spanish parents or perhaps, as a different census has it, in Florida of German and French parents. Raised in an El Paso Catholic orphanage—we do not know how she got there—she was bilingual, had become acculturated as a Mexican girl, and lived her life as a Mexican woman.[5] Her choice of racial identity was remarkable, forswearing the advantages that an Anglo persona could have brought her, but her passionate faith made it not really a choice after all. Mexican people were her family, and none other could have recognized and accepted her spiritual passion.

The other Clifton-Morenci Mexican women admired her education, her resourcefulness, and the sense of autonomy she communicated–the product of her convent rather than family upbringing. As she came to the church to help every day, and Mandin grew to rely on her and to use her as a conduit for information to the other women, she became familiar, almost a staff member.

Margarita was what Mexican American Catholics sometimes called a *beata*. Technically a *beata* is a woman in the process of achieving sainthood. A term apparently first used in medieval Spain to recognize the religious significance that devout women created with their lives outside the church's institutions, a concept like that of the *beguine,* it points to women who dedicated themselves to manual labor and charitable service.[6] But Mexicans occasionally used the term to mean someone they considered deserving of sainthood–an example of the irregular, unorthodox folk Catholicism they practiced and against which Mandin knew he had to struggle. Sometimes *beatas* might become mystics, unsanctioned religious leaders, but they might also be popular community leaders or healers. In fact, Margarita's piety and dedication threatened to overwhelm Mandin–a visitor from an age of feminism might have thought her better priest material than he was–because he preferred a more moderate tone. But she had made herself indispensable, and he was hoping for the best. Señora Chacón was a *rezadora*–she took charge of the prayers at occasions such as wakes. She came to the church for adoration of the host every day so that the Blessed Sacrament would not be alone. (Indeed her husband, Cornelio, resented the amount of time she devoted to the church.)[7] And she was also a *celadora:* she decorated the church, kept its records, and supervised the cleaning and repair of church and residence.[8] The El Paso orphanage had given her education as well as intense religiosity, and her primary source of status in the community was as a teacher. She conducted classes in catechism, basic reading, and writing–English as well as Spanish–for Mexican children in her own home.

In El Paso six years earlier she had met and married Cornelio Chacón, when she was eighteen and he was substantially older.[9] He was a runaway, a Mexican migrant fleeing peonage and seeking a better future through American opportunity. We wonder why Margarita did not become a nun, how she met Cornelio, what he offered that was more attractive than the possibility of staying with the El Paso sisters. It seems he was a man of purpose and possibly even charisma:

From peonage he had raised himself to a good, steady, high-paying job in the smelter. He was something of a community leader, too: an officer of the local Sociedad Zaragoza, a fraternal benevolent organization affiliated with the Alianza Hispano Americana (the leading Mexican benevolent society) along with, for example, Clifton's only Latino deputy sheriff, David Arzate, and Mexican businessmen such as Enrique Holguín.[10] As a couple they were highly unusual—a marriage between a Mexican man and an Anglo woman was a rare occurrence not only in Clifton but anywhere. But no one seemed to think of Margarita as Anglo.

Señora Chacón's classes were one of the few instructional opportunities for the Mexican children in Clifton-Morenci. In the 1880s, when the population was much smaller and segregation less rigid, the children of the better-off merchants and workers went to the local elementary school. Now the number of inhabitants had mushroomed but since the growth was largely among Mexicans, the town government did not provide enough schools. The Chase Creek school hired Gregorio and Jesús Rodríguez, father and son, to cover the Mexican classes of the first three grades, but the majority of the Mexican children were not in school. Señora Chacón's teaching not only served religious and educational purposes but also allowed her to earn money independently as she collected small fees from her pupils' parents for her classes. As a teacher she belonged to a great Mexican tradition, a tradition of women's autonomy as well as of female commitment to cultural uplift and economic mobility. In parts of the U.S. southwest, Mexican women, mostly unmarried, played a major role in organizing *escuelitas,* small schools, or *escuelas particulares,* in places where they were not publicly provided for Mexican children. These little schools frequently combined religious and literacy training. Some such women were intellectuals and activists, like Sara Estela Ramírez of El Paso, a poet, political speaker, and supporter of the Partido Liberal Mexicano, an early manifestation of the Mexican revolutionary movement.[11] There is no reason to think that Señora Chacón was a political intellectual, but, especially since she came from El Paso, center of Mexican liberalism, she may well have known herself to be part of a respected and seemly occupation for a woman. Certainly the El Paso nuns had provided for her models of female autonomy, activism, discipline, commitment to a cause, and skepticism about men's inevitable supremacy.

Margarita had seen to it that every arrangement was perfectly in place before the children arrived. Each woman made or purchased some new clothing for the child she was to get, and had been told, accordingly, the age as well as name; and each family now had a letter authorizing pickup of its child. The families had been asked for a contribution to defray travel expenses, but they were not much more forthcoming with this money than they had been in response to any other financial appeal from Sacred Heart. The women had, however, brought cooked food to the church for the babies and the sisters. Margarita had checked with the station and learned about the delay, informing the others more or less when to expect the train. Ever scrupulous and self-sacrificing, she volunteered not to come to the station but to stay at the church to make sure everything was ready.

When the train pulled in, Father Mandin stepped on board to consult with the head sister, Anna Michaella. He had thought to take all forty children to the church, but she vetoed this plan for several reasons. The children were all very tired. Then, too, she had just learned how far Morenci was, and that there was no way to get the children there before the next day, and she did not want them to sleep on church pews (even before she realized that the pews were just rough benches). To lessen confusion and stress, Sister Anna Michaella decided to send out only the sixteen children destined for Clifton homes, with three Foundling Hospital women and George Swayne, and to keep the twenty-four headed for Morenci to sleep on the train, since they wouldn't be able to get there until the next day anyway. Sister Francis Liguori, and three other Foundling women would remain on the train with the Morenci group.

The father asked some of the Clifton ladies at the front of the crowd at the station, those who had gotten themselves closest to the train, to help him lift the children down from the car, onto the platform, and into the wagons. Or perhaps these ladies pressed forward on their own, without being asked, reaching to lift the lovely children from the steps of the car. Mrs. Wright, Mrs. Abraham, Mrs. Parks, and Mrs. Simpson were bursting with curiosity and eager to help and made their way to the front of the crowd, as the more reserved and deferential Mexican women stepped back. Laura Abraham, wife of the owner of the Clifton Hotel, the biggest and finest hotel in town, later said that she had immediately asked for the privilege of taking one of the orphans, assuming that requests for children would be accepted on the spot because she had probably read some of the many newspaper stories about the famous orphan trains that described lineups of children waiting to be picked. Mr. Swayne, she said, had replied that, before any distribution of the children, strict inquiry would have to be made into the standing of the people who wanted them and their ability to care for the children.[12] Mrs. Gatti was certainly neither deferential nor reserved in her eagerness. This is how she described her approach:

> There was a large crowd at the depot; and I thought to myself, "I better get where I could see the babies good." So the car pulled up a little ahead, and I goes to work and climbs the box car—not exactly a box car, but a flat car that you load lumber on—and [I] gets a peak at the children and jumps down and goes up to the butcher shop and tells Mr. Gatti, "Oh, but there is some lovely children in that car over there."

What is it, one might ask, that made these women "ladies"? Their status might have been unintelligible to a New York man like Swayne or a foreigner like Mandin. (A woman might have picked up the distinction more quickly.) It was not a distinction based, as it might have been in England or the East, on delicacy of manners. Clifton's "ladies" were accustomed, often, to hard manual labor, building, digging, cleaning, as they faced mud slides, scorpions, and gunfire. And some of them, like the irrepressible Louisa Gatti, could be as fit and sassy as an adolescent boy. The markers of ladyhood here had less to do with behavior than with appearance and ethnicity. Clifton ladies dressed differently from the Mexican women (although everyone's clothes were perpetually dusty): the "ladies" wore hats but no serapes, dresses and skirts often store-bought, of colors and plaids but not solid black, boots instead of sandals. Their skin was lighter, their hair worn twisted on top of their heads. And they spoke English.

In any case the Anglo women were eager to see and hold the orphans, who were beautifully decked out, the girls in what Mrs. Wright described as "little white French dresses" and the boys in sailor suits. They certainly were a pretty sight: the girls all had ribbons in their nicely combed hair, the boys even had little sailor caps, and they all wore shiny black lace-up boots. The littlest, Elizabeth Kane, to be two years old the following day, was absolutely irresistible with her chubby short legs encased in black lisle stockings.

In these few minutes an agitation began to roil up these observers—an agitation that was to plunge the towns into a furor nearly as intense as that over the massive mineworkers' strike the year before. In fact, for the Anglo women, the events of these days were more disturbing than the previous year's strike, and seemed as momentous. Father Mandin as yet had no inkling of a problem, and it seems doubtful that the dozens of others at the station did either. Certainly the sisters did not, nor did Agent Swayne. In fact, it is not clear exactly at what point the events became defined by participants as a problem because, of course, history is told from afterward not from beforehand.

The problem as the ladies began to construct it right there at the station was that the lovely orphans were Anglos, not only elegantly dressed but also blond and light-skinned, and most of the crowd at the station was Mexican. The Anglo ladies began to suspect that these Mexicans were the prospective parents for the lovely white orphans. The Anglo observers did not understand the Foundling Hospital procedures or that the children were all spoken for; they expected the orphans to be up for grabs. Their sudden desire to acquire children for themselves might have been supported by some misunderstood words, although it seems more likely that wishful thinking rather than loose talk was the source of the misunderstanding. Laura Abraham "took one of these children in my own arms and held it until all had been placed in the hacks; and as I held the little one I handed it to Mr. Swayne, and I said, 'I'll keep this one'; and he said, 'Not tonight,' but gave me the impression I could have the child if I applied for it the next morning, in that tone of voice." Muriel Wright recalled that "we were anxious all this time to hold these little children . . . and I said, not only once, but a number of times, 'Wouldn't you love to have this little one and that little one'; and Mr. Swayne was there and I heard him say, 'No hurry madam, we will be here two or three days.'" At this time Swayne had no idea what the prospective foster parents looked like and might well have thought these Anglo ladies were they, just a little overeager, and he wanted them to take their children from the church in an orderly fashion.

The excitement at the station no doubt increased the children's agitation. Naturally, they were uneasy, scared, possibly panicky: over the last week they had lost some of the original anxiety at being pulled away from the orphanage and begun to feel comfortable in their car, but now they had abruptly been dressed in new clothes, handed from one strange woman to another, placed high up on a buggy, then trotted off down a dusty, rutted road. The sisters soothed them until they arrived at the church a few minutes later, then lifted them down from the wagons, and placed them on the rough pews of a small, dark church with instructions to sit and wait. Father Mandin directed all this with gestures, unable to make his words understood by the sisters, except when Señora Chacón was nearby to translate. The church was not familiar: even its crucifix was different; the adobe walls and the father's costume were foreign. And soon some of the crowd from the station came in, staring at the children and whispering among themselves.

2

Mexicans Come to the Mines

Adíos mi patria querida:	Good-bye, my beloved country,
yo ya me voy a ausentar	Now I am going away;
me voy para Estados Unidos	I go to the United States
donde pienso trabajar.	Where I intend to work.
Me voy triste ye pesaroso	I go sad and heavy-hearted
Ga sufrir y a padecer	To suffer and endure;
Madre mía de Guadalupe,	My Mother Guadalupe,
tu me concedas volver.	Grant my safe return.
Pues yo no tengo la culpa	For I am not to blame
que abandone así a mi tierra	That I leave my country thus;
la culpa es de la pobreza	The fault lies in the poverty,
que nos tiene en la miseria.	Which keeps us all in want.
Ya con ésta me despido	And so I take leave
de mi Patria Mexicana,	Of my country, Mexico.
he llegado a Ciudad Juárez,	I have reached Ciudad Juárez
¡oh Virgen Guadalupana!	Oh, Virgin of Guadalupe![1]

CLIFTON SHOULD HAVE BEEN A GOOD FIT for the orphans, because nearly everyone there was an immigrant. The Chiricahua and Western Apaches were the native "owners" of the land—but as soon as large-scale profits could be squeezed from the mines they were expropriated by a combination of capital and political clout. The mines pulled in immigrant workers from Britain, Italy, Spain, Germany, Canada, Mexico, and China, and migrants from practically every state, but the overwhelming majority came from Sonora and Chihuahua. No other mine or smelter had such a high percentage of Mexican workers, not even those much closer to Mexico like Bisbee or Douglas. So despite the 165 miles to the border,[2] the orientation of Clifton's population was southward.

Even today one approaches Clifton and Morenci almost always from the south. Highway 191 (formerly Route 666, but they changed the name a few years ago because of protests from fundamentalists) winds down from the north over the Mogollon Rim, but it is a slow, picturesque, and not much traveled route, and there was never train service from the north. By car you come up from Tucson, from the southwest, through Safford and the former Solomonville, once the county seat, or from the southeast from El Paso; by train a spur takes off northward from the Southern Pacific at Lordsburg, New Mexico. But you always come from the south. The southern orientation reflects the topography, of course, and also the human geography.

Until a century ago all travel in the area was oriented north-south, not east-west, and it was arduous because there are no navigable rivers for hundreds of miles. The first political center from which Arizona was governed was Mexico City, the capital first of Spanish and then independent Mexico. Explorers and traders came from the south and returned to the south. The nearest port was Guaymas, on the Gulf of California, and virtually everything eaten and used in the mining camps came from or through there: foods like flour, beef, beans, sugar, barley, corn, and vegetables from Sonora; manufactured goods from Europe. This stuff came at first by pack train, and hundreds of Mexicans earned a living as muleteers; then the Atchison Topeka and Santa Fe Railroad connected Guaymas to Tucson and the Southern Pacific in 1882.[3]

The labor market was also primarily a north-south enterprise. As Clifton and Morenci lie on the northern edge of the Sonoran highlands region of rich mineral deposits, experienced miners were, naturally, found to the south. Skill and experience underlay the prominence of Sonorans in 1870s and 1880s mining, but the 1890s takeoff of industrial copper production changed the conditions of their employment drastically. As absentee ownership and a longer chain of management command distanced supervisors from their men, workers were hired anonymously, en masse, and then discharged in bulk when copper prices dropped. An entirely new frontier was developing, an industrial frontier with a new and distinct border proletariat.

In other mining camps, even nearby Bisbee and Globe, the mine-workers were primarily Anglo migrants. Further from their American or European homelands, their visits "home" were few, while the mainly Mexican workers of Clifton-Morenci retained ties with their homes, tightening the bonds with frequent visits. The new labor market they entered was created both by Mexican underdevelopment and by U.S. development—which are of course closely and causally related—and they combined to create a borderlands migrant labor force and a bor-der culture. It was not an intermediate culture but an integral working class with a unique identity and composition, including some distinc-tive gender and race structures. The revolutionary years of the next decade would affect this class profoundly, and many of these border workers would become passionately patriotic Mexicans, but their labor and cultural experience was transnational.[4] Migration impressed itself not only on their fundamental life expectations but also on the con-sciousness and social organization of Clifton-Morenci's majority Mexi-can population, and migration helps to explain their involvement in the orphan episode.

Cornelio Chacón, foster father of Jerome Shanley and Katherine Fitzpatrick, was such a migrant, perhaps even a "typical" migrant. We know he had been a "peon"—a worker usually bound to his employers, unfree to leave, subject to corporal punishment—and had run away to the United States through El Paso, but that is all. His son Juan Chacón died just before I first went to Clifton, and his grandchildren do not know his history. No scholar ever interviewed Clifton-Morenci migrants. So I pieced together a composite "typical" history from the migratory experiences of similar people in similar towns.[5]

Consider the migration patterns of the Hoyos and Córdoba families. When Consuela Hoyos's husband, Ramón Córdoba, was killed, she moved in with her husband's sister and brother-in-law. This household reflected not only her in-laws' sense of responsibility for her, but also the fact that the Hoyos and Córdoba families had long been close and had moved from one Sonoran mining town, Cananea, to another, Agua Prieta, at the same time. Her son Carlos Córdoba apprenticed informally in the workshop of his uncle, a blacksmith. Since Agua Prieta is right on the border, it was not surprising that in this shop

Carlos not only learned traditional smithing but also became familiar with American inches and yards, tools and parts, drilling and machining. When he was fifteen he began a six-year series of job trips to United States, working in mines, railroads, and agriculture. For a while he worked near Douglas, stayed in a company dormitory, and returned home on weekends. Then he went to Phelps Dodge in Bisbee in the maintenance department, keeping track of tools; then he picked tomatoes in California and worked on the railroad; then returned to mining. During this time he was joined by one of his brothers, and they came home less frequently. Their money, however, arrived regularly and helped support their mother and sisters, one of whom was working as a seamstress. Carlos and his brother bought their mother wood for floors and tar paper for the roof of her house, and installed them. They bought her a sewing machine, a cast-iron stove, and a hand mill. Having lived so close to the United States for so long they were quick to understand and love cars, and they jointly bought one while in California, which they proudly brought back to Agua Prieta. They continued returning and sending money to their mother's home until she died.

In the first decades of industrial mining, these Mexican workers spanned not only nations but also economic systems: they were both workers and peasants. Santiago Aguirre was one of thousands who lived that double life. He had worked in mines in the United States, Sonora, and Zacatecas. When he married in 1903 he was a mine paymaster, a job requiring education, recording the quotas and piecework men accomplished, and at times he even substituted for American workers on vacation. As his nine children were born he and his wife, Antonia Peralta, frequently moved back and forth between the El Tigre mine and the Sonoran village of Bacerac, where his wife's family were smallholders. His wife wanted whenever possible to be with her mother during childbirths. Antonia's oldest brother, José María, kept the family land and passed it to his youngest son, while all the other siblings went to the mines, probably brought into their jobs by Aguirre. This generation retained a peasant core from which individuals ventured out into wage work. In the next generation, Luis Aguirre, Antonia's son, became exclusively a wage worker, both in mines and in agriculture, still sometimes migrant but always close to his peasant cousins, who were themselves migrants, or commuters, in another way: they regularly came to the El Tigre mining camp to sell

beans and chiles and would leave their mules in the corral of Antonia's house while there. Gradually, Luis lost track of who actually
kept the plot of land in Bacerac, as its value, no doubt, declined ever
further.

Carlos Córdoba, Santiago Aguirre, and Clifton foster-father Cornelio Chacón were part of a mass migration, smaller than the nearly
contemporaneous African American Great Migration but nonetheless
a history-changing event. The whole American working class formed
out of four great diasporas—from Europe, Africa, Asia, and Mexico;
and while the Mexican was numerically small compared to the European, its impact on the U.S. Southwest was greater than the numbers
suggest, and this region constituted more than half the North American
land mass. There was no need for *coyotes,* guides to sneak illegals
through the border; there were no border markings (save a few stone
pillars here and there), no immigration control, and thus no illegals.
Lacking border control, the United States had no reliable immigration
figures from the turn of the century, but there are some good estimates:
perhaps 50,000 in 1900, up from under 1,000 a year in the previous
decade, increasing to 60,000 in 1907. Observers in Bisbee estimated
higher, between 60,000 and 100,000 a year at the turn of the century,
but they were not counting how many Mexicans traveled the other
way, returning to Mexico. Governor Kibby of Arizona reported in
1907, "What proportion of those Mexican immigrants remain here
permanently is impossible to say. They are passing to and fro all the
time between Sonora and Arizona."[6] The 1900 census counted only
14,000 Mexican residents of Arizona, doubling to 30,000 in 1910,
almost certainly a substantial underestimate.[7]

THE FORCES THAT IMPOVERISHED MEXICANS and literally forced
them out of their native land ("underdevelopment") were the same
forces that turned the rapidly expanding and industrializing United
States into a veritable magnet for labor ("development").[8] The U.S.
victory over Mexico in midcentury hastened the dispossession of the old
Mexican inhabitants of what was now U.S. soil and also, ironically,
accelerated Mexican industrialization by bringing in American capital.
Porfirio Díaz seized power in Mexico in 1876 and opened his country to
U.S. investment—some might say, plunder—giving away 134,500,000
acres of land, one-fifth of the area of Mexico, to personal friends and
foreign speculators. Large landowners enclosed peasant common lands

(ejidos) until 1 percent of rural families owned 85 percent of the land and 96 percent of Mexicans were landless—one of the largest land grabs in history. (The enclosures were enforced, in Mexico as in the United States, by a new product: barbed wire.) "Push" is too gentle a word for this process. Its operation was brutal. By the 1890s many displaced peasants had been forced into itinerancy, wandering, usually by foot, sometimes hundreds of miles in search of work.[9]

Thus these former peasants came from a Mexico already being radically transformed by capitalism, and they did not usually move directly from peasant labor in Mexico to industrial work in the United States. Rather, they typically migrated in two stages. They often headed first to northern Mexico, where debt peonage was weaker—though still predominant on haciendas—and the wage-labor market stronger. As a result, the Mexicans who entered the U.S. mines were often not peasants but had been proletarians in their home country, although even as miners many had been peons.[10] But this new working class was by no means detached from the peasantry. Sonoran and Chihuahuan peasants hung on to their remaining lands and often developed a kind of family mixed economy: men began commuting to mining jobs, hoping thereby to accumulate wages that could be invested back in their villages.[11]

The investment subsidized by Díaz poured not only into land and industry but also into building the infrastructure of modernization, railroads. Railroads had a multiple impact on the border working class. By lowering transportation costs, they created the conditions for the profitable extraction of nonprecious, low-concentration ores like Sonoran copper. They also displaced many workers: muleteers who had driven pack teams, handicraft workers whose markets were eroded by manufactured goods, peasants who could now be undersold by food and meat shipped from the vast commercial haciendas.[12] At the same time, they created a new demand for laborers—indeed, railway work became the single most common job drawing Mexican peasants into wage labor as they replaced Chinese workers in the period 1880–1920.[13]

Then the railroads carried Mexicans into industrial labor, in their own country and in the United States. In 1880 there was not one railroad going anywhere north of Zacatecas; by 1884 you could travel by rail from Mexico City to Chicago, and before the turn of the century there were 22,000 railroad cars carrying approximately 70,000 passengers from Mexico into the United States every year. A railroad ticket north was so valuable that many peasants pawned their last pig, even the crossbeam of their house, for a train ticket to Nogales or El Paso.[14] The same train that carried the foundlings to Clifton no doubt picked up some of these hopeful miners at Lordsburg. In the Mexican *corridos,* as in the African American blues, men sang with love and pain of trains and riding the rails.

Corre, corre, maquinita,	Run, run, little machine [engine?]
Por esa línea del Quiri,	Along that Katy line,
Anda a llevar este enganche	Carry this party of contract laborers
Al estado de Kansas City.	To the state of Kansas City.
Ese tren a Kansas City	This train to Kansas City
Es un tren muy volador,	Is a flying train,
Corre cien millas por hora	It travels one hundred miles an hour
Y no le dan todo el vapor.	And they don't give it all the steam.
Vuela, vuela, palomita,	Fly, fly little dove,
Párate en ese manzano,	Light on that apple tree.
Estos versos son compuestos	These verses are composed
A todos los mexicanos.	For all the Mexicans.[15]

Just as Mexicans followed the Chinese into railway work, so the expulsion of Chinese workers from the mines pulled the Mexicans underground. Early entrepreneurs had hired Sonoran miners first but soon turned to the Chinese, whom they believed to be more easily exploitable. Like the Mexicans, Chinese men had moved eastward from their California entry point, working for the railroads and doing a little prospecting on the side. The Chinese worked hard, skillfully, cheaply and, employers believed, "were not afraid to work at any depth and with little shoring of the roofs of the tunnels." But both "American" and Mexican workers thought that the Chinese depressed wages and working conditions (exactly the charge against Mexicans in the white camps) and sought to prevent this by excluding rather than organizing them. Miners staged armed uprisings against the Chinese in every western mining state and most of the companies capitulated, expelling them from the mines and employing them only as cooks, servants, and laundrymen.[16] (In 1882 the Chinese Exclusion Act prohibited further Chinese immigration.) Then the label of docility fell on the Mexicans, a label they had not worn in the placer-mining era. Sylvester Mowry, an early mine owner and propagandist for investment in Arizona and Sonora, reported that his "own experience has taught me that the lower class of Mexicans, with the Opata and Yaqui Indians, are docile, faithful, good servants . . . They have been 'peons' (servants) for generations. They will always remain so, as it is their natural condition."[17] Mexicans replaced the Chinese as the designated cheap labor.

About the alleged docility, we will see more soon. Mexicans took low wages precisely because, to them, it was high wages. As you rode the rails north from Mexico City, wages went up as the demand for labor went up: In 1900 common laborers earned 23¢ a day in the interior, 88¢ in Juárez, and $1.00–$1.50 on the frontier. The prevailing wage on Mexican haciendas for agricultural labor was 12¢ a day, while in the United States clearing land paid 50¢ a day, railroad and agricultural labor $1.00–$2.00, and mining work $2.00. In mining alone the pay rose from 37¢ to 75¢ a day in Guerrero up to $2.00 a day in Sonora, the highest in Mexico.[18]

Moving from Mexican to American mines was easy because Americans owned both. Mexico attracted half of all U.S. foreign investment up to 1910, and mining accounted for two-thirds of this investment in 1902.[19] By 1910, three-quarters of active Mexican mines were U.S.-owned. Within Mexico, American-owned mines paid better than Mexican mines; across the border they paid better yet. Mexican miners could simply transfer to American mines with the same owners, such as Phelps Dodge or Anaconda. As a result, migrants did not stay long in the Mexican mines. One mine manager from Chihuahua complained that he had imported eight thousand workers from Zacatecas and elsewhere in Central Mexico but that within a year 80 percent had left for the United States.[20]

Profitable mining was jeopardized by scarcity of labor power. High wages and grapevines were not enough to reel in workers, and the mine managers resorted to direct recruitment. In the 1880s the Lesinskys' foreman from Clifton, Don Antonio, rode through Sonora recruiting workers, encouraging them to bring their families in order to stabilize the labor force. Professional headhunters, *enganchistas* or *enganchadores*–literally, hookers–used saloons and hotel parlors in the border towns or in Sonora and Chihuahua as recruitment offices; or they stood on rear platforms of northbound trains and exhorted villagers, promising high wages and offering to pay transportation costs. Those recruited and possibly even the recruiters would have been surprised to know that the U.S. Alien Contract Labor Law of 1885 prohibited recruitment of workers in Mexico, which was standard practice.[21] The gangs of workers were placed on northbound trains, while the agents held the tickets, the cost of which was passed on to the American employer, who deducted it from the workers' pay. They traveled in parties under a *cabo,* or boss, often in cars with locked doors or even armed guards. But frequently the workers took the train rides into the United States and then lit out on their own, dumping *enganchadores* in order to keep the full wages for themselves.[22]

The greatest seductive power of the United States, then as today, came from consumer goods, and these too were brought by the railroads. As early as 1879 an Arizona newspaper explained that the labor crisis in Sonora arose because the peons wanted shoes, Levis, and flannel shirts. Saying "it's American" was a universal form of bragging, as was the opposite: "Hecho en Mexico, mal hecho" (If it's made in Mexico, it's badly made).[23] Peddlers conveyed goods from railroad depots to the remotest villages; peasants rode the Nacozari-Douglas line into the United States to shop.[24] Villagers became regular customers of the railroad commissary cars. The mining companies promoted consumption through the dazzling array of items and the credit they offered in company stores, producing an upward spiral of desire for goods and for jobs to pay for them. As one Texas Anglo "expert" on Mexicans described it, "Most of them came north with no money and little clothing, sandals (huraches) [*sic*] instead of shoes, wide sombreros, and blankets wrapped around them instead of coats. They are returning with rolls of money, often several hundred dollars, with good suitcases in their hands and most of them are dressed in the dearly-loved blue suits."[25] The allure of consumption transformed not only individuals but northern Mexican society and culture as well. Several states attempted to ban the *pantalón* (loose cotton pants) and require the wearing of American-style slacks; beer replaced tequila as the most popular drink; American railroad workers introduced baseball, and it soon became the most popular sport in Sonora, forcing many bullrings to close.[26] Consumption and wage work rose together in a spiral: money was once a meager, hoarded supplement to a peasant economy, but now wages became fundamental and desirable, and this further loosened the hold of the villages on their young men.

MOST OF CLIFTON-MORENCI'S MINEWORKERS came from the Mexican north, bringing its distinct culture with them. The pull of things American was greater for the *norteños* than for southern and central Mexicans, and not only because of proximity. *Norteño* was not only a geographical expression, although its unique cultural content arose from its regional identity. In contrast to the heart of Mexico, the north had lacked a vigorous urban life, a strong sedentary Indian culture, and an economically vigorous church; its large estates were mainly in secular hands. As a result, the conservative alliance between church and Indians common in the south was missing and, instead, anticlericalism prevailed. Sonora and Chihuahua were sparsely populated, partly because they were desert highlands, partly because of the Apache raids, but also for political reasons. Sonora and Chihuahua had been run for most of the nineteenth century by a few *caudillos* who drew their Indian and *mestizo* subjects into nearly constant warfare. War with the Apaches, anthropologist Ana María Alonso argues, had elaborated a warrior culture, an internally strained masculinity in which the superiority and manliness of the Mexican *norteños* depended upon an ideological contrast with barbaric Apaches. The normative Mexican feeling toward Apaches was complex: hated and feared, never disdained, the Apaches were known as brave and powerful but wild; the *norteños* called them *broncos,* the same word applied to undomesticated animals. By contrast *norteño* masculinity had to combine valor and honor, bravery and rationality. Thus the Mexican usage *gente de razón,* people with reason, in contrast to the *indios bárbaros.*[27]

Except for the indigenous population, *norteño* relation to the land was different from that in the south: land was more commoditized, and peasants' bonds to particular lands were weaker.[28] These Yankees of Mexico were perhaps more individualistic and entrepreneurial than their compatriots, more restless, a set of qualities the more imbedded because they were about masculinity, manliness, gender, and proving oneself.[29] So perhaps the *norteños* were quicker to seize the opportunities offered by American copper, less reluctant to leave their *patria.*

The *norteños* liked to consider themselves more "like" the Americans not only temperamentally but also in a discourse about "color" that became part of their regional identity. *Norteño* superiority over the southern *chilangos* was expressed as the superiority of whiteness over brownness, to the point that the whiteness became a "nature," signifying bravery, independence, and rebelliousness, honoring a personal conduct that was hardworking, democratic, egalitarian, and open to individual achievement—here their Yankeeness. Their valorization of whiteness was not a U.S. imperial construction, though perhaps it was a Spanish one: from the eighteenth century and probably earlier, being white conveyed status, and becoming lighter was synonymous with upward mobility. A racial drift defined as upward emerged as the elite became whitened; Hispanicized *mestizos* and mulattoes were said to *blanquearse,* bleach themselves. This bleaching was a social, not a skin-tone, process: high status made a family white no matter what the individual skin colors. Indeed, in the eighteenth century *norteños* re-wrote their history to deny their interbreeding with Indians, thus furthering the possibility for mixed-blood people to become "white" socially.[30]

Lightness of color had special salience for *norteñas* because it fashioned definitions of beauty and decorum. Women's sexual modesty and chastity was part of lightness. Indeed, lightness shaped the very identity of "civilized women," distinguishing the *norteñas* from Indian women. Equally it distinguished *norteñas* from southern Mexican women: In the north they cherished more the (white) Virgin Mary than the (brown) Virgin of Guadalupe. Some women used honey and lemon juice to try to lighten their skin. As manufactured cosmetics became available, *norteñas* bought preparations from the United States that bleached hair and skin, curled hair, and lifted noses; more recently, they surgically narrowed their noses.[31]

The new wonders of manufacturing also beckoned women because they offered new organizations of labor. Industrially milled wheat flour from the United States became particularly desirable. *Norteños* soon came to prefer flour to cornmeal and consumed a disproportionate share of the country's wheat.[32] Cast-iron wood stoves offered such advantages that younger generations of women soon lost the knack of repairing and reshaping adobe ovens when they cracked, became misshapen, or collapsed.[33] Sewing machines were being promoted throughout the region by the first decade of this century: through agents of the big corporations like Singer, who advertised in *norteño* and Arizona Spanish-language newspapers, or through U.S. company stores in Mexico and Arizona. With these machines women could replicate fashions they saw in the papers, save considerable time in sewing for their families, and earn by sewing for others. Many Mexican village women acquired treadle machines before 1910.[34] This not only offered single women a way to earn, but also considerably changed married women's options for contributing to the family economy and, arguably, increased their power within their families.

The openness of Porfirian Mexico to American capital and goods has been figured as a sexual metaphor of Mexico's (female) subordination. But in another way "America" also lay open to Mexican laboring men. These migrations were easier in 1904 than they are today. "Both American officials and entering aliens understood that it was the labor needs of the American Southwest that defined Mexican migration to the U.S. and not laws drawn up in Washington."[35] The migrants were not so much going into a foreign country as joining other communities of Mexicans (*México de afuera,* they called it) or, more specifically, of *norteños* or, even more specifically, relatives and neighbors.[36] In a perspective that became more conscious and articulate during the Mexican Revolution, they conceived of themselves as moving from free to occupied Mexico, or even as returning to a land from which they had been driven, first by Apaches, later by the even more unrelenting gringos. And for many, their identification as *norteños* was as strong or stronger than their identity as Mexicans, so they were not truly leaving their country either.

Norteño society, economy, and culture continued to shape the activities and experience of the migrant workers while in the Arizona mining camps.[37] Gradually the term *norteño* itself migrated to refer to those Mexicans who had worked and lived in the United States. The *norteño* land-inheritance system, for example, was not merely a factor expelling these workers into migration; it continued to shape their lives in the receiving location. Individual family land estates were typically so small that, divided among the children, they would become useless. Instead, one son would commonly inherit the land, quite possibly through negotiation with the rest of the family. Sons awaiting or excluded from inheritance might still continue to have economic as well as social attachments to their village. Often they sought cash wages in order to be able to purchase land, now an actively traded commodity in Mexico. Perhaps they thought to accumulate some cash to open a saloon or, observing the general increase in commodities, a small grocery in the village.[38] In the short term, their ability to send cash or bring prestigious consumer goods "home" raised their own status in the eyes of their compatriots.

At first the work was in the United States but the workers' goals were in Mexico. The earnings were a means to a homeland dream.[39] Their wage labor was purely instrumental and these migrant workingmen were, in economist Michael Piore's analysis, "the closest thing in real life to the *Homo economicus* of [neoclassical] economic theory." That is, their only goal in the United States was to maximize earning. Early on in their careers of migrant labor, male workers tended to live austerely, saving surprisingly high proportions of their very low wages—for example, Mexican workers often sent home 40 percent of earnings.[40] Postmasters reported to a federal investigator around 1905 that a significant part of their work involved making out money orders for Mexican workers to send home; fifteen years later sociologist Manuel Gamio counted these money orders: 5 million pesos the first year, 9 million the next; $23,000 in one four-month period.[41] The most common beginner migrants were single male lodgers, not only sharing rooms but often doubling or even tripling up in beds when they worked for around-the-clock operations such as the mines. Their only nonessential expenditures in Clifton-Morenci were liquor, gambling, and, occasionally, prostitutes.

The men's unqualified devotion to earning was qualitative as well as quantitative. They displayed a flexibility regarding their labor that reflected not only its alienation but the fact that their social identity remained primarily located in Mexico. Their self-identification as temporary residents of the United States created an unusual gulf between work and identity. That disconnection allowed them to perform work and occupy jobs in Arizona that might have been undignified, beneath their self-image, even humiliating in Mexico. "A Mexican is not particular about the kind of a job he gets . . . He is willing to shift from job to job . . . while the Italian doesn't like that."[42] Any work in the United States brought prestige, because of the higher wages (especially mine work, which offered the highest wages available) and the consumer goods, but there were deeper reasons too. There was pride in being a part of advanced, industrial, even technological production, in having worked in the largest mines, built the most modern railroads. Fusing temporary relinquishment of identity with prestige, Mexicans often made ideal employees from the employers' point of view. Many Mexican men worked in maintenance, as cleaners and janitors, doing "women's work," which would have been demeaning to them in Mexico; they could accept the work with equanimity not because

America had a more relaxed sexual division of labor, but simply because they were not at home. "If I'm going to do that sort of work, I'd rather do it over there. Then, I can come home and be myself." Similarly, "I work there: Then at home, I am king."[43]

There is an engaging perversity here. These new immigrants, often uneducated, from rural and generally agricultural backgrounds, supposedly steeped in communitarian and "traditional" values,[44] came to the United States and behaved . . . like radical individualists. Far more than those who had been American workers for a generation, the migrant workers were the true rational actors, unimpeded by "culture," seeking only personal profit maximization.

If these characteristics had not been enough to make the migrant Mexican laborers ideal workers, another aspect of their economic and geographical position made them employees from heaven: the fact that part of the costs of maintaining and renewing (that is, reproducing) their labor power fell on a different economy and society, Mexico.[45] In theory, wages are set by many factors, among them the actual cost of living. Presumably wages must provide at least for subsistence not only of the worker but also of his non- or lower-earning family members. But when the worker's children, wife, aged parents, and other dependents are two hundred or more miles away in another economy, working the land and maintaining themselves partly on nonwage resources, the worker is often able to survive on lower wages than could a worker whose family lives two blocks from the mine or smelter. Dividing production and reproduction between different economies had great advantages for employers in the dominant economy. The copper employers did not need to provide wages that could keep children properly clothed for attending school in all seasons, buy fuel for Clifton's cold winters and food for a family at inflated company-store prices, satisfy the desires of women and children attempting to dress like "Americans." The migrant laborer, straddling two nations and two economies, could view the dollars in his weekly pay envelope in terms of what they would buy in Mexico. While employers might not have conceived this migrant-labor system in precisely these terms, they certainly appreciated the fact that Mexican workers accepted wages half to two-thirds those of "American" workers and that they had to pay "American" wages for only a limited number of skilled positions.[46]

The Mexican workers *had to* travel back and forth, because they had responsibilities in Mexico. Payroll records suggest that in 1902 the majority of the Clifton-Morenci Mexican mineworkers "quit"–that is, left–three to six months after their first hire.[47] Itinerancy was not uniquely a Mexican pattern; it was common throughout western mines on the part of Anglos as well, and some found the whites less reliable and more likely to run out on a contract than the Mexicans. But the Mexicans who quit also came back. Their southward trips had a variety of purposes: they wanted to visit home; they wanted to return home when they had accumulated enough money for a particular purchase (thus the desire for consumer goods also encouraged labor transience); they missed their wives and children; they needed the satisfactions of return to a place where they were respected. Transience was also seasonal, as some miners returned to their village lands during planting and/or harvesting season.[48] Quitting was also the predominant form of protest, one inextricably involved with the personal need for honor. The Mexican migrants often returned to the same mine, but they also frequently moved from mine to mine in the search for better conditions (and higher wages, of course). Employers learned that they had to keep a roster of workers much larger than the number actually needed.

Mine and smelter supervisors seem to have missed the rationality of migrant workers' choices and instead believed that they were fickle, irresponsible, and immature. In the naturalizing metaphors of a Texas employer: "A Mexican is just exactly like a bee. The bee will go into the fields and forest, running through the flowers, and gets his honey from the whole of it, and he will stay there until the honey plays out–then he is gone."[49] His metaphor was not correct, because miners quit even before the "honey" was "played out," but their aspirations, which remained in Mexico, were invisible to employers. Some constructed romanticized and primitivized Mexican cultural attributes to account for this: "A Mexican has more reverence for home, family life, father, mother, brother, and sisters than the American. Men meet and they kiss each other and they love their home and not only that, their home means the place they came from and all the community, because it is married and intermarried."[50] Such "reverence" was often real but it was accompanied by strategic economic goals. Failing to recognize them, some employers came genuinely to believe that Mexicans did not want higher wages, inasmuch as higher wages did not induce them to remain on the job. "As soon as they get an increase of wages, they simply work fewer days and spend what they make . . . the higher wages we pay down there the less we get out of it."[51] "The average Mexican cannot stand prosperity," concluded one article of advice to mine employers.[52]

But the system was not stable because the migrants in Clifton-Morenci, as everywhere, displayed a tendency toward settlement. In fact, the classic immigration distinction between sojourners and settlers, migrants and immigrants, is only useful in hindsight, because in the actual lives of workers, settlement is never definitive until death.[53] Workers don't know what their future holds. Some intend to settle permanently but become unbearably homesick, or are affected by unforeseen family changes back home; others intend to return home but can never create the business or buy the land there that they dreamed of. This back-and-forthness was not disorganizing but permanent for many Mexican miners. They lived in a border culture (and many of them in twin towns that straddled the border, like Douglas and Agua Prieta, Bisbee and Naco, El Paso and Ciudad Juárez); they were not so much binational as they were border people, as if border itself were their nationality.

IN SITUATIONS OF CIRCULAR MIGRANT LABOR, work and home, labor and its renewal are separated; settlement reunifies the separated. Both migration and settlement rest on the work, needs, and choices of nonemployed members of the working class, especially wives, mothers, sisters, older children. Wherever there has been migrant labor there has been pressure toward settlement, which comes both from those in the "host" economy and from those at home. In the first stages of the Clifton-Morenci camp, men lived in tents, shacks, or barracks, and they lived poorly, their quarters often dirty and disorganized, their food unhealthy and unsatisfying—conditions that encouraged spending leisure time in saloons and enabled them to send so much money home. But it was difficult to live this way for long. Not only did men long for women, they longed for wives, and the presence of a few women only intensified that feeling. They missed their children no less.

The trend toward settlement became noticeable to employers after about 1905. In 1908 a railroad official reported the change like this:

men who had been in the United States and returned to Mexico began to bring back their families . . . Most of the men who had families with them did not go back the following season, but some of the men without their families did, and some of them came back the next year with their families . . . So the process goes on, with . . . a larger proportion of women and children among the immigrants each year, and a larger proportion remaining in this country.[54]

As a few women arrived, they often seized the opportunity to earn money by opening lodging- and boarding-houses, which not only met a need but also created a major improvement in quality of life for the mineworkers. Women also opened little restaurants in their homes and prepared box lunches for the workers, providing the Mexican food that the men missed so much. A few of them taught, like Cornelio's wife, Margarita.

Like all large-scale migrations, that of Mexicans to the United States was not always the result of harmonious family decisions; on the contrary, family conflicts sometimes sent people north from Mexico. Mexican patriarchy was already being wounded by modernization, and the mass male migrations further unstrung the patriarchal loom. Men's migration created contradictions in women's situations—subordinated, yes, but frequently on their own, running the household and a small plot, shop, or other source of earning. Husbands might leave for America without their wives' consent or even consultation, at times suddenly, in response to an offer of a ride, a job, or a companion. Their remittances home sometimes became scarcer and smaller as their absence extended. Doubting their husbands' defense of migration as a good economic move, wives were fearful of abandonment, and with reason: some men set up new households with other women and quit supporting their Mexican wives. (These were not the *casas chicas,* the girlfriends' households, that so many Mexican men kept and so many Mexican women had to accept; these were desertions.) In one *corrido* a man and his American girlfriend argue about the money:

Pues por qué les das a ellos	Well how come you give them money,
ningún servicio te dan,	They don't do a thing for you,
yo te lavo, yo te plancho,	I wash and iron your clothes, so
venga el cheque para acá.	Give me that check.
Mira, no seas ventajosa;	Look, don't take advantage,
tú gozas de lo mejor;	You enjoy the very best;
supiste que era casado	You knew I was married
y que tenía obligación.[55]	And had an obligation.[55]

In the patriarchal families of northern Mexico, the son's departure for an American adventure became a rite of passage, a step toward an autonomy that could span the cultural requirements of continued subordination and individual manhood.[56] Cornelio Chacón, who went on to become a community leader in Clifton, was likely such an assertive youth when he left home. Migrant workers were disproportionately young: by one count only 7 percent were over age forty-five.[57] The presence of return migrants meant that many boys imbibed over the years a migration culture which made it seem inevitable that they too would go someday. And their motives were by no means exclusively or even mainly familial; many longed for travel, challenge, change. These migrations often arose from a "broken patriarchy," in which traditional community restraints were unraveling and the patriarch could no longer pass on a viable mode of living to his sons and daughters.[58]

So migrants were searching in part for new ways of achieving masculine status, and mining attracted them not only because of its high wages but also because those wages increased the manliness of mining work and culture. Mineworkers were proud of the strength and skill and risk taking that their jobs required, and showed it in their "stride and strut," their mining lingo, their organized drilling contests.[59]

Although 93 percent of Mexican migrants in this period were men,[60] within the whole pool of migrants, mineworkers were most financially able to bring family members. This too was a source of pride, and not exclusively masculine pride: many mineworker families in Clifton-Morenci sat for studio photographs, family portraits to be framed and also sent home, the men always in suits and the women in hand-detailed fine dresses. Women were typically left behind at first, but not necessarily for long. And when they came, they were not just "brought" like furniture—the different stories were highly individual. Some no doubt nagged to come; a few even came on their own, perhaps even against their husbands' wishes; some came at their husbands' insistence against their own preference; some came without men because they were widowed and sought ways to support children. Pasquala Esparza fled to Ciudad Juárez and then El Paso fleeing her husband's brutality to herself and her daughter.[61] When María Hernández was first widowed, she went to her parents; but then her father drowned in a desert flood, and she moved from Chihuahua to the Sonoran mining town Pilares de Nacozari, where her grown sons, working in the mines, could help support her and the young children.[62] The fact that women contributed so much did not mean that they were entirely happy to be there. Women also longed for their homeland. As one miner's wife, who moved between Cananea and several Arizona *minerales* (as the Mexicans called the mining camps) explained, "My dream, and my husband's too, is to go back to our beloved Mexico, especially now that my children are growing up, for I want to give them a true Mexican education."[63]

Despite these loyalties and longings for homeland, settled Mexican communities evolved in the mining camps. Migrant men began to create an alternative, binational gender system in which men with American jobs and experience could claim higher position in the male hierarchy.[64] These binational men did not need to choose between their Mexican villages and their American jobs. In fact, Mexican village land actually became increasingly concentrated in the hands of successful U.S. migrants, because they used their earnings to outbid those with less cash. They saw their homeland not only as a land of recreation, not only as a place where their success would be appreciated, but also as an investment opportunity.[65]

Women's and children's presence planted settlement in Clifton-Morenci. The towns were growing extraordinarily rapidly, doubling in size between 1900 and 1910 from about 2,500 to about 5,000 each, and a significant part of this growth was created by the in-migration of women and the in-migration or birth of children.[66] By 1900 the Clifton-Morenci Mexican workers were far less migratory than their Anglo supervisors knew, a misunderstanding that was to prove costly to management, who expected dissatisfied mineworkers to quit, not to stay and organize for higher wages. Not only were there many settled families in this Mexican camp, but proportionately more Mexican men lived in families than did Anglo men.[67] The adult female population is a good index, because in mining towns the lack of women's jobs meant that few women came except to be with husbands. In Clifton-Morenci there were proportionately more Mexican than Anglo women.[68] More Mexicans than Anglos lived in couples.[69] And the proportion of children in the population was by no means as low as that in stereotypical mining camps with a primarily itinerant male population. For example, in the 1880s the Montana, Idaho, and Arizona camps had 10 percent or fewer children; Clifton-Morenci in 1900 and 1910 had 32 to 37.5 percent children.[70] More Mexican couples had children (82 percent) than did Anglos (70 percent).[71] To these we have to add the female-headed households, typically headed by widows, the great majority Mexican.[72] The overwhelming majority of Clifton-Morenci Mexicans lived in family households.[73] Those who did not lived mainly as lodgers, and more of these were Anglo than Mexican.[74]

It would be hard to say when the copper workers shifted their sense of "home," when the trips south became "visits" instead of "returns." Probably the travelers themselves could not pin down the moment of the shift unless it occurred through a sacred event such as marriage or a birth. I found immigration information for only five of the forty Mexican adoptive fathers, and they had been in the United States between ten and thirty-five years, the women often coming later. Of the Clifton-Morenci mineworkers in general, most seem to have married in Mexico. Pablo Medina, smelter hand, had worked in the United States twenty years, and after the first nine years brought a woman back with him; they had been married ten years in 1900–it was not unusual for the Mexicans to live in informal marriages and regularize them later, perhaps under pressure from the priest; she'd had five children, but only two survived. Jesús Valencia, age thirty-eight in 1900, had worked in the United States before and after his marriage eighteen years previously; his wife had only recently arrived, yet they had a total of fourteen children (of whom ten were living).[75] But Cornelio Chacón, a true border man, had lived in the United States for nineteen years and found an American-born wife in El Paso. Some found wives in Clifton. Such was the story of Jesús Frias, age twenty-two, who had come to Clifton as a two-year-old boy; he married Manuela, twenty, who had been in the United States five years. Similarly, Santa Cruz Lara, a smelter hand, was twenty-three in 1900 and had been in the United States for three years when he married Concepción, who had been here for nine years.[76] And there were families in which the entire group came at the same time, most of them nuclear families such as that of Julio and Guadalupe Maldonado, who arrived in Morenci in 1890, or the extended Durán family, who arrived in 1895, a group composed of a fifty-five-year-old mother, her son, twenty-seven (listed as head of the family), her daughters, twenty-five and nineteen, and four of her grandchildren.[77] And we must not forget the 22 percent of Clifton-Morenci Mexicans who migrated from elsewhere in the United States–mainly Texas and New Mexico.

Settlement did not stop the traffic back and forth across the border. Women's own unique desires and family strategies created strong incentives, despite the difficulties of the journey. Women often went home for childbirths, if they could, and to tend to ailing kinfolk. Children were moved back and forth between family in Mexico and in Clifton according to their ages, their needs, and the changing configurations of family health and prosperity. Teenage sons might be sent to work in the mines and smelters of Arizona or in the fields in Mexico; girls might care for houses and family members wherever they were most needed. People went home to bring important consumer goods, protect their inheritance, plant or harvest a crop, rest. They also went home because they were homesick, because of the impossibility of choosing between opportunity and community, freedom and isolation.[78]

Despite the continuing travels, settlement began to create community. A mining camp grew into a town. There had always been sociability among the workers, of course, notably in the saloons, but soon it became more purposeful. Workingmen, led by ambitious types like Cornelio Chacón, created mutual insurance societies. Women cooked and thus patronized grocery businesses; they cleaned and decorated and thus patronized hardware and housewares stores; they sewed and thus patronized fabric and notion stores; and in these stores and on the streets outside them people gathered and talked and created a town. The women's presence reduced the numbers of prostitutes and saloons. Women raised money for their church and planned weddings, funerals, fiestas. And the Mexican workers were proud and optimistic about what they were doing: earning good steady wages, buying lots, building houses, developing a community of orderly, respectable, hard-working families.[79]

October 1, 1904, around 7:30 P.M.

Sacred Heart Church, Clifton

THERE WAS NO DOUBT that the crowd of women at the Sacred Heart Church picking up their babies was, in Clifton's way of seeing people, 100 percent Mexican. But this identification was not yet evident to the sisters. The only identification that mattered to them was, were they Catholics? The nuns again asked Father Mandin about this, and they were satisfied that he had recruited parents only from among communicants.

Despite the commotion among the excited women in the church, despite his poor Spanish and poorer English, Mandin felt in control, thanks to Señora Chacón's careful record keeping. He could never understand why, later, the records turned out to be inconsistent about which Mexican family had which orphan. The sisters had sent a precise assignment list to Mandin, and when some Clifton parents withdrew and others volunteered, Margarita carefully recorded the changes and presented revised lists to the sisters.

That Saturday night, each prospective mother had a paper assigning her a child. One by one each woman pulled hers out from within her shawl and handed it to the padre. Then he compared it to a list that Swayne had. Then the sisters found the child with the right tag, and the woman left with the child. Some of the children's tags had special health notes, and all gave a name and birth date.

Later, at the trial, the nuns claimed that they had already begun raising objections at this moment of initial distribution because the mothers seemed "not as fair as we had hoped for." At some point,

the Foundling Hospital representatives said, they had adopted a policy of trying to place children with parents who "matched" the looks
of the children. Swayne testified that "the first three persons coming
for the children were objected to, on account of their dark complex-
ions, and their faces plainly showed that they were of Indian blood.
The balance of the people were well-dressed and well-mannered."
The sisters stated that they had bowed to the father's authority. Louisa
Gatti, wife of a local rancher and butcher, testified that "the sisters
looked at the lady, this Mexican woman, whatever you call her; and
she says, 'No, father'; she says, 'this woman is a little bit too black for
that, for the color of this baby.' Then the father and Mr. Swayne
persuaded her to give it, and she did."[1] But all this came out in
after-the-fact testimony, and by that time Swayne and the sisters were
trying to acquit themselves of blame and put it all on Mandin.[2] Mrs.
Gatti's mission in this testimony, of course, was to hang onto three-
year-old foundling William Norton; and she would have sensed, if she
had not been actually coached, that it would be safer and more effective to castigate the priest, now gone from Clifton, than the sisters.

Now comes a blackout, a virtual power failure for the historian.
There are no survivors to interview. No statement, letter, or recollection by a Mexican mother survives to hint at how this process felt to
her. Was she pleased with her child? Was her excitement only happy
or also accompanied by trepidation? Who went first or last? Did they
leave individually or wait to walk home together? Which children
could walk and which had to be carried? We can only imagine. The
children were beautifully clothed and groomed in what any Christian
mother would understand to be Sunday best. The older ones knew
what was happening, although without as yet any hint of the emotions
that would accompany their final separation from the sisters and their
brother and sister orphans. The younger ones experienced a more
inchoate anxiety. All of them sensed the importance of the occasion
and did their best to sit still on the too-large benches. It looked like
musical chairs in reverse as one by one the seats were emptied.

As the mothers walked home with their new children, eager to
display them to family and household members, they were warmed by
righteousness, by their pride in having been able to do this act of
devotion and charity, but chilled by just the least bit of anxiety and
defiance, not exactly anticipating trouble but knowing they had done
something daring. They experienced themselves as both Mexican and

American. Enacting motherhood in a manner both powerful and self-effacing–what could be more Mexican? Mothering an American child–what could be more American? No strangers to race talk and Anglo chauvinism, they teetered on an edge, between patriotism and treachery.[3] As Mexican mothers, they were bringing alien Americans into their families, motivated by charity and by self-interest. To take in a poor motherless Catholic child from the sisters was surely a virtuous act, and yet they knew it was also an assertion of female authority. To bring a white child into a Mexican home was to reenact and continue the original construction of Mexicanness out of race mixing, *mestizaje,* between the Indians and the Spanish, but it was also a way to become American.

Most likely the new parents had already chosen *padrinos,* godparents, for their new babies. It was an honor to be asked to be a godfather or godmother, and virtually impossible to refuse, although the commitment entailed financial responsibilities that were far from trivial. The bonds of *compadrazgo,* godparenthood, could be stronger among the adults thus connected than between adults and children; the relationship strengthened friendship–indeed, transformed it into kinship–and adults thus united typically addressed each other as *compadre* or *comadre* rather than by name. In preparing for their foster children, the mothers chose godparents carefully, using the *compadrazgo* system to round up support for the initiative they had taken–*comadres* often served to strengthen women's influence–and to provide insurance against the costs of bringing additional children into poor families. Godparents would buy clothes, pay some of the costs of communions and other fiestas, help in cases of illness, desertion, or widowhood. *Compadrazgo* enlarged the community of those with an emotional investment in the project of taking in and nurturing the children.[4]

Jerome Shanley and Katherine Fitzpatrick were lucky enough to be taken together, and as they held each others' hands they could not have guessed at their power: they transformed the childless Margarita Chacón into a mother. Margarita was able to come round to the church daily in part because she had no children, and she wore black because she had just lost another pregnancy. After six years of marriage, she still had no living children; six years later, in 1910, she reported having given birth seven times, but only one baby, then seven months old, survived.[5] As she walked back to North Clifton holding Jerome's hand and carrying Katherine, she saw how frightened they were and talked to them, in English, about the life they would have here. They were right for her, she thought, as she was a "mixed-race" woman. They were right for her, too, because she was an orphan herself, and now she sought to meet her own needs as well as those of children, to relieve her own loneliness. She was with children often, those of her good friend Estéfana and those she taught, but they only increased her craving for her own.

Virginia Galván, wife of Silvestre Galván, stage driver and saloon owner, one of Clifton's Mexican elite, took in an orphan, although she had three teenagers and a ten-year-old at home; but she too had had personal grief: five of her ten children had died. Both Galváns had been born in Mexico but were among the Clifton area's earliest residents, having arrived in 1869. They had been married twenty-four years.[6]

The youngest child, Elizabeth Kane, who would be two years old the next day, went to Refugia Apodaca. Elizabeth was probably too young to understand that she was being permanently separated from her big sister, Hannah, who was being sent to Morenci, but even the temporary separation, possibly the first in her life, must have been frightening. Refugia, like many of the new mothers, cannot be identified with certainty. Apodaca was a common name in Clifton, and I could not determine her immediate family, but since most of the Mexican foster families were among the elite, she may well have been related to Emiliano or Emilio Apodaca, of the next generation, who became the first Mexican to graduate from high school in Clifton and went on to become a lawyer—through correspondence school!—and eventually a president of the national Alianza Hispano Americana.[7]

The oldest girl, Marie Mack, five years and two months, went to Roja Guerra, a fifty-year-old-widow who ran a seventeen-room boardinghouse with her five grown children.[8] Could Guerra have been looking for child helpers to replace her own?

Abigai de Villescas, with her husband, Andrés Villescas, who worked at the smelter, took in almost-four-year-old Anna Doherty. Abigai was elderly to become an adoptive mother by Clifton's standards of the time: she was forty-seven, and Andrés fifty-one. She had had two children of whom one was living although not with them—likely the child was grown. They had been married fourteen years, both born in Mexico, but had lived in the United States for at least several decades. We don't know whether Abigai was related to Josefa Villescas, who was assigned Sadie Green, age three. Clifton-Morenci had many Villescases, some of them well-to-do like Romulo, from a pioneer family, who started as a railroad worker and opened a successful open-air vegetable market, or Julián, who ran a Chase Creek saloon. But there was no trail left by Josefa.[9]

Another orphan[10] went to Lee and Refugia Windham, one of Clifton's intermarriages. Windham was known in town as a formerly boozing, whoring cowboy who had settled down and had now been with Refugia for years; the priest had insisted they marry in order to adopt an orphan, and they had complied early in 1904—in other words, they had been planning for this child for months. He was a registered voter, thirty-six years old, ready for a family, perhaps. He worked at the smelter for $2.50 a day.[11]

Two-and-a-half-year-old Josephine Corcoran went to Angela Flores, recently married to her long-time partner, Juan Esquivel, who also called himself John Maxwell. He was himself a son of the classic sort of border intermarriage, between an Anglo man and a Mexican woman. He was a good earner, working at the Shannon Copper concentrator mill earning $3 a day; we don't know if he got a high Mexican wage or a low Anglo wage. Neither John nor Angela was foreign-born: he came from New Mexico, she from Texas. They lived in a neat, frame house in La Baranca, the old east side of town.[12]

Four-year-old Joseph Ryan went to Baleria and Ramón Balles. The boy had not had an easy life: after his birth in September 1900, his mother kept him for a full eight months before abandoning him to the Foundling Hospital, where he spent the next three years. The Balleses were also a relatively upscale family, Ramón having been educated in the Clifton elementary school; now they were thrilled to have "José," as they immediately renamed him. Married nine years and childless, Baleria was lonely. Her husband was at work fifteen hours at a time, sometimes day, sometimes night. Loneliness may not have been her only incentive, given the reputation of an infertile woman; Ramón confided to Sister Teresa Vincent their hope that a child would "prevent elders from thinking negative thoughts that sometimes beset them, or doubts that sometimes come between couples." This couple already had the child's education planned: "we were aware that we must set him a good example, especially since we will send him to school a distance from here."[13]

Gabriella Welsh, two-and-a-half, and Edward Gibson, four, went to Trancita Alvidrez and her husband, Francisco, a smelter worker.[14]

Francisco was beginning to build what was to become a prominent Mexican family: his son Frank became a businessman and a political "big wheel" in Clifton, the first Mexican to be admitted to the Elks, in the 1950s.[15] In 1904 the Alvidrez home was multigenerational. The sixty-year-old father Alvidrez also lived there, contributing to the family economy by cutting and hauling wood and doing occasional jobs at the smelter; he was a registered voter and a Civil War veteran who, according to today's Clifton lore, served with Kit Carson.[16] Francisco Alvidrez, Jr., was *padrino* to at least one child born (to Francisco Saénz and Andrea Andujo) in 1900, another hint of status.[17]

The oldest child, Henry Potts, went to Josefa Holguín, a seamstress married to Rafael Holguín, who worked at the smelter and later at the concentrator as a liner, a skilled job. Rafael Holguín and Francisco Alvidrez were friends and coworkers. Josefa was Mexican-born, but Rafael came from Texas. The big age difference between them—she was nineteen, he was thirty-one—was not uncommon here. They had no children. In 1904 they had only been married two years, but in 1910 they still had no children, suggesting a fertility problem they may have already guessed at by 1904. In their house in Shannon Hill lived Juan Delfino, Josefa's brother, who worked in the smelter; Cecilia Delfino, Josefa's sister, who went to school; José Gómez, a lodger, who worked at the smelter; Juan Acosta, an elderly lodger. Rafael Holgúin was going to become a person of note in Clifton, and the orphan affair would help put him in that position. "An abrupt, aggressive, determined type of an individual, not easily intimidated, and a good worker and provider," remembers Al Fernandez.[18] He communicated that he was someone to be reckoned with—for example, he was a registered voter; he was on the short list of Mexicans whom James Colquhoun, Arizona Cooper's manager, invited to public events; eventually Holgúin was able to quit working for the copper company and became the town's garbage collector. Josefa, too, was known: she made nice clothes for some of Clifton's elite like the Palicio family.[19]

But in 1904 they were just a relatively new couple suddenly acquiring a six-year-old blond, blue-eyed boy who came with a tag that said, "allergic to spicy foods."[20] We wonder if they had preferred a school-age child to a baby or if the specific assignments of children were more or less random. In any case, owing to Henry's age, Josefa found that she could communicate with him by sign language. She had made two suits of clothes for him and stocked up cookies and toys.[21]

I could identify twelve of the Clifton homes where the orphans were first placed, and judging from these parents, the mothers at the church were by no means a cross-section of Clifton's Mexicans. They were better off than average, their husbands more ambitious or more lucky; they were all probably legally married. The census enumerator listed them all as literate, which also marked them as an aristocracy among Mexican workers.

The transactions at the church were mainly a women's affair. Only mothers, no fathers, picked up the children. And a group of Anglo women had come to watch, smaller than the crowd at the station because most of them did not feel comfortable coming into the Mexican church. Louisa Gatti was there, perhaps because she was less inhibited, perhaps because she and her Italian husband had actually come to Sacred Heart for some weddings. There were a few men around: Father Mandin and George Swayne were comanaging the distribution of the children with the sisters. The church sexton, Mr. Lewis, was there. One other man who might be considered Anglo was present, Eugene Fountin, a Frenchman who had lived eight years in Clifton, working for five or six years as a refrigeration engineer for Arizona Copper. Born a Catholic, he never went to church, but he had heard about the orphan placements from his wife, who did occasionally attend mass, he said.

Despite the men's presence, the tension in the church was created by the main protagonists in this incident: three groups of women—New York nuns, Clifton Mexicans, and Clifton Anglos—all concerned for the children's fate. Two of the groups were united by religion, two of the groups by "race." But they did not all recognize the alignments. The New Yorkers did not feel bound to the Anglos by whiteness. The Anglos did not understand how the Catholics felt about preserving the young souls for the faith. When I first told this story to friends, several said, it shows that race trumps religion. But that is not quite right. To the Clifton Anglos, religion was not an issue; the majority of them were not churchgoers and, although most were Protestants, among their number were some who were born Catholics and Jews. To the sisters religion remained the overriding issue, although they would come to "see" that white Catholics were better than brown Catholics as they learned the Anglo racial system. And the Mexican women had not yet learned how intensely Anglos felt about racial borders.

The three groups of women, shortly to become near violent antagonists, were strangers to one another. The New Yorkers, tired first-time visitors to a completely new kind of town, were less perceptive, less able to detect social nuances, than they would have been in the East or Midwest. Most of the Anglo women did not know any of the Mexican mothers, although they might well have seen them often. The Anglos saw them as an undifferentiated, unindividuated group. When asked later, "what kind of Mexican women . . . were those who presented these tags?" Louisa Gatti answered: "They were dirty faces, and wore black shawls over them and they had ragged dresses on." Questioner: "Do you know these Mexican people who got these children–do you know anything of them personally?" Mrs. Gatti: "No, sir. There are so many Mexican women around there I don't know one from the other . . . they are Indians; they are not real Mexicans." (In Anglo racial talk in Clifton, most of the time "Mexican" was pejorative enough, but here Mrs. Gatti was pulling out all the stops, marking them as maximally inferior.) The Mexican mothers knew a bit more about the Anglos, as subaltern groups often learn to observe closely those with more power. Besides, women of their community worked as maids in Anglo homes. They had some understanding of nuns, because of their faith, but not of the religious and racial concerns of New Yorkers.

The Anglo women came to the church out of curiosity and, possibly, to see if they might get an orphan. Neither their expectations nor their motives were fully formed. Louisa Gatti went over to the sexton: "I says to this Mr. Lewis, I says, 'I would like to have one of those babies.' I says, 'I am not a Catholic, but,' I says, 'my husband is a Catholic; and also his father, my father-in-law.' 'Well,' he says, 'I'll see for you if we can't get you one . . . take a seat.'"

Why did the Anglo women want the babies? Some of them faced infertility too: Mrs. Wright had been married five years and had no children, Mrs. Pascoe had had one child who died, Mrs. Simpson had had two children who died. Rebecca Tong had already been trying to adopt a child for some time. Some had the baby hunger that so often moves women whose children have grown, like Mrs. Reed, who had one married daughter, or Mrs. Freeman, who had three married daughters and one sixteen years old. But they not only wanted the babies, they were beginning to think it wasn't right for the Mexicans to take the babies, and it is hard to know–perhaps even hard for them to know–which came first. They were beginning to fume when one by one the Mexican women emptied the church of orphans.

The orphans were literally drawing Anglo women out of their homes and into an adventure in which they felt that they had an obligation to lead. Excitement was stimulating aberrant and even disorderly behavior. Louisa Gatti continued her narrative:

> while I was staying there waiting to see if I could get a baby, here stops in Mr. Gatti, my husband, and he come over towards me, and he says, "Old lady, I want some supper." "Why," I says, "here John, here's the key. Go home and get your supper yourself. It's all ready." He just told me, "No, come on." I says, "No, I want a baby." As I jumped up the father caught my arm and he says, "No, don't go yet; I am going to give you a baby."

But Mr. Gatti spoke with the priest in French—John Gatti was of French extraction although born in Italy—and reported to Louisa that she was mistaken, all the children were spoken for, and took her home. Similarly, Eugene Fountin claimed that after his wife had first heard of the orphans, they had talked it over and decided to take one, and that he had come to the church with this in mind. But Mandin had told him that he was not suitable because they were not good enough Catholics.[22]

A similar proceeding took place in Morenci the next morning, Sunday: Awakened in the railroad car at 5 A.M., washed and given breakfast, the remaining twenty-four orphans traveled in five wagons with Mandin and all the Foundling representatives nine miles up the mountain to the Morenci Holy Cross Church. The children were taken to the nearby home of one of the prospective parents, where they stayed while Father Mandin conducted a mass. Then he and the Foundling group went into the rectory and passed the children out as they had in Clifton, to families all "well-dressed and well-mannered," in Swayne's recollection.[23] But some anxiety must have already been in the air because Sister Anna Michaella, showing the influence of Anglo comments the previous day, decided that nine of the prospective parents did not look right and turned them down. So the sisters had nine children with them when they checked into the Morenci Hotel late Sunday morning.

Even before this, while the nuns and the twenty-four orphans were sleeping or nervously lying awake in the railroad car, Clifton was buzzing. Rumors developed quickly and by huge leaps away from the truth.[24] Anti-Catholicism mingled with anti-Mexicanism in these rumors so that I can only wonder how Anglo Catholics like the Gattis and the Fountins reacted. It was said that twenty orphans had died en route to Clifton owing to negligence, and it seemed there were few limits to the Catholics' callousness: "Some of the children taken sick on the train, it was asserted, had been given to Indians along the latter part of the route in order that they might be gotten out of the way before dying."[25] There were reports that the Foundling regularly sold children like cattle, in carloads.[26] And that this was the way the Catholics periodically got rid of the illegitimate offspring of the nuns and priests.[27]

The Anglos became convinced that the Mexicans had bought the children from the priest. "As each smiling Mexican took his child, he or she paid to the priest a sum of money ranging from two dollars up for each child."[28] Since the New York Foundling Hospital asked for some of the expenses to be paid locally, Father Mandin had asked for contributions from the prospective parents. Some Anglos said they actually saw money given to the priest in exchange for the children. The most "authoritative" such claim came from Charles Bull, editor and publisher of the *Copper Era,* Clifton's newspaper, and his affidavit is so, literally, incredible that the reader inevitably extends some skepticism also to the reliability of his newspaper. Bull said he

> heard an old Mexican woman say to him [the priest] in the Mexican language "Quiro [*sic*] uno Muchachito" (translated into English means: "I want a little boy"). That said Mexican woman repeated the said language several times to which the said priest made no reply, nor paid any attention whatsoever, until the said Mexican woman handed the said Priest some money which she held in her hand, consisting of several paper bills and some silver coin . . . that when the said Mexican woman handed the said money to the said Priest, said Priest immediately entered an adjoining room, and emerged therefrom with one of the said infant children, and gave it over to said Mexican woman who immediately left with said infant in her arms.[29]

(Several witnesses had the idea that legal-speak required putting "said" in front of references to individuals.) Others told stories less embellished by "saids" or by exaggeration, and confined themselves to the claim that they heard Mexicans say that they had paid good money for the children. Laura Abraham complained that the sisters distributed the children "as they would deal so many packages of merchandise," but she offered no observations to back up her judgment.[30] John Gatti, the only

Anglo who spoke French and could therefore communicate accurately with the priest, later testified that the priest said he took up a collection for costs but got so little it wouldn't even pay for a hack from Clifton to Morenci. Mandin himself said, in an interview with a Tucson newspaper, that he paid forty dollars of his own money for the children's provision and got a total of thirty dollars contributed by his parishioners to pay for conveying the orphans from Clifton to Morenci.[31]

The Anglo gossip targeted Mexican mothering particularly. The Anglo women worried that the children were being fed Mexican food. (Clifton-Morenci Anglo disdain for tortillas and beans was no more ignorant than that of New York "Anglo" for garlic or pasta or that of San Francisco "Anglos" for dim sun.) The Anglo women accused the Mexican mothers of sexual immorality, calling them prostitutes, bar women. (Given the typical domesticity and religiosity of most Mexican women, these accusations seem far-fetched.) The most urgent rumor was that the orphans were in immediate danger. Someone had seen "a drunk Mexican staggering down the street with a bottle in one hand and a foundling" in the other. Someone else had seen a Mexican woman feeding beer to her foundling. Several knew that the orphans had been given to women of the "tenderloin" district.[32] Another offered: "Would I be allowed to tell what I seen that morning? . . . I seen a Mexican going along with one [orphan]; it must have been ten o'clock [Sunday morning], with a bottle of whiskey in one hand, and a little child in the other; and it was crying, and wanted to go home. That was what started me so quick to rescue; and the child wanted to go home, and he was staggering along with the bottle of whiskey, and wouldn't go home." (If the child was crying to go home, surely it meant the Foundling, not the foster family's house.) Another charged, "The filthy Mexican youngsters began to maul them over, the old people kissed them and breathed into their cheeks their filthy, tobacco-laden breath . . . Most of the Mexicans are unwashed and infested with vermin."[33]

The orphan story the Anglo women were collectively composing resembled several other classic American folk parables: captivity narratives, like the memoirs of white women captured by Indians, which had flourished throughout the preceding century, and stories of white slavery, which were to become widespread melodrama a few years later. The crux of all these narratives was, innocent white people were the captives of dark people who would mistreat them. Both captivity and white-slave stories offered not only thrilling accounts of ordeals but also stylized discourses through which authors shaped cultural representations of evil and immorality in racial forms. (The white slaver, often literally a Jew or an Italian, was always figuratively nonwhite.) The captivity stories exhibited an anxiety about the white person turning "injun," disrupting what was supposed to be a biologically ordained whiteness by revealing its malleability.[34] The stories also fashioned a form of pornography that was respectable even for women writers and readers, shivery tales of women ravished by savage or depraved men, and although the Clifton captives were but toddlers, the sexual innuendo of the rumors was unmistakable: dirty and drunken men and immoral women dandling and kissing the children, showing off the babies in saloons, for example. The racialization of both sorts of narratives used pornography to mark, in degrees of outrage, the gulf between the savage and the white. Tales of kidnapped children constitute an international folktale genre, with racial outsiders, such as gypsies, often accused of kidnappings.[35]

The atrocity stories repeated by the Clifton Anglo women established the need for a rescue operation by marking the babies as victims and making them the responsibility of their fellow whites. The Anglo women had no moment of doubt as to the orphans' racial identity, yet their label might have surprised the sisters. In New York, the children would have been called Irish; they would have been white if compared to African Americans, but it wasn't their primary identity. Neither Cliftonians nor New Yorkers thought or talked much about the generic idea of "race," preferring the concrete categories that mattered in daily life. In New York the dominant ones were Irish, Italian, German, and Hebrew, along with Protestant, Catholic, and Jewish. In Clifton, to both Anglos and Mexicans, the operative categories were: Anglo and Mexican. There were subtleties, exceptions, and subordinate categories in both places: Jews, Italians, Irish, and Spanish people in Clifton who in the most exclusive contexts might be not quite as "white" as the English, Cornish, and Scottish elite. And the Anglo women busy discussing this outrage included Laura Abraham and Mary Quinn, who later identified themselves as Catholic. And the Jewish Abraham brothers were at the peak of Clifton society, second only to Arizona Copper's top managers. But the Anglos did not refer to Mandin's church as the Catholic church or Sacred Heart; they called it "the Mexican church," and they did not attend. Had some of the orphans been dark-skinned or black-haired or Italian-named, or had they been fewer, there might have been some ambivalence about the appropriateness of their placements. But since they were blonde, and so numerous that it seemed all Clifton-Morenci was involved, the children became *simply* white.

The most arresting rumor was that the Mexican mothers who volunteered to take orphans had asked the padre to request light or fair babies. Sister Anna Michaella testified later that, in addition to specifying that "there should be no negroes, or any indians sent, or Chinese," the priest had asked for "light complexioned," "fair" children.[36] She made this statement when she was trying to blame Father Mandin for everything, and whatever correspondence between him and the Sisters of Charity may once have existed has been misplaced, so we cannot know if this was true. But if she said it, the Anglo townspeople might have believed and rumored it as well. And it might have been true, completely consistent with the Mexicans' desire for things American, for mobility, for lighter offspring. There is of course a vital difference between what "light" meant to the Mexicans and what "white" meant to the Anglos: the former was a shade of complexion, a calibrated measure of status; the latter was a more totalizing divider, a mark of all-around superiority. Thus a desire completely rational—even laudable—to the Mexicans seemed pernicious to the Anglos in part because of a misunderstanding, a literal mistranslation. The heart of the conflict, however, came from perfect understanding: The Mexicans wanted to move up. Not only especially ambitious individuals but the mineworkers as a group aspired to an Anglo standard of living. The Anglos wanted the Mexicans not to move up, grasping, however unconsciously, that their own standard of living benefited from Mexican subordination.

Who was spreading the word of this threat to the children's welfare? Perhaps the outspoken Louisa Gatti, after she gave John his dinner; likely also some of the others who had been at the train station or the church. Muriel Wright, who had seen the children come into the station, encountered many Clifton people because she helped out at her husband's saloon. Her father-in-law, Arthur Wright, was a justice of the peace and an investor in several local mines. Mrs. Johnnie Parks, who had also been at the station, knew everyone, her husband being a Clifton deputy sheriff and the younger brother of the Graham County sheriff, James Parks. Together the Parks brothers owned substantial

geland and cattle. Etta Reed's husband ran a furniture store. May
___pson was the wife of a locomotive engineer for the Arizona and
New Mexico—the copper company's private railroad—and she happened to be living in the Clifton Hotel at this time (why we don't know),
which put her at the center of much social traffic. Her sister-in-law Anna
Riordan was married to a railroad conductor and hotel-and-saloon
owner, so she was no doubt also in the center of local gossip when she
helped out at the bar. The Abraham sisters-in-law, Mrs. Jake and Mrs.
Sam, wives of the manager and owner of the Clifton Hotel, respectively,
were plugged in as well.[37] The women constituted a network of female
community leaders. All were married to men for whom entrepreneur-
ship was a goal if not a current identity: those husbands who held jobs
as skilled workers like Riordan and Simpson were saving and investing
to become businessmen. Many wives "helped out" in their husbands'
businesses, where they took in and gave out a great deal of local
information. Theirs was a fairly tight community, bound by kinship as
well as friendship. From the central positions they occupied, they could
organize the town's knowledge of events rather quickly.

By the next morning these women had constructed a full-fledged
emergency. Creating that emergency meant, in large part, arousing
men. The women had to negotiate a delicate strategic and tactical
problem, actually a conflict between tactical and strategic imperatives.
To right this wrong against the children, which the Anglo women had
defined and thereby created, it was necessary to develop tactics for
direct action; but in formulating such action, the women had to be
cautious not to overstep a normative line into the male sphere, because
doing so could have subverted their strategic alliance with men and
with, shall we say, more conservative women. The very use of a term
like "conservative" holds up to view the complex political meanings of
this episode. What is conservative here? The Anglo supremacy being
defended was hardly traditional in these parts, given that they were all
recent immigrants and that Mexicans had occupied a social status
closer to equality just a few decades previously. Nor was the women's
leadership a tradition to be conserved. In the political terms of 1904,
organized conservative women were quite indignant about women
stepping into male-sphere activity such as law and politics. The Anglo
female child-savers of Clifton had to move carefully, although their
care came from a practiced tending of men's egos and gender proprie-
ties rather than from planned maneuvers. So let us notice how the

sexual division of labor and leadership were manifest, changing but not too much.

It happened that two of Clifton's deputy sheriffs had gone to the county seat, Solomonville, on business, including Mrs. Parks's husband, Johnnie. Early Sunday morning, as the angry buzz among the Anglos continued to escalate, a group of citizens telephoned to Sheriff James Parks's office and asked that the deputy sheriffs be sent back to Clifton pronto.[38] The community agitation escalating this Sunday morning preempted any thought of church among these infrequent churchgoers. By about 1 P.M. the group that had called Solomonville managed to find another deputy sheriff in Clifton, L. Jeff Dunagan. (If there was an Anglo hero in this episode, or even an Anglo who behaved somewhat better than most, he is it, despite some pronouncedly clayish feet that would be revealed by later events.) A committee of five men appointed itself, not yet calling itself a committee: Sam and Jake Abraham, Mike Riordan, Tom Simpson, and Harry Wright. All five were husbands of the Anglo women leaders. This group requested—insisted—that Dunagan go to Morenci and immediately arrest George Swayne and Father Mandin. For what crime? It is not clear what they imagined—possibly selling babies or endangering children. In other words, they pulled out all the big guns immediately, not even hesitating to interfere with a priest's authority over Catholic children. But Dunagan had been a deputy during the massive strike of 1903 and seen several thousand armed Mexicans amassed in the center of Morenci, and he had no enthusiasm for starting trouble. Perhaps Dunagan discussed developments with Sheriff Jim Parks, perhaps not, but at any rate he had the sense to demur at this point, explaining that he could not arrest anyone without a warrant. The committee, however, wouldn't take no for an answer, so Dunagan agreed that he would go up to Morenci and "bring the people down . . . to get the fact of what they had done." One of the committee, Tom Simpson, eventual father of orphan Anna Doherty, went with him.

3

The Priest in the Mexican Camp

THE YOUNG FRENCH PRIEST Constant Mandin had arrived in Clifton only eight months earlier, an outsider from across the sea, from another continent, another language, another of Clifton's many transatlantic immigrants. Yet even as a newcomer he was supposed to lead, to shepherd, to protect his flock, not to adapt himself but to transform others. His Latinness made him a border person in his own way: "white" like the Anglos, but belonging to the Mexicans, a guardian over the Mexicans and, when necessary, an ambassador from them. Mandin mixed an outsider's ignorance and a novice's innocence with a need to learn quickly. Unable to take anything for granted or to naturalize what he saw, his observations can help the outsiders from across a century of time imagine this raw mining camp in 1904.

Father Mandin's assignment to Arizona seemed to fulfill his most celestial aspirations. When he was recruited from his seminary in the Vendée, France, by Bishop Granjon of Tucson, when he was roughing the journey from civilization to the savage frontier, nothing forewarned him that he would become a fall guy in a racial conflict or flee his first post in a narrow escape from lynching. Instead he regarded Clifton as a lucky, dream-fulfilling opportunity and challenge.

It was not at all strange for a Frenchman to be sent to Arizona—virtually the entire Catholic clergy of the area was European. Under Spanish rule, Franciscan missions, directed from southern Mexico, ran the diocese of Sonora, which included the Arizona and California territories. Under Mexican rule the Franciscans withdrew, putting a local Mexican clergy in their place, but the Durango see was unable to supply enough priests to cover this vast territory. To the Franciscans of central Mexico the north had always seemed an uncivilized but also unsullied frontier, a religious void, reflecting its desert landscape–devoid of Catholic discipline but also devoid of corrupting European influences. (This view ignored the fact that priests throughout Mexico engaged in unseemly and unorthodox sexual practices.)[1] As missions sent by a religious order were replaced by a secular clergy–that is, one administered through the diocesan hierarchy–financial support declined. The missions to Arizona and New Mexico territories continued to receive some backing from the French Society for the Propagation of the Faith, but local priests were mainly on their own financially, dependent for their livelihoods and the building or upkeep of churches on what they could collect from parishioners. Upon U.S. annexation, a negotiated division of territory gave jurisdiction over these southwestern lands to the St. Louis see, where the French clergy constituted a major influence. St. Louis distrusted the Mexican pastors, many of whom had allegedly supported or even led Mexican revolts, tolerated or even participated in heretical religious practices, and never demonstrated much loyalty to the French church. As eight new dioceses were created in the area, from Galveston in 1847 to Tucson in 1897, the clergy continued nearly 100 percent European, mainly French.[2] The bishop during the orphan incident, Henri Granjon, wrote up his annual reports in French and computed his budgets in francs.[3]

The territory, dependent on long-distance management, was understaffed. In 1880 there was one priest per 10,000 square miles in Arizona. The bishop calculated his 1904 population at 160,000 (40,000 Catholics, 90,000 heretics, 30,000 infidels), and there were twenty-eight clergymen, or one for every 5,700 people; in France there was one for 690. The Tucson diocese alone was two-thirds the size of France.[4] "Typically *padres* rode into these isolated settlements at the end of the day, gathered the *rancheros* and their families for some devotion, instruction, and confessions, and then celebrated Mass the following morning before saddling up for a day's ride to the next *rancho*."[5] These padres tried to re-create their European churches, to restore what they believed had been a glorious age of Spanish control by shepherding their communicants as, they believed, the Mexican clergy had failed to do. They were pleased to find that their neglected

Mexican flocks had managed to keep alive the teaching of catechism and prayers, however incorrect, incomplete, and lacking in understanding.[6] But religious orthodoxy and deference to the church were shaky at best in Sonora and *nuevo México;* anticlericalism thrived and the peasants had fallen into what the French saw as erroneous "folk Catholic" customs. The Mexicans rang church bells for civic occasions, conducted costumed and noisy public processions, brought food and music into cemeteries. They decorated churches with *retablos*[7] and carvings, painted and hewed in "primitive" manner, with "staring eyes and raw colors . . . whose features looked like those of the people themselves in the dark mountain villages of the north," and their art used Indian symbols such as lightning, arrows, and deer along with the cross. They adored irregular saints and the Virgin of Guadalupe. The Franciscans had encouraged, even propagated, many of these practices as a way of converting Indians. When Americans took over, the St. Louis see condemned these customs and charged its priests with stifling such syncretism.[8]

One of these irregular saints arrived in Clifton just a few years before the orphans did, like them a romantic and desirable refugee, and her story reveals not only the magnetic pull of folk Catholicism but also the fluidity and Mexicanness of the racial order there. Like the children, Santa Teresa de Cabora was an orphan, a spiritual, metaphorical orphan, an illegitimate child of Mexico.[9] As I got to know her during several years of research, I began to appreciate what her story tells about culture and social life in old Clifton. Santa Teresa is a multiply contradictory fable: in race a light-skinned mestizo beloved by Mexican peasants and Indians and Clifton Anglos; in class the illegitimate daughter of a servant and a lord, who then became a big money maker as a healer; a Catholic mystic whose prophetic charisma recalled the Old Testament; a quintessentially Mexican revolutionary heroine who ended in the care of wealthy white Americans; a prophet whose own personal life seemed shaped by immaturity and even opportunism.[10] Like the orphans, she came by train, and the trip made her white.

The future saint Teresita was born Teresa Urrea on a hacienda in Sinaloa in 1873, the illegitimate child of the *patrón,* Don Tomás Urrea, and the fourteen-year-old daughter of a Tehueco Indian ranch hand, Cayetana Chávez. An outspoken liberal, the don had to flee the vengeance of Porfirio Díaz and in 1880 moved his household to a new property, Cabora, near Obregón in today's Sonora. When Teresita

reached sixteen, he called her into service in his new home, now run
by another mistress, Gabriela Cantúa. Here the girl became an informal apprentice to Huila, an old *curandera,* or healer, who found Teresita
talented at the work. Huila soon noticed that Teresa could exert a
powerfully calming effect on the ailing through touch and a hypnotic
gaze. Often described as beautiful, with light skin and chestnut hair,
she also played guitar and sang, and soon the whole ménage adored
her. One day (possibly after escaping an attempted rape) Teresa lapsed
into a "seizure," alternatively described as a coma and an epileptic or
cataleptic fit, from which she was expected to die, which was later
understood as a mystical experience. On the fourteenth day, already
dressed for burial, some say, she awoke and reported a visitation from
the Virgin, who told her that she must use her special powers to cure
and comfort the people. Like some medieval female mystics and many
revered Mexican women healers, Teresa would henceforth ignore
clerical authority to develop her own spiritual authority for healing.
She became also a prophet in an Old Testament tradition: in repeated
trancelike meditations, Teresita could summon power to heal even the
most severely crippled, to see the future, to speak the truth.

As evidence of her powers accumulated, her father, the skeptical
freethinker and Mason Don Tomás, was forced not only to acknowledge her ability (although he believed that there was a nonmetaphysi-
cal explanation for her cures) but also to reorganize his hacienda to
accommodate the supplicants who came—and to profit from their
needs, selling them lodgings and provisions.[11]

Thus an illegitimate peasant girl's faith overwhelmed a lord's secular-
ism, but hers was an unruly faith. Teresa drew the masses not only
because she healed but also because she denounced the corruption and
pretentiousness of the church, on this point not defying but following
her father's anticlericalism. "I spoke much to the people about God,"
she said a decade later, "not about the church, or to tell them to go to
church . . . I told them what I believe: that God is the spirit of love."[12]
The Mexican church denounced her visions. But hers, of course, was a
deeply Catholic anticlericalism. As her devotees accumulated throughout the region, their religiosity strengthened a peasant-Indian determination to resist the land enclosures of the Porfirian regime. Teresa
proclaimed that God intended the peasants to own the land. Mexican
peasants had a long tradition of choosing and honoring irregular saints,
a practice that was escalating in the 1890s as their immiseration deep-

ened. On Christmas in 1891, an armed rebel group of Yaqui, Tarahu-mara, and Mayo peasants came to pay homage to Teresa and then, holing up in the village of Tomochic, defeated a Porfirian armed force with the cry "*Viva la Santa de Cabora.*" In the church they replaced the saints with images of Teresa. Soon afterward a replenished army of *federales* burned Tomochic to the ground, letting the women and chil-dren burn to death inside the church. "Remember Tomochic" became a battle cry in the Mexican revolution that overthrew Díaz, and several Indian revolutionary groups became known as the *Teresistas*. No matter how earnestly these early Mexican revolutionaries tried to harness Teresa's powers to their desperate need, Teresa herself resisted and repeatedly denied, no doubt honestly, any role in inciting rebellion or desire to do so. Nevertheless in 1892 a second guerrilla army of rebels claimed Teresa as their inspiration, and the governor of Sonora arrested her, then deported her and Don Tomás. They went first to Nogales, Arizona.

But whether Teresa Urrea desired it or not, she had become the peasants' Joan of Arc, and the border could not hold back her invol-untary nurturance of their rebellions. Crowds followed her in Nogales and then in El Paso. So Don Tomás took her further from the border, to Clifton, in 1896.[13] Here he established profitable dairy and firewood businesses, but the greater income continued to come from Teresa. Anglos soon discovered her healing work and understood from the Urreas' many distinguished Mexican guests that this was a family of status. As luck would have it, the six-year-old son of one of Clifton's wealthiest citizens, banker Charles Rosecrans, was rapidly becoming paralyzed from "cerebro-spinal meningitis." Clifton physician L. A. W. Burtch could do nothing, but Teresa could, and in three weeks the child improved to a degree recognized even by Burtch, who became a believer in her powers. Teresa, now twenty-three, became a pet of some of Clifton-Morenci's most prominent Anglo women, while con-tinuing to heal many Mexicans. The situation was difficult for the Clifton priest, Father Timmermans, because he could not credibly condemn as false the "miracles" of this "saint" so beloved by so many.

Teresa's holy persona remained connected to worldly Mexican na-tionalist and revolutionary politics.[14] A close family friend, the liberal activist Lauro Aguirre, promoted Teresa through the anti-Díaz newspa-pers he published, *El Independiente* and later *El Progresista,* from El Paso, and he collected stories about her into a book, which circulated widely among the politicized Mexican workers and exiles in the United States. She was an odd choice, indeed, to be a darling of Clifton society. But the combination of Teresa's powers, her light skin, and her father's wealth and education opened doors into white social life, and they were invited to the best dinners and balls. These social occasions were attended by upscale Mexicans as well; and to appropriate occasions, Father Timmermans was invited. We see the status of elite Mexicans in the fact that Teresa could not speak English at all well—even after her three years in Clifton she needed a translator in order to heal.[15] Many Anglos, by contrast, knew Spanish—you could not do much business in Clifton-Morenci in English.

The Anglos' willingness to accept Teresa's Mexicanness, and the Mexicans' view that her powers came from another world, must account for everyone's forgiving attitude toward her ill-judged marriage to miner Guadalupe Rodríguez in 1900. She somehow fell in love with Lupe, remembered as tall, fair, and handsome, but Don Tomás forbade him to see Teresa. On June 22 he showed up at the don's house with the local justice of the peace, aimed his rifle at the don, and demanded permission to marry Teresa. The don refused, but Teresa went to Lupe's side, declared that she was twenty-seven and that it was her will to marry him, and the justice read the ceremony. The couple then retired to Lupe's lodgings near the Metcalf mines, where they sang and danced all night. The next morning he insisted she accompany him to Mexico, and when she reminded him that she dared not return there, he pulled a gun on her and tried to force her to go. (Some suspected that he was a Porfirian agent sent to capture her, others that he sought to collect a bounty for her.) She escaped and a posse of two hundred captured and jailed him, eventually committing him to an asylum in Phoenix. Or so the story goes—with little documentation. Might she have colluded in this forced marriage and kidnapping, as a way of defying her father without taking responsibility for such an un-Mexican act? Yet she had predicted, even before leaving Cabora, that the man she chose for a husband would be cruel and would attempt to kill her.

The marriage episode alienated Teresa from her father but not from her patrons. Mrs. Rosecrans took her for a rest to San Jose, California, and there began to sell Teresa's spiritual and healing exploits. Soon this marketing propelled Teresa to national attention. (California was sparking a national revival of apostolic healing, and Teresa was a forerunner of Protestant evangelist and healer Aimee Semple McPherson of the

1920s.) A San Francisco sleazy businessman offered her $10,000 for a five-year contract, and under his auspices she traveled around the country for several years on a "Curing Crusade." In one location he had her compete in a beauty contest wearing a tacky costume and crown. During this time she gave birth to two daughters. Returning to Clifton in autumn 1904, after the orphans came, she used her money to build a large two-story building intended to serve as a hospital. But her curative powers diminished, the standard fate of female prophets no longer chaste.[16] She died in 1906, among the Anglos, without her father or any of her Mexican people. Yet she died a Mexican and a Catholic death: of consumption, the name then given to the disease that killed most miners; and she died at age thirty-three, as she had long predicted, just like Christ and so many other female saints.

Teresa de Cabora constructed a life and a career out of the cultural materials she had access to as a border person, and these building blocks embodied the contradictions that characterized the U.S.-Mexican border at that time. A heroine to Mexican peasant revolutionaries and a darling of Arizona Anglos; a Catholic who pioneered the evangelical techniques popularized by Protestants; an illegitimate, half-Indian servant girl who came to dominate the economic and political activities of her wealthy aristocratic father; a woman bearing herself with the submissiveness revered in the Madonna, yet ambitious and assertive in her work. Well known to all the individuals we will meet in this orphan story, she not only symbolized their concerns but also influenced them. In 1896 when she arrived in Clifton they all knew that racial lines were still pliable or, more accurately, that class and celebrity could make one white, in Arizona as in Mexico. No one was surprised that Teresa Urrea became white through a kind of adoption, while losing none of her Mexicanness, which was so charming to the Anglos and a source of pride to the Mexicans. Indeed, her posture in this "adoption," as in her marriage, remained so passive that there was no hint of her being blamed for deserting, much less betraying, her people. Rather her accomplishments benefited all. Certainly her healing career served as a symbolic reminder that people at the grass roots (and notably women) could reshape their spirituality beyond the dictates of the church.

THE CLERGY WHO TRIED TO CONTROL the adulation of Teresa were even more foreign than she was. Mandin's predecessor, Peter

Timmermans, was the first pastor assigned when Clifton became a parish in 1894, a man "intrepid" and "soul-weathered" enough to take on such an apostleship.[17] Born in Flanders in 1867, orphaned at six months, ordained in Louvain, Timmermans was recruited there by the first bishop of Tucson, Peter Bourgade. At first Timmermans said no, because he longed for a hard, rugged mission—his heart was set on China; persuaded to give Arizona a six-month trial, he concluded that it was "tough enough." "Upon arrival in Tucson . . . [in] 1891, all I found was poverty . . . I was lodged in a shack of brush in the rear of the priests' residence . . . a room with a dirt floor; only a hole in the wall served as a window and a piece of the door. There were no chairs, only an orange crate." This was luxury compared to the Solomonville-Clifton circuit he took on three years later, a territory stretching 276 miles. He visited the sick, traveling often a day and a half by horse, once in the saddle for twelve hours at a stretch, carrying seventy-five pounds over steep and slippery mountain paths; sometimes he ran out of water. He recalled being lost in the desert, able to see nothing but a ribbon of dust on the horizon and the waves of heat. He built a church in Clifton with his own hands, he claimed, and when it was destroyed in a flood he built another. Perhaps he was aggrandizing his holiness in performing this punishing work, and in telling us about it, but maybe he had to build it himself—we know he was not pleased with the devotion of his parishioners. He never received a salary and had great difficulty collecting contributions—the better-off Catholics did not come to mass, and those who did were poorer than he had believed possible. He did not enjoy walking by the saloons with the drunken miners and gun-toting cowboys leaning near the doors.[18]

Timmermans could survive the wild west but not its industrial transformation. After his district was divided and he moved to Clifton in 1900, the sulfur fumes from the smelter made him sick (although the manager, James Colquhoun, claimed they had healing properties).[19] He returned to Belgium on sick leave. The bishop could not let Clifton-Morenci go unpriested. This Mexican camp, as the twin towns were known jointly, was unique among Arizona mining towns for its high proportion of Mexicans and, therefore, of Catholics. So in February 1904 Constant Mandin was sent as a temporary replacement, for his very first assignment, young and bewildered and excited. He had been recruited by the second bishop of Tucson from a seminary in the Vendée, where he had been born twenty-five years earlier. Like most of the Catholic missionaries of this period, he was attracted by the prospects of adventure as well as the deliverance of souls from darkness; his parents owned a wild-west novel, *Bandits of Arizona,* which he read while at university. Like Timmermans, he wanted a "hard rugged life" and the thrill of holding off the "redskins." Mandin had the confidence of the weapons training he had gotten during his required ten-month service in the French Army, and then Bishop Granjon had tempted him to Arizona precisely by emphasizing its dangers with stories of "the long horse back rides through the deserts . . . the Indians, the snake dance, the Apache raids and . . . the life of the pioneers who had to hold their plow with one hand and their gun with the other to repel the attack of the warring red skin."[20] His later recollections of his early Arizona days were as nostalgic as those of the secular cowboys.

Thus the pastor dealing with the orphans was eager for adventure and as anxious to prove his Arizona manhood as the next man. He came by ship and then train, of course, and perhaps the vast plains and desert flowed together with the vast ocean as they had for his bishop before him: "In place of the liquid plains of the ocean, it is the unending plains, barren and dry, of the great American Southwest that your giant locomotive will break through . . . for the locomotive has a prow made to cut through the resistance not of salty waves, but of cattle and horses strayed onto the tracks. Most of the time the monotony is the same as it is at sea. To the right, to the left, lonely, endless distances tire the gaze. Above your head is an immense blue hemisphere seared during the long hours of the day by a burning sun."[21]

Did Clifton's wildness live up to his expectations? Mandin had anticipated a lawless, violent town, and in their recollections the oldtimers relished bolstering that reputation. "There were many hard and tough characters who made their headquarters there," one remembered. It was a "rip-roaring, money-mad, wild-western mining town [with] little law except gun-law," recalled another. Mandin might not have felt disappointed. As in all mining camps, regardless of the men's ethnicity, bar brawls were virtually nightly events, and they frequently spilled over onto the streets, escalating from rough rivalry to rage and from fists to knives or even revolvers.[22] The deputy sheriffs frequently arrested those using weapons, kept them in jail overnight, and occasionally prosecuted them. Other violence was "domestic" and since virtually everyone owned a firearm, this too could escalate danger-

ously. Just as Mandin arrived, Frank Lane was arrested for the rape of
Pearl Childress; the grand jury refused to indict him, suspecting a more
voluntary relationship; Pearl's husband then shot and killed Lane; but
the town sentiment was with Childress, the newspaper reported, so a
conviction was unlikely.[23] Perhaps even before his arrival Mandin had
heard several versions of the capture of Augustín Chacón, a legendary
outlaw, Arizona's public enemy number one, in Morenci in November
1902. Chacón claimed just before Sheriff Parks hanged him that he had
killed fifteen Americans and thirty-seven Mexicans, but the Mexicans
in the mining camps considered him one of their esteemed, noble
bandits and sang his praises in their *corridos*.[24] The mining camps were
violent because they were male enclaves, their homosocial culture of
rivalry and aggression dominant because there were not yet enough
women and families to challenge it with respect for discipline and
vested interests in peace.

Still, when Mandin arrived the old-timers might have told him that
Clifton was peaceful compared to what it had been, as in the days of
Kid Louis and his strong-arm gang, who during one period averaged
a killing a day. "There was a Sheriff, Justice of Peace, Mayor and a
Town Council of a sort, but if they were not all members of Kid Louis's
gang, they were so afraid of him that they done what he said"; the
company doctor, however, insisted that the killings had never averaged more than three a week.[25] In the 1890s local authorities offered
five hundred dollars for an Apache scalp, and one was displayed,
properly desiccated, in the Blue Goose Saloon. All the men and some
of the women owned rifles if not pistols, and there was easy access to
dynamite. The Arizona Rangers and the *Denver Tribune* labeled Clifton
the toughest town in the territory, with Morenci not far behind. Cattle
rustlers and horse thieves were familiar patrons of the bars. Justice of
the Peace Boyles was busy, hearing sixteen case of criminal violence
in one summer month of 1904, and these only the misdemeanors,
almost all for fighting or shooting in the air outside bars.[26] But there
were no murders, so the old-timers must have been right that Clifton
had become tamer.[27]

Mandin worked and lived in the heart of Clifton's uncivilization, his
church at one end of Clifton's most untamed street. When he first
walked the half-mile along Chase Creek from the railroad station to his
new home, he was taken aback by the crudeness of the church,[28] a
structure of rough and uneven bricks. The inside seemed to Mandin

gauche, decorated in an unmatched and unartistic combination of the coarse and the finished. There were no windows. A small organ and a lathed-and-varnished railing stood on top of an unfinished plank platform. Clifton's poor women contributed what they had: a few lace doilies, not fine quality, lay next to plain muslin, clumsily tacked. His room was spacious but rather barren, although he could hardly complain about the woman who scrubbed it daily and supplied him with water. (He soon learned the cliché about fastidious Mexican housewifery.) There was, of course, no indoor plumbing, but the worst trial was the lack of good food. He was expecting hardship, of course, and had not anticipated fine meals, but he had not imagined eating without good bread and wine and cheese.

He was astounded, too, by the proportions of the town as he first explored it. There is not much flat space for building in Clifton, just the narrow valleys created by Chase Creek and the San Francisco River, enclosed by steep cliffs and hills. It was as if the mountains had stepped apart slightly to make room for a few people but stubbornly refused to move further. Five neighborhoods had squeezed themselves in—the east side, a strip east of the Frisco River just wide enough to hold one row of buildings and one street, the oldest district, where miners and smelter workers lived on the hillsides and drank in the saloons; North Clifton, a strip upriver on the west side of the Frisco, where the better-off workers and managers lived; Chase Creek, a narrow strip along a tributary of the Frisco, mainly Mexican, where a rapidly expanding, raucous business district vied for space with the houses that climbed up the hillsides; South Clifton, then known as Hill's Addition after its developer, the flattest and broadest residential area, the home of the "best" Anglos; and a new neighborhood for the poorer workers, Shannon Hill.[29] Chase Creek consisted of a creek, usually dry, paralleled by a dirt road—which meant, depending on the season, either dust, mud, or flood—with building entrances usually four to six feet above street level to protect them from floods. Every six months Rosario (Challo) Olivas plowed the street with his team to smooth the ruts (later the town acquired a one-cylinder Fairbank-Morse steam roller to follow up). In the dry season C. C. Reed—one of the Anglo adoptive parents—sprinkled it with water from his wagon weekly, to hold the dust down, but the ladies' boots still often sank into the dust, and the black skirts of the Mexican women were turned gray.[30] For some short distances there were plank or concrete side-walks, but they were discontinuous and pedestrians had to walk in the street along with the horses, burros, and occasional buggies—there was no way to keep clean while venturing into Chase Creek and you had to be always watching for holes, garbage, and the horse and donkey droppings. (The terrible smell was as much human as animal, however, as there was no system of sewage disposal other than outhouses, many of which had no underground pit.) If you could momentarily look up, you would see the electric lines overhead, the steep hills, and the smoke from the smelters. When an inversion held the air still, the sulfur fumes drizzled painfully into one's nose and throat; the sulfur dioxide gas combined with water to produce sulfurous acid and it stung and burned. "I felt that some demoniacal fiend was there injecting boiling lime into my lungs," one visitor to a smelter town wrote.[31] Everyone in Clifton then tried to stay inside until the winds came up and cleaned the air.

The one- and two-story buildings had once been mainly wooden, but the boom of the last few years had brought brick buildings, some with Italianate stone facades, and a variety of stores with brightly painted signs: restaurants and rooming houses, tailor, grocer, barber, butcher, baker, shoemaker, watchmaker, attorney, and stockbroker, clothing and dry-goods stores, drugstore, five and dime, laundry, and stage coach office, and La Tienda de Un Precio, the one-price bargain store. Timmermans had once had to go to Solomonville for many of his purchases but no longer. In Clifton's relatively temperate climate—cool, compared to other parts of Arizona, because it is so high—commerce spilled out of doors, and there were men who earned their living literally on the streets: draymen, who delivered freight from the railroad depot in wagons; Chinese hawkers, who sold the produce they grew from baskets suspended from a pole across their shoulders; "drummers," traveling salesmen, who sold dishes and shoes from trunks on the street; prompters, who solicited passers-by into the stores; *leneros* and *aguadores,* peddlers selling wood and water from their burros—most all of them announcing their offerings loudly. Some services appeared only itiner-antly in Clifton, like those of Dr. P. Kornblum, "Graduate Optician of New York and Chicago Colleges of Ophthalmology," who could tempo-rarily be consulted at the drugstore, or Dr. H. A. Schell, promising to cure headaches with his spectacles, who could be seen at the Clifton Hotel.[32] Street life was thick and news traveled quickly.

During the orphan affair two hubs of communication served the two sides of the town: the church for the Mexicans and the Clifton Hotel for the Anglos. The Anglos, mostly Protestants, did not need a church for their social and community activity, because they had other locations, both commercial and civic, such as the Library Hall. But Mandin noticed, nevertheless, that the Anglos were not on the whole a church-going group. The French, of course, could be pretty casual about the church, when they weren't downright anticlerical, but Mandin was used to the intensely religious Vendée, and his education led him to expect Protestants to be pious and sectarian. But there was only one Protestant church in Clifton, and it was not well attended. The Clifton Hotel had been the heart of the town's goings-on for several decades already, housing a barbershop (shave fifteen cents, shampoo twenty-five cents, haircut twenty-five cents), saloon, and billiard hall. Back in the 1880s, "It was built of undressed 1-inch lumber and surmounted by a canvas roof. Each room was divided from its neighbour by sheets of cheese-cloth nailed to scantlings, and the ceiling was conspicuous by its absence. It had mysterious powers akin to what is now known as wireless. A whisper at one end of the row could be easily heard at the other; and that is how it came to be known as Telephone Row. In summer time it acted as a Turkish bath during the day, and in winter it filled the role of a refrigerator during the night, and it was to local scorpions what the Riviera is to the Parisian." On Sundays the meals came with wine, which "had the consistency of crude oil and the soporific quality of chloroform. After a hearty meal sluiced down with this ambrosial nectar, the thirty odd boarders walked to their seats under the verandah, and there promptly fell asleep."[33] Things had improved by 1904: the rooms had walls, the parlor had good rugs, the scorpions were fewer, although by no means extinct, and the wine was a bit better, but it was still the place to go for Clifton news.

The priest searched in vain for a bar in which to sip coffee. Whatever his moral or drinking habits, he soon observed that the saloons were the uncontested town centers, the heart if not the brain of the organism, and they produced enough violence and vice to keep even a non-Protestant, nonprudish French pastor steadily dismayed, attracted, and justified. (Although most of the Chinese had been driven out of Clifton, a few opium dens hung on and attracted customers of all nationalities.)[34] Selling liquor was more profitable than mining to individuals without much capital; liquor was a lucrative import because of its high value in relation to the space it took up, so bar owners were often also liquor dealers. In the earliest days a bar was merely a plank laid across two barrels in a tent serving homemade mescal,[35] but by Mandin's time some of the Anglo east-side saloons had beautiful polished bars and titillating paintings. There were fifteen bars listed in the 1905 *Arizona Business Directory,* seven in Chase Creek alone, and these were just the well-established ones; the book did not list Rocky Jones's bar, the Old Buffet, La Favorita, or Cesario Cárdenas's and Jesús Cobo's places. Saloons provided many services beyond selling drinks for a bit (twelve and a half cents): they frequently served as banks for miners, keeping and lending money, and often offered baths, feed yards, libraries, and lodging, which further increased profits. Mandin heard that church services had been held in the bars. Most of Clifton's prominent businessmen got their start by opening bars. Ipolito Cascarelli, one of Clifton's wealthiest, began with a saloon and was soon vice president of the Metcalf Bank, major rancher, real estate dealer, and landlord.[36]

The main activity in the saloons was gambling—stud poker, monte, keno, and blackjack in the Anglo bars, Rifa and Panguingui among the Mexicans, punchboards everywhere. The saloons took a cut and paid a licensing fee of $30 per month, payable to the sheriff, collected by his deputies—a good way of keeping informed (and an opportunity to rake off a bit?).[37] There was also plenty of outside gambling, betting on the cockfights run by "El Turco" (a Turkish immigrant), badger baiting, and rooster chasing. In Morenci in 1903 cockfight promoters built a small amphitheater at the cockpit in order to promote contests with other towns; one match between Morenci and Clifton had a $200 jackpot.[38] Jackpots of over $300 were not unusual, although most workingmen were more likely to put in $1 and feel like a champ if they won $5. Methods of cheating were numerous and often simple. Professional gambler Laureano Matellan, who said he was unable to do mining labor because of arthritis, eked out a living by marking cards with an invisible paste that he could see when he looked through his green visor.[39] The gambling and the cheating gave rise to most of the fights. Yet the saloon keepers, whose establishments stimulated the violence, often gained stature from their roles as mediators, referees, or attendants to the fallen.[40] For this reason as well as because they accumulated property, saloon keepers were prominent among town leaders and, notably, law officers. And law officers became saloon

keepers–like Graham County Sheriff James Parks, who bought the
Barnum Saloon in Clifton, featuring its first billiard tables.[41]

The female bar workers did not attain similar prestige. The bars
hired women–for very low wages plus tips–to sing, flirt, induce the
men to buy drinks, and dance with patrons for a price. Every Anglo
saloon had a nickelodeon, which played constantly, five cents a tune,
and the old-timers still remember the songs: "all of the beautiful tunes
of those days–'Turkey in the Straw,' 'The Old Gray Mare,' 'Johnny Get
Your Gun,' 'The Ballad of Mother McCree,' 'La Cucaracha . . .'"[42]
Prostitution was sometimes part of the deal between the woman and
the bar owner, sometimes a form of moonlighting needed to supplement low wages. Every mining town had its row where prostitutes'
"cribs" were located, often just shacks, in which the women (barely)
earned their living. In some larger mining camps, like Tombstone, a
few madams operated large and elaborately decorated houses, but not
in Clifton,[43] partly because Clifton did not have the wildly skewed sex
ratios, such as five men to one woman, of other mining towns. James
Sing, one of the Clifton Chinese, once ran a house, and it was rumored
that his women were virtually slaves, but then in the mining camps
virtually all except the Chinese would go to any exaggeration to vilify
the Chinese, especially in terms of morality.[44] There were at least two
publicly identified "houses" in Clifton-Morenci. At some point PD in
Morenci opened a brothel, part of its full-service company town,
known as the Green House because the building was green,[45] but in
1904 the women operated without company sponsorship. In 1900
census taker James Langerman wrote "prostitute" or "public woman"
in the occupation column beside ten Mexican women in Morenci and
six women (Anglo, Mexican, and Japanese) in Clifton. How do we
imagine the conversation that led to this identification? Did they tell
him they were prostitutes? Unlikely. Did he consider it common
knowledge? More credible. Perhaps they were hard to miss. One
old-timer recollected how differently they dressed, in skirts up to their
knees; the "nice" women hesitated to go to Chase Creek, but when
they had to shop there they often walked down the center of the street
in the dust or mud, rather than on the plank sidewalk, in order to avoid
contact with women of ill repute.[46] Of course, Anglos sometimes
maligned any Mexican women who worked in bars. But the claim of
some Mexican American Clifton residents that the early prostitutes
were all Anglo seems unlikely too.[47] For all women, the existence of

prostitutes served to mark off the dreadful fate that lay beyond the bounds of respectability.

As they were everywhere the prostitutes in Clifton-Morenci were vulnerable to violence, legal persecution, false accusations of thievery, and many worse risks.[48] Yet there are Clifton whores-with-hearts-of-gold-and-happy-endings stories. Today old-timers recall that prostitutes often mothered the men, gave away money to the poor, and ended up marrying respectable cowboys, and while these memories may have been polished up over the years, there are some documented cases, from other mining towns, of kind and respected prostitutes. For example, in nearby Silver City, New Mexico, Bessie Harper paid for coal and food for the poorest families. Since Bessie was the extremely prosperous owner of a house, this may have been as much an investment as a sacrifice for her;[49] but it may well be that even poor prostitutes were motivated to good deeds in efforts to transcend their evil reputations. Some prostitutes married and became housewives, possibly fully respectable ones, but many received pretty rough treatment and did not move up in the world.

The prostitutes and saloon women formed a small but notorious subculture and sometimes offended the law not through sexual transgressions—prostitution was legally tolerated—but through disorderly conduct. In 1904 the local courts heard five cases against women for fighting, several including groups of women, all leading to convictions and fines of ten dollars per individual. Lupie *(sic)* García must have been well known, arrested in August for "vulgar and obscene language," the next day for fighting with Ynes Miranda, and in December for fighting with Ysaval Rocha. Abilena Ray, Mattie Mosley, and Yee Him were arrested in December for smoking opium.[50] These cases were trifling compared to the nearly daily trials of men for violence and disorder, but they explained why "respectable" women, Mexican and Anglo alike, avoided the streets near the bars. The distinction between women's respectability and disrepute was underlined by the numerous prosecutions of men for "using vulgar and obscene language in the presence of women and children."[51]

Prostitution was not the only moral disease Mandin thought he had to cure. Plenty of couples lived in sin, although we cannot know how many because we cannot trust that the census taker knew or cared.[52] Free unions were respectable and common in Mexico, especially among the poor, accounting for up to half the couples in rural Mexico, around one-quarter in urban Mexico, and these patterns traveled to *el norte*.[53] One historian computed that in Arizona mining camps in 1864, the single largest group of women were Mexicans living with men to whom they were not married. This proportion declined over time, but unwedded couples were still common in the early twentieth century.[54] The wife of one of the territorial supreme court judges who heard the orphan trial found these informal relationships common in the mining towns.[55] Meanwhile, within the church declining financial support—and venality—induced priests to charge high prices for weddings, adding yet another reason not to bother.[56]

The parents who took orphans were all formally married because Mandin insisted on it, and perhaps he and Timmermans lowered their prices in their campaign to clean up the town. Timmermans had required Juan Esquivel (aka Maxwell) and Angela Flores to marry in church, which they did on November 9, 1903, although they already had two children born in December 1901 and June 1903.[57] Timmermans was intent enough on marriages to perform weddings between a Catholic and a non-Catholic "cum dispensatione Disparitatis Cultus."[58] But Clifton's Mexicans did not flock to the church despite the padre's pressure, because the unmarried state by no means made them outcasts or even unusual among poor Mexicans.

CLIFTON'S MEXICANS AND ANGLOS kept themselves mostly separate but not always or everywhere. To the historian today as to the outsider then, the rules seemed inconsistent and confusing. To Mandin Arizona's racial system was like a cloud that dissolved when you reached for it. Indeed, his ignorance was later defined as the root of the problem by the Anglos—he did not understand "what the Mexicans were really like." He may not even have grasped what a "Mexican" was. In defending himself later he wrote that the applicants for orphans were not "negroes. I did not see the husbands but the women were white."[59] A historian writing thirty years ago blamed the "misunderstanding" on Mandin's being French: "being a true Frenchman [he] apparently had all the Gallic obliviousness of his countrymen to racial and ethnic distinctions."[60] But of course he wasn't oblivious; it's just that there was more than one racial-ethnic system in the world.

He understood himself to be traveling to a colony to proselytize the natives, but he did not comprehend the native identity. He may not have fully recognized Mexico's national independence, and he and the nuns all claimed later that they thought the people were "Spanish." It is true that this population sometimes referred to themselves, when speaking English, as "the Spanish people" or, possibly, "Spanish Americans," as had become common in New Mexico. Yet when speaking Spanish it seems likely that they called themselves, as they do today, *mexicanos*. (The word *hispano* had not yet entered the Clifton-Morenci vocabulary.)[61] To this group there was old Mexico and new Mexico, but both were Mexico. When they heard "Americans" speak of "Mexicans," they knew that this term "Mexican" had some faulty implications: it implied foreignness when that was not the case; and it was pejorative. Another term they heard more and more frequently was "half-breed," a nasty but commonplace label applied by whites. Unlike the Mexican *mestizo*, a word with no pejorative connotations referring to the mixing of Spaniards and Indians that formed the Mexican people, the ugly Anglo phrase "half-breed" was first applied to Native Americans and was always derogatory: it meant "mongrel" and carried the assumption that a blend of origins was somehow inferior to a single one.

Today the nomenclature about the people of the U.S. Southwest with Spanish, Mexican, and Indian backgrounds is notoriously shifting and contested; books about the Southwest often begin with apologias for an author's choice of labeling because there are, indeed, choices: Mexican, Mexican American, Latino, Chicano, Hispanic, to cite just the English-language options. The Clifton-Morenci camp obscured the categories yet more because it contained several scores of "Spaniards," different in complicated ways from "Spanish people"–some Spaniards had immigrated directly from Spain, while others "stopped off" in Mexico before coming to the United States.[62] In 1904 one might have heard different dialects of spoken Spanish; today the outsider can learn to distinguish Spaniards from Mexicans only by asking. But Mandin could barely speak Spanish; he continually misspelled Spanish names in his baptism, marriage, and death records; perhaps he could not distinguish Castilian from Mexican speech.

Language was hardly Mandin's only obstacle to understanding Clifton's racial categories because these were riddled with exceptions–but then race is like a language, structured out of irregularities as well as rules, the inconsistencies as numerous as those of English grammar. Race has often been supple, mobile, even contradictory, but in small towns in particular, social categories coexisted with singularities, and people got themselves defined as individuals rather than as members of groups. Because of this specificity, racial orders arose as microsystems and, like microclimates, the more remote the area, the more specific the microsystem. Originally influenced by several different racial logics, the Clifton-Morenci system then grew on its own.

Although most peoples have some concept we might call "race," what they mean by it varies. In most parts of Latin America, race talk was primarily about *physical appearance*—where a finely calibrated range of terms defined people from dark to fair. In the United States "race" developed in the context of slavery, influenced particularly by the slaveowners' desire to hang on to as many slaves as possible. So in this country "race" became a matter primarily of *ancestry,* focused on blacks and whites. The law came to define anyone with even a "drop" of black "blood" (as if it were blood that carried "race") as black: the law of "hypo-descent."[63] Over time there were important changes in this system, tending from the complex toward simplification. Early on in the U.S. system numerous categories of descent were in use—for example, quadroon or one-quarter black, octoroon or one-eighth black; in Latin U.S. cultures, as in Louisiana, there were even finer distinctions—a *griffe* or *sambo* was three-quarters black, a *sacatra* or *mango* seven-eighths black. But intermarriage soon multiplied the number of categories beyond a workable number. After slavery the U.S. conception of race evolved further, responding to the imperatives of maintaining white supremacy and white denial of widespread "race" mixture. Given this practice, the in-between racial categories shriveled and died and the United States came to adopt a binary system: everyone was either black or white.[64]

A third system thrived in Mexico, using race words primarily to designate *class position or social status*. Appearance and ancestry were subordinate meanings in Mexico, a country dominated by *mestizos*. Mainly using a tripartite as opposed to a binary system, most Mexicans categorize people as Indians, *mestizos,* or whites. In practice these labels usually conform to appearance and ancestry but can also directly contradict them, so that an urban professional would likely be called white despite dark skin and Indian or *mestizo* facial features. Where formal physical description is necessary, as on a passport, individuals may be bureaucratically categorized as *blanco, obscuro, or muy obscuro;* in the vernacular they may be described in finer gradations and metaphors like *café con leche*. This was the system most Clifton-Morenci Mexicans had grown up with.

Most adult Americans today were taught that race was a biological matter, that there were three races—Caucasian, Negro, and Mongolian. Apparently, it took the global migrations and mixings of the last half-century to make visible the arbitrariness of these or any categories, and in the last few decades the study of race has been radically transformed by the understanding that systems of racial classification are always socially and historically constructed. No racial classification can yield consistent descriptive or biological groupings. Race is a "pigment of the imagination," says sociologist Rubén Rumbaut,[65] and the imagining is social and cultural, not individual. Clearly human beings display a variety of physical attributes, and those from groups that have lived near and reproduced with one another usually appear more similar than those from more distant population groups. But differences between groups are rarely greater than differences within groups, and no set of racial characteristics can be detailed that will accurately predict the popular impression of who is white, who black, who Asian, who Mexican. Nor do racial groupings rest on some consistent set of invisible biological features, such as blood or capacities.

But the new awareness of historical and global instability in racial categories—the new critical race theory—does not mean that race isn't "real." To the contrary, it is as real as slavery, Auschwitz, the U.S. immigration quotas. As real as this orphan affair. Race is a social fact, one with great force. It is both "a constituent of the individual psyche and of relationships . . . and a component of collective identities and social structures."[66] Race is a strong, hot idea—unlike categories such as body type (mesomorph or ectomorph) or temperament (witty or quiet). The categorizing work of race seems always to involve power, subordination and superiority, inclusion and exclusion, and frequently gain. Perhaps race talk is most vehement when possession of power is unsettled or contested. In Clifton in 1904 that was the case—not at the very top, of course, where the copper company managers ruled, but just underneath, where entrepreneurs, managers and foremen, skilled workers, and a few farmers and ranchers hung on to their positions, threatened by the enormous social changes put in motion by the copper companies.

Race segregation was under construction in Clifton in 1904. It was completed by, say, the 1920s and then remained fairly intact until well into the 1950s. In the 1890s, when Clifton had perhaps a thousand people, Anglos and Mexicans mixed often and Mexicans could command status and respect. Although the races were hardly equal, numerous Mexican artisans, businessmen, muleteers, skilled miners and smelter men mixed with Anglos socially. The Lesinskys depended on Mexican foremen and managers. Intermarriage was widespread and not disreputable–Louis Lesinsky and Johnny Ward (for whom Ward's Canyon is named) were among the many Anglos with Mexican wives. In the 1880s the list of "American" students at the elementary school included Carlos and Frank (Francisco) Alvidrez and Tomás and Ramón Balles[67] (Francisco and Ramón were to become foster parents for that one fateful day). In 1894 45 percent of the registered voters in Clifton, Morenci, and Metcalf had Hispanic names.[68] A decade later segregation was curtaining off the Mexicans, but it was still a loosely hanging drapery. For example, a few Mexican children went to school, mostly in segregated classes, but only for the first three grades, and they were kept out of the predominantly white South Clifton school.[69] The Anglos developed segregated clubs, fraternal organizations, and saloons on the east side and in South Clifton. There were formal public balls for whites, while Mexicans held dances much more frequently, usually outside in the Mexican neighborhoods. The Mexicans had their own drinking places, bars in Chase Creek and some private houses where women sold drinks, and no whites would go there. But the system was not yet thoroughly rationalized and the town's various spaces, businesses, and institutions had varying practices. Anglos and Mexicans both frequented the Italian saloons run by the Spezia brothers and the Siriannis, and Mexicans went to the bar owned by Hugh Quinn (who ended up taking one of the orphans) on Chase Creek.[70] Whites patronized Mexican entrepreneurs and craftsmen–electricians, plumbers, carpenters, schoolteachers, locomotive engineers, and barbers. Mexican activities–performances, marriages, trips, illnesses–were frequently reported in the local paper, and the Mexican elite still sometimes mixed with the Anglo elite at large formal events.

Additional diversity had once worked to undermine neat categories and to place some groups even below the Mexicans. It is by no means only elites who use racial hierarchies against "others"; subaltern groups also initiate and manipulate racial identities to define insiders and outsiders. But diversity was now declining. The pacification of the Apaches muted the anti-Indian hysteria of the other settlers. Still more consequential was the exile of most of the Chinese. In 1883 they made up one-quarter of Clifton's miners and were treated with the utmost callousness. James Colquhoun remarked that "if occasionally a few were killed no questions were asked, and the work went on."[71] Mexican and Anglo workers joined forces to drive out the Chinese and now only a handful were left: about sixty-five in Clifton in 1900, all male. They were commercial vegetable gardeners par excellence; they competed with Mexican women for laundry customers; and they cooked at the best restaurants. A few were commercially quite successful, proprietors, for example, of six Clifton eateries, including that in the Abrahams' Clifton Hotel. Still, even owning a business could not bring them respect, and several Chinese businessmen were not even named in the business directory but referred to insultingly as, for instance, "French Restaurant, Chinaman, E Clifton."[72] The great majority of the Chinese worked in servile positions as domestics, launderers, or private cooks. One Anglo old-timer, son of the city judge, recalls being "programmed . . . to not be respectful towards these people," harassing them mercilessly, chanting "Chink Chonk Chinamen," stealing the ritual food that the Chinese left on graves at funerals.[73] But their numbers were so small that the Mexicans no longer had racial inferiors to raise their own racial status. Although all other groups, including the Mexicans, expressed negative views of blacks, there were not enough of them either–possibly several score in Clifton-Morenci–to serve as the standard of racial inferiority.[74]

Before Clifton-Morenci assimilated to the southwestern Anglo-Mexican binary racial system, the camp developed its own three-part racial classification, and this was the system that predominated at the turn of the century. This racial logic replicated neither the American nor the Mexican system but created a unique triplet: at the bottom were poor Mexicans; at the top were "Americans"; in the middle were prosperous and usually light-skinned Mexicans, Spaniards, and other dark or "Latin" European immigrants–I call this group, for want of a better name, "Euro-Latins." They were not (yet) clearly white or nonwhite, and if we remember to look at this racial system through Mandin's eyes, it is no wonder, as they included many with olive skin, black hair, and Latin language.[75] The Euro-Latins remind us that whiteness is by no means an obvious or universal concept. The group was, in 1990s terms, more a racial and class category than a religious one; true, the Euro-Latins were Catholic, but so were the numerous Irish in Clifton and an occasional French or French Canadian immigrant; and few of these men went to church anyway. Clifton-Morenci contemporaries categorized people variously but usually in three groups. The copper companies delineated three formal wage groups: Mexicans, Italians and Spaniards, and whites, but there was slippage between the nonwhite groups and some Italians earned the Mexican rate.[76] Anglos sometimes referred to "Mexicans and Italians" as a group; a Morenci resident recalled her school class in the early twentieth century as "five white boys and the rest were Mexican and Italian."[77] As one law officer described a Morenci scene in 1903, "pretty big crowd—mostly Mexicans, but a lot of Dagoes, Bohunks, and foreigners of different kinds—no whites at all."[78] Patterns of sociability also pointed to a "Latin" identity that included Mexicans. For example, the many single Italian miners in Morenci more often lived in Mexican than in Anglo lodging houses. Intermarriage among Mexicans, Spaniards, and Italians was common.

The orientation toward a three-category system may have been influenced by the racial culture of Mexicans, but the whites were pushing back, leaning strongly toward the binary. Many of Clifton's Anglos might have said that two categories were the "American" way, especially since a disproportionate number of them came from the South, supporters of the Confederacy and then of Jim Crow. They frequently transposed antiblack discourse to Mexicans.[79] Ironically, if Mexicans had appeared in the plantation South, they might have been classified as white or at least not black; but the southern whites' Jim Crow ideology was making Mexicans the equivalent of blacks in the Southwest.[80] Meanwhile in Clifton-Morenci, Euro-Latins were learning the value of whiteness, which required distinguishing themselves from the Mexicans. By 1904 the drift was already toward a new form of the American binary, Anglo or Mexican—in its uglier form, gringo or greaser.

The massive immigration from Mexico might have altered the drift toward the binary, by distinguishing newcomers from long-term Mexican residents of the U.S. Southwest. This distinction prevailed for a long time in, say, New Mexico and southern California, but not here. Whether they were old-time residents, new settlers, or seasonal migrants, no matter how the *hispanos* tried to distinguish themselves from the immigrants, the mines and mills and smelters paid them all the "Mexican wage" and gave them "Mexican work," and the Anglo clubs excluded them—thereby exerting on them a centripetal force. There was no term "Mexican American," and to the Anglos, citizenship didn't matter much anyway: large proportions of the Anglos were immigrants and to them "Mexican" was a racial-ethnic, not a national, designation, while to the Mexicans *mexicano* was in considerable part a term of nation and patriotism. Ironically, Mexican and Anglo uses tended to converge over time: Mexican and *mexicano* both meant, part of the Mexican *people*. As a Texas Congressman put it in 1921, "In Texas the word Mexican is used to indicate the race, not a citizen or subject of the country . . . 250,000 . . . were born in the state but they are 'Mexicans' just as all blacks are Negroes though they may have five generations of American ancestors."[81] In other words, the Mexican identity of the time—part national, part racial—was shaped both by Mexicans and Anglos. Anglo discrimination helped create a new truth because the way the Anglos treated the Mexicans was in part what made them separate, un-American.[82]

Although Mandin's work as a pastor introduced him rather quickly to hundreds of people, it did not make it easy for him to learn the race structure of Clifton. Only a fraction of his parishioners attended mass and those who did were virtually all Mexican women. A few non-Mexicans showed up for the odd baptism or marriage, and the race categories used in Mandin's parish reports to the diocese replicated those of the U.S. census, categories that labeled Mexicans white: under the heading "family heads (white)," Mandin listed 7 "Americans," 4 Italians, 12 Spaniards, 156 Mexicans; under "family heads (nonwhite)" he wrote a zero.[83] When Mandin went up to Morenci to hold mass, his communicants were even more overwhelmingly Mexican, as was the overall population: Clifton was 54 percent Mexican, Morenci 69 percent. Italian and a few other non-Mexican names appear in the Sacred Heart records: Giuseppi and Nicola Capelli, Joe Cicerelli, Francesco Mazzotti, Antonietta and Domenica De Grazia, Severino and Luciano Gagliardi, Salvador Sirianni, Carlo Vieta, John Dougherty, Hugh and Mary Quinn, John and Anna Micetich—and we don't even know if any of these were churchgoers, since the records indicate only that they conducted their marriages and baptisms at the church.[84] So not only was Mandin's parish almost entirely Mexican, but the others were so overwhelmingly Spanish and Italian as not to stand out.

If Mandin did not yet grasp the Mexican identity, he had even more difficulty grasping the white. For most twentieth-century American whites, whiteness as a racial identity was invisible because they considered themselves, simply, the norm, like some aboriginal groups who called themselves "the people." Because "whites" had greater power, they labeled, described, and understood "nonwhites" as departures from the standard or, worse, specifically marked as inferior.[85] But who could get to be part of the standard?

In the turn-of-the-century United States there were two primary meanings of "white": In the East Coast version, the superior race in the early nineteenth century had been Anglo-Saxons, including primarily northern Europeans, and as the century went on other peoples who came to the country were registered as separate races—the Irish, Italians, Slavs, "Hebrews," and "Hindus," for example.[86] Gradually most of these groups worked their way into whiteness. In fact, "whiteness" arose when diverse peoples, largely from Europe, subsumed their identities of origin as subcategories of white or, rather, when they turned their identities of origin into ethnicity rather than race.[87] The western version of whiteness expanded to take in many of these other races even more quickly—Jews and Slavs, for example. In Clifton-Morenci the Euro-Latins were the last to be included as white, but they did eventually make it, and the orphan affair helped them achieve that acceptance. Part of what made the West a land of opportunity was the chance to become white. But throughout most of the Southwest, especially Texas and California, that chance was denied to Mexicans; whites made them nonwhite. The circularity of this racial definition was, of course, the essence of the process: those secure as whites got to say who else could be white.

In Clifton's earlier decades Mexicans were not exactly white but not nonwhite either.[88] As Cliftonians poured in from many different racial cultures, it was as if the imperative to categorize the population was temporarily in abeyance. To Spanish, French, Irish, and Slavic immigrants, Mexicans were one among many groups of foreigners. "Not white" meant the Chinese.[89] Even African Americans were not definitively unwhite. Not a single mining camp in Arizona ever banned blacks, while most prohibited Chinese and many excluded Mexicans.[90] In some places in the U.S. Southwest, blacks were white and Mexicans were not. Making the southwestern mines into "white man's camps" at the turn of the century meant keeping out Asians, southern and eastern Europeans, and Mexicans, while blacks were sometimes accepted as miners.[91] James Young, a black man at the Contention mine in nearby Tombstone, remarked, "Si White and I were the first white men in Tombstone after Gird and Schieffelin."[92]

Race had another peculiarity in the West, one that rewrote history:

here "white" usually meant "American," and "American" came to mean "white." At that time "Mexican American" would have seemed an oxymoron to the Anglos. No matter that many of the Mexicans had lived on this soil far longer than the Anglo immigrants, longer than the African Americans had lived in the Unitd States; the continued immigration from Mexico into *México afuera*–U.S.-occupied Mexico–redefined the whole category as one of outsiders, aliens.

Becoming nonwhite involved not only economic and political punishment for Mexicans but also psychic and social trauma because the superiority of lightness ran deep in Mexican culture too. Mexicans found it easy enough to understand the importance of being "white" to these Americans. But given the Mexican tradition of "racial" mobility, of becoming lighter as a part of the *meaning* of moving up, it must have seemed to them particularly galling that Anglos began, around the turn of the century, to deny them that possibility. In this interdiction on social fluidity the orphan affair was to become a major enforcer, at least in this small location.

The vigilantes later said that Mandin did not understand "what the Mexicans were really like." They meant that he did not look upon the Mexicans as "nonwhite," that is, inferior and alien, and that he recognized significant social differences among them–class, cultural, religious differences. He distinguished among these differences to find what he considered moral, stable, superior homes for the orphans. His very individualization of the Mexicans, his apparent reluctance to think that they were all alike, was what the vigilantes blamed him for. Mandin was an innocent, a newborn in relation to Clifton's racial system.

But although his innocence remained unsullied by Anglo racism, he had his own Gallic, Roman Catholic version of Orientalism. He was influenced by his bishop's racial views, which were in turn influenced by the Mexican racial system: Bishop Granjon trisected his flock as white people, Mexican "half-breeds," and Indians.[93] In his use of "half-breed," he was taking in the Mexican *mestizaje,* but he was applying it to all the Mexicans, not just part of them as the Mexicans meant it. And he probably did not understand how pejorative the word became when rendered in English, since he was more positive about the Mexicans than the Americans were. The French clergy's racialist view of the New World appreciated Mexican piety and the fact that the Catholic spirit and mysteries infused many of them. But it rested as much on a sense of superiority as did the American outlook, albeit a superiority emerging from different cultural values. Mandin likely picked up his bishop's Gallic distaste for American "civilization," a Dostoevskian contempt for its commercial, competitive, ambitious, nonspiritual essence, and his assimilation of the Mexican sensibility to that of the French—"The Latin blood and Gallic character adapt perfectly to apostleship in Mexican lands."[94] But this view of Mexicans is at best condescending, at worst racially infantilizing: Granjon saw Mexican society as a kind of "rural Spain of old, somewhat mixed with Anglo-Saxonism and a relic of Aztec Survival." He spoke of "the naive simplicity of this race of children . . . 'Ignorant as slaves and more courteous than princes,' [as] it has been said of these fine native peoples . . . another similarity with the Middle East. The home is perhaps only a miserable hut, a *jacal,* there is inside perhaps only a crust of bread, and for sleeping, only an old sheepskin spread on the ground. No matter; all this is yours, the *jacal,* the crust, and the sheepskin."

Granjon's Catholic racialism was limited to the cultural. The bishop evinced no interest in the people's appearance, innate capacities, or ancestry. As a result he considered these racial traits fragile, vulnerable to contamination and damage. The bishop lamented the pernicious impact of Americanism, of the "selfish manners of the 'invader,' as they call the American in their ballads," on the traditional Mexican patterns of hospitality, generosity, civility, "this beautiful urbanity, completely natural and so gracious."[95] The long-term Mexican residents of New Mexico and Arizona, too, experienced the Anglo newcomers as unmannerly and crude. "Society was different in those days to what it is now. The men were more gentlemanly, the ladies more gentile [*sic*]."[96] But while the Mexicans condemned the Anglo domination over their lands, the bishop feared the Anglo infection of the people.

Prominent in the invaders' attack, Mandin knew, were the efforts of Protestant missionaries, a new Reformation "loaded with gold and astounding promises," already converting some Catholics in this region.[97] Local priests saw "Americanization" and the Interchurch World Movement to "Christianize" the Mexicans as two aspects of the same menace.[98] Protestant missionaries' attitudes to the Mexicans resembled Catholics' in some respects—viewing them as childlike, benighted—but the Protestants lacked the Gallic sense of style. They regarded Mexican formality of address, for example, as showy insincerity, effeminacy, signaling dishonor and treachery. As missionaries, they had to believe in the acquired, cultural nature of these traits, because they needed human souls to be malleable. So, like the Catholics, they also had to beware of contamination. Obsessed with manliness as were so many American men at the turn of the century, the Protestants worried about Mexican seduction of Anglos, about "going Mexican" as a form of degeneration.[99] Mandin found little of this anti-Catholicism or missionary zest for conversion in Clifton, where the Anglos seemed content to leave the Mexican religion alone, because, it seemed, the Anglos did not have much religious energy at all. They treated Mandin with respect, as they had Timmermans, as an ambassador from the Mexicans, worthy in status by dint of his position, although he represented only a minor people, not a major power. But the bishop's awareness of the Protestant drive would affect his indignant and determined intervention when the foundlings were kidnapped.

Mandin had to confront, however, another corruption: Mexicans were undependable, undisciplined Catholics even without Protestant blandishments. The young priest faced direct rejection—the anticlericalism of many Mexican men, especially wage workers—the poverty of Mexicans and their disinclination to contribute to the church, and their attachment to some seriously unorthodox beliefs and practices.[100]

Combined, this Mexican resistance to authority, attraction to the unorthodox, and openness to Protestant competition increased the attractiveness but also the negotiating power of the Mexicans in relation to the Catholic clergy. The unreliability of the Mexicans, like that of any fickle clientele, modulated the padres' approach, if not their commitment, to suppressing popular unorthodoxies. The search for control reinforced an already familiar pattern in which priests like Mandin addressed themselves almost exclusively to Mexican women and children in raising money and building parishioners' devotion.

What did it mean to the young father to preside over women? We can guess that his sense of the institution, of his institutional position, and of his job was not the same as that of his flock. Even his own, partial, apprehension of the situation was divided: Reciting the Mass to a church filled mainly with women and children, his nervousness receded, his confidence in his sprouting authority grew, his pleasure in his status swelled. Yet the men's absence taunted him, like a silent chorus his mental ear could not filter out, an implicit challenge to his potency. Bringing those men to mass—which meant, of course, to some acceptance of subordination—was an obligation that, however distant, remained a measure of his success. Thus the very enthusiasm, loyalty, hard work, and deference of the women reminded him, occasionally but recurrently, of what was missing. Perhaps over the years other padres like Father Timmermans could gather up a full sense of accomplishment from the combination of women's devotion and institutional stability. But Constant Mandin was too new to feel such ease. What's more, his yearning, however inarticulate, derived not only from his understanding of women's lower rank, an inferiority only made more visceral by their eagerness; it derived not only from his need for higher-status parishioners to boost his own pride; no, it came also from a longing for male company. What was missing was not just the camaraderie of the seminary and the ordinary and reassuring friendships of youth, although he was indeed lonely in Clifton, but the contagious and delightful aspects of sharing in the fellowship of the superior sex, the true congregation and leaders of the faith.

The bishop of Tucson was uniquely attractive in this regard, an intellectual, composer of fine writing, and connoisseur of sumptuous living—part of his disdain for things Anglo. He exchanged luxurious gifts with one of his few wealthy Anglo Catholic patrons, William Brophy, head of the PD company store in Bisbee. Granjon received cases of Chianti and other good wines, which he looked forward to enjoying in his new private dining room and kitchen, and in return he sent a Lyonnais tapestry and books "of profound thoughts and literary merit." He anticipated his four-week vacation on Lake Chapala near Guadalajara, where he planned to "live there in the water, day and night, like ducks, by way of contrast from this our hyper-dry and hot country."[101] The Clifton cowboys and landscape brought a thrill to Mandin, but Granjon's was the destiny he preferred, the kind of company he craved, and certainly the source of the approval he wanted.

October 2, 1904, Afternoon

Morenci Square and Clifton Library Hall

ARRIVING IN MORENCI, Deputy Sheriff Jeff Dunagan and Tom Simpson proceeded according to the hierarchy of authority. First they drew in the town boss, Charles Mills, superintendent for Phelps Dodge, "a grim and dominant man, whose subordinates took no action without his knowledge and consent."[1] The chief tactician for the copper companies against the 1903 strike, he would know how to manage trouble. It wasn't hard to locate him: if he was not in his Detroit Copper office, he had to be either in the bank, of which he was director, located in the Morenci Hotel, or in the exclusive Morenci Club, all on Morenci's central square. Since he was a bachelor he would not be at home. Morenci Anglos who had watched or heard about the placement of the foundlings had already gotten to Mills, so he had independently decided that there was a problem that needed fixing: "I have been waiting for some of the authorities to take hold of this," he said. Then the three of them went to the Morenci Hotel.

Answering a knock on her hotel room door, Sister Anna Michaella found two armed men, one calling himself a deputy sheriff. He said that an error had been made in placing the children. Then she heard the crowd in the railroad yard outside the hotel, which had by then grown to over a hundred and were, in the words of the understandably nervous sister, "very indignant and excited."

The Clifton men demanded to talk to Swayne since, to them, it was obvious that the only man in the expedition would be in charge. They assumed that Mandin had no authority–was it because Mandin had no confidence and could be made to back down easily? Or was it because he was indebted to the copper companies for contributions to keep his work going?[2] Soon joined by H. B. Rice, assistant manager of the Detroit Copper company store and member of the Territorial Legislature, and Dr. Tuthill, Detroit Copper doctor, the men could not at first find Swayne (who was having his first bath in days), which made them more annoyed. When they finally rousted him, they insisted on speaking with him privately, without the sisters.

Mills began the talking and his was the recognizable, understated voice of power, speaking as if his own decisions were the ineluctable laws of nature: He explained that "these people [the Mexicans who had received the orphans] . . . were indigent, had no trade, no means, and didn't draw sufficient salary to support families or educate them either; that they didn't educate their own children . . . that five or six of them would stop in the same room . . . didn't even have a bed to sleep in." He explained, as if it were a matter in which he was only an observer, "the feeling that was there between the white American people and the Mexicans . . . he thought it advisable . . . to be advised by the people [sic]." They asked Swayne if he could not reassign the children to white people, and he refused. Meanwhile a crowd outside the hotel continued to grow.

The "people" later insisted that Swayne had only himself to blame. He could have backed down, they thought; and had the delegation talked first with the sisters alone, the sisters might well have backed down. Perhaps a "compromise" might have then been accepted: had the sisters immediately offered to take all the children back to New York, the crowd might have been persuaded by Mills and the deputies to back off. But the men excluded the sisters from discussion, so there was a man-to-man confrontation. Dunagan and Simpson had revolvers tucked in their belts. The committee's demands and the noisy crowd outside made Swayne more obstinate. Perhaps he recalled some of the vicious anti-Catholic mobs of the East and felt his moral and manly obligation was to defend the faith. He insisted that he knew his business and that the children had been placed and would stay placed until the sisters had a chance to investigate the homes, and that the Foundling Hospital did not propose to be dictated to by "the people." Simpson "told him it wasn't right placing them with the Mexicans that way, the lowest class in the whole community." Mills said that it was a disgrace to the American people to place white children with people like these. Swayne answered, well if that was the case he was ashamed to be an American. Someone then dared Swayne to repeat those words to the by now extremely large crowd, but this dare he did not take, so Dunagan, Simpson, and Mills returned to the lobby. While Simpson went off to telephone Jake Abraham in Clifton (who had a telephone in his hotel) about what was happening, Dunagan and Mills of course had to let the crowd know about Swayne's refusal to cooperate, and that was when things first got ugly.

The crowd did not share the committee's determination to deal only with men and was shouting insults and threats against the nuns as well. It flowed into the hotel lobby, and soon there were 100 people in the hotel lobby and 300 outside. These were the citizens in arms: several hundred in a town of approximately 735 Anglo adults, even allowing for exaggerated testimony, was an impressive mobilization.[3] Mills managed to get them out of the hotel and brought Swayne and the nuns down, probably to scare them. On the way down he informed them that if they did not reclaim the children, the crowd would do so and that might lead to worse trouble because there had already been "trouble" between whites and Mexicans a year ago. Seeing the armed mob convinced the New Yorkers that his threat was not a bluff. The crowd would not let any of them explain their point of view, demanded that they leave town immediately, threatened them with tar and feathers; and several in the mob called for a rope. Tom Simpson, who later adopted Anna Doherty, was among the most threatening. As one of the sisters described it, "In the street a sheriff sat on horseback, with a revolver, like the other men. Women called us vile names, and some of them put pistols to our heads. They said there was no law in that town; that they made their own laws. We were told to get the children from the Spaniards [the sisters could not get straight the difference between Spanish and Mexican] and leave . . . If we did not we would be killed."[4] The nuns were terrified and the terror worked. Dunagan and Mills took the Catholics back inside and ordered them to recall the children. Dunagan assured them that he would make sure the children would be protected once in the sisters' care, and that once the Morenci children had been collected, he did not foresee any trouble in Clifton. So they acceded.

The nuns capitulated at this moment because they were, literally, under the gun. They were not cowards, but they knew when to make a tactical withdrawal from a battle they could not win. They were taking another step as well, neither backward nor forward but into a different racial system, one that required acknowledging that a "mistake" had been made. When they conceded this error in newspaper interviews and at the trial, they blamed it on Mandin. He was an easy scapegoat because he was young and new and because blaming him fit their resentment at their subordination to the hierarchy. But by ascribing the error to Mandin, they were from this moment on aligning themselves with the Anglos' view that Mexicans were not white and that white children should go only to white people. It was not a long step because their own racial sensibility had noted that the parents were not "as fair" as they had expected. Yet at the moment of giving over the children, Mandin's word had been enough to reassure them that the Mexicans were okay. In explaining the color difference to themselves, they could have used a Mexican-style racial system in which upstanding, respectable people were white enough, or a three-category racial system in which Irish orphans and Mexicans would have been an acceptable match. Had they done this, their later grievance would have been that children were kidnapped from their rightful parents. Instead they acceded to the set of rules that framed the Anglos' grievance and claimed that the children had been wrongly taken from the Foundling Hospital's custody, that their Clifton-Morenci placements had been only temporary, and that they wanted to re-place the children in other, better families. Of course the "better" families would still have been Catholic, white Catholics, so they were not betraying their religious commitment. Nevertheless, here in Arizona they were faced with a contest between a Mexican Catholic and an Anglo Protestant racial system, and they went instantly, instinctively, with the latter. There is only one possible explanation: they followed the system outlined for them by those who they could see had power in these towns. It is stunning how quickly they accepted this system, something only possible if "white" already had power-laden meanings for them.

The nuns conceded to taking the children—taking them back to New York, they thought. Even then it took the side-by-side appearance of Dunagan and Mills, and all the authority that they could jointly summon, to quiet the mob long enough to hear the announcement that the children would be collected. Dunagan said he would escort Swayne and the padre back to Clifton to do the same, but the crowd vetoed this plan: they would not let Swayne and Mandin leave Morenci until all the children were reclaimed. So Swayne set out, accompanied by the priest and Sexton Lewis, who knew the paths and the locations of the Mexicans. It was not an easy route in the best of weather, and it was now evening, and a thunderstorm was releasing sheets of wind-driven rain: "we went all over those hills and notified every one of those families that the children was required to be delivered to the hotel within an hour. They got them back pretty near in that time." Swayne reported that he "found every home neat and clean, furnished with modern furniture, brass or iron bedsteads, musical instruments, pictures on the walls, portierres [*sic*] at doorways and curtains on the windows."[5] But of course this testimony came weeks later when he was trying to lay the basis for the suit to get the children back.

The children began arriving at 7:30 P.M. "A drenching rain had set in, and the sight of the foster parents bringing in the little ones dripping with rain was a sight not calculated to quiet the crowd," one newspaper reported.[6] The crowd was of course illogical—it wasn't the Mexicans who had chosen to expose the children to the rain—but no more so than the Detroit Copper boss. As they came in, Mills had Dunagan read out the names of the Mexican families to whom they had been given, then Mills looked them up in his payroll ledger and announced their wages, to show how little each man earned.

Even the return of the children did not quiet the crowd. As Swayne, Mandin, and the sexton were returning, a group of men rushed at the priest, punching and pushing him.[7] Someone said, "We want to take him down and fix him up." Swayne made himself out as the hero, reporting that he shot back, "'Nothing of the kind . . . he has done no wrong and you will not touch him,' and stepped in front of the *padre*." Dunagan had to rush in and persuade the men to let up on account of the "bad spot" it would put him in if anything happened to the padre.[8]

A good law-enforcement officer? Maybe, but reserve judgment until the end of the story. Even at this point he was not honest with Swayne and Mandin. He delayed taking them to Clifton until about 10 P.M., because he was waiting for a telephone call from Clifton, the specifics of which he did not tell them. Swayne and Mandin believed they would go to Clifton, get a night's sleep, and round up the children in the morning. But by 10 P.M. the Clifton posse was already out collecting the children.

While Dunagan and Simpson were on their way to Morenci, the agitation in Clifton had converged in an "indignation meeting" at Library Hall, which had been built for the town by the Arizona Copper Company a few years previously. We know little about this meeting, and for good reason: its participants afterward realized how incriminating it could be. Here emerged the lineaments of hysteria and mob rule. Shouting, frenzied citizens demanded direct action without regard to procedures of law. They called out "all the dirtiest names possible." The "hoodlum element," as one source described the most threatening group, had brought a bucket of tar, a sack of feathers, a long rope, gasoline, and coal oil, "as some of the rough element advocated burning at the stake . . . Billy Hamilton, saloonist and gambler, dominated the meeting and talked a great deal and inflamed the hot headed element to such an extent that it looked like a lynching for some time."[9]

Women were among the most vocal participants, and their influence turned the crowd's fury in a different direction, less violent but equally decisive and dramatic. Muriel Wright was among those who called upon "the good citizens of the town . . . [to] rescue these babies." Women convinced the crowd that the matter was urgent, that the children were at immediate risk. The frenzy was, of course, contagious, and those who arrived calm or thoughtful left too agitated to ask questions or hang on to critical faculties. A feverish rage against Mexicans poured out, including much that had nothing to do with children's welfare. Testifying in a "can you top this" spirit, some of the citizens competed to tell the most sickening or outrageous stories about Mexicans. The outcome was a "decision to hold the children at all hazards, law or no law." As the citizens told and retold stories about how disgusting and dangerous was this and that Mexican family for a white child, distinctions among the Mexicans disappeared entirely. The decision became, "if we were going to take one, we might as well take all."[10]

When Simpson telephoned about 3:30 P.M. to say that Swayne had refused to cooperate, it did not take long for a committee of twenty-five to appoint itself. The group included two other deputy sheriffs now back in town–Johnnie Parks and Gus Hobbs–as well as Sam and Jake Abraham, Mike Riordan, and Harry Wright, all local businessmen; George Frazer, smelter superintendent; the loquacious deliveryman Neville Leggatt; and more men who remain unidentified.[11] It would soon be clear that this "committee" was a posse: It did not include women, it did include law-enforcement officers (who seemed less cautious than Jeff Dunagan), and it organized itself for action. But was it a legal posse? Were Parks and Hobbs acting in an official capacity?

Did Sheriff Parks deputize, or authorize to be deputized, any of the other men? Probably not. The possemen were so cautious about what they said afterward, and began covering their backs so quickly, that we have to assume they were uneasy about the legality of what they had done.

But that evening nothing qualified their certainty that they were in the right. The committee of twenty-five moved decisively because the citizens had confidence in what they were doing. They knew they were the citizens, and citizenship to them was not passive but made them responsible for law, order, and justice in the territory. At the trial every single one of the twenty-seven witnesses, the lawyers for both sides, the judges, and the newspaper reporters were in perfect agreement about who the citizens were.[12] In referring to the posse, nearly everyone said, the *citizens* of Clifton have decided to take back the babies, or even the *people* of Clifton have decided. There seemed to them a truly American democracy in the posse, containing as it did the highest and the lowest among the "citizens" of Clifton. Membership in "the people" had nothing to do with place of birth, as several of the "citizens" were born elsewhere and several of the Mexicans had been born in the territory. Nor was naturalization the issue: Some of the Anglo immigrants were naturalized, some were not, just as some of the Mexicans were legal citizens and some not. Besides, territory law at that time allowed anyone to vote who had the intention of becoming a citizen, and at least one of the Anglo adoptive parents seems to have taken advantage of that leeway.[13] Women had a special kind of membership in the citizenry: exempt from and not eligible for military or posse service, they were nevertheless full "voting" members of the decision-making body despite their legal disfranchisement. Only Mexicans were not counted among the citizens that night.

The "citizens" always said they had to take *back* the foundlings. This "back" speaks vividly of their racial assumption: that because the foundlings were "white" they belonged among Clifton-Morenci's Anglos. In this symbolic language, they reversed history, making it seem that it was the Mexicans who had stolen the children and were holding them like contraband.

There had been posses in the area often before, aimed at cowboys, Apaches, gamblers, strikers. Mexicans had participated in some of them. This posse was different because it sealed a new boundary around citizenship, eliminating some holes and gaps where the fence was down. This posse made whites citizens and made Mexicans not white. It took in Jews, Irishmen, and French Canadians, but not Mexicans. Even Euro-Latins were in, like John Gatti. What had been flexible became more rigid; what had been fuzzy became clearer; what had been porous became impenetrable; what had been complex became simpler. There were whites and nonwhites.

On another frontier at this time, in South Africa, such a conception of citizenship was called an *herrenvolk* democracy, a democracy of white men. Clifton's whites did not develop the "master race" ideology or the apartheid regime that enforced it to the same degree as the South African Boers. But Clifton's whites shared with the Boers not only a sense of racial superiority but also a feeling of entitlement to the land on the basis of their identity as pioneers, sweating it out in rough conditions, defending themselves from wild animals and violent Indians, seeking a fortune in a new world.[14] Their increasing emphasis on white superiority reinforced not only their self-righteousness but also their sense of participation in a democratic brotherhood.

In fact, the posse was not a democracy even among white men. In Morenci everyone knew Mills was the boss. In Clifton matters were more indirect. Colquhoun was subtler than Mills in exercising influence; Colquhoun's subordinate George Frazer participated in the posse on the same footing as several prominent businessmen, while Colquhoun himself stayed aloof from this disturbance. Yet few thought Neville Leggatt, the deliveryman, who spoke with a "Dooley dialect," equal in importance to George Frazer, the smelter superintendent.[15] In testifying later about his role, Leggatt was obviously proud to have been included, but he also saw himself as an onlooker, not a decision maker, regarding how things happened. When asked in court about how the Library Hall meeting got arranged, he did not deem himself a peer: I "went around to the various citizens and asked them what they were going to do, and the citizens told me they were going to have a general meeting at the library." Of course, in the courtroom all the possemen evaded responsibility. Mills dodged his accountability in a different way: the Mexicans wouldn't be adequate parents because they got paid too little, he said; but they got paid too little because he paid them too little. Of course he didn't see it this way: he had long ago learned to complete the vicious circle in his head: they got paid so little because they didn't deserve, want, or need more. Whatever the cause, their Mexican standard of living was too low for white babies.

And on that subject—what white babies need—surely the women were the experts. They were animated by intense maternal bonding experiences. At the trial, the attorney for the Foundling asked each Anglo mother if she would be willing to give the child back to the sisters if she thought such was the child's best interest; each mother said no. Many of the Anglo mothers and would-be mothers spoke of falling in love with an orphan as if transported, helpless in the hold of a higher force. A Morenci Anglo woman watching as the Mexican families brought the children back to the hotel wrote, "I picked up the Dear little Baby Girl Catharine . . . My Heart went out to the little one I showed her to my Husband and said if we get her I will think God has sent us a little angel through the Dear Sisters. The Dear little one was crying and I picked her up and as I talked to her she put her arms around my neck and looked at me with those Big Brown Eyes, and I know I could not [illegible] my arms any more but the Sister asked for her and I gave her back, but I felt as tho she was already mine."[16]

That the white women felt duty-bound to rescue the orphans resulted, contradictorily, both from their authority over a domestic sphere that certainly included children's welfare and from their stepping out of the domestic into the public, political sphere. What's more, their actions symbolized and furthered the unity of domestic and political spheres. The women's domestic authority forced the men to act, because manliness required them to defend women and children.

4

The Mexican Mothers and
the Mexican Town

THE CLIFTON ORPHAN STORY plays like a theme and variations—
every particular repeats a central motif. Consider the young wife Margarita Chacón, a woman of the border, a crossover in a land where
everyone crossed, symbolically in perfect harmony with Clifton's history: Born an orphan, she would mother orphans. With no experience
of a father, she served the father devoutly. Raised to be flexible and
servile, she became a carrier of Mexican obstinacy and dignity. The
stereotype of the Mexican woman, she was probably not by birth a
Mexican. It is lucky that these oppositions in her identity are so perfectly thematic, because Margarita Chacón must speak for four dozen
other silent individuals. From the Mexicans who took in the orphans,
the historical archives contain exactly two letters, written by one man,
to the Sisters of Charity. Not one Mexican testified at the trial. There is
no oral history, not a single shard of evidence beyond these two letters
of their weeks of preparation, of their one day as foster parents, of how
it felt to have their new children kidnapped by vigilantes with Winches-
ters. As for Señora Chacón, she has had to be reconstructed from slivers
in the legal records and the recollections of her grandchildren.

The reason for this intensive interpretation is that Señora Chacón
represents the best lead in a mystery: why did the Mexican women of
Clifton-Morenci want to take in New York orphans? Everyone around
the events knew the adoption was a women's initiative. At the trial, the
Anglos referred to the women by name—as Margarita Chacón and not
Señora or Mrs. Chacón—and they almost never referred to the men.

Only two fathers' names could be found anywhere on the Foundling Hospital's list. The priest negotiated with the women only and admitted that he had not even met their husbands.[1] As if replicating the gender order of New York City's Catholic charities, where women ran services for children, in Clifton the whole project belonged to Mandin and the Mexican women's church. What drew them to unseen New York Irish foundlings? We will never know each individual's innermost motivations, but we can track the collective sources of their willingness to take on this burdensome act of charity. Taking in the foundlings was for them truly a border action, that is, an action produced by the intersection of their Mexican heritage with their American future, perhaps by their loneliness and distance from kinfolk, certainly by the opportunities and the constraints of work, marriage, motherhood, and race culture.

ORPHAN TRAINS seem distant from us now, an artifact of a time without child protection legislation, without the new psychological science that warns us of the complex emotional problems of children who could not bond with a parent. So if we imagine ourselves in the position of these Clifton-Morenci Mexican women who offered themselves as mothers, we admire them but we may also be surprised. They offered to feed, love, and care for one more child although they were poor; they knew nothing about the children, who might be troubled or sick or crippled; and they were not accustomed to the adoption of strangers.[2] One of the criticisms directed against the orphan trains was that they delivered children into virtual servitude, that the "foster" families were often seeking free labor. But these prospective mothers knew that these Catholic orphans were just toddlers, many years from being able to work; and in this mining camp, where few people farmed or ranched, there was little productive work children could do.

As to adoption, it may have been stranger to the Anglos than to the Mexicans. Legal adoption in the contemporary American sense—taking a child into a family so as to legally obliterate the rights and duties of her or his natal family, and so as to make her or him legally undifferentiated from a "natural" child—is an extremely recent phenomenon. Massachusetts passed the first state law allowing this kind of adoption in 1851, and twenty states had followed by 1875, but in most of the United States such adoptions were practiced commonly for the first time in the twentieth century. In Latin America the practice of

U.S.-style modern legal adoption was an even later development. Traditionally in most countries, adoption produced parent-child bonds that always remained different from biological ones; parents could, for example, "adopt" a child without the biological parents having to relinquish her or him. In most cultures and among Mexicans in particular it was commonplace to take in the children of kinfolk, while taking in strange children was rare. The child-placing agencies did not expect their foster parents to adopt legally, and there was so little paperwork in most agencies' programs that different families could have had varying understandings of what they were committing themselves to, how permanent the arrangement was, and what obligations, if any, were legally enforceable.[3] The general vagueness about adoption in the early twentieth century explains why few of the Clifton-Morenci orphans were immediately legally adopted by their Anglo parents, despite the incentive provided by the custody struggle. The Mexican parents, we must assume, had equally vague expectations, possibly quite different from the Anglos'. For all, the flexibility and simplicity of what was offered by the orphan trains, the lack of bureaucracy mediating the relationship between parent and child made adoption more inviting than it is today. The process could fulfill longings without the decision and labor involved in legal adoption.

Most important, children were a blessing. This traditional view was being modified in industrial conditions where children cost more than they could contribute to the family economy, and the blessedness did not mean that couples wanted as many children as possible. Still, some felt insufficiently blessed. Many Clifton-Morenci families were childless—30 percent of the white and 18 percent of the Mexican—and almost certainly not by choice. Some of this infertility resulted from repeated miscarriages; at least one woman suspected that the sulfurous air around Clifton-Morenci caused her to become sterile.[4] At this time, and especially in the peasant communities from which many of the Mexicans came, childlessness was a painful economic and personal failing, especially for the women. Still, the children were, we know, also taken into families that had other young children.

Families also suffered another kind of loss: in more than half the Mexican families and a fifth of the Anglo families at least one child had died. Mexicans suffered much higher child mortality rates than Anglos: 28 percent of Clifton Mexican women (in Morenci 33 percent) had experienced the deaths of two or more children, as compared to

11.5 percent of Clifton Anglos (in Morenci 12 percent).[5] Mexican infants were usually entirely dependent on breast milk, and a mother's supply was not always reliable, especially if she was exhausted or malnourished. Sometimes they fed babies donkey milk in desperation to save them.[6] Although fertility was high and small families were regarded as a misfortune, as in many societies of great poverty and high infant mortality, Mexican families were not large on average because of the high death rates. Still, they were considerably larger than Anglo ones: the former averaged 3 children per household (this excludes grown children living elsewhere), the latter 1.7 children per household.

Since children did little remunerative labor in Clifton-Morenci, naturally the orphans were sought out mainly by those families who could best afford them. Mexicans in Clifton-Morenci were, of course, economically and socially stratified, as are all modern populations. Mexican men in Clifton divided into three classes: a small group of entrepreneurs—shopkeepers or ranchers mainly—several dozen at most, a middling class who often mixed with the Euro-Latins; proletarians who worked in the mines, mills, or smelters; and the poor self-employed who earned a living through casual labor or peddling. The second group, which took in the great majority of the Mexicans, contained further status and wealth variation within it: A few were high earners at the company, making $3.00 a day, top wage for a Mexican (the standard rate for a miner was $2.25 a week after the 1903 strike). Cornelio Chacón belonged to this group. At the bottom were casual workers whose wages were low, a group that frequently overlapped with those whose behavior was not respectable in terms of Mexican community standards— notably those who drank and caroused a lot. These class, status, and wealth distinctions mattered, and the more elite Mexicans did not usually socialize with the poor or the disreputable. Mexican women were similarly stratified, according to their husbands' earnings and behavior but also in terms of their own standards: they judged themselves and one another with stringent measures of housekeeping, dress, piety, and deportment.

Twenty-five years earlier Mexicans had dominated the businesses of supplying the mining camps with daily needs—vegetables, meat, flour, dairy, wood, water, liquor, tools, virtually everything. In those days before the railroad they either produced the goods themselves, making men's and women's work equally important in these old farming or ranching families, or they freighted it by mule or burro (the freighting business was virtually in Mexican hands). Moreover, many of this elite were not immigrants but had been born in the land that now belonged to the United States, in Texas, New Mexico, or "A.T.," Arizona Territory. By 1904, however, Anglos had taken over all but the smaller businesses, a displacement and expropriation that extended throughout the Southwest as Anglos poured in.[7] The remaining Mexican entrepreneurs were barbers, shoemakers, grocers, peddlers of water and firewood, and the women less often worked in these businesses. One group of Mexican families lost their farm and ranch land when Phelps Dodge managed to get control of the water, without which the land was useless.[8] But in 1904 a few were still operating: Primitivo Medina survived as a rancher and dairyman because at a good moment he bought the ranch of Sheriff Jim Parks's brother, located on the Coronado River, right on the stage-coach route. A few Mexican landowners to the east in the Gila Valley built a toll road from Solomonville, charging ten cents per horse and ten cents per wagon and providing water and food at the toll house.[9] There were just a few Mexican professionals—Jesús Martínez, a doctor; Arturo Elías, the Mexican consul (although a naturalized American citizen), who occasionally stayed in Clifton; and perhaps one should count David Arzate, deputy sheriff and saloon keeper, who translated at court.[10] Quite a number of Mexicans were foremen or labor subcon-tractors.

In previous decades, Anglo old-timers, businessmen who dealt with Mexicans, and anyone moderately observant understood these class divisions. In 1904 a few of these families were still socially accepted by Anglos as Spaniards or "a better class" of Mexicans, but the number was declining. In a remarkable process of unlearning, many Anglos were primitivizing Mexicans as classless, a pure type, just "Mexican." During the orphan affair most of the Anglos would revert to that decivilizing fallacy. When the Anglos at the Clifton orphan trial referred to the Mexicans always in the aggregate, differentiating neither individuals nor subgroups among Mexicans, their testimony showed that to Anglos "Mexican" had come to *mean* poor, ignorant, degraded.

MEXICANS LIVED in three neighborhoods: Chase Creek, Shannon Hill, and—the best location at that time—North Clifton. North Clifton and Shannon Hill offered some flat terrain on which to build; flat land not only provided more room in which to spread out but also saved the labor and expense of shoring up the houses with timber and stone, not to mention having to climb up and down steep stairs for every venture outside the house. But houses in North Clifton, on low ground right next to the river, like those in Chase Creek, were more vulnerable to floods than some of the *jacalitos,* little shacks, on stilts on the hillsides.

The first housing in Clifton consisted of adobe and ocotillo (a cactus with long canes that can be used for fences and roofing), or tents emulating those of some early Indian miners, or gunny sacks stretched over frames of tree branches with brush-and-mud or flattened tin-can roofs (the mud being fixed with a binder such as chopped straw), or caves, partly natural and partly excavated, in the hillsides, usually with an adobe room as a foyer. With the railroads came lumber, which did not wash away in the heavy rains or require constant maintenance like the adobe. One-by-twelve boards supplied the most common siding, and scrap lumber supported the steps dug into the hillsides. The poorer frame houses were made from reused or cast-off boards and pieces of boards and waste metal, stuffed with brush to fill in the cracks. A poor but resourceful miner might make a chimney of coffee cans telescoped one in another. A few of the best houses were made of stone with the usual wooden *vigas* (beams) holding up the roof. The mine-workers' range of building materials was, of course, greatly expanded by pilfering from the companies' vast supply yards. Most houses had two rooms, not counting a small *ramada* or roofed shed, which served as the kitchen; as immigrant Mexicans adapted to the colder winter temperatures of Clifton, the kitchens migrated indoors or the *ramadas* were enclosed. Some poor homes had no windows, and none had more than a few, and they were just openings, possibly shuttered but without glass or screen. Virtually every house had a fenced *corral* for animals, plants, or general use. In town the houses were close together; farther out there would be more room but few men wanted long treks to work.[11]

Inside, the floors were almost always dirt, tightly packed down, regularly sprinkled to suppress dust, and swept. Many of the poor used packing crates of various sizes and shapes for chairs and tables; others relied on homemade rough wooden benches; still others had carved, heavy furniture. The first mattresses were *petates,* made of grass, replaced by American mattresses as soon as possible. There would be a large clay *olla* for water, several five-gallon *tinas,* tins, for carrying water and washing dishes, and many other jars and large cans for storage of *masa* (dough) and *nixtamal* (cooked maize or wheat ready for preparing the *masa*) as well as other liquids and foods. In warm weather containers storing meat, fruits, and vegetables would be covered with wet cloths to keep them cool, but as soon as they could afford it the women got wooden ice boxes. There would be a heavy iron *comal,* or griddle, for cooking the tortillas, a *metate* for grinding and a smaller *molcajete,* or mortar and pestle, for grinding chiles (they needed two separate tools so the chiles wouldn't stain and flavor the tortillas). Cleaning tools in immigrant homes might include wrapped bundles of cactus fibers for sweeping or grass roots for scouring, but women soon preferred store-bought brooms and soap.[12]

The work and daily lives of wives like Margarita Chacón were dictated by the mine and smelter schedule. The individual jobs women did—the tortilla making, the cooking, the breast-feeding, the sewing—seem preindustrial if examined as separate tasks, in contrast to the industrialized men's work. But that appearance would yield a misunderstanding; industrialization had transformed women's labor and its meanings. The copper companies shaped women's schedule, budget, working conditions and tools, purchases and diet, health and medical care, even family size.

Almost all the plants operated round the clock, so men returned home, slept, and ate at various hours, and depended heavily on women's labor. There was neither electricity nor gas in these homes; women cooked on wood stoves and created light with kerosene lamps and candles. You could see these dim lights at almost any hour of darkness. Women arose as much as several hours before the men and children in order to feed the stove, heat water, and prepare breakfast and lunch buckets; with switching shift work, breakfast might be required at any time of day. With several men in the house working different shifts, a common occurrence, a woman might have to provide a constant succession of substantial meals. Starting in the late morning you could hear the clapping sound of tortilla making wherever you walked.

The labor connected with water was ubiquitous. It had to be fetched in buckets and carried a good distance from wells—this was often a children's chore and could well require a walk of a mile and a half.[13] The drudgery of fetching and heating water for baths and laundry was particularly heavy because the silt from the smokestacks settled everywhere, and the men and their clothes came home filthy every day—they had no showers at work—and it required lots of water to get them clean. There were not many items of clothing, besides, because these were usually made by hand—no one had a sewing machine yet—so doing laundry could not be postponed. It was the hardest piece of housework, the first to be sent out if the family had a cash surplus, and housewives later greeted the possibility of owning a washing machine with nothing short of passion. In these early days of the century the wash was done on a scrub board, in the creek or river if it contained any clean water, or in a tub laboriously filled by the bucket.[14] One Anglo described his memory of his maid doing laundry: "We had large, steel corrugated buckets. These containers were coal black on the outside and snow white on the inside from the soap. After the clothes had boiled for some time she took them out and literally beat them to death with a long piece of wood. It was an all day job to wash and put the clothes out to dry . . . we [sic] managed to keep very clean."[15]

Local water was not only difficult to get but often dirty with sediment. One pioneer recalled "that on the rare occasion that any one indulged in a bath, a whisk broom was needed to brush the sediment off the body." Those who could afford it bought their drinking water from *aguadores,* who delivered it on burro-back in leather or canvas bags (one Clifton woman sewed all the bags for them); they might charge $4.00 per month or 25¢ a bag.[16] The Clifton Water Company had already begun a city water system, digging a forty-foot-deep well about four miles north of town and installing pumps. Houses with indoor plumbing could pay a connection fee and then a regular charge (there was no metering): the standard rate was $2.25; for households with bathtub or livestock, $3.00; with lawns or trees, $4.90. But in 1904 few Mexicans could afford indoor plumbing, and besides, the pumps did not reliably bring water up to the houses on higher ground—that problem was only solved later, when the company hired Pete Gámes, a self-taught genius of a plumber and blacksmith from Sonora.[17]

Even with the water scarcity, housewives were ever scrubbing, sweeping, straightening, and decorating, and the hard work paid them back with pleasure and pride. Mexican women gained a reputation here, as elsewhere, for their dedication to cleanliness—beyond cleanliness, in fact, to beautification.[18] Every woman's home was ornamented with small shrines, pictures of the Virgin or the Virgin of Guadalupe or Christ or Teresita with a small shelf and a candle underneath, or hand-painted *retablos.* Walls were sometimes covered with newspaper or magazine pictures and a calendar.[19] Virtually every woman's home had flowers, usually grown in pots or large cans in which the right soil and water could be maintained. Even the most racist Anglo memoir I read commented on Mexican women's superiority to Anglos in their dedication to beautification, especially with flowers: "the home is blessed with the saving grace of flowers . . . The Mexican women are ahead in this particular, and it is not uncommon to see in front of their mud-hovels tiny spaces enclosed by cactus or brush fences and blazing with colour."[20]

Mothers were equally proud of their child-raising work, measured by the beauty and *disciplina* of their offspring. These well-behaved children represented substantial maternal labor. Nothing is more draining than pregnancy, nursing, and infant care, especially when combined with the round-the-clock provision for men, yet Mexican women between the ages of eighteen and forty were doing such labor more often than not. The worst burden fell on the younger women, who did not yet have older children to help with the rest of the work. What children could contribute was gendered, and daughters helped more than sons: a son would be expected to fetch water and wood, but a daughter of eight or older could do that work *and* cooking, cleaning, baby care. Some mothers took children back to Mexico to be cared for by kinfolk until they were old enough to marry or work. Clifton-Morenci elementary schools were just beginning to take in Mexican children at the turn of the century but the majority still got no formal schooling. Active young children at home had to be constantly protected from the hazards of the mine, mill, and smelter sites and girls had to be constantly supervised. And they had to be trained to show respect for their elders, defer to their father in all things, and learn their catechism well. The standards for well brought-up children were high and the opprobrium laid on the mothers of *hijos mal criadas,* badly brought-up children, had a sharp bite.[21]

Norteñas felt themselves far from civilization, so they tried to recreate the civilized foods of their homeland; they tried to grow what they could not buy in order to make the traditional *tamales de elote* (fresh corn) in late summer, *tamales de carne* at Christmas, *buñuelos* (fried cakes) for New Year's, and *capirotada* (bread pudding) for Lent. Their horticultural work included not only growing foods–figs, apricots, grapes, pomegranates, squash, chiles, corn, cucumbers, melons, even citrus–but also taming wild plants for healing purposes, such as mesquite pods and wild greens, *verdolagas* (purslane) and *bellotas* (acorns), and *manzanilla* (camomile) for tea.[22] Most families kept chickens, and those with more space might try to keep a goat or pig or two as well.

Supplementing the *tienda de raya*, company store, with what you could grow was essential to the budget. The men's work, especially that in the mines, made them ravenous; their caloric requirements far exceeded those of men performing less demanding labor. Those who cooked knew this well, and their knowledge was confirmed by scientific nutritional calculations offered by efficiency experts to mining employers in the next decades. Calories burnt per hour could triple between "active muscular exercise" (200) and "very hard muscular exercise" (600), so that a miner of only 120 pounds could easily require 6,000 calories a day. Buying that much food would far exceed his income.[23] Consider the account of Filiberto Vásquez at the Arizona Copper company store. His wife Felicitas spent $35.05 during March of 1910 (the earliest date from which I found such an accounting), which would have been deducted from his earnings of $49.50 except for the fact that he already owed the store $52.30. She bought for a family with five children—we don't know if there were any boarders. Here are some of her purchases (in dollars and cents):[24]

Eggs	.45	Garlic	.05
Cheese	.25	Prunes	.10
Milk	.25	Rice	.25
Apples	.10	Flour	2.50
Cocoa	.25	Lemon	.10
Cakes	.35	Tomato	.15
Sugar	.25	Vinegar	.10
Coffee	.20	Corn	.25
Beef	.60	Tobacco	.05
Vermicelli*	.15	Lentils*	.15
Garbanzos*	.25	Oatmeal	.15
Benas	.25	Potatoes	.25
Chile*	.10	Sopolio	.15
Onions	.25	Soap	.35
Lard	.85	Baking powder	.20

* These items were misspelled in the company store ledger, suggesting the clerk's unfamiliarity with these foods. No Mexicans held these sales jobs in the company store.

During the month Mrs. Vásquez bought beef five times, each time in smaller quantities than the first purchase, spending a total of $2.25, plus one purchase of unspecified "meat" for 15¢.[25] Chicken was not sold by a butcher because most Mexicans raised their own chickens or bought live ones, but since Mrs. Vásquez purchased eggs, she probably had no chickens.

Then there were the other necessities. Children's shoes at the Arizona Copper company store were 75¢ and $1.25 a pair, men's undershirts and drawers 75¢ each, flannel was 8.5¢ a yard and gingham 16.5¢. The lowest grade tobacco was 60¢ for eight ounces.[26] It was not easy to manage all this on wages averaging $2.25 a day. Small wonder that pilfering building materials from the companies was standard, a kind of gleaning to which the workers and their families felt entitled.

Shopping in this small town might have led to a great deal of sociability but few women actually went to the stores: most goods were bought from peddlers or ordered from a company-store man—like Neville Leggatt—who stopped by to take an order in the morning and delivered by wagon in the evening. Numerous peddlers would come by each day: the dairyman, the water man, the wood man, the company-store man, providing a different kind of sociability, a steady stream of visitors it seemed. At times whole herds of burros moved noisily along the streets. The Arizona Copper company store delivered on a wagon, the Detroit copper company store on a string of mules or burros, in *alforjas,* saddlebags. Items of furniture were carried by one or more men. Many women patronized the Chinese vegetable men, who sold by far the best produce not only here but in most Arizona and Sonora mining towns. When they walked through the town, they wrapped the vegetables inside wet burlap sacks, loaded in two large bamboo baskets that hung, balanced, weighing about one hundred thirty pounds, from their shoulders on a six-foot pole of tickwood. "He placed a towel in its center for padding. He crouched, placed the padding on one of his shoulders and straightened up. With the baskets off the ground, they started to sway up and down. He timed his first step with the upswing of the baskets and started to walk with a wobbled gait. He was continuously in motion and only stopped to make a sale. As he approached a house he would yell like all hucksters do, '*sandía, tomate, chile.*'"[27] Luther Hulsey brought the ice on his wagon, pulled by two horses; it had a bed of lumber onto which fifty-pound blocks of ice were loaded each morning. The company store provided cardboard panels with a two-by-four-inch window; attached to its back was a circular revolving piece with printed numbers from zero to one dollar; you turned the attachment to indicate an amount. If the panel showed twenty five cents, Hulsey would cut a twenty-five-pound piece off of the big block and carry it into the house with his ice tongs. Most people left coins for the amount they ordered and authorized him to come in and put it directly in the ice box.[28] The *leñeros,* firewood peddlers, were usually in business on their own: since there was no other fuel, and since there was no way any owner could monopolize the wooded land, the demand seemed endless and many families earned their living this way. The men went into the hills to cut the mesquite—or juniper if they could find it—farther and farther away as the sparse trees were used up, chopped it, and carried it by burro through the streets to sell. You could buy a *cargo,* a whole load or a cord, for somewhere between $1.15 and $1.50, depending on whether it was juniper or mesquite, or a sack for about 25¢.[29]

Mining camps once seemed to feature classic male-breadwinner families, since these towns, usually far from cities, offered few jobs for women. But there was no way men could support their families single-handedly in a town where the average worker's wage was around two dollars a day and prices were unusually high because of the high cost of transportation. And anyone who had observed the lives of women in mineworkers' families would have known better. Family economic need had a complex relation to family size: at first, the more children, the more the woman needed to bring in; as the children grew older, they could also earn, relieving the pressure on their mother a bit. The logic of the situation, a bit crazy from the standpoint of the modern urban family economy, was that the younger the children, the less the mother was able to devote herself to family care. The housewife's classic "scrimping" would not do; many women and most mothers had to earn. (Anglo women were less pressed because their men's wages were higher.) Mexican men also had to supplement wages, often with the fish and small game they hunted in off hours—virtually every household had a rifle—but the women were small entrepreneurs.

And not all the mothers had male wage-earners to help them. Women commonly ran families on their own, in Clifton-Morenci as in Mexico. In 1900, 9 percent of families were headed by women, 80 percent of them Mexican, and there were numerous other husbandless mothers who did not head households but lived with kinfolk.[30] By 1910 female-headed households were up to 17 percent, a figure consistent with other mining towns.[31] Most female heads were widows, despite the fact that many widows returned to Mexico; some had been deserted, some separated, a few divorced. Only about one-third of the female household heads had working sons or sons-in-law. Others sent daughters out as domestic servants. But Clotilda Ward was on her own with three young daughters. The widowed Onofria Marques had four children age nine and under. Eighteen-year-old Olfina Díaz with three- and one-year-olds was divorced, an extremely unusual status for a Mexican woman.[32] How did they manage?

For almost all, the answer was that they "took in."[33] Most commonly, washing and sewing. Frequently, boarders and lodgers. Occasionally, someone else's children. Many Arizona Mexican women remembered the labor of taking in laundry: carrying water, heating water, scrubbing, hanging, heating irons, ironing; as Carmina García put it, the Mexican women took over laundry when the Chinese left. A widow described her work: "I washed and ironed here for a long time, honey . . . This porch had a bar from one wall to the other and that's where I ironed and hung the clothes. That was my life, washing and ironing . . . heating the iron on the stove . . . At midnight I would be hanging clothes . . . By five o'clock I was already up . . . I even went for firewood on the hill and carried it on my back."[34] Then "I ironed and ironed and ironed . . . Standing . . . At it and at it and at it with that iron."[35] The children picked up the dirty clothes and delivered the clean to customers. The women made their own children's clothes out of flour sacks but sewed fine linen and woolens for hire. One illiterate seamstress kept her accounts in a neat little book, drawing a circle to stand for one dollar and a half-circle to stand for fifty cents.[36]

Some women took in "tricks." Sixteen women listed in the census as prostitutes, and no doubt more who were unlisted, earned in that manner. Several probably had bosses, such as the two who lived as lodgers in the household of a saloon keeper. One group of four prostitutes in Clifton lived together in interracial partnership: one Mexican, one Japanese, and two Anglo women. Another headed a household with her two young daughters. One lived with her miner father. Assuming that these women were in fact prostitutes, community members probably saw them as *both* disreputable and as honest working women. Other sex workers were able to set limits. One told Manuel Gamio, an extraordinary Mexican anthropologist (twenty years later, but completely relevant to turn-of-the-century Clifton-Morenci), of a dancer-for-hire's delicate balance of feelings:

> My work consists of dancing as much as I can with everyone who comes. At the beginning I didn't like this work because I had to dance with anyone, but I have finally gotten used to it and now I don't care, because I do it in order to earn my living . . . Each dance is worth ten cents . . . Besides there are some who will give you a present . . . This work is what suits me best for I don't need to know any English here . . . It is true that some men at times make propositions to me which are insulting, but everything is fixed by just telling them no . . . One man whom I liked a lot here in the hall deceived me once. He was a Mexican. But since that time it hasn't happened to me again. My mother takes a lot of care of me so that I won't make any bad steps. My sisters do the same.[37]

Two-fifths of Clifton-Morenci's miners and smelter workers were single men, utterly dependent on hiring women not only for sex but for food and rest. In these towns, as in many similar ones, boarding and lodging were usually divided between different locations and both required much female labor. Few Mexicans had the room for a group of lodgers: in 1900 in Clifton 22 percent of the male-headed and 18 percent of the female-headed Mexican households kept lodgers, but the great majority had only one or two. (In Morenci, with more single men and fewer women, it was 41 percent and 13 percent, respectively.) Most lodgers were kinfolk, but they still paid, and what they were paying for was by no means simply the use of a bed—in fact, they often did not have exclusive use of a bed but shared it, especially among workers who slept at different times of day. Lodgers usually also got their clothes washed and mended, their socks darned, their bath water heated, their money guarded, their illnesses tended, their loneliness and sadness eased. Women frequently did errands their lodgers could not accomplish because of the limited hours of company stores (typically, 9 to 5 and payday evenings) and other businesses—buying personal necessities, sending letters and money home. Providing board is less visible to the historian today because no one reported it as a "job" to a census taker, but it was the dominant way in which single men got fed. Men would typically arrive for a meal just before and just after work, then leave for the job or for the bars, and sleep at another house. At the entrance to the home would be a table with a water pitcher and bowl and towels for the dirty miners (more laundry); shifts of men seated themselves at long tables and benches, possibly constructed of boards. Most women fed just a few people beyond family members but there were several big boarding houses: in Morenci Vicente Aja and his wife fed twenty-five men, although the dining room could only hold twenty and the rest had to wait their turn on the porch. Women also sold "box lunches," typically packed in a metal two-layered bucket, for men to take to work, or prepared food they could peddle at the bars. Mothers often took in extra children, most often those of kinfolk, but also sometimes those of neighbors—perhaps while the parents returned to Mexico—and occasionally Anglo children.[38]

Women sold many other goods and services. Some women provided healing and midwifery skills (although many pregnant women preferred to return to Mexico for confinements) for low fees. Midwives almost certainly also provided abortions; although I have not been told of this practice in Clifton, it was done in other mining towns—and, I would wager, in every community—with herbal abortifacients and knitting needles.[39] Women sold eggs, chickens, home brew, anything they could make. And mothers functioned as general contractors for their children's labor, both directing them in the home and finding out-of-home jobs for them. In large families, the older children might each have responsibility for one of the younger. Kids could sometimes earn a few cents delivering lunches to the smelter, and one enterprising girl carried the lunches as she delivered laundry, thus reducing her trips.[40] Among the very poorest there was out-and-out child labor, most often in the mill in Morenci. The ten-year-old son of lone mother Leonida Lopez worked as an ore sorter, as did the two youngest sons of laborer José Maria and Refugia Vargas.

Women who could leave home to earn were limited not only by the scarcity of jobs but also by their family's and community's standards of respectability. Anglo single women could teach or work in copper company offices, but Mexican women were not hired. Working in bars or even in restaurants was out of bounds for most "respectable" Mexican women. This limitation derived from patriarchal customs of women's sequestration: they should remain *casera,* at home, and young women should be always chaperoned.[41] Some women resisted and bent these rules, of course, but they were reinforced by harsh gossip, both Anglo and Mexican, libeling the morality of women working in service jobs in public places.

What was left? Domestic service and sewing.[42] There were a few small dress-making shops where several seamstresses worked together.[43] The great majority of those working outside their homes, single or older women, went to other people's homes to cook and clean. Here they encountered the trials typical of domestic servants: low pay—twenty-five to fifty cents per day, poor working conditions, no protection from excessive demands, humiliating supervision. The employing housewives complained of them in exactly the same way that eastern housewives complained of Irish domestics, alleging that they stole and worked slowly and malingered.[44] Employed mothers relied, of course, on their daughters to do all the housework—cooking, cleaning, shopping, child care.

Even play meant work for women, but cherished work, the work that made Clifton home. Women planned, cooked, decorated, and cleaned up for all the many fiestas and religious celebrations, not to mention more casual sociability. The secular, patriotic holidays, the Sixteenth of September (Mexican Independence) and Cinco de Mayo (Battle of Puebla), they never missed; some of the extremely numerous religious fiesta days had to be passed over, but they tried to mark El Día de San Juan, El Día de San Pedro y San Pablo, Sábado de Gloria (Easter), the Fiesta de la Virgen Guadalupana, and Christmas.

Among the most cherished celebrations were baptisms and communions. Just as families lavished all they could afford on these events, at which scores of friends and relatives would be served extravagant meals, so the mothers expressed their love and pride in sewing elaborate clothing for the children: for baptisms, long robes and caps finely stitched and trimmed with lace and ribbon; for the girls' communions, individually designed and fitted dresses with delicate smocking, lace, and ruffles, a flowered bridal-style headpiece and veil. And the boys needed suits.[45] Throughout the year women were raising money and sewing for such events.[46] The funerals also took a lot of work, and they came too frequently, especially considering the relative youth of the population, because of mining deaths and infectious disease.

Clifton's Mexicans also relaxed more spontaneously. On fair evenings you could hear a guitar and a folk song or *corrido* no matter where you walked. Several families gathered with beer and singing the Saturday night the orphans arrived. Music and dance were, along with beer and mescal, the central components of celebration in Mexican Clifton, and there were house parties every week, which could be held anywhere that someone could provide a guitar and a flat space for dancing.[47] Some women turned their *corrales* into patios, surrounding them with plants and candles or *candelarias* (candles in bags), and charged a small fee for parties or even weddings.[48] The children danced until they fell asleep, sometimes literally under foot. Except for the singing and dancing, socializing tended to segregate by sex, as it did among people of virtually all cultures at the time. The men smoked and joked and drank and sometimes became raucous and vulgar, or sentimental and contemplative. The women also loosened up but they rarely drank.

Such sociability provided not only the relaxation that allowed work to continue but also the community bonds on which all depended. Here in Arizona almost everyone pined for distant kinfolk in Mexico, Texas, and New Mexico. The loss was economic as well as emotional. How did one survive without the give and take among people whose mutual obligations never ended? By creating an alternative infrastructure of mutual support. Mexicans, out of necessity, had a flexible and tenacious kinship structure for this purpose, the *compadrazgo* or godparenting system, which could extend and deepen networks of mutual aid. As *padrinos* and *madrinos,* adults assumed material responsibilities for their godchildren, helping to provide for the observance of special occasions, such as communions and weddings, and for emergencies, as they simultaneously formalized their friendships with parents.

Since the poor live best by helping each other, working-class people throughout the world have organized mutual benefit societies, commonly with ethnic identities, and Mexicans in Clifton-Morenci created particularly dense networks of such societies, known as *mutualistas.* Clifton had four Mexican societies: the Sociedad Progresista Auxilios Mutuos, incorporated as a sickness and death mutual benefit society; the Unión de Obreros, also described as a benefit society, but probably a company-sponsored one; the Sociedad Juárez Protectora, which was proscribed as a "secret revolutionary society" by the Mexican government in 1908; and finally Lodge 2 of the Tucson-based Alianza Hispano Americana, at that time the leading Mexican organization in the United States. The Zaragoza Society, of which Cornelio Chacón was an officer, was an affiliate of the Alianza, possibly an alternative name for Lodge 2 or possibly an additional chapter. The Alianza was created in Tucson in 1894 by elite Mexican families, a defensive reaction to the appearance of a chapter of the American Protective Association, a national nativist and anti-Catholic organization. But workers soon became the backbone of the Alianza's membership. Its first lodge outside Tucson was in the mining town of Florence, its second was in Clifton, with Metcalf and Morenci added by 1902. Other early locals were in railroad employment centers. The Alianza grew to 1,171 members in twenty-two chapters by 1907.[49]

Better-paid, higher-status workers and artisans usually led the lodges. With dues in working-class lodges at about $1 per month and frequent fund-raisers, these societies could help their members with emergency loans, contributions for the needy, and above all insurance for illness, death, and funeral expenses. The Alianza paid a $1,000 widow's benefit and $200 burial benefit to a widower. The societies provided political leadership as well. They urged Mexican workers to become citizens and exercise their right to vote, protested the corruption of local government—such as the Morenci justices of the peace who, they alleged, pocketed fines and court fees—and challenged discrimination and abuses on the basis of a solid understanding of American law. They commonly sponsored educational projects such as schools, reading rooms, libraries, and newspapers, and created job and business "networking" opportunities for members. With women's help they sponsored *bailes,* dances that were central features of Mexican community life. In Clifton the Alianza held dances almost every month, with an orchestra of about thirty including violins, guitar, accordion, saxophone. The girls wore festive long dresses and there were sometimes contests for best dancer.[50]

Mexican women worked hard for these lodges but also established independent women's organizations through the church. At some point two sodalities were organized in Clifton, the Ladies of the Sacred Heart and Los Esclaves de María—neither church records nor memories tell us exactly when. These took on particular projects, usually raising money for church improvements. These groups dignified the activity of women and created for them a sphere of authority. Going to the church, even at night, was always respectable and appropriate for women. The priest's dependence on women was undeniable and his requests uncontestable. In a culture characterized both by anticlericalism and devotion, as this one was, church was a site of women's activism and authority.[51]

The working-class identity developing in Clifton-Morenci exerted a mixed influence on Mexican women's social status. As Clifton-Morenci

Mexicans shed their identity as alien "sojourners" and constructed a new one as members of a settled working class, their consciousness was composed simultaneously and inextricably of class and racial-national understandings. There were outliers–white or Euro-Latin workers–but for the majority of the population one identity, Mexican, was mapped neatly onto another, worker. The solidarity that resulted not only included but also depended on women's sense of membership, to see families through those periods without income, to face down substantial threats, and to pressure other workers not to break that solidarity. That sense of belonging was hard to avoid in company towns like Clifton and Morenci. But this class identity reinforced women's subordination in some ways. Opportunities for women's economic independence were rare, and those that achieved it usually did so by moving away. Because of the lack of opportunities for women's economic independence and the high level of danger and exertion in the men's work, mining camps seem to have been more patriarchal than other working-class communities. The class organizations–unions and brotherhoods–were men's organizations, and the struggles they fought, victorious or defeated, bonded the men in ways that confirmed their manly sense of themselves as heads of households, *jefes* of the family. There were of course as many ways to be a *jefe* as there were men, and many preferred more egalitarian family relations. What's more, male headship did not by any means imply female subordination on all issues, and as in every society and family, beneath and in between the appearances of traditional male dominance were man-woman and parent-child conflicts, sometimes violent and sometimes so subtle that even the participants were unaware of the power struggle at their core. There were negotiations, haggling, complicated interactions, and sometimes beatings, with outcomes not always predictable.

So we need to hold in our minds a complex picture of the marriages of those who volunteered to take in the orphans: women typically submitted when men insisted on their authority, and sometimes men insisted violently and women were badly hurt, but sometimes women used men's dependence on their labor to negotiate from positions of considerable power. Men and women functioned in a patriarchal family culture, yes, but this does not mean that one side had all the power and the other side none.[52]

Women complained most about men's drunkenness. In earlier decades, when the miners were mainly single and migrant, payday binges were virtually universal, and there were no significant ethnic differences–the whole camp got drunk on "rich day" (payday). In one of Arizona's white camps, the copper company estimated that drunkenness during working hours cost it a thousand dollars per month.[53] With increased family life in Clifton-Morenci, drunkenness declined somewhat as men found other forms of relaxation, but the damages caused by alcohol remained fearsome; the health costs did not stand out because mine and smelter injuries took a high toll first, but alcohol-related violence occurred at least weekly, and drink made men more likely to respond to women's assertions of theirs and their children's needs with beatings. The very fiestas that women so lovingly fashioned created mixed expectations for those with husbands or fathers prone to violence.

The most violent men didn't need a party to set them off; an ordinary night at a saloon was enough, and the most brittle men didn't even need liquor. It is safe to assume that wife beating has gone on in every community in the United States, possibly more extensively in the generally violent culture of mining towns, among all racial-ethnic groups, and we know about only those cases that came to the attention of the courts: some because they led to murder, others because the women actually brought charges. A Metcalf Mexican miner stabbed his wife and ten-year-old daughter to death in July 1903.[54] In Morenci Tibusia Martínez alleged that Andrés Rodríguez "came home drunk and drove [her] and the children from the house." He was convicted and sentenced to forty days in jail, a heavy sentence for this court.[55] The Clifton justice of the peace–lowest level of the American court system in Arizona, which normally heard cases involving property of one hundred dollars or less and misdemeanors–heard several complaints every year. In the two months just before the orphans came, three domestic violence cases were heard in Clifton, two of them involving Mexicans. In August Candelaria Talamantes brought charges against Yginio García, who was convicted and fined twenty-five dollars, a standard fine for Clifton's justice of the peace, equivalent to that imposed for drunk and disorderly charges. Rosa Luján, obviously very frightened, charged Joe Luján with threatening to murder her, and Justice Boyles ordered him to file a five-hundred-dollar bond to keep the peace, suggesting that his violence toward her was a continuing problem. (One wonders if he could possibly have raised such an amount.) As if to deny Mexican men any appearance of a monopoly on violence, W. H. Carpenter murdered his wife Rada Carpenter, after she tried to leave him because of his brutality, and then killed himself.[56]

Recorded cases are always just a fragment, of indeterminate proportion, of the incidence of violence against women. But they provide evidence of something else that is equally important: women's willingness to bring legal complaints. Women do not bother when they believe they have nothing to gain, and they have often had nothing to gain. In the United States women individually and in organizations campaigned to get wife beating criminalized throughout the nineteenth century, and by the end of that century they had achieved at least *de jure* success, although neither police nor courts would usually punish offenders enough to deter them. Mexican women in particular have seemed to many observers to accept a certain amount of beating with resignation; indeed to some scholars Mexican men's violence against women seems so normative that it is not mentioned, though it appears vividly between the lines.[57] But the evidence suggests that many women displayed no such resignation. Even in extremely patriarchal societies women (and children) resist violence with energy and resourcefulness, relying on gossip, family networks, threats, guns, knives, and occasionally poison to protect themselves or intimidate their assailants. Turning to the courts—or in this case to the justice of the peace—meant using a new country's tool for an old job.[58]

PROSECUTING A PARTNER was, however, also a part of a process that by no means yielded only positive benefits. Some call the process Americanization, some modernization, some marketization, and in truth it was all of these—American capital was the closest, most dynamic, irresistible force bringing a commercial-industrial economy to Mexico and the U.S. Southwest.[59] Mexicans of both sexes ardently sought out American consumer goods but also complained about America and lamented the loss of their homeland culture. On the one hand, they did not like the impolite and hurried forms of American speech and interactions, and they missed the fresh fruit and flowers; they were offended by disrespect for women and the elderly and by weak coffee and chicken that wasn't fresh. Like Granjon, they sensed the contagion of American culture, which made the Mexicans themselves "greedier and more selfish."[60] On the other hand, they loved beer, Coca-Cola, blue jeans, higher wages, and opportunity. Both sexes sang this litany of love and hate.

Many observers considered women the Mexicans' primary modernizers, through their desire for new consumer goods. (Some considered this a compliment, others an accusation.) Certainly women longed for American fashions and cosmetics—as well as for health care, indoor plumbing, gas ranges. Adopting the orphans could plausibly be labeled an aspect of this Americanization. Although it is not clear that women were more hooked on installment buying than men, or that consumption was more central to modernization than wage labor, it is certain that Americanization accelerated family and gender change among many immigrant groups as they confronted this land of dollars. Mexicans in the United States displayed a variety of responses, progressive, conservative, and contradictory, and prominent among them was women's exploration of new possibilities. Evidence of their restlessness shows in the Mexican American press's fretful preachments about the sacredness of women's traditional place and denunciations of their temptations to desert family. "Luxury," editorialized *La Hormiga de Oro,* an Albuqerque labor socialist weekly, in 1904, "is the major enemy of the home and the woman." And "What more could a man have than a wife who is prudent, loving, faithful, domestic and accepting [*resignada*]?" The Alianza newspaper blamed women's lack of virtue for men's frequenting saloons. Girls' education should feature domestic labor, the Albuquerque newspaper *La Bandera* prescribed in the midst of a small flurry of worried editorials about the impact of education on women's place: "The most elevated knowledge could never replace this modest science,"[61] that is, housewifery. Integrated into a new discourse about the work ethic, one which attempted to redefine manliness and honor in terms of hard work and discipline, was a chorus about housekeeping, featuring paeans to cleanliness; one editorial gave women housekeeping instruction: sweep the whole house, stairs, and patios daily, dust the furniture, shake out the bedspreads, remove the cobwebs—thus obeying Saint Augustine.[62] This discourse crossed class lines, appearing both in employer-owned papers aimed at disciplining labor and in labor-movement newspapers.[63]

But mixed with this hold-the-line gender chorus were grudging acknowledgments of the need for improvements in women's position: letters to the editors questioning the absolute value of gendered traditions, editorials acknowledging women's public-sphere contributions as part of a "new womanhood," and outraged reports of violence against women. The woman slaves of yesterday have disappeared forever along with the caste system, declared Morenci's *El Obrero*. "The modern woman is a moral and intellectual persona, a factor . . . in all social activity, scientific development, art, industry, progress and the prosperity of the nations."[64]

Soon the Mexican revolutionary movement would bring anarchist-feminist ideas to masses of Mexican workers on both sides of the border. Following in the tradition of Mexico's women educators and labor leaders, teacher Sara Estela Ramírez spoke and wrote throughout south Texas on behalf of the Partido Liberal Mexicano (PLM), starting in 1901. Her feminism remained elusive, her prose more airy than pithy: "Rise! Rise into life, into activity, into the beauty of truly living; but rise radiant and powerful . . . You, the queen of the world, goddess of universal adoration; you, sovereign to whom homage is due, do not confine yourself in your goddess temple, nor in the boudoir of the triumphant courtesan . . . Only action is life."[65] But her presence as an emancipated woman and a political leader carried a clearer message. By 1910 Ricardo Flores Magón, leader of the PLM, was regularly denouncing unequal pay, sexual harassment, and women's political subordination in the PLM newspaper distributed throughout the Southwest, and soon the first Chicana feminist organization formed, the Liga Femenil Mexicanista.[66]

These changes were contested because matters of power and resources were at stake. When Manuel Gamio interviewed immigrants—two decades later, but his records are still the best source—their views about gender divided to some degree along sex lines. Men disliked American women and what America did to Mexican women. Carlos Ibáñez did not like "the system of the women here. They are very unrestrained . . . control their husband . . . the Mexican women who come here also take advantage of the laws and want to be like the American women."[67] Pedro Chaussé, an educated white middle-class Mexican, a man whose status might well have attracted an American woman, thought the same: "the American girl is too proud and cannot adapt herself to the idea of the home which the Mexican has had since the cradle."[68] Elías Sepulveda was born in Nogales, Arizona, but still would not want to marry an American because they are "ambitious and free . . . when the husband comes from his work he has to buy the groceries and then help her in the kitchen and even wash the dishes . . . The Mexican women are hard workers and do all that one wants."[69] Popular *corridos* repeated these views:

> From Mexico have I come
> Just to come and see,
> This American law
> That says women are boss.

Or

> If their husbands go to a bar
> For some fun or pool playing,
> And if his woman finds out
> She complains to the judge.[70]

Domingo Ramírez from Cananea liked to go out with American girls who "give one kisses that get one all excited, while the Mexicans don't even want to allow themselves to be kissed. But if I were to marry I would marry a Mexican girl because they are obedient and are grateful for everything . . . know how to work in the house . . . The American girls do everything they want to and they don't pay any attention to their husbands."[71]

Strikingly, the women told Gamio exactly the same thing–from a different perspective. Dolores Sánchez de Fuente, a sweatshop worker from Mazatlán, complained that her Mexican husband was domineering, cruel, and arrogant and drank and smoked marijuana too much. "Sometimes when the husband remembers that one doesn't work as hard over there he wants to go, but she remembers that there the women are not as well protected by the law and that if he has never struck her here it has been for fear of going to jail. She thinks that there he would beat her."[72] Beware of translating the Mexico-to-United States transition as one from patriarchy to freedom. Mexican women had their sources of power, and the United States had plenty of male tyrants. But American norms were freer. Señora Campos, of a different class position than Sánchez de Fuente–white and elite–liked the United States because of the goods, comforts, and privacy it offered: "Here she goes with freedom to the grocery store, clothing store . . . and buys whatever she wishes without anyone paying any attention to her." But she disliked "the liberty and way of behaving of the young women . . .

by which her daughters have been influenced."[73] A study of Tejanas found them resisting husbands' sexual infidelities and drinking at cantinas.[74] Just as American popular culture and consumer goods penetrated into Mexico, inviting emigration, so did "American" standards of gender relations also invite emigration. Señora Ceballos came to the United States fleeing a husband who beat her and forced sex upon her, a man she'd been forced to marry at fifteen. Arriving in Los Angeles, she told her story of woe to women at a Young Women's Christian Association (YWCA) who sheltered her. "She understands that here woman has come to have a place, like a human being, which is what she really wanted when she was in Mexico."[75] Elena Torres de Acosta, a *mestiza* from Guadalajara, came to the United States on her own because of "spiritual suffering" from her husband's infidelities, the kind of affairs said to be resignedly tolerated by Mexican women.[76]

What women loved about the United States was by no means limited to American men's allegedly greater restraint. They also appreciated a culture that seemed to them, despite its hypocrisy, a bit less punitive and fearful toward female sexuality. They appreciated a different sensibility among women. Several women recalled with bitterness their sexual ignorance and shame about menstruation, sex, and childbirth, an ignorance that continued when they entered marriage, an ignorance imposed upon them by women, albeit women perpetuating a patriarchal helplessness. "Like I say, it's like they kept us completely in the dark. I didn't know, when I was going to have my first child, well, excuse me, I said to her: 'How is this baby going to be born?' . . . I was very desperate . . . my mother told me: 'Wait daughter, be patient.'" These women admired the greater openness of their American daughters.[77]

Gender is not a system of men stepping on women. It is the social and cultural meanings given to sex, and everyone participates in the construction, confirmation, alteration, and constancy of gender. Precisely because of the sexual division of labor, women are usually more active in communicating gender to other women. They transmit traditions and innovations. In America, immigrants commented, Mexican wives were using contraception, often with husbands' approval; but we can guess that it is not through men that they learned about modern contraception or gained the courage to try it.[78] Many women recalled–with some nostalgia, true–girls' rebellion against the strict chaperonage imposed on them by family members.[79] Nor did Mexican opinion about the "modern" gender order divide neatly between men and women. Gamio found that men he called "assimilated" had more egalitarian views toward women, and several associated Mexican patriarchy with the oppression of children as well as women.[80] That no men discussed American standards of maleness probably derived from the silences of their interviewers.

The fact that Mexicans associated gender change with Americanness is complicated, in part because it follows a worldwide pattern in which colonial powers sometimes brought "women's liberation" to their colonies. Thus class and ethnic resistance to domination could seem to require loyalty to traditional family relations. Moreover, the rise of Chicano nationalism a few decades later sometimes brought with it a revalorizing and rehonoring of patriarchal family forms; it "idealized the [sexual] division of labor, romanticized the double-standard, ridiculed nontraditional feminine behavior as a form of cultural disloyalty."[81] Only a few scholars have examined open-mindedly and critically the attractiveness of American gender standards on the U.S.-Mexican border,[82] and most studies of Mexican-Anglo intermarriage and "interracial" families have avoided looking at male domination, women's subordination, or power contestations. But these issues are vital to understanding the orphan story because it too was about gender and "race mixture."

Anglo-Mexican intermarriage was common throughout the Southwest, attributed mainly to the shortage of Anglo women. The incidence was highest during the earliest period of U.S. ownership of the region, when Anglo women were scarce; declined thereafter, particularly sharply as Anglos made Mexicans into an alien race; and increased again after about 1945.[83] The 1864 Arizona territorial census counted only eight non-Hispanic, non-Indian women. In Pima County, where Tucson is located, for example, Mexican-Anglo unions accounted for 23 percent of all marriages in the 1870s, 19 percent in the 1880s, and 12 percent in the 1890s.[84] Throughout this variation there was a continuity: Anglo-Mexican couples consisted almost exclusively of "white" men and Mexican women.[85] In the Clifton-Morenci census and the Sacred Heart Church records for 1900–1904 the Chacóns were the only Mexican man–Anglo woman couple. The scarcity of Anglo women does not explain why Mexican women failed to match up with Mexican men. The ellipsis here stems from a Victorian notion that men choose, women comply. But even assuming—falsely—women's passivity, their parents' choices still need explanation.[86]

In other parts of the Southwest, in the nineteenth century, there were substantial economic inducements for white men to marry into property-owning, politically powerful *hispano* or *californio* families. In this marital commerce, women were the legal tender, exchanged in the process of consolidating ownership and creating new capital.[87] The social outcomes of these exchanges provide further evidence for economic motives, as the "mixed" couples tended to assimilate to Anglo America,[88] perhaps suggesting that women's greater pliability made it their task to acculturate. But these motives and patterns were absent from Clifton-Morenci where there were few wealthy *hispano* families and many Anglo daughters of wealthy or influential parents. What then explains relationships between working-class whites and Mexicans? Here the economic incentive was women's, because they could benefit from white men's wages. Consider some of the intermarried Mexican women in Clifton-Morenci: Jennie Buttuer was married to a butcher; Carmel Nellton to a smelter foreman; Maria Lesry to a hoist engineer; Carmen Bruner to a salesman; Angel Springer to a barber; Josefa Erskine to a painter. Two-thirds of the intermarried women in Clifton-Morenci in 1900 had husbands with higher-status jobs than a Mexican could get, and to this we must add the likelihood that the other one-third got the usual higher white wage for the same work. The distribution of these economic motives may explain why half of the intermarried couples lived in Mexican neighborhoods and a third in mixed, usually Mexican-Italian neighborhoods; only 17 percent lived in distinctly Anglo neighborhoods,[89] suggesting that here the woman defined the sociability network (as we might expect), or found the housing for the couple, or that the husband had been taken into the Mexican community. Any explanation points to women's influence and initiative.

Add to economics the near constant, near universal attraction of lighter color. But this again provides an incentive only for Mexican women, not Anglo men. Among the upper-class intermarriages in the eighteenth and nineteenth centuries, the *hispanas* involved were usually light-skinned, so at least there was no disincentive for the men. The working-class women of Clifton-Morenci were occasionally darker but perhaps this mattered less to men who did not see themselves as climbing into an elite. There was a significant gender difference in the attitude toward lightness: among women its value crossed class lines because it was assimilated to standards of beauty, and women seemed to appreciate lighter-skinned children more than men did.[90] So we have another reminder that it is impossible to appraise racial motives or hierarchies without figuring in female as well as male action and subjectivity.

The least certain motives have to do with gender power relations. There are volumes of racialized discourse about Mexican women's passivity, subservience, and sexual availability and Mexican men's machismo. But those volumes come from ill-informed, stereotypical, external, sexist, and often racist perspectives; the critical literature examining gender in Mexican American relationships is still sparse. Yet how can we ignore gender in thinking about intermarriage? What we are discussing is precisely the meeting of male and female on the most intimate terms, in relations whose rapport or discord derives from gender cultures.

Whites' racist anti-Mexican discourse was directed primarily toward men. Not only did it go softer on Mexican women, but a form of Orientalism rendered Mexican women particularly attractive to men, even trophies, so that marrying a Mexican woman was by no means a low-status move for a white man.[91] The "greaser" label was part of a slander that Mexican people were dirty, but it coexisted with the impression that Mexican women were extraordinary housekeepers, taking great pride in the cleanliness and beauty of their homes and children.[92] Possibly the greatest pull of Mexican women on Anglo men, although the most tricky to delineate, was the belief in their greater submissiveness than "American" women, a belief that remains to this day.[93] A Kansas City priest in the 1950s explained that he encouraged marriage between Anglo boys and Mexican girls because these marriages were stable, owing to the men's satisfaction as a result of the women's subservience. The other way round would not work, he believed: because of male jealousy, because she is considered trash who has been rejected by Anglo men, and because of the husband's "stress trying to maintain his traditional role and expectation as an authoritative husband in a situation over which he actually has little control."[94] But this unilateral story of intermarriage, one that reckons only men's motives, not only works to reinforce women's subordination, but does not fit the facts as well as a bilateral interpretation. Mexican women were also attracted to American men because they saw there the promise of American-style marital behavior—more acceptance of women's autonomy in public and private, a less entrenched double standard regarding sexual and economic fidelity (those mistresses, those *casas chicas,* took money as well as love out of the household), and a lesser emphasis on personal honor and domestic authority. Hardly least important, white men could bring home white men's wages.

So perhaps these intermarriages represented racial, class, and gender bargains: Men wanted sex appeal, housekeeping, yieldingness; women wanted lighter children, a better standard of living, less machismo. But without much evidence, such speculation is suspect, resting as it does on stereotypes. For example, were Mexican women really more pliable? Could anything be less measurable? Consider the fact that women in Mexico enjoyed more legal rights than most in America, and some of these were incorporated into laws of the Arizona Territory. Sons and daughters usually inherited equally. Property acquired during marriage was community property and women's previously owned holdings did not necessarily fall into their husbands' hands. Women kept their own names. They could sue on their own behalf. In Colorado and New Mexico—where Mexicans were more numerous and their legal culture more established—women were accustomed to turn to courts in marital disputes, and sometimes won. Men as well as women were sometimes punished for adultery,[95] and the Clifton-Morenci court records show that Mexican women tried to use local laws against their male partners. The system of *compadrazgo,* continuing robustly in Clifton-Morenci, provided them with institutionalized networks of support in addition to those of husband or family of origin.

A more modest, weaker conclusion has more certainty: that women's very attraction to Anglo men as a way of reducing patriarchal control was in itself a symptom of their degree of autonomy from patriarchal control. This is not peculiarly Mexican—it is true everywhere, because patriarchy is a contest, a dynamic, not a consistent and stable set of procedures. So the question about whether Mexican women were subservient is entirely a wrong question; wrong because universalized, abstracted, and perhaps not ever answerable. What we need to know is actually simpler: whether Mexican women saw some opportunity, in some directions, for improving their position by taking what Anglo gender culture offered along with what Mexican gender culture offered.

Was not taking in the orphans a taking in of a piece of Anglo culture? At the least it was another move that marked the limits of patriarchal control over women—and, quite possibly, pushed those limits outward. These women were not, on the whole, accustomed to acting without their husbands' permission, so this orphan plan was a step out of line. This is not to say that the men disapproved or were defied; it is to say only that the women took the initiative in this undertaking, defining it as belonging within their sphere of authority, and that, in taking the initiative, they enlarged that sphere. Questions about that process involve unknowable aspects of these marriages: did the women have to beg and plead to get their husbands' permission? Did their husbands compute that one more mouth to feed would not make much difference? Were the husbands honoring a lonely wife's whim, or did the wives argue that such a child might be an asset? Whatever the answers, the results remind us that the authority of Mexican husbands did not mean the powerlessness of Mexican women.

Whether these were mutual decisions or men's indulgence, it was women's desire that brought the orphans to Clifton. They desired, first, to be good Catholics, to have the opportunity, one not often given to the poor, to help the unfortunate in a truly grand gesture. Surely it seemed to them sad that these motherless children should languish in an orphanage. For Margarita Chacón this sadness was also her own, a flood of memories of rows of cots, sisters in habits walking single file to prayer, silent meals at long tables. Perhaps she told her friends, making them feel what it was to be an orphan, or perhaps she merely encouraged others to join her in this act of charity, an act that would bring respect to their families and in some cases status to their ambitious husbands.

The women also wanted to please the new priest. He was young and they could enjoy flirting, but mostly he brought them into positions of some importance as they helped orient him to his new community and teach him his new language. He was their spiritual father, but they were also his mothers. Through him, too, they could become leaders among women; and through such leadership they could strengthen the church, assure their children's devotion, perhaps even lure their husbands into the little adobe structure on Chase Creek.

They also desired a new child. For some that yearning was a powerful, longstanding loneliness; for others, it was the baby hunger that arose after their children had grown or left; for still others, it was a desire to repeat the greatest satisfaction of a womanly life. An orphan child escalated the importance of their motherhood, made them centers of attention within the community. Those asked to serve as *comadres* and *compadres* were honored and excited to meet their new wards. As any childbirth was an adventure, this was an adventure of multiplied value: comforting an orphan, gaining a child who was a magnet for community interest, without the dread of childbirth—a dread not just of the pain but of staring death in the face.

And then there was the special yearning for a light child, a yearning they did not know they had—or actually did not have—until one was offered. Appreciation of lightness had been part of their Mexican culture. As girls they longed to be lighter themselves; as mothers they longed for lighter babies. Lightness was not mere aesthetic prejudice but stood, however subconsciously, for material hopes: for prosperity, health, security, status. Today we may contemplate this preference with a shudder and understand it as learned racism. If in turn-of-the-century Mexico a critique of racism was not yet widely articulated, there was no lack of awareness that the light were more and the dark less powerful. But now in Clifton-Morenci light had become "white," not a description but a rank, a caste. Marrying into whiteness was no longer a realistic option, but adopting whiteness—who knew what it might lead to? Such a child might go to school, might learn perfect English, might marry a white man or earn a white man's wage. Perhaps not, but it could hardly lead to anything bad, and the child would at the very least be admired among the Mexicans. Such a child might make the whole family whiter. Such a child might become a true *americano*. If so, it would be an achievement accomplished by the mothers.

October 2, 1904, Evening

The Hills of Clifton

THE POSSE HAD A HARD NIGHT. In some neighborhoods the Mexicans lived high on the steep hillsides and the men had to climb up crudely dug footholds, sometimes without timbers to hold the soil. It was difficult to find the way in the dark, and several men slipped and cursed. After about 8:00 it began raining, and the paths quickly became muddy. Several men carried rifles rather than Colts,[1] and the rifles made them even clumsier. They were not entirely sure which families actually had the orphans and approached several houses in error. Once they had collected a child, one of the men returned with her or him to the hotel, and eventually there were only four men left. That last group was soaked and tired.

But they had no thought of turning back. The women had convinced the men that they had to protect the babies, and the men had become equally committed to the task. For some there was the added sweetness of revenge for the previous year's fear of the Mexican anarchists. Others, like Leggatt, who had been somewhat sympathetic to the strike because he knew so many miners, did not share that desire for vengeance but enjoyed the recognition of his citizenship. They all liked the good fellowship of the posse and the chance to show their grit in this way. Their enthusiasm, and perhaps a touch of defensiveness, showed in their later justifications of their actions and their lengthy commentary about the nature of the Mexicans.

Nothing could be more symbolic of the nature of the posse than its composition: white men of nearly every status in Clifton, top to bottom.

As if to underscore their titular equality in citizenship, Neville Leggatt and George Frazer–the deliveryman and the smelter superintendent–were the key witnesses at the trial to describe taking the children away from the Mexicans, and they were in total agreement as to its justification. Leggatt knew he had been essential to the posse because he was the only one who could find his way to each house on that dark and rainy "very wild night." He had helped get things organized since he was always the town messenger, giving and getting news at each stop.

At the trial he would feel proud to be a key witness, explaining the justification for taking the children, as important as George Frazer before the court. In his testimony Leggatt passed lightly over the way the library meeting got arranged because he knew he wasn't a leader and because he sensed it was a tricky issue. But he gave long and detailed testimony about the Mexicans who had first gotten the orphans and about the Anglos collecting them. He liked to think that his knowledge of the Mexicans was now getting respect: "They are half Indians and the lowest kind; they work for anything; two dollars, some get three dollars . . . and I know taking out the provisions and everything it never amounts to more than eighteen dollars, and that amounts to a whole month." When asked what he knew about them "intellectually," Leggatt answered, "They cannot either read or write." All the witnesses claimed that none of the Mexicans could speak English.

Frazer was sure that he knew the Mexicans too, since so many of them worked for him at one time or another: They were all very poor, lived in coarse adobe homes or small frame houses, roughly ten feet by twelve feet, had "no intellect, and they are moral [*sic*–he meant immoral but the court reporter got it wrong], some of them. [They] generally drink up everything they can . . . come to work never washing their faces from one week's end to the other . . . come the next morning with the marks of the perspiration on their faces yet. I have sent them home and told them to wash their faces." The last statement was particularly startling, coming from Frazer, because just a year before, one of the workers' leading strike demands was a changing room with showers.

Tom Simpson, a locomotive engineer, had not been with the posse because he was up in Morenci, but he also believed himself qualified to testify about the Mexicans, having lived in Clifton seventeen years:

> Well, its a mining camp, and we have the renegades of Mexico and of Arizona; that is, down in Guaymas and about there, what we have to

contend with . . . they all live in those little shacks about the size of 8 x 6, or 8 x 10, and most of them have no floor in them at all . . . you see they . . . all get very little salary . . . about two dollars a day, some of them two and a half, and very few of them gets three . . . [They have] five or six people staying in one room . . . [yet] they are very extravagant in the dry goods department.

This kind of condemnation, evoked by the necessities of defending the posse's actions, was not the manly anti-Mexicanism that formed the standard small talk of so many Anglos in the U.S. Southwest. That talk constructed Mexican men as feminine, attempting to erase them as military or economic rivals. The Anglos of the posse had participated in endless repetitions of the major tropes of this chorus: Mexicans were cruel, to animals, women, and other men; they were cowardly and treacherous and could triumph only through betrayal and a knife in the back; they were natural thieves and had no respect for property; and they were indolent. The source of this degeneracy was that they were half-breeds.[2] The inferiority of the Mexicans—especially their moral inferiority—was a foundation of the Anglos' right to be there and to have what they had. The inferiority of Mexicans was part of the Anglos' individual identities, their egos, as brave, rough, and honest westerners, identities constructed against a number of others—not only Mexicans but also Indians, easterners, and women. That's why the trope was so durable that it was still being repeated by Texas's most distinguished twentieth-century historian, Walter Prescott Webb, in 1935:

> Without disparagement it may be said that there is a cruel streak in the Mexican nature . . . This cruelty may be a heritage from the Spanish of the Inquisition; it may, and doubtless should, be attributed partly to the Indian blood . . . The Mexican warrior . . . was, on the whole, inferior to the Comanche and wholly unequal to the Texan . . . The whine of the leaden slugs stirred in him an irresistible impulse to travel with rather than against the music. He won more victories over the Texans by parley than by force of arms. For making promises—and for breaking them—he had no peer.[3]

By contrast, the foundling affair twisted the gendered meanings of anti-Mexicanism a bit; owing to the foundational role of the women, the posse's discourse was itself somewhat feminized. The Anglo husbands had understood that the defense of their kidnapping rested not on valiance and honor in battle but on respectability in the home, in the women's sphere. The Anglos' main criticism now was that the Mexicans were "greasers." The origins of that old term had nothing to do with personal or household cleanliness, but in the nineteenth-century western context it had begun to express a fusion of moral and domestic uncleanliness.[4] This new axis of condemnation, focusing on housekeeping, drinking habits, and sexual respectability, was largely a creation of women and yet another aspect of Anglo women's influence. In another context Leggatt and Frazer might have chortled over tales of out-of-your-mind drunkenness and would not have measured a man's worth by the house he lived in.

But when it came to individual Mexicans, the Anglos' so-called knowledge became fuzzier. And because they were not certain what a proper Mexican home might look like, they could not back up their allegations with any specific observations. They tried to avoid showing these major gaps in their knowledge by answering even specific questions about individuals with hazy generalizations. Frazer said he knew the Mexicans thoroughly, but then confessed it was "not by name," and as he and Leggatt were led by their lawyers, step by step, in recounting their mission that night, they actually had little information to offer. They had gone first to the house of Francisco Alvidrez—although they identified the orphans as belonging to the women, they identified the houses by the husbands' names because they didn't usually know the women's given names. Leggatt said it was a three-room adobe, Frazer that it had one adobe and one lumber room. (The Anglos spoke of adobe as a symbol of low living, although Anglos in the region had themselves once lived in adobe houses, and just a few years later Mabel Dodge and her crowd would make them fashionable in the Taos area.) Leggatt knew that Alvidrez was a "wood man," translating *leñero,* meaning that he cut and sold wood for heating and cooking, going far into the mountains and carrying it out by burro or mule, of which he owned quite a few. But Frazer said he used two old horses. Sometimes other wood men stayed in his house—Leggatt said, "I believe that they call them 'Cousins' or something of that kind." Frazer testified that Alvidrez was among "the lowest class Mexicans that we have in the town . . . I couldn't say as the place was filthy, but still it wasn't clean. The corral where they keep their burros and mules was right against the door of the house . . . He is an old man probably 65 or 70 years old, and we give him work at the smelter some times as a case of charity."

They were wrong not only about Francisco Alvidrez's status but even about his identity because they knew so little about the Mexicans. Leggatt was describing Francisco's sixty-year-old father. But his son, a well-paid smelter worker, was more likely the one who took an orphan, and he must have spoken English adequately as he had attended elementary school in Clifton. Both Leggatt and Frazer were sure the household was dirty, and Leggatt specified that they had only minimal furniture—"a bed, a couple of chairs and a table"—but it turned out on cross-examination that neither man had ever been inside the Alvidrez house, nor any Mexican household. They would not have known that Alvidrez Junior had already assumed the honor and responsibilities of being a godfather. In contrast to Leggatt's and Frazer's claims, the Foundling Hospital attorney had visited and found the Alvidrez family in a good home and comfortable circumstances.[5] Frazer claimed that Francisco Alvidrez had asked that the children be taken away, saying he could not afford them, but Trancita Alvidrez, his wife, denied this and said she wanted the children back.

Their next stop was at the home of Lee Windham and his "Mexican woman," whose name they did not know. They related the Anglo Windham's old reputation as a drunken, unruly cowboy: Leggatt called him immoral, a drinker and a gambler; Frazer called him shiftless but never drunk. They also slurred his wife. Her ex-husband, Costelo Gonzalez, they claimed, still worked at the smelter along with Windham, a proximity they found distasteful; and they made much of the fact that she had lived with Windham for five or six years before they married. Leggatt labeled her a prostitute. The Anglos used such terms loosely when talking about Mexican women. Depending on the context it might have meant a woman who worked in a bar, or lived with a man without legal marriage, or had a boyfriend—or it might have meant any woman not a "lady." Father Timmermans, interviewed by the Foundling Hospital attorney before the trial, denied these charges of immorality and said that Refugia Windham was "living a good life." Despite his generalizations about the wretched homes of the Mexicans, when pressed regarding Windham's establishment Frazer said that they had two small adobe rooms, about ten by twelve each, and adobe floors: "They sprinkle it every morning and sweep it to keep it dry and hard ... The walls are whitewashed and plastered." Despite the possemen's claims at the trial that all the Mexicans gave up the children willingly, Refugia Windham was still heartbroken about losing little

Sadie a month later and burst into tears when interviewed by the Foundling Hospital lawyer in November; she told him that she wanted the child but did not want trouble with the Anglos and that was why she let them take Sadie.[6]

The posse then proceeded to the home of José Bonillas, also allegedly a drunkard married to a prostitute. Leggatt said they had late-night parties. He testified that he had "seen them at times when I used to go around there at 5 o'clock in the morning on the butcher wagon. I have seen a whole crowd in the room. There was there a lot of other women singing, and bottles of wine there." Simpson had seen Bonillas "up town . . . in the Italian saloon." The sisters' lawyer pointed out that two of the Anglos who seized and kept the children ran saloons and asked, "Are there not a lot of good people who get drunk and gamble sometimes? . . . Do any of these people who now have the children drink and gamble?" In response Leggatt withdrew to the Anglos' first line of defense: "I guess they can afford it and those other people could not afford it."

Another house was John Maxwell's and Angela Flores's. Leggatt called her, too, a prostitute and pointed out that she and Maxwell (also known as Esquivel) had lived together for a few years before getting married. According to Eugene Fountin, the padre had insisted: "[Maxwell] said his wife went to the priest, and the priest asked her if she was married; and she told him no, she had a man but she wasn't married; and the priest told her she had to marry this man by the church to get the child." By the time he said this, Eugene Fountin had taken the Anglo women's point of view, because his wife too had asked the priest for a child; and he was particularly peeved because Maxwell "wasn't as good a Catholic as I was." The Foundling Hospital attorney found, to the contrary, that Angela Flores's frame home was clean, that she was a "good woman and very much grieved that she lost the child . . . given to her." She showed the attorney the clothing she had made for the child, which included two red flannel skirts, two white skirts, one undervest, one red dress, one elastic waistband with garters and attachments for underclothing, and a great deal of cloth that she had not yet sewn when Josephine was abducted.[7]

When the posse came to the Chacón home, Leggatt really wished he had not had to take the children from Margarita. She was for him and several others in town the good Mexican woman, her image practically virginal. Perhaps, too, some of them identified her as not "really" Mexi-

can despite her marriage to a Mexican, her life exclusively among
Mexicans, and her central role in the Mexican community as teacher
and church leader. He was so uncomfortable at her house demanding
the children that I wondered whether they were actually acquainted or
whether her devoutness made him feel ashamed. He specified that he
had known her for fourteen months. Probably he had seen the group of
Mexican children she taught in her home. At her house, he said, "I told
them I was sorry I would have to take them away from there because
they were honest people." But the committee had decided "if we were
going to take one, we might as well take all."

Leggatt considered Margarita above any reproach but not so her
husband, Cornelio, who was often "drunk on the streets raising Cain."
Among the series of dubious accusations, this was one of the most
dubious, given Cornelio's community leadership in a mutual benefit
society. It raises the question, could the posse's anger have been
provoked by particular individuals' assertiveness in protesting discrimination or in seeking advancement? Leggatt admitted that Chacón
got "pretty fair wages–$3 a day–[as a] skimmer," which put Chacón,
like Maxwell, at the highest earning level among Mexicans working in
copper. Frazer lumped both Chacóns with the "lowest-class" Mexicans
although, as Cornelio's employer, he probably knew that Cornelio was
a high earner. He knew that the house was mortgaged and that Chacón
owed debts to several men, including Frazer himself and Crum the
butcher. He commented that the walls were papered in this adobe
house, without appearing conscious that this hardly matched his pejorative description of the family's class position.

Fountin condemned Margarita Chacón with a particularly odd claim,
untrue as far as I can determine–she "is not a very good character . . . her
mother is married to a nigger, and her sister is a half-breed nigger." A
racist anxiety about Negroes attached to this case throughout the country as several newspapers published a photograph (reproduced in this
book) of one of the Mexican homes in front of which stood a Negro-look-
ing boy. (His appearance could have come from a mixed-race relationship, or he could have been simply a dark Mexican.) The many white
southerners in the area so frequently compared Mexicans to Negroes–
perfectly logical, after all, to compare one subordinated group to
another–that the connection became common local discourse.

The Mexican parents never had the chance to rebut these insults in
court, but if they had they might have referred to the nightly carrying

and heating of water to prepare the mineworkers' baths; their husbands' fluency in English, and perhaps their chortles about overhearing management conversations which took place on the assumption that the workers could not understand; the jars in which they squirreled away coins to pay for the children's lessons with Señora Chacón. The women would have recalled their hours of housecleaning, not to mention the work they did cleaning Anglo houses. Or would they have been so disgusted by these "experts" on "what Mexicans were like" and their slurs that they would have disdained to comment? In fact the Anglos could not "see" the Mexicans. They were looking at working-class and entrepreneurial families but saw only an underclass. The Mexican parents were mainly from the highest-paid stratum of Clifton-Morenci workers, which meant they were an aristocracy of labor among their people "on the other side." Quite a few were U.S.-born. The women were pious, charitable, devoted to their church, and you can be sure that their adopted children would have been regular churchgoers; the men included leaders of fraternal organizations, and at least several of them were registered voters. Among those who were immigrants, the very fact of their being here signaled their ambition, and there is no doubt that educating their children was a priority.

The possemen later claimed that the Mexicans relinquished the orphans quite willingly, although Leggatt excepted Margarita Chacón. Were they simply lying to protect themselves legally? Or could they have been honestly reporting the situation from their standpoint? They believed they knew the Mexicans, and conceived of themselves as wanting only the best for the Mexicans, so of course they were sure that they knew what the Mexicans wanted and above all what was in the Mexicans' interest. Frazer claimed that Alvidrez told him, "Take the children away, George; you know I can't support them. You know it takes me all my time to support myself." Leggatt said, "after these children were taken away they themselves said they were glad it was done. They said they could not give them the homes those children have [with the Anglos] if they tried to." If these lines do not have the ring of truth, Frazer's report on the response of Lee Windham's woman sounds more convincing: she "just looked at us a little while and said, All right." The Anglos missed resistance also because of the strength of their sense of mission. When Leggatt testified that Señora Bonillas objected, "Who is going to pay me the money I paid the Priest for this child?"[8] to him it merely showed her greediness and disinterest in the

child itself. When Tom Simpson allowed that Trancita Alvidrez said
she was giving up the child because she had no choice, it did not shake
his conviction that she really didn't mind.

The Mexican parents had their own reasons for not trying very hard
to correct this Anglo narrative. It was mainly men who met the
possemen at their doors, and they were not about to let the Anglos
provoke them into a battle they would surely lose. The very strategy
and tenacity they had displayed the previous year led them to pick
carefully their fights, the terms and arenas of conflict. And the chosen
fights were likely to be on men's terms, around men's issues; these
adoptions were not as high on their list of needs as higher wages and
safer working conditions. The adoptions were, after all, the women's
scheme, not theirs.

But their restraint did not mean that none of them minded. "We
been married 9 years and we haven't got no family nothing but us two
and when Joseph arrived to our house every thing seem to be glad and
now every thing look sad but we can't help it now is taking away from
us now," Ramón Balles wrote to the Foundling sisters. This letter was
in English but he might, of course, have had someone else translate for
him. In a second letter, a month later, in Spanish, his style was more
flowery and his grammar more accurate:

> Let me assure you that we have not forgotten José, especially at dinner.
> Also, we feel very sad . . . Sister, our house is empty without José. His loss
> is deeply felt. A house without a child is not a happy home! Especially
> for the ladies, because in our situation, we [note his royal "we"] must
> work fifteen hours . . . With the child, José, here my wife had some one
> to keep her company, to offset moments of sadness . . . We loved the child
> more than we loved our home.[9]

Not everyone could swallow the vigilante violation of their homes
and families with such self-control. No posse member ever testified
about collecting Henry Potts from Rafael and Josefa Holguín, and we
can guess why: Rafael refused, went into the house and came back with
his gun, and said, "The only way that you can take the boy is over my
dead body. If you prefer to use force, before you get me, I'll get a
couple of you. You decide." Holguín had a reputation as "an abrupt,
aggressive, determined type of an individual, not easily intimidated,
and a good worker and provider." Luckily, a more "benign" member
of the posse responded, "Rafael, we are trying to let the court decide

if the church had legal authority to have the children placed for adoption. We are trying to avoid trouble. Would you be willing to return the boy to the priest if he asks you?" Holguín agreed, and the priest came and affirmed that the case was "under litigation and that if the court decided what the church did was legal the boy would be returned to him." A man with a temper, Holguín was also ambitious and prudent. Josefa packed up into a satchel Henry Potts's two sets of new clothes that she had made and a bag of cookies and passed him to the priest.[10]

At another home, not mentioned at the trial either but reported in the *El Paso Herald,* a parent "required to see the papers for the authority of the vigilantes to take the child . . . Whipping out a Colts [*sic*] the rescuers said, 'this is the paper and the law.' The Mexican shrugged his shoulders and turned away while the rescuers took the child."[11]

With such a shrug, perhaps, patience and strategic thinking conquered anger, but it remained in the store of bitterness Clifton-Morenci Mexicans had to carry. Only one Mexican published a response to the kidnapping, and he lived in Benson. Mariano Martinez wrote,

> My parents were born in this Territory. I was raised in Tucson . . . educated in the public schools, and I always considered myself an American . . . The Mexicans applied for and complied with the requirements for the adoption of the American children . . . They are able to write and speak both the Spanish and English languages, and they do not butcher it as do your so-called 'Arizona Americans,' who are composed of Swedes, Norwegians, Servians, Canadians and Dutch, who , . . make out of this portion of the United States a dumping ground. Probably the only claim you have to call them 'Americans' is that they have blue eyes, red hair, a face full of freckles and long feet. The 'low-down' Mexicans whom you refer to . . . have absolute respect for law and order . . . without having to resort to mob violence.[12]

5

The Anglo Mothers and
the Company Town

THE ORPHAN RESCUERS BELIEVED they were acting not only properly but nobly. Whatever nervousness troubled Deputy Sheriff Dunagan or PD supervisor Mills, they reassured themselves that they were acting to protect the welfare of children and to preserve peace and order in the community. In these beliefs they were enacting the spirit, if not the letter, of democratic government, as vigilantes did throughout the United States. They may not even have noticed that they had been mobilized by women and could even be said to be doing women's bidding.

In constructing and then purveying an alarm about the danger to the children, Louisa Gatti, Muriel Wright, May Simpson, the Abraham sisters-in-law, and some other Anglo women were assuming a responsibility of citizenship. In their vigilance in noting the danger and then acting to protect children at risk, they were performing a public duty and thus making themselves citizens. In a small way, they were redefining female citizenship. Throughout the world, women have aspired to and reached citizenship, or a piece of it, through defending children's welfare. Historians mainly study this activity in its formal, institutional mode, reconstructing the contributions of women who created orphanages, compulsory education, child welfare agencies. Such female political cultures usually started locally, in church, clubs, and charity, and Clifton's Anglo women were in their own modest way developing such a political culture.

Of course their motives were in part self-interested, both as individuals and as members of their class and race. Not only did they have vested interests in a segregated industry that kept their husbands in an elite position, but they also ended up keeping the children themselves. Of the eight women who led in organizing the kidnappings, seven took orphans. Of the sixteen Clifton couples who eventually seized and kept one each of the orphans, at least seven women led in organizing the kidnappings, and others may have played a role that is not preserved in any of the documents. But self-interest does not negate their commitment to public good, diminish the public significance of what they were doing, or distinguish them from many other child welfare activists now much revered. For what virtuous acts are not framed by how their doers see the world? It might seem that saving children is a universal value, free from bias. But some of the bitterest arguments are about what constitutes children's well-being and a good upbringing.

It is not possible to distinguish morally between an impersonal commitment to protect children and a personal desire to rescue one of them: both are ways of saving children, both originate in a maternalist sensibility about women's capacity and responsibility. Maternalism can range from a style of personal relations to a program for social responsibility. For these women it had not become consciously political, did not lead to a platform for institution or state building. Yet precisely in being so personal, in translating from sensibility to desire to irresistible force, the women's actions did build the power of the state. For nationally renowned urban reformers, maternalism helped construct protective legislation and a federal agency such as the U.S. Children's Bureau. The Clifton-Morenci women's contribution to state building was by comparison insignificant, but similar local efforts cumulatively helped create a legal precedent for how to adjudicate child custody disputes, a precedent that used racialized and class-ridden assumptions to determine what was in the best interests of a child. This means, then, that the orphan affair also helps us address another crucial question: what were women's unique stakes in racial power structures—in whiteness?[1]

To understand how female maternal desire led to male armed compulsion, we need to become acquainted with women's efforts toward "civilizing" the frontier. They called upon "family values" in strategizing to pacify the riotous, violent mining camps. Indeed, it seemed that the very rowdiness of the mining camps created an unusual respect for female gentility.[2]

Many of the Anglo women leaders had a sense of belonging, pride, and entitlement, which arose from their identities as pioneers, settlers who had experienced hardship. Prominent individuals and families of this group had been in the area for several decades, at least before the railroads—a significant marker in the definition of "pioneer." The Abraham brothers arrived with their father, who was the first manager of the Arizona Copper company store, in 1874; Laura (Sam's wife) came first to Silver City, New Mexico, as a child and had been in Clifton twenty-two or more years. Mr. and Mrs. Pascoe came to the area in 1880, Tom Simpson in 1879, Sheriff Parks and his family also in 1879, Henry and Rose Hill and the George Frazers at least by the 1880s. Mrs. Wright, Mrs. Reed, Mrs. Pascoe, and Mrs. Fountin had been in Clifton itself only three to five years, but the old-timers set the norm and created the confidence behind their collective sense of entitlement.[3]

The discourse about pioneering was a formative narrative chorus in American history, with some distinctly female form and content. Consider the themes in the following excerpt from the memoir of a Clifton woman, Sarah Butler York:

> In the spring of 1873, a party of sixteen persons, four women, seven men and five children, started from . . . Missouri . . . Our train consisted of covered wagons, drawn by oxen and a herd of cattle, driven by the younger men who were on horses. Our long, tedious journey required four months . . . Nine miles a day was the average distance we covered . . . On stormy nights the men did the cooking while the women and children remained in the wagons or tents . . . wood for cooking was our greatest problem and it was some time before the women would consent to use a fire made of buffalo chips . . . We . . . passed large herds of buffaloes . . . and saw many antelopes. Our men killed several antelopes and two buffaloes on the way and the fresh meat was very acceptable . . .
>
> When we came through the Sioux and Fox Indian Reservations in Western Kansas one of the men missed his dog . . . he went back to look for it . . . the Indians took him into a tepee where the dog was tied; no doubt they were preparing to have a feast of dog meat. The government had built good stone houses of two rooms for these Indians, but they would not use them and were living in ragged tepees nearby. They had used the floors and the window and door casings for fires. . . .
>
> [After staying a few years at the base of the Colorado Rockies, they found they could not get title to that land, so continued further southwest in 1877.] . . . we boarded an ox train, which consisted of sixteen immense

wagons, each drawn by ten or twelve yoke of oxen. . . . The man who owned the train promised to make the trip in six weeks but on account of having poor oxen and encountering stormy weather, we were almost three months on the way. . . . The drivers were all Mexicans. . . . They were good to the children and would want to hold them. This would have been a rest for me, as I had to hold my baby all day to keep her from falling out of the wagon, but they were so filthy and infested with vermin I didn't dare allow them to help me . . . We learned a few Mexican words, the alphabet and how to count. Mr. Chandler said we were not to ask the meaning of their songs as we could enjoy them better not to know. Since we were so long on the road our provisions gave out and we had to use the same food provided for the Mexicans; beans, flour, coffee, bacon and dried fruit. . . . One Mexican did die one night in the wagon next to ours. We heard him moaning and calling on God to help; it was bitterly cold and no one went to him . . .

　. . . we [lived] for a year in a Jacel [*jacal*] house, made by setting posts close together in the ground and daubing them with mud. It had a dirt roof and floor . . . my husband was engineer in the smelter, for over two years, then he took a herd of cattle on shares from Harvey Whitehill, sheriff of the county, and moved them out on the Gila river.[4]

Pioneer narratives such as this were constructed over time. Clifton's "pioneers" came in the ninteenth century, but most of the accounts of their voyages were produced several decades later, well into the twentieth century, when the personal nostalgia of old age had combined with the collective political valorization of a frontier gone by. The pioneer narrative, subspecies southwestern, Anglo, and female, featured labor, fortitude, and resourcefulness: the hardships, tedium, and discomfort of travel; the impediments to maintaining life and health on the trip; the drudgery, exhausting effort, unaccustomed demands, and need to develop unprecedented skills in the harsh conditions of the frontier; the irregularities in sexual division of labor that often developed as a result; strange foodstuffs; the loss of the seasons and flowers; difficulty in keeping clean and maintaining civility in dress and habitat; illness and death in the absence of medical care; the men's aspiration to move from location to location and their scorn for wage work as opposed to economic independence.[5] These chronicles, like those of other groups of women who traveled from the metropoles to the colonies, defied some conventional female virtues and turned some alternative female virtues into sources of self-respect. The resulting honor roll was sometimes internally contradictory, as are most value systems: toughness and stamina; optimism in facing many setbacks; courage and ability to survive alone or with little companionship; the innate delicacy of "true ladies"; adaptability to new and strange living conditions; resolute fidelity to higher standards of refinement, albeit standards that were temporarily in abeyance.[6] The challenges they met and conquered (or endured) came from two sources: the roughness of the natural environment and the coarseness of its "natives." In a rich and contradictory interpretation of their experience, pioneer women simultaneously reaffirmed female delicacy and celebrated their own defiance of delicacy in withstanding and transcending the roughness of the frontier.

After the initial voyage, repeated trips back home reconfirmed these meanings of pioneerhood. Throughout the last century, travel continued to offer hardships; even after the railroads came, the trips were dirty and hot, or cold, with poor sanitation, and plagued with delays. Anglo women frequently traveled unaccompanied by men, who could not be spared from their employment. Whether or not they experienced harassment, they must have worried about it. Yet their manless ventures only increased their pride, courage, and sense of independence. Even getting to Tucson was a significant expedition, and Tucson was far from a metropolis (it had about 10,000 people in 1904); you had to go to Los Angeles or Kansas City (each with a population of about 200,000) or Denver (perhaps 160,000) to get true big-city opportunities.[7] Yet Anglo women in small places like Clifton and Morenci traveled a lot. They typically went to see relatives, to escape the tedium and cultural desert of the mining camps, and to shop where better clothing and furniture could be had. They took their children to boarding schools in Tucson, Phoenix, or even California—in 1904, there was no high school at all in Clifton-Morenci. These voyages through the western wilderness reinforced their "civilizing" mission. Their vision limited by the blinders of their expectations, they gazed upon arid open lands, rough "native" settlements, and debased communities where Anglo women had not yet done their job, and these sights confirmed the urgency of their work and the value of their gentility.

Wearing the status of "pioneer" like a tiara that honored their social position, in writing their memoirs these women were not recalling fixed memories but living myths, already considerably different in the telling from renditions that might have been offered during the events described. These narratives, sought out and published in the pioneers' old age, as a form of homage, fused boasting and modesty in stylized form. Sarah York's narrative was written thirty to forty years after the events, reconstructed under the influence of a female form of Progressive Era celebration of U.S. expansion and entitlement to control the continent (even beyond the continent: by this time the United States had conquered its first overseas colonies). The Progressive womanhood ideology included white women's claims to leadership not only in domestic uplift and reform but also in international "civilization" through empire.

Although the new womanhood discourse was city-bred, it traveled well and found friends everywhere, including Clifton-Morenci. Local newspapers discussed and editorialized about women's rights, simultaneously denouncing "feminism" and influenced by it. Clifton's *Copper Era* covered President Roosevelt's "race suicide" pronouncement fully: the avoidance of reproduction by educated women is creating a dangerous, dysgenic tendency for the best American "stock" to produce too few children while the inferior produce too many; the woman who avoids her maternal destiny, "whether from viciousness, coldness, shallow-heartedness, self-indulgence . . . why, such a creature merits contempt as hearty as any visited upon the soldier who runs away in battle."[8] Roosevelt's vitriol pointed at urban, elite women forsaking marriage and motherhood in favor of higher education and professional or reform careers. "EDUCATED WOMEN UNFIT FOR WIVES," headlined the Solomonville newspaper in 1904.[9] Yet organized women, creatively, used his own rhetoric to justify all sorts of public-sphere activity in the name of bettering motherhood or advancing child welfare.

This political culture, like all others, expressed and helped shape America's foundational racial structures. The internal logic of the white-woman-as-civilizer claim paralleled that of some woman suffragists that "the woman's vote" could counteract black power, signifying that womanhood was white and blackness was male. In the big northeastern and midwestern cities, white women "civilizers" increasingly marked immigrants, not blacks, as the objects of their uplift efforts. In the same period "pioneer" women developed a similar uplift agenda in the West. Particularities of southeastern Arizona, notably the extreme ferocity of the Apaches until their final suppression in 1886 and the lack of large old agricultural Mexican communities, were interpreted by the "pioneer" women as legitimations for their high, "civilizing" mission. The pioneer talk of the early twentieth century echoed historian Frederick Jackson Turner's concept of the frontier as the meeting place between savagery and civilization.[10] The Arizona Territorial Legislature sought statehood, it said, "In behalf of that band of pioneers who have wrung from the savage this fair land of Arizona, in behalf of the citizens of Arizona, who have fought its battles and developed these conditions under which we now happily exist."[11] Looking back upon their earlier rough living and working conditions from the vantage of a finer, cleaner, and more technologically advanced experience in the early twentieth century, pioneer women projected an ideological mirage that Anglo life had always contrasted sharply with the alleged dirtiness and vulgarity of Indians and Mexicans, their food, family patterns, housing, religion, morals, work habits, and craftsmanship. Progressive women reinvented pioneering as an act of civilizing, which in turn was inescapably racialized.

Anglo pioneer narrators sometimes registered the presence of Mexican residents when they arrived, but they did not consider those residents pioneers. Indians were present as obstacles to the pioneering, never as pioneers themselves. Indeed, a substantial part of what pioneering *meant* was racial: that which had to be braved, endured, and transformed was the low civilization of the earlier inhabitants. Pioneer talk inverted the power relations of U.S. conquest of western North America, representing the eastern migrants as victims, the native westerners as aggressors.[12] This reversal provided a frame in which women's courage could be recognized, as in the yarns about women with rifles defending self, home, and children against terrorizing Apaches, while maintaining fealty to women's "true" fragility and dependence. But women's conquest stories were more often social, emphasizing the culture and cleanliness they brought. Their narratives reversed also the racial logic of East Coast Americanizers: those reformers identified themselves, by the early twentieth century, as virtually indigenous residents facing immigrants of inferior ways of life. In Clifton everyone was an immigrant, but only some counted as pioneers, as the authors of progress.[13]

Occasionally, later in the twentieth century, a Mexican pioneer might be acknowledged, but at the turn of the century only Anglos were pioneers. Pioneer talk encoded a racial system considerably different from that in the urban Atlantic and Midwest. "Anglo" was a larger category here than "white" was there. Jews, for example, were within the circle, not even near the margins. German Jews had been central in the development of the Southwest in the late nineteenth century, making fortunes from government contracts to supply the Indian-fighting armies. Henry Lesinsky, founder of Clifton, had in this way tripled his capital from $100,000 to $300,000 in six years.[14] The Abrahams were recognized leaders within the Clifton-Morenci business community, not just its Jewish sector, and their hotel was a headquarters for commercial networking. Laura Abraham was not Jewish, but in Clifton her marriage was not an intermarriage. Jews were not only accepted but accepted as Jews. In 1903, for example, Judge Mashbir gave a talk to the Ladies Literary Club, in his Solomonville courtroom, on the persecution of Jews in Russia.[15] A latent Anglo anti-Semitism remained and no doubt could have been activated under the right circumstances, but it was stifled by the unifying force of other alliances and enmities, and by the visible benefits of Jewish investment.[16] Mexicans, if they harbored anti-Semitic feelings, seemed to conflate Jews with Anglos in general, resenting the "prying, obtrusive and calculating manners of the Yankee and the Jew," which had forced out the "dignified, grave and courteous bearing" of the old Mexican merchants.[17] As the Jews had always been Anglos here, so too the Irish. Henry Hill was Clifton's richest capitalist, at the acme of its society, and Hugh Quinn, saloon owner, was as Anglo as the Jewish and WASP businessmen. Some of the Euro-Latins, located between whites and Mexicans, even laid claim to pioneer status, such as Ippolitto Cascarelli, Fermin Palicio, and Antonio Spezia, and John and Louisa Gatti's rise to prominence during the orphan affair moved them closer to Clifton-Morenci's pioneer ranks.

"PIONEER" WAS A RACIAL TERM but not exactly a class term. Those of modest as well as those of high circumstances could be pioneers. And the vast majority of these Anglo settler women worked hard, dirtying and roughening their hands, quite unlike urban ladies of this time. Yet class structure was to play a large role in creating the prominent place Anglo women were able to occupy in Clifton's progress. This does not mean that upper-class women led. In fact, those who led in the orphan affair did not include any women who could be placed at the very top of Clifton-Morenci wealth and power. Charles Mills, *mayordomo* of Morenci, manager of Detroit Copper's operations, was unmarried. Elizabeth Scott Wallace Colquhoun, wife of the Scottish manager of Arizona Copper, did not participate in the "rescue" of the orphans. Rather, in Clifton, as opposed to Morenci, a strong small business class was holding its own against the huge absentee copper lords, and the women of this class took the lead.

Louisa Gatti was a perfect example. Born in the Arizona Territory of German parents, married to an Italian immigrant, she differed sharply from both Mrs. Abrahams, Etta Reed, and Muriel Wright in education and refinement: she spoke an ungrammatical, coarse English and did not comport herself like a lady. She was not genteel. These characteristics combined with her husband's nationality, had kept her at the edge of Anglo women's society. But the events of 1903–1904 may have had a doubled personal meaning for her: not only did she acquire a new son but she also slid into a more central and secure position among Clifton-Morenci's Anglos. As race lines grew firmer, class—when viewed as a matter of culture—mattered less.

Mrs. Colquhoun's son, James Clifton Colquhoun, gave a privileged child's view of Clifton's class hierarchy in his biography of his father:

> The other houses in [his] row were occupied by senior staff of the Company, always addressed as "Mr." . . . Then there were the heads of departments, whose christian names were used in place of "Mr.": Archie Morrison and John Grimes in the concentrator; George Fraser[18] in the smelter; Mike Reardon on the railway . . . On the opposite side of the river from our house there were many more buildings: dance halls, saloons and gambling dens, of which our side was completely free. I well remember the music and other weird noises which at night drifted across the river. The workmen were Mexican; although there was a time when they were Chinese.[19]

The women ringleaders were mainly wives of men Colquhoun could address by their Christian names—a neat and succinct measure of status—but they were not his employees. Rather, they were small businessmen and artisans, distinct from both the big capitalists and their managers at the top and the wage workers at the bottom. The women who set the indignation meeting in motion were wives of hotel keepers, an undertaker, a locomotive engineer, and owners of saloons, a furniture store, and a lumberyard. The richest among them were wives of ranchers, like Parks and Gatti, who were producers as well as merchants. Wives of PD or Arizona Copper employees were not leaders in these events. (The only exception was Mrs. George Frazer, who saw the orphans arrive at the railroad station and got an orphan herself, but was not vocal in spreading word of the crisis or at the indignation meeting.) Nor did professional families lead in the citizens' meetings or posses—Clifton's lawyers and doctors and their wives apparently stayed home.

But this class of entrepreneurs was by no means homogeneous, unconflicted, or stationary. In many pioneer locations, an elite group of bankers and businessmen, usually Protestant, Republican, and of northern European origin, presided over the community.[20] In Clifton-Morenci, two factors altered that structure: the presence among the elite of copper company employees, working for absentee capital, and of southern Democrats. Here the small businessmen had an ambivalent relation to the copper barons: on the one hand, virtually all commerce owed its livelihood to provisioning the copper works; but, on the other hand, the copper companies threatened to violate, even roll over, the interests of the business community. If businessmen formed a top edge of the "middle class," the bottom was occupied by skilled workers, although the boundary was fuzzy. Many of the businessmen, like the undertaker Pascoe and the builder Freeman, also worked with their own hands. And many skilled workers, like Simpson and Riordan, railroad conductor and engineer, respectively, were on their way up—planning and investing for a future as businessmen, not workers or professionals. Most ambitious men aspired to economic independence, not to waged or even salaried labor, although some were beginning to sense that independence was not likely in Clifton-Morenci given the absorption of the copper companies by giant international corporations.

The predominance of business-class women as leaders may have arisen from their daily life experience, for among this group women's labor was particularly essential and public. The commercial viability of shops often depended on the unpaid labor of wives and older daughters. These middle-class women often worked twelve- to sixteen-hour days, on their feet constantly. Women waited on customers and cleaned the shops and workshops. They managed inventory, ordered goods and supplies, kept the books. Hiring help would, in many cases, have wiped out profits. And where could one find hired help to whom one could entrust the resources of the business? What employee could be relied on to provide the warmth, familiarity, and personal touch that made customers comfortable? Who could report gossip, network, and keep up with new products that Cliftonians would buy? When the seven businessmen's wives who were among the leading agitators informed all of Anglo Clifton that there was a crisis with the orphans, they were doing the same thing they did in their shops, and they were using the public confidence they had developed in part from that work.

And yet, when the dust settled, Clifton's upper class had received a share of these valuable orphans without having done the "work" to get them. Somehow orphans came into the hands of Henry and Rose Hill—he was Clifton's biggest real estate developer, creator of "Hill's Addition" (later known as South Clifton), a member of the Graham County Board of Supervisors, and vice president of the First National Bank. Harry Laskey, a department head for Detroit Copper, took a child, as did J. G. Cooper, treasurer of Arizona Copper. It was as if the rough proceedings of expropriating the Mexicans' foster children had replicated the larger expropriations of class.

These class categories are helpful only if they are used to define relationships, not static positions. Classes are pulsating organisms, ever moving and changing shape, and Clifton's middle-class heart was beating particularly fast and hard in this boom time for mining, rapidly increasing its wealth, consolidating its power and position. With hindsight we can see that this "old middle class" of independent businessmen was destined to give way to the new class of employees, but in 1904 copper's dominance had not yet had that effect. The mining camp was in the midst of its greatest decade of economic growth thus far. Its 1910 population, about 4,900 in Clifton and 5,000 in Morenci, had doubled since 1900. Arizona Copper profits multiplied seven times between 1894 and 1903, and its works at this moment were the largest in Arizona. Detroit Copper in Morenci, soon to overtake Arizona Copper, returned 36 percent on investments in 1909 and 1910 (the earliest years for which figures are available).[21] Both companies were building at an unprecedented rate, employing many kinds of laborers in addition to miners and smelter and mill workers. Arizona Copper was building not only a bigger industrial plant but also flood control embankments, new schools, and a town library. The company store in Clifton could not supply the rapidly growing demand for consumer and construction goods, so smaller sources of mercantile capital were investing heavily. Indeed, in the early years of mining the merchants who supplied mining towns got rich faster than the mine prospectors and developers.[22] Although the mines were leaping ahead, the local businessmen were still doing well. Chase Creek seemed continually under construction in these years. Clifton's First National Bank organized in 1901, and Morenci's Gila Valley Bank in 1902. Louis Ferber, one of the Jews so prominent in this early mercantile development, had opened a brokerage in Clifton. Four Anglo law offices (largely dealing with land, water, and mining claims) and five mining engineering and surveying offices flourished. Arizona Copper's Arizona and New Mexico Railroad began its daily passenger service in 1901.

Clifton's bourgeoisie, if we can call it that, was somewhat divided politically. Clifton-Morenci usually had a Democratic majority, which was typical of western mining camps, but in Arizona the Democrats were differently composed: Most of the Mexican mineworkers could not or did not vote, and a significant proportion of the elite were Democrats, in part because so many of them were of southern U.S. origin. (By contrast, in Rocky Mountain mining camps the elite was usually Republican.) Clifton-Morenci also had a substantial Republican minority—the party split was usually about 60/40, depending on the particular electoral contest—so the camp was by no means a solid Democratic bloc. Democrat Judge P. C. Little ran unopposed in 1904, for example, and Democrat Sheriff Parks won by a slightly greater margin, but in the Congressional election, Clifton went for the Democrat and Morenci and Metcalf for the Republican.[23] Between 1903 and 1906 Clifton even had two newspapers, as a Democratic operation tried to compete with the mine-dominated Republican *Copper Era.* (The mine owners in Morenci also published a Spanish-language paper, *El Obrero,* aimed at the Mexican workers.) Nationally, attitudes toward nonwhites, however conceived, divided the parties, but in Clifton-Morenci dependence on Mexican and other foreign labor produced convergence on a pro-immigrant position, until the 1903 strike temporarily fractured that unity.

Unity also prevailed across party lines on the question of statehood. Virtually every Anglo in the area wanted Arizona to become a state and resisted joint statehood with New Mexico, primarily because of hostility to incorporating New Mexico's greater proportion of Mexican citizens. Ironically, this very racism led Congressional leaders to oppose statehood or to propose it on terms Arizonans would reject. Senator and historian Albert Beveridge, ardent racist supporter of U.S.

imperialism and chair of the Committee on Territories, feared state-hood for a variety of interlocking Progressive reasons: conviction that statehood was a scheme of big business interests, who would control the state government and provide enormous subsidies for their pro-jects; anxiety, shared by the president and by Gifford Pinchot, chief of the U.S. Forest Service, that statehood would result in spoliation of the natural resources of the territory; and prejudice against Mexicans and Mormons, Beveridge's most enduring, passionate, unbending convic-tion. A joint Arizona–New Mexico state would have diminished the relative size of the Mexican vote, but it would have increased it for the Arizonans.[24]

The largest fissure among Clifton's capitalists pitted mining against every other interest. The economic activity second to mining was ranching, and its substantial capital investment and profit would have been itself cause for celebration–and criticism from other smaller interests–were it not for the dominance of copper. In 1883 the Clifton newspaper reported stock-raising profits of 100 to 500 percent. Graham County's 1902 livestock assessment calculated $470,000 and $111,000 in horses, not to mention mules, burros, hogs, goats, and sheep.[25] The orphan incident featured an interesting reversal of a typical western film or novel plot, in which ranching interests often threaten to trample the civic rights and virtues of townspeople; here, by contrast, the ranchers allied with the white townspeople in the orphan affair, while big capital (mining) either remained a bystander or tried to cool them off and defend law and order.[26] Conflicts of interest between mining and ranching surfaced repeatedly, the main one fought over water, as the mines and ore-processing plants sought to quench their ravenous thirsts. Many Mexican farmers and ranchers had been effectively dispossessed by the loss of their water supply, and Anglo landowners were trying to fight back against similar threats. Water rights disputes frequently reached the courts. An environmental protection movement developed, based on economic self-interests. Just as the orphans arrived, ranchers and farmers were organizing to limit the slag and tailings dumps, which damaged land and water. The *Copper Era* threatened that ranchers and farmers "cannot help them-selves by killing the mining interests" and caricatured the California "Anti-Debris Association," which was protesting such dumping.[27]

A conflict over the incorporation of Clifton as a municipality pro-duced similar alignments. Clifton's middle class was eager for incorporation at the turn of the century. Particularly those concerned with public health—hundreds had died from typhus, dysentery, and malaria before about 1900, and there was an epidemic of typhoid the year the orphans came—wanted a taxation system on which to float public bonds and with which to develop sanitation measures and hire a town health officer. But Colquhoun and his staff opposed incorporation because of the tax burden it would impose on Arizona Copper, and they managed to stave it off until 1909.[28] (Morenci never incorporated.) The copper interests resisted separating off Greenlee County from Graham County for the same reasons, and held off the imposition of state taxes on their property and copper production for many years.[29]

DESPITE THESE SIMILAR PATTERNS and a common boom in investment and productivity, the political economies of Clifton and Morenci were diverging. Morenci was becoming a formal, legal company town, the provincial capital of a private kingdom. By 1915 PD controlled major newspapers in five Arizona towns and cities—Tucson's *Arizona Daily Star,* Phoenix's *Arizona Gazette,* Douglas's *International Gazette,* Clifton's *Copper Era,* and Bisbee's *Daily Review,* not to mention its Morenci Spanish-language paper. It "influenced public school curriculums, manipulated lawyers and doctors, and even intervened in church politics to eliminate liberal ministers."[30] Today Morenci remains one of the few specimens of 100 percent company-owned towns left in America. Clifton was a company town in a more indirect sense—its economy depended on Arizona Copper, but independent entrepreneurs continued to thrive by supplying its population.[31] Metaphorically the twosome can be compared by thinking of Morenci as a state-controlled, and Clifton as a mixed, economy, with a copper barony functioning as the state in both cases.

The key to Morenci's history was the region's shortage of labor power in relation to the potential profits of copper extraction. Company towns are complex and expensive operations, established only when a steady supply of labor is not otherwise available. They are most commonly found in mining camps, which are often remote from large population concentrations. Copper was more likely than gold or silver to produce company towns because profitable copper extraction required massive capital investment, unlikely to be risked if the labor force was unreliable.[32]

If Clifton seemed not quite civilized at the turn of the century, Morenci was barbaric. It was literally just a "camp." Its violence and vice won Morenci the name "Hell Town." Miners lived in tents or crude shelters and prepared meals over outdoor fires. There was no sanitation system whatsoever. One resident of that era reminisced, "one might think Morenci had a corner on tin cans, as every where one looked they could be seen piled in heaps. Fresh fruit and vegetables were almost forgotten commodities, consequently every one resorted to canned goods. After using the contents the cans were thrown out the back door, provided the house boasted two doors, and allowed to accumulate until a big rain came and washed them together with loose rocks, old shoes, bones and other refuse, pell mell down the canyon."[33] Shallow outhouses leeched into shallow wells; many shacks and boarding houses lacked outhouses altogether and dumped refuse into gulches; the density of population was too great for natural decomposition to break down the waste. In summer heavy rains carried filth into the creek and river and started "plague season." The mine management in the 1880s and 1890s preached to the miners on the virtues of cleanliness and sanitation but did little to remedy these public health hazards. Just months before the orphans came, Detroit Copper for the first time hired a team to clean up the litter in Morenci canyon.[34] Then in 1897 a fire destroyed most of the Morenci shacks and provided Detroit Copper's superintendent, Charles Mills, a chance to build an orderly settlement from scratch.

Today's Morenci is a direct product of Mills's vision, and visiting it is a startling experience for the outsider who has not grown up in a company town. It is not incorporated, yet it is the most corporate of towns.[35] Phelps Dodge owns all the land, every building, every facility, and virtually every service except the U.S. mail and the schools. PD owns the only significant store, PD Mercantile, a supermarket that sells food, clothing, hardware, furniture, and appliances; it owns the movie theater, the gas station, the motel, the restaurant. A few small private shops rent from PD—a beauty parlor, a video rental store, a pizza parlor. It owns all the approximately twelve hundred houses, renting them to employees, who are required to vacate upon leaving PD employment—retirees have six months to get out. PD runs the water, sewer, fire, and ambulance services. There is a public school district with elected commissioners, but that is the only element of representative government.

Today's Morenci is a completely different town than Old Morenci, of course. The old town was several miles further from Clifton, fifteen hundred feet higher, built, like Clifton, in the crevices and canyons among mountains that were steadily more hollowed out by the mines. When June Nash entitled her study of Bolivian miners *We Eat the Mines and the Mines Eat Us,* she was using a workers' metaphor about the way that mining simultaneously supports and devours the miners. In Morenci the relationship was not metaphorical: the mines ate up the town. In 1937, PD sent in the first steam shovel to begin the process of transforming a mine underneath a mountain into a pit. Between 1965 and 1982 every last Morenci dweller was evacuated, and every foot of dirt and stone that was the Old Morenci fell into the vast open-pit mine, its shimmering colors announcing its position as the jewel in PD's crown.

The source of this treasure was Mills's ability to multiply mining profits, and his company town was critical in the process, because the profits depended on creating a town livable enough to attract and hold a work force. In addition to the usual sources of labor discipline, he used stores and the credit they offered to supply the workers, keep them in debt, and supplement his profits; and his control over the living environment helped him discipline his workers and reduce their ability to organize against him. He established the Morenci Water Company in 1898 and the Morenci Improvement Company, a housing construction operation, in 1900. He had a new townsite leveled and graded farther up the canyon. By 1901 he had built over fifty residences of three to five rooms each, renting for $12–$20 per month, and a forty-two-room lodging house with a barber shop and bath. The private homes soon had electric lights and outdoor bathrooms. In 1905 he had the outdoor latrines removed from the better residential areas and replaced with indoor toilets. Later in the century several PD operations, notably water, electricity, and the hospital, were extended to Clifton as well, and PD Mercantile became the major store for both towns.

In the early twentieth century these benefits were reserved almost entirely for management and the minority of Anglo workers. The Anglos paid for their homes and utilities out of wages that averaged 150 perent those of the Mexicans, in addition to the bigger differential created by the segregation of jobs themselves. In 1903 Detroit Copper's list of foremen included no Mexicans. Even the locker rooms and showers the miners finally won remained segregated until the 1950s. The company town gradually took in the Mexicans, and encouraged family houses, not only to attract workers but also because management believed that men with families would prove more stable, harder-working, and less likely to strike or quit. (The next chapter will show this to have been a poor prediction.)

But the company town was strictly segregated. At first Mexican workers paid ground rent for dwellings they built themselves. When the company provided housing for Mexicans, it did so in a separate townsite, Newtown, referred to by the whites as "Tortilla Flats"; Stargo, the Anglo townsite, was so off-limits that well into the 1950s if Mexican children went there to play, PD security officers would run them off. When PD provided Mexican houses, they were all just two rooms, no matter how many children in the family. Blueprints (from another PD company town, in Tyrone, New Mexico) illustrated this way of thinking—that Mexicans did not need or desire better homes. The plans provided for nondetached Mexican homes, each 20 feet by 10 feet, which consisted of two rooms—a kitchen and a living room, 10 by 10 each—with no bathroom or indoor plumbing; the cost of construction was $525 per unit, and they rented for $6 a month. There were two models for "American" families: a three-room semidetached house 30 feet by 20 feet, with living room, bedroom, enclosed porch, kitchen, closet, and bath, at a cost of $1,827 per unit and a rent of $18 a month; and a four-room detached house 37.5 feet by 21 feet, with living room, dining room, bedroom, front porch, sleeping porch, kitchen, enclosed rear porch, closet, and bath, at a cost of $2,547 per unit, and a rent of $27 per month.[36]

The Anglos appreciated the order and cleanliness of Mills's company-town-in-the-making, women pointing with particular enthusiasm to its reduction of lawlessness. "Man may go alone into places taking chances for his own welfare, but he will hesitate when it comes to taking mother, wife, sisters and children . . . the fact that the . . . Companies own . . . the land upon which the town is located, thereby prohibiting the location thereon of any vicious or lawless element . . . discountenance and debar of itself any attempt at invasion by the undesirable class."[37] This morality was of course a matter of zoning: Mills's regime exiled saloons, dance halls, and prostitutes from Stargo to Newtown.

The power structure of Mills's copper republic of Morenci announced itself with a large central plaza, an industrial restatement of a classical form, whose size, hierarchy, and architectural style delivered unmistakable messages. Overlooking and triangulating a large railroad freight station and switching operation stood three massive, multistory "public" buildings: the company store, the Morenci Hotel, and the Morenci Club, built in 1899, 1900, and 1901, respectively. The club and hotel were designed by architect Henry Trost of El Paso, who introduced into Arizona the mission revival style—an amalgam incorporating the horizontal lines of the prairie school with Spanish-Moorish flamboyant, curving decoration.[38] Luxurious, slightly whimsical mansions, of graceful proportions, were situated disconcertingly next to half-loaded flat cars, stacks of lumber and pig iron, and men in sombreros and dirty pants wheeling barrows or leading strings of burros—the disorderly, dirty, accoutrements of the southwestern industrial age. The juxtaposition recapitulated the contradictions of Anglo life in the copper camp—hardship and luxury, sweat and finery, masculine camaraderie and feminine stylishness; the refinements were the more valued because life was so hard. The club was for members only ($1.25 per month) and entirely off-limits to Mexicans. One woman who grew up in Morenci described the color of another woman to me by saying, she was so white, she could walk into the Morenci Club— and she was referring to the 1940s at the earliest.[39] The club featured lectures, a ladies' exercise class, billiards and pool, bowling, baths, a library and reading room "containing all of the prominent dailies, scientific papers and magazines of the country," a game room, a bar, and a gym. The club's most expressive feature, from the outside, was its second-floor veranda facing south and the plaza. There gentlemen sat in colonial-style outdoor furniture and took in the sun, their drinks, and Morenci's high cool breezes as they surveyed the industrial motion below; and they could be seen from below by the men who worked for them.[40]

The hotel provided a second, more bustling clubhouse, not only for visitors but also for local professionals and managers since it also housed the bank, the post office, the telephone company, and the Morenci Water and Improvement Companies. Here along with twenty-three spacious and elegant guest rooms, lighted by electricity and heated by steam, with electric call bells and private bathrooms, was a beautiful lounge featuring a massive stone fireplace, a ladies' parlor, and a restaurant with "cuisine of the highest character." You could eat here and charge the meals to your company store account, to be deducted from your pay envelope, if you could afford the prices.[41]

To the region's promoters these buildings stood for the ultimate retort to those who criticized modern "soulless" corporations. "The 'soulless corporation' ship, launched some years ago by the agitating jaw-smiths . . . appears to have stranded somewhere on the sands of despair, and a long way from the handsome port of Morenci; for here may be seen one of the most substantial evidences of what men with souls may do in behalf of the social conditions of their employees."[42] An odd statement, regarding two buildings from which the over-whelming majority of employees were excluded, but one which be-comes more comprehensible when we add the third building, the company store. This institution provoked universal passions, whether positive or negative, because it made absolutely direct the connection between class status and luxurious consumption that was still a novelty for many in the American middle class. As anthropologist Josiah Heyman put it, "Such [company] towns are an extreme, and otherwise rarely encountered, distillation of the wage earning situation in which foundational aspects of the labor market are repeated endlessly outside of work, leaving little or no way of constructing diversified sets of social involvement. One knows exactly how a person stands in corporate power from the size of the house," the clothing, and the purchases.[43]

Despite its remote location, in 1904 the Detroit Copper store could rival any other company store in the United States for size and variety of goods relative to the population served. A massive building that an architect has described as "Industrial Romanesque with traces of Gothic Revival and Chicago School," built of steel girders resting on limestone pilasters and walls, it was the largest department store in Arizona.[44] Polished wood and glass counters in a high-ceilinged room 75 feet by 150 feet, displayed its goods in a manner still new to those who shopped at traditional stores: clothing, shoes, jewelry, patent medicines, food, hardware, liquor, kitchenware, and furniture; miners' wives could see fine imported items next to the rough necessities they purchased on credit. The store's supremely efficient design, symboliz-ing and practicing a new rationalization, was cause for admiration among Arizona boosters and customers:

Leaving the main salesroom and proceeding to the basement, it is here manifested the masterly forethought which worked out the details of this remarkable warehouse of sales distribution . . . The trains of the Morenci South R. R. [PD's private train line] comes [*sic*] directly to a platform from which goods are received and discharged directly into the basement. A steel trolley takes the meats upon hooks to a scale, where being weighed, are conveyed on same into a cold storage room, having a capacity of 50 beeves . . . Butter, lard, eggs, etc., are each given seperate [*sic*] rooms and kept in perfect condition . . . You will witness no noise, confusion or unusual bustle on the main floor in filling orders, no slamming down till covers and throwing of scoops into barrels, for this has all been provided for in the basement. Here is a corps of able-bodied, active young men, all busily engaged filling the orders sent down by the salesmen . . . Think of this business balanced to a penny every night before the bookkeepers go home. Think of upwards of 1,000 employees, with pass books, with credits in them from 50 cents to $25.00 . . . and yet at the close of business every day, precisely what the company owes every man, or what he owes the company is known to the office . . . Reports in military precision are placed in the manager's hands daily, so that he is in constant touch with every branch of the business.[45]

If at first it seems odd that all the public buildings were segregated except the store, a bit of contemplation shows that the system thrived because everyone could see the imported brie (literally) next to the beans. In such a store the goods tell a story of stratification as vividly as do the mine, mill, and smelter divisions of labor. And in such a bookkeeping system, the worker would not win many arguments with management over how much he owes.

How I wish I could report all this first hand. I try to visualize the carefully watered pitch where the cricket team played in its whites, the servants bringing drinks to spectators, the wooden and glass counters of the old store, but it is all gone, into the pit. There are few clues to the past in today's Morenci: The New PD Mercantile is like a Kmart or a SuperSafeway, only distinguishable by the fact that it sells T-shirts, baseball caps, and key rings with PD slogans and insignia.

In 1904 rationalized company-built Morenci had only just been constructed, and most people still lived in haphazard worker-built Morenci. Yet Mexican men built the company houses, and many Mexican women knew them intimately because they worked as maids for the white women; in this colonial economy, even working-class white families were typically able to hire Mexican women for as little as twenty-five to fifty cents a day. Most Mexicans shopped in the old way, for there were still many independent small merchants and peddlers. Morenci had two mills grinding *nixtamal,* Chinese green grocers, Mexican grocery stores, barbers, a tailor, Chinese launderers, and pool halls, just like Clifton.[46] The difference was that in Morenci, where independent businesses were fewer and smaller, they were also over-whelmingly Mexican; because there was not much future in business here, and because there were fewer Anglos, independent Anglos did not enter commerce. Even the Mexican workers increasingly relied on the company store for their staple foods and consumer goods. Since many Mexican shoppers–especially women–could not find the time and energy to walk with their children up and down the steep hills to the store, or did not feel comfortable actually entering the glittering emporium, they placed and collected their orders when deliverymen like Neville Leggatt stopped by. The colonial culture was growing. Once a year a PD event welcomed all–a Christmas celebration for the children on the central plaza, beneath the club, hotel, and company store. One child in each family would bring a gunny sack to carry home the gifts–typically three or four oranges and apples, a box of crackerjacks, and a small gift. It was a much anticipated event for the children, but at least one mother had mixed feelings as she recalled that PD deducted one dollar from each worker's pay envelope to pay for this party.[47]

A CANOPY OF COLONIALISM sheltered and enclosed both Morenci and Clifton. Even the foundations and walls of this mining camp were formed out of relationships that can be characterized as those of internal colonialism–a colony of the United States within its borders.[48] Achieved by conquest, the southwestern colonial territory featured racial discrimination and segregation, a culture in which education could be achieved only through deference to Anglo norms and self-righteousness, and substantial disenfranchisement of the colonized. The fit between class and race categories was very close in Clifton-Morenci, modified by the incorporation of a small Mexican American elite into the middle classes and some white workers into the proletariat. Prominent in the 1970s, disputed in the 1980s, the internal colonialism theory illuminates well the structural position of Anglo and Mexican Americans in Clifton-Morenci society and economy in the early twentieth century.

By identifying a connection between Mexicans in the Southwest and colonial subjects abroad, the internal colonialism theory reminds us of the global context of U.S. annexation of Mexican territory—a context of worldwide colonization in which Arizona has parallels with, say, Puerto Rico and South Africa. It disputes, by contrast, the parallel between European immigration into the eastern United States, which became the paradigm for most scholarship on ethnicity, and the Mexicans who came to work in the southwestern United States. No matter that particular Mexican mine workers made individual, free choices to "immigrate," their experience in the United States was structured by that of earlier Mexican residents who were involuntarily incorporated. Mexican American identity and discrimination against Mexican Americans were shaped by the U.S. conquest of Mexico and the consequent supremacy of Anglos. Correspondingly, the Anglo identity and experience in the Southwest were shaped by the U.S. conquest of Mexico and the consequent subordination of Mexican Americans.

Internal colonialism produced a distinctive racialized labor system. It featured a dual or segregated labor market and a dual set of working conditions for whites and Mexicans; the use of Mexican workers as a reserve labor force, drawn in and expelled to fit the needs of capital; and the use of peonage, or extraeconomic forms of coercion to control the labor force. The last feature obtained mainly in the virtually indentured Mexican labor in agriculture and on the railroad, but some aspects of it also pertained in Morenci—for example, PD's control of the police force and authority to evict and banish anyone it considered objectionable. Clifton-Morenci's economic success rested on a typically colonial system of absentee-owner exploitation of natural resources, accomplished through hiring labor at below-subsistence cost in relation to the economy from which the capital comes and to which the profits go. The colonized workers in the system were geographically excluded from the power to change occupations readily. Their labor was cheap because of their connection to a foreign but nearby and less-developed economy, that is, these workers sustained themselves, in part, through dependence on a nonindustrial family economy in Mexico. Anglos, using a deeply ingrained predilection toward racial explanation, translated this international economic relationship into a sincere belief that Mexicans inherently needed less to live on and did not crave the comforts that whites needed in order to work well. Thus Anglos saw no injustice in the dual wage system. By 1917 Clifton-Morenci copper workers had won a promise to eliminate it. But to the extent that it ended the dual wage system, PD merely shifted almost all "unskilled" jobs into Mexican hands and reserved skilled or managerial positions for whites. Then the dual wage scale merely relocated and reappeared as a differential between mining camps: in Clifton-Morenci, because it was a Mexican camp, wages were well below those paid at the white camps such as Bisbee or Globe-Miami.

Internal colonialism, as developed thus far, has been an imperfect theory. By explaining white supremacy on the basis of economic self-interest, the theory cannot explain irrational aspects of the racial system, such as white unionists' hostility to including Mexicans, and is vulnerable to the well-known critique of Marxist theories of imperialism, that is, that imperialism did not produce net profits for the metropoles. By using "race" or "nation" as its fundamental category, it cannot explain the fact that PD paid more at (white) Bisbee and yet maintained excellent profits there, or that PD worked as hard to suppress unions in the white camps as in the Mexican camp. Internal colonialism theory can miss the ways in which racial definitions and the many discourses that helped create them are often independent of class relations. The theory usually ignores culture entirely and never fully considered gender. But the recent scholarly emphasis on deconstructing colonialism, taking note of its internal variety, contingencies, and contradictions, should not blind us to the theory's useful work in pointing to general underlying structures of power and profit.

Internal colonialism explanations work better for Clifton-Morenci in particular than for the whole Southwest. At the turn of the century the Mexican camp might have seemed a textbook case for the theory: wages could be low because they had a higher value in Mexico; the workers could be sucked in or blown away as management needed; racial stratification was the fundamental organizing principle of two completely separated labor markets; and the future was . . . apartheid.

The structural differences between Clifton and Morenci point to different models of colonial settlement. Old Morenci was like a state-owned economy. The model means, of course, categorizing Phelps Dodge as a state, which is not much of a stretch: PD was indubitably the government in Morenci, and it wielded tremendous state power throughout Arizona. In Clifton power was more diffuse, its concentration in the hands of Arizona Copper both weaker and more veiled. Copper officials wore that veil in Clifton as a sign of respect for Clifton's other men of standing, but those independent businessmen and employees chose not to lift it, for to pierce the copper company's disguise was to reduce their own status. The orphan incident was to reveal both the differences between these two systems of colonialism and their likeness.

What I like most about the internal colonialism analysis is the accuracy of the imagery it elicits: associating Clifton-Morenci with foreign colonial society and culture, with India, South Africa, Algeria, Cuba–capturing exactly what I saw in the old pictures and heard in my interviews. As in Third World colonies, race corresponded not only with the class structure but also with the geography of this Mexican camp in 1904. If you walked between Anglo and Mexican neighborhoods, the changes in sights, sounds, smells, language, children's games, and etiquette seemed like foreign travel.

But these border crossings were not symmetrical: Mexicans daily walked into white territory–mines, mills, smelters, houses–where they worked for whites, often under white supervision. To survive they needed to know a great deal more about Anglo life and Anglo individuals than most Anglos did about Mexicans.

And yet many Anglos believed the opposite. Part of the basis of the Anglos' sovereignty, as could be heard over and over in their justification for kidnapping the orphans, was their confidence that they knew "the Mexicans," what they were like, and therefore how to manage them. This colonial knowledge provided the whites with the confidence they needed to operate the camp, because although the Mexicans were in general no more natives of these parts than the Anglos, the Mexicans were more numerous, usually more efficient in coping with the terrain and climate, and more essential to the economy. The mining managers and foremen discussed the best personnel and supervision practices, as their wives did in relation to their servants. Storekeepers and saloon owners–the whole small business group–had to know Mexican tastes. Many plebian Anglos, like deliveryman Neville Leggatt, needed knowledge of the Mexican community to do their jobs. Believable claims to intimacy with the Mexicans could prove a remunerative asset, as the copper companies employed spies, from at least 1903, to report on the Mexican workers' discontents and organizing. The Anglos all used a bit of Spanish and prided themselves on their knowledge of the Mexicans' food, fiestas, religious holidays, superstitions. Above all the Anglos' assurance that they knew "the Mexicans" supported their poise as governors, their identity as superior to the "natives" who were not really natives.

For colonialism shaped Anglo as well as Mexican identities. In much of the United States, whiteness tended to be invisible, which was a large part its source of power in this democratic country. The white citizen became the norm, his or her countenance, culture, and bearing the universal taken-for-granted mode of being, so that others became not simply different but lacking. In Clifton-Morenci, by contrast, whiteness was more visible because whites were the minority. Often labeled "Americans," whites here benefited from the joining of race, nationality, and citizenship, which endowed their composite identity with a proud and explicit sense of superiority. Moreover, Clifton-Morenci's whites were led by a self-conscious elite that set standards to which others aspired and/or deferred. The very poverty of the "natives" and the very roughness of their living conditions seemed to steer the "colonizers" toward ever greater luxury and ostentation. One mining historian compared this managerial caste to that described by W. Somerset Maugham his stories of the South Sea Islands: "local administrators–congregated in a tight, friendly clique–[who] maintained their identities as wardens if not as nabobs . . . Unlike pillars of the community in more traditional, familiar American settings, the mine and smelter operators felt no compulsion toward demagogic propriety . . . they had acquired gracious and hedonic tastes."[49] For the poorest Anglos, whiteness became a standard to live up to, and thus also a source of anxiety.

Women helped reconstruct this colonial culture. They were less influential in the early days, the "pioneer days," but by the time of the full-tilt profits in the 1890s they were a force to be reckoned with. When segregation was constructed in the first decades of this century, Anglo women left their mark on the system. Sharing with Anlo men a material interest in a colonial labor market, which provided them with cheap domestic servants, but often opposing these same men's raucous cultural taste, the women's influence introduced sexual, familial, and domestic standards of respectability as demarcators of status. It was women who fully spliced class status to whiteness. They stigmatized intermarriage and reduced its incidence, in a kind of gender contest by which they challenged Anglo men's patriarchal colonial privilege to marry and make "white" their Mexican wives. They made *mestizaje* increasingly an embarrassment. Dress, etiquette, house furnishing, even to the point of luxury, began to define class and race position. Some of Clifton's Anglo women maintained friendly, even respectful relations with Mexican neighbors; many of them continued to work at the same kinds of harsh household labor that Mexican women did—lugging water, scrubbing clothes on a washboard, heating an iron on a wood stove in the heat of summer; some of them even worked side by side with their maids. But socializing was impossible. One woman recalled, "there was an awful line between the Mexican people and the Americans. You weren't supposed to associate with Mexicans at all . . . you didn't go on parties or things with them . . . Some of the Mexican young folks would try to crash the white dances and some of the white would try to crash the Mexican dances and there would be some trouble."[50] As Wallace Stegner wrote about a lady in another mining camp, "she met on the trails brown-faced men and women who saluted her with grave courtesy and moved aside for her to pass . . . she was tempted by the pictures they made, but would no more have thought of making companies of them than of their burros."[51]

True, the delicate white woman who shuddered at the roughness of the "natives" has been used as a symbol—and blamed—for colonial racism to an exaggerated degree. Women could not rival men's power in the economic and political processes that defined Clifton-Morenci hierarchy. But little power is not the same as no power. Anglo women took some significant and effective initiatives in developing the white culture.

As with all colonial "civilizers," their efforts had contradictory aspects: they initiated some modest projects to improve Mexican welfare; they tried to make Clifton-Morenci more hospitable to women in general; and they helped construct and maintain segregation and inequality. In emphasizing ladylikeness, which they defined primarily in terms of Anglo style, they shoved Mexican women toward the margins, interpreting Mexican poverty as an absence of respectability. In emphasizing sexual propriety and law-and-order, they worked to pacify a violent camp but also to redefine previously nonracialized male behavior—drinking, gambling, rowdy fraternizing, and whoring—as unworthy of whiteness. With children as a priority, they campaigned for schools and public health improvements, which benefited Mexicans as well as whites, though never equally. And most ominously for our story, in extending their standards of decorum to include children's dress, nurturance, and behavior, they moved Mexican kids out of their category of the well-mothered.

The comforts of a servanted household gave many Anglo women not only ease but also the free time to elaborate social life and—not least—to operate as citizens in the public sphere. As citizens they built an infrastructure of organizations and activities that "civilized" and colonized Clifton-Morenci. In these efforts there was a significant distinction between Morenci and Clifton: ironically, the mixed economy of Clifton, the very ways in which it was less colonial than Morenci, created a larger civil society in which there was more room for women to exert power.

THE LEADERS OF ANGLO FEMALE SOCIETY did not seem to be chasing power. They seemed more intent on improving the town, defining their social position, and setting a standard for civic life through moral rules, dress, decorum, and entertainments. Incorporating hardship and rough labor, they thrived on the challenge of producing a gracious lifestyle in this uncivilized spot.[52] Some even brought in luxury. They bought oysters imported by John Gatti from Louisiana.[53] Their fine furniture came, before the railroad, by ox-team from Kansas; Mrs. Louis Abraham's Steinway piano, seven-foot-high carved mirror, bedroom set, and grandfather clock arrived that way, even as her husband was driving the mules that pulled the first boxcars of ore down to Clifton from the Morenci mine. They gave elaborate teas on tables set with silver sugar bowls and spoon holders and cream pitchers and "casters"—units that held salt and pepper and a bell for ringing the servant. They paid calls upon one another in the afternoon wearing white gloves and elegant dresses, held afternoon card parties at which they played progressive whist, and had teas and "Dutch lunch parties." "If the lady of the house was not home the visiting lady would leave her calling card in the slot reserved for it" or present it to the Chinese or Mexican servant. "They'd call on one another, you know, make about a five minute call and leave a card . . . every time they returned the call, they'd come and you'd go back and it was very formal."[54] These conventions were not frivolous. Emotionally and symbolically they represented the triumph of decency and civilization over filth (of all kinds) and violence. Paying these calls involved trudging along dusty or muddy streets without sidewalks, avoiding the drunks and prostitutes, dodging the burro droppings. A woman from an earlier mining town offered a vivid description of the contrasts:

> John comes up from the lowest depths of the mine, where he daily runs
> the risk of suffocation by the extreme heat, besides other chances of death

. . . then he changes his clothes, and drives off to a mill in the cañon . . .
I chance to meet him on C Street, in the course of the day, so busily
engaged in conning the stock report, or talking "rock" with some eager
millman, that he does not see me. However, that makes no differences,
as I am going to a lunch party, and afterwards to call upon a friend, and
do a little shopping.[55]

A few elite women defined the pinnacle of Clifton society, and most
Anglo women could participate in this high society only occasionally
and up to a point; their hard domestic labor and modest budgets gave
them less time for clubs and calls. Even women with fine furniture and
servants often had no clean water and no way to escape the sulfur
smoke. Even those with Mexican hired women often worked alongside
them, scrubbing away the daily dust, sewing shirts, dresses, and linen,
reconnoitering against centipedes and scorpions, driving flies from
screenless rooms, carrying firewood, and baking and "putting up"
fruits and vegetables in the heat of the summer. The wife of Clifton's
judge cooked, like everyone else, on a wood-burning stove and emptied the dripping ice compartment from the icebox. Most housewives
killed, plucked, and cleaned their own chickens. Some of the richer
men sent their wives to cooler climates in the summer and formed a
Summer Widowers club, but most wives stayed in Clifton twelve
months a year.[56] Their men were making money, but not by sitting at
desks in suits.

In this era without mass popular culture, far from the usual itineraries
of circuses and theater, Anglo women organized many parties, dances,
and balls. "Galloping two-steps, gliding waltzes, hoppy polkas, the
gracious schottische, lively quadrilles and lancers, as well as the Grand
March which was always the first number on the program," recalled
Rose Ferber (the sister-in-law of Clifton merchant Louis Ferber), and
Mrs. Louis Abraham (sister-in-law of Sam and Jake) of sister mining
camp Silver City remembered the same dances and the "good orchestra . . . a whole Mexican family, the harp and cornet and violin and I
believe the mother played the guitar . . . You know they do love music,
Mexicans."[57] Some of the balls were extraordinary events. The Masons
sponsored their annual dance on George Washington's birthday: the
men imported costumes of velvet with lace cuffs and lace on the shirts
and white wigs tied with a ribbon in the back; the women had their hair
done like Martha Washington, "up on our heads with puffs . . . And all
powdered white." They had three hundred dollars' worth of roses

shipped in. Friends from Bisbee and Douglas would come up for two or three days on such occasions to provide help with the decorations and food, and at other times Clifton-Morenci women would return the visits. They usually hired a Mexican band but did not serve Mexican food, which they considered low, and spent money instead on the "daintiest edibles and fruits." These balls were open (to all who felt welcome) and advertised in the newspaper.[58] Once a year from the 1890s until after World War I, James Colquhoun invited all his department heads, along with other local men who counted and distinguished outside guests, to an annual "smoker" at Library Hall. The 1901 event was catered by a San Francisco firm and attended by over a hundred in evening dress, at a cost of over a thousand dollars. In April of the year of the orphans, Sir William Menzies and other directors of the company came from Scotland to inspect, and Colquhoun gave a dance for two hundred, including the governor and James Douglas of Phelps Dodge. The governor reminded everyone that he had been a Rough Rider with the president and went on to suggest that Colquhoun shared Roosevelt's best qualities; Douglas received the greatest applause when he reprised the heroic history of Morenci and the risks PD had taken in developing it. The town's most important business was transacted here: Colquhoun detailed his conditions for lending support to the town's incorporation and more or less directed the town's Sanitary Commission to get something done toward cleaning up the foul Chase Creek and Frisco River.[59] When a congressional delegation came to Arizona to investigate the statehood issue in 1905, a luxurious private train took it to Metcalf, where a mining stope (a horizontal excavation) had been lighted and transformed into a banquet hall; "well-trained Negro waiters in dress suits" served the congressmen and local bigwigs an elegant meal.[60]

Clifton's elaborate Anglo social life required extensive organization. Both Clifton and Morenci had several musical groups—bands and choral societies—and although one could find an occasional Mexican guitar and an Anglo banjo or mandolin together in a bar, the organized bands and orchestras were segregated. So were the numerous sports teams: not only baseball and boxing but, owing to the Scottish and English influence, rugby and cricket. Formal fraternal and sororal organizations flourished especially well here, no doubt in part because the relative isolation of the community stimulated associational life, and they were strictly segregated.[61] By 1904 men had established lodges of the Odd

Fellows, Improved Order of Red Men, Grand Lodge Masons, Knights of Pythias, Elks, Ancient Order of United Workmen, and Woodmen of the World. (The Rotary Club did not come to Clifton until 1937, and the Elks long remained Clifton's largest businessmen's group.) Photographs show the Anglo men groomed and dressed just like those in the Alianza, but the groups were strictly segregated. And the fraternal groups did similar work. Like the Alianza, the workmen and the woodmen provided life and funeral insurance for their members. The more elite Anglo fraternals were primarily social and service clubs, although they too would sometimes raise money for a member's care. They staged elaborate, decorated, and costumed rituals, usually secret, and members moved from initial ignorance through layers of mystery, from the outer margins to the innermost exalted circle. They were fun-loving, often hard-drinking clubs for hard-working men. They gave (and their wives organized) dances and carnivals, sometimes to raise money for charitable work, admission charges typically one dollar. Yet they were also dead serious about their hidden rites, and even their meetings were purposeful, "networking," creating the bonds of loyalty that made the town run. The Masons were the most Republican and the most elite. But they all created some fraternity across class and political party lines—never across "race" lines—and this was a vital part of their function. Mine managers socialized with employees and local businessmen, Democrats with Republicans with Populists with Socialists. Indeed many fraternal lodges forbade political discussion, so great was their commitment to brotherly harmony. In Morenci, all the orders met in the Morenci Club, except when the 1907 Grand Lodge Masonic convention, emulating the Congressional banquet of 1905, also met in an underground stope.[62] Virtually every man in the posse belonged to at least one of these groups.

These clubs were exclusively Anglo, and included Jews, Irishmen, Slavs, and Germans. As always in Clifton-Morenci, the line grew fuzzy as you moved further south in Europe. Some Italians were in. Spaniards usually were not. The first Mexican got into the Elks in the 1950s. The Catholic Church was not unhappy with this particular form of anti-Mexican discrimination, as it detested and feared the attraction of these orders, all of them, in its view, tainted by Freemasonry. Father Mandin described the Anglos in Clifton as *either* Protestants or Freemasons.[63] (The Mexican Church had long experience with Freemasonry, a germinator of anticlericalism, so some Clifton-Morenci Mexicans would have been familiar with the movement. Mexican Masonry was not a working-class movement, but some of Clifton-Morenci's Mexican businessmen might well have liked to join.)[64] Many fraternal orders today flirt with racial ambivalence and attraction to the exotic, such as the Shriners with their Muslim names and imagery. In 1904 Arizona, the Improved Order of Red Men insinuated, not at all subtly, the temptations of the forbidden: Dedicated to preserving the customs, legends, and names of the Indians, the lodges were called tribes, met on a lunar schedule, in wigwams, where they lit council fires, referred to money in their treasury as wampum, and named every "paleface" member for a bird, animal, or other natural organism. Their ritual consisted of stagings of imagined American Indian rites. Claiming to be the largest fraternity of purely American origin, its bylaws provided that the "Americanism of the order is the true American spirit which . . . stands for equal rights for all." Red Men were required to be white.[65]

The Red Men were performing a kind of blackface, mirroring the original style common in minstrel shows, which were also popular in Clifton. Old-timers both white and Mexican recalled with delight the blackface actors who came to perform. The schools put on their own versions:

> I was Mr. Bones and Donald was Mr. Rambo . . . We had exaggerated costumes with big bow ties which sat right on our adams apples, allowing it to bob up and down as we talked. We had painted black faces. We waved our white gloved hands around and exchanged quips . . .
>   Interlocutor: "Where you boys goin'?"
>   Mr. Bones: "I'se gwoin' to the store."
>   Mr. Rambo: "How's I gwain' to find you all?"
>   Mr. Bones: "I'll tell you what—if I gets there fust I'll draw a white line. If you gets there fust you rub it out."[66]

Louis Abraham was a local star of amateur blackface productions, playing the bones and singing.[67] Mexicans and Anglos in the audience all cheered.

The racial messages of minstrelsy circled and doubled back on themselves just like the winding, looping road from Clifton to Morenci and the intricate racial understandings of Clifton's Anglos. The apparent imitation of African Americans was of course an invention, not a facsimile. This effigy simultaneously belittled and envied, disdained and feared the culture of an enslaved and subjected people. That blackface was being performed where the subjected ones were Mexican—not only here but throughout the West, where minstrelsy accompanied political battles over free soil and Manifest Destiny—made its meanings more ambiguous.[68] Anglo ambivalence toward Mexican culture—contempt and attraction—became more vibrant as the century progressed, as segregation was accompanied by Anglo appropriation of Mexican food, dress, crafts, and housing design. Already in Clifton Anglos absorbed Mexican know-how in the domestic, industrial, and construction arts, although without shaking Anglo certainty about their "civilizing" mission.

What could rival minstrelsy as an example of a spectacle meaning different things to different audiences? To the whites, watching and enacting blackface—or Indian face—was about establishing whiteness. The enjoyment was doubled in knowing that the performer was not black; had the performers not been white, the joke would have been less funny and the repetitiveness of the shows tedious. Indeed, the audiences' delight in reiteration of the same musical and visual tropes suggests the repetition compulsion children demonstrate in playing with truly frightening experiences, like peek-a-boo as the representation of disappearance and return. To the Mexicans, minstrelsy served as a reminder that there was a racial group which virtually all considered yet another step down.

In this respect it is not incidental but integral that minstrel shows were frequently a project of the fraternal orders. Those societies did not so much honor a preexisting boundary between white and non-white as maintain and even occasionally move it, shifting some of the marginal population to insiders and others to outsiders. That inclusion was of particular value to those whose whiteness was perhaps uncertain—the Irish, the Jews, the Italians. Arizona's Jews pioneered in the development of fraternal orders disproportionately to their numbers, and the societies' rituals were rarely Christian in content or tone.[69] Morris Goldwater helped establish the first Masonic Lodge in 1865; Jake Abraham was one of the first officers of a Globe lodge established in 1880; Sam Abraham was a founder of the Clifton Elks. Avid joiners, small town businessmen often belonged to many groups, even serving as an officer for several.[70] As the isolation of the frontier diminished, the earlier enthusiasm for Masonic and other secret societies with a great deal of ritual was overtaken to some degree by engagement in groups like the Elks, which emphasized networking, community improvements, and boosterism. But all these groups did boundary construction work, racial work. Membership certified whiteness.

GENDER BOUNDARIES were often also under construction around the fraternal orders, like fences planted on sandy soil, along guessed-at property lines, then leaned against by the animals they were corralling. When the lodges presented events that included family members and outsiders, women did the work. Itching for recognition and inclusion, they were rejected by men who loved the benefits of exclusively male space and bonds. But the men also needed assistance and domestic tranquillity. So women established their own auxiliary groups: Clifton chapters of the Order of the Eastern Star (Masonic), Crescent Temple Rathbone Sisters (attached to the Knights of Pythias), and Rebekahs (Odd Fellows).[71]

The tussle between the sexes was often sidelined by other priorities: the women's own pleasures in creating a female space and bonds, and the call to clean up their towns. But these very priorities also served to advance women's power, supplying a base for women's claims to moral authority in the community.[72] Clifton-Morenci's wildness cried out to women to civilize it. "The wilderness must be redeemed inch by inch into garden."[73] Before their garden could be planted, it had to be cleaned of garbage, pollution, and immorality. Blocked from temperance agitation by the fact that so many of their husbands were saloon owners, they focused on prostitution, and although their success in reducing its extent and visibility derived primarily from the in-migration of women and families rather than from moral or religious rebirth, they nevertheless felt proud of this moral improvement. Similarly, their campaign for schools, churches, and a medical clinic gained success primarily from the copper companies' needs, but they nevertheless experienced these institutional gains as an achievement.

Still, one of the major resources they needed to maintain their activism—money—reentangled the club women with their husbands. The patriarchalism of the mining camp took in Anglo as well as Mexican society, but the fact that so many Anglo women worked as their husbands' business partners probably gave them some clout. In addition, the Anglo women cultivated the view that because they had sacrificed so much in coming to the wild west, their husbands were indebted to them, debts which they could collect when necessary. Invoking the pioneer identity, one club member recalled, "Now any

woman who would brave Indians and lawless men . . . to be with her
husband in a rough mining town was not at all daunted with the
thought of raising money for a clubhouse . . . could any man refuse
when his wife said, 'John, I want $25.00 for our new clubhouse?' When
his guilty conscience reminded him that the little woman had no
running water, electric lights or indoor plumbing?"[74]

The women's clubs, like the men's, enforced racial boundaries. The
segregation seems not only sad but also ironic in hindsight, because the
Anglo women shared most of their values and priorities with Mexican
women. All the women were committed to "civilizing" their community through church and schools, to training up clean and disciplined
men and children, to fostering good health and good manners. All
were extremely hard-working as they fought off the dirt, the vermin,
the sin. Some of both groups of women consulted Teresita when an
illness or ailment was unusually threatening. Most were far from family, sometimes lonely, needing to replace kinship with communities of
church, neighbors, and friends. The women's tastes in leisure were
similar too: they shared a love of music and dancing. Meanwhile
"American" and Mexican cultures were influencing each other. All the
Anglos soon picked up a bit of Spanish, and many liked some Mexican
food and Mexican music. In some parts of New Mexico, Anglo and
Mexican women actually became friends, and the Mexican old-timers
taught the Anglo newcomers about how to cook and keep house in a
strange environment.[75] But here their lives were becoming completely
segregated. Indeed, the very "civilizing" of Clifton-Morenci, through
the construction of schools, churches, municipal improvements, and
organizations—in other words, "progress"—intensified the barriers. The
upshot was that the Anglo women were able to get themselves defined
in the history books as civilizers, while the Mexican women were not.

In some ways these fences were less necessary than those among
men, because the Anglo women saw the Mexican women as more
completely different—confined, uneducated, priest-ridden, downtrodden—than the Anglo men saw the Mexican men. The women of both
groups looked at each other across a "gender frontier,"[76] a border
drawn by different gender practices along with religion, language,
food, and class, all making up "race." The orphan story is a tragedy
generated from silence, created because two groups of women could
not speak to each other.

Mexican and Anglo women shared a civilizing priority: the church.[77]

They all believed that church was a core part of the woman-friendly culture they sought. Here the Anglos had farther to go because until the turn of the century Protestant Clifton-Morenci was unchurched.[78] Clifton's Anglos were not particularly religious and made few distinctions among Protestant denominations; Jews joined Christian clubs and married Christian women, and even differences between Protestants and Anglo Catholics were muted in Clifton-Morenci. Whites mainly used public buildings for their worship: the Episcopalians met in Library Hall, and the Presbyterians conducted services and Sunday school in a schoolhouse until 1901, when they took apart an unused Tombstone church and reassembled it in Clifton. George Frazer sponsored a Baptist congregation starting in 1905. Women were the heart and blood of these church groups, lobbying, staffing, organizing, and fund-raising to start them and keep them going, and although they got substantial support from the copper companies, they worked to get it. Colquhoun paid for putting a belfry on the church, but when the Presbyterians hired their first minister in 1902, Rev. Curry Love from the coal fields of Pennsylvania (picked because he would understand a mining town), they had to raise his one-thousand-dollar yearly salary.[79]

Another priority shared by Anglo and Mexican women was, of course, schools. Their ability to create them differed, however. A one-room school for white children, funded by private subscription, was initiated (in part by Sheriff Parks's mother) in 1882, serving Clifton, Morenci, Metcalf, and Guthrie, and by 1889 it received some county funds. At the turn of the century the copper companies built schoolhouses, a result both of civic demand and of efforts to recruit more skilled labor. The heroes of these early schools were the teachers: largely single women, recruited often from far away, paid sparingly, expected not only to teach but to organize schools from scratch. One of the early ones, Mary Elizabeth Post, came by "mud wagon"—a stage that consisted of a canvas-covered wooden wagon—from San Diego; her school was a tiny adobe structure that had previously served as courthouse and jail.[80] Another, Sheriff Parks's sister Jennie, went at age nineteen to teach in a Mexican school in San Jose, near Solomonville.[81] A few teachers were local: Mrs. Reardon, probably Mike's mother, taught the Clifton school in the late 1880s, while also serving as postmistress. There was at best one teacher to a school. In 1894 Miss Harriet Gillespie at Morenci had 70 pupils, and in 1910 the average ratio was still 43 pupils per teacher. In 1901 Graham County's female teachers were paid, on average, $58.75 a month, the male, $64.09.[82]

But women's common interest in schooling for children did not create a common agenda. White and Mexican students were always separate and unequal. By 1904 Clifton had a school census of 595 and a daily average attendance of 281, or 47 percent; Morenci 670 and 180, or 27 percent, respectively. Morenci spent much less ($3,600 or $5.37 per student) than Clifton ($5,620 or $9.45 per student), almost certainly because more of the students in Morenci were Mexican—which also accounts for the lower attendance.[83] Although there was no high school yet, there were four elementary schools, segregated both internally and between schools: North Clifton, mixed but with separate classes for Mexicans and Anglos; South Clifton, all Anglo; and two Chase Creek schools, one Anglo and one Mexican. The inefficiency of running two Chase Creek schools led the Greenlee County Board of Supervisors to propose consolidation, and a special election was held in November 1905. But this would have meant desegregation, so the vote was 24 in favor and 496 against, a feat accomplished with the help of Arizona Copper. "All Mexicans in the employ of the company were filed into the polls by companies, and in most cases their ballots were handed them already filled out. There was much loud talk and ugly threats but peace was finally restored without bloodshed."[84]

There is no record of the role of Anglo women's groups' in this school controversy, and the Mexican women did not engage in public civic activism. The most elite Anglo women's organizations, such as the independent woman's clubs, established at the turn of the century not only in Tucson and Phoenix but also in the mining towns of Bisbee, Douglas, and Florence, were just beginning to engage in politics. These clubs affiliated to the newly organized Arizona Federation of Women's Clubs in 1901, in turn becoming part of the powerful national federation, and they were active lobbyists. Educated and secular, these women were attracted neither to hocus-pocus rituals nor to auxiliaries of male lodges. They were oriented to service, reform, and self-culture, and their large social events often served to raise money for their projects. Such clubs did not come to Clifton-Morenci until years later.[85] But the elite clubs and the fraternal and sororal societies were not entirely dissimilar. In both, members had to be voted in and could be blackballed, making status a major motive for seeking entrance. Some joined out of temperance motives, some from a desire for self-improve-

ment, everyone sought community, and many discovered their desire
for a project only in the process of club activism. There was an opening
for women here, which allowed the expression of a latent desire to act
and to make a contribution, a desire for respect. That unruly desire
sometimes yielded a militant, campaigning spirit in their undertakings.
Some of their projects could be done by their own volunteer labor:
civics and literary self-education; keeping the jail clean and fit; decorating the schools; creating small libraries; visiting the sick. Some
projects, however, depended on mobilizing others, agitating for regulation or government spending: kindergartens; public libraries; maintaining sidewalks and grading streets; kinder treatment of animals,
especially the burro; sewers; pure food and drug regulation. Mrs. E. G.
Ord of Bisbee—we have no such document from a Clifton leader, but
we know that the Clifton and Bisbee women were in frequent communication—enunciated their persuasive style in 1903 in language that was
(literally) flowery, but her combative tone is unmistakable:

> Which one of our citizens would hesitate to risk his life to rescue a child
> from flood or fire? Not one . . . But how few of these same men take
> thought enough for the constant danger which threatens their children
> and ours to DEMAND sewerage . . . Because this way was good enough ten
> years ago, it is NOT good enough now . . . We may plant our trees and
> flowers to try to teach our children the beauty of decoration before they
> have learned the beauty of cleanliness, but we are simply scattering rose
> leaves over a charnel house.

Mrs. Ord blamed the town's shortcomings on men: "whatever advantage may be gained, must come through the help of GOOD MEN . . . We
have come it is said to the day of the new woman. But the new man
must be with us too."[86]

These mining-camp women's clubs, sororities included, were part of
a national movement toward women's organization and reform activism. Even in remote Clifton there were hints of the cryptofeminism
lurking beneath the apparently disinterested goals of much women's
Progressive Era reform. The auxiliary groups like the Eastern Star
derived not just from women's jealousy of men's secrets but also from
their refusal to be left out. The quiet or not so quiet conflicts they may
have had with their male master groups can be guessed at from a
conflict that did erupt in the Presbyterian congregation, Clifton's most
important Protestant group. Women consistently raised most of the

money for such groups. In 1901 the Ladies Aid Society Bazaar raised $243 for the church (out of an annual income in those years of approximately $484), which they decided to use to buy a cloth for the communion table, linoleum for inside the front door, and a reflector lamp for outside. Apparently they spent the money without first seeking the approval of the church fathers, thus provoking a crisis. The visiting minister, Reverend Cromb, knowing how dependent he was on their work, took their side at a meeting, moving that "the finances of the church be turned over to the Ladies Auxiliary . . . since the ladies had to be depended upon to raise the money for the church, it was only right that they should have the disposal of it. Mr. Cooper moved that while not disparaging the service of the ladies in raising the money, the financial department should be left in the hands of the trustees." Mr. Cromb's motion carried, although it was rescinded in 1910 in a backlash movement.[87] This small tempest was no doubt the buzz of the white women's groups for a while.

We should not expect to find in Clifton the distinctive women's political culture that permeated the big-city women's reform communities. Clifton-Morenci had few of the educated, unmarried women who constituted the core of Progressive women's reform activism. With the exception of a few schoolteachers, librarians, and clerks, most Anglo adult women were married, identifying with their husbands' interests, just as their husbands identified with theirs. There was little overt gender conflict, and whatever covert conflict occurred may well have looked rather like Mexican gender conflict.

The opening to women's activism created by Clifton-Morenci's needs differed from those of the big eastern cities, which have been the basis for most generalizations about Progressive reform. There were fewer signs of temperance agitation here, not surprising considering the centrality of the saloons to local commerce. In most big cities, Societies for the Prevention of Cruelty to Animals had arisen several decades earlier, and humane campaigns then went on to protecting children from cruelty; but here there was a racial discourse about animals, with Anglos frequently accusing Mexicans of mistreatment of the beasts of burden on whom they so depended.[88] Yet in other respects these small-town women were in tune with the major themes and issues of the urban white women's Progressive social reform agenda, and their work displayed the standard Progressive spectrum from progressive to conservative. Giving priority to public health measures, such as sewerage,

street cleaning, and food and drug regulation, was consistent with Pro-
gressivism's most progressive impulses. Health campaigns predominated here because in these congested small camps, everyone's safety
was threatened by the lack of sanitation anywhere. We wonder if it was
women who persuaded Mills to undertake the cleanup of Morenci in
1904–1905. At the other end of the spectrum, a conservative, lady-
bountiful approach dominated their ministering to the poor, transformed now by the Progressive racial consciousness that fused charity
with Americanization and with training for class-specific jobs. The
Anglo women provided fuel and food for poor mothers, clothing for
poor children, cooking and budgeting classes for Mexican mothers, and
classes in serving for the Mexican girls. One Anglo schoolteacher engaged in Americanization work found the "Spanish" women particularly eager to learn how to make cakes. They promoted vocational
training in the schools for the Mexican children.

Above all, they shared with mainstream, national women's Progres-
sivism a maternalist stance. That is, they emphasized children's welfare
and women's unique responsibility and capacity for understanding
children's needs; and they positioned themselves as mothers toward
less fortunate grown women to whom they could teach the science and
soul of homemaking and motherhood. As women came together in
Clifton-Morenci, child saving was gaining influence. The orphan trains
served to communicate to westerners the pitiful plight of children of the
eastern urban poor. The anti–child abuse movement had conceptual-
ized child neglect as a major evil, asserting that poverty, poor nutrition,
poor health, and lack of supervision could damage a child just as
beatings did. The president and other legitimators of official moralism
preached the primacy of motherhood to civilization. Even organized
feminism had shifted its central message from one of equal rights to one
of women's special maternal contributions to culture. Thus when the
orphan train arrived the Clifton-Morenci, Anglo women already had a
frame, even the outlines of a picture, into which they painted foundlings
abused by inadequate mothers.

As it was everywhere else in America at this time, their maternalism
was racialized. How other than racially could these Anglo women
understand what they perceived as their superiority to the Mexicans?
All social difference was becoming racial in America. The entire
working class was being transformed into a race alien to the putatively
Anglo-Saxon Americans. The poor were daily becoming more racial-

ized. The western pioneering project was racial. And nothing was more racial than the cause of protecting and saving children, especially since "race" was continually understood in a doubled and contradictory manner, referring at once to those who were alien and to the whole "human race." Frequent slippage between these meanings allowed white racial superiority to become, not oppression but salvation, a joint project in which elevation to the "white" standard was a form of benevolence toward nonwhites. "Racism," a word that did not then exist, would have meant to the Clifton-Morenci Anglos, had they heard it, that white supremacy was good for everyone. As they believed, Republicans and Democrats alike, that imperialism aimed to benefit the conquered and registered President Roosevelt's association of imperialism with woman's duty to civilization. The women's Improvement Club from a nearby mining camp, Florence, threw a "colonial party" as its first function, to raise money for putting up street signs.[89]

It is difficult to sever "race" from religion in America at this time. In New York, Jews and Irish Catholics were marked by most Protestants as racially "other," perhaps "white" but yet another race. In Clifton-Morenci, race and religion were better distinguished. Yet although Jews and Anglo Catholics were popular and respected by the Anglo elite, the place was by no means free of anti-Semitic or anti-Catholic residue. The anti-Catholic American Protective Association racked up significant influence in the western states, and several anti-Catholic "exposés" circulated widely, such as Margaret Shepherd's *My Life in the Convent,* 1892, and Charles Ciniquy's *Fifty Years in the Church of Rome,* in its fortieth edition by 1891.[90] Their scandalous stories about clerical drunkenness, sexual immorality, and venality would reemerge soon as explanations for the disposition of the orphans. Mexican women's devotion and financial support for their priest only lowered them in Anglo eyes. Elsewhere, anti-Catholicism connected closely with child-saving imperatives, and some of that association was brought to Clifton by eastern women. For the East Coast elite, "orphans" were almost definitionally Irish Catholics. So, even more universally, were the impoverished and often lone mothers whose inadequacy to the task of child raising urgently necessitated intervention. Both as creed and as institution, Catholicism was to the elite a benighted system, a pernicious influence toward dependency, alcoholism, and shiftlessness—a logic that fit, of course, with the hegemonic elite understanding that poverty grew from moral failings.[91] Children's salvation required their removal from such influences.

Clifton-Morenci Anglos were self-contradictory about Catholicism. The high-status Catholics, like real estate developer Henry Hill, an Irish immigrant, or H. L. Laskey, Detroit Copper's converter foreman, and the several white Catholic families that got orphans (Hugh and Mary Quinn, John and Louisa Gatti, the Kellys, and the Laskeys), did not count as Catholic: to the Anglos, they were simply not defined in religious terms; and since they rarely, if ever, attended mass, the Mexicans and the padre did not consider them Catholic. The Anglo Catholics identified their religion only later, in defending the vigilante group against the accusation of religious bias at the trial. Still, there was no explicit anti-Catholic discourse in building the Anglo consensus to kidnap the children. The discourse was about race.

And race was inextricable from the Anglo women's convictions about what was good for children, although we cannot know their precise thought processes. Perhaps they "saw" bad parenting because the parents were Mexican, or perhaps they observed some Mexican parenting customs that they did not like. Perhaps they just considered it disrespectful for the Mexicans to want white children.

A crucial maneuver in the racial discourse about the orphan affair was the erasure of respectable Mexicans. The Anglos believed that all of the eventual white parents were reputable and worthy of respect, but they did not or could not see that so were many if not most of the Mexican parents: hard-working, honest, disciplined, devoted to family, chaste, appropriately manly and womanly. The orphan rescuers also performed a reverse maneuver, denying the existence of poor and disreputable whites. Many of these resided in Clifton and Morenci, and although they were most likely to be single men, some were families with children. Either way, the discourse generated an un-inflected, unqualified equation of whiteness with virtue.

Ironically, one component of the Anglo women's sense of racial superiority was their desire to advance women. They believed that Mexican women were poorly treated. Althought their discourse about Mexican women's victimization was in part a projection of their own complaints, it was also a way of distancing themselves from Mexicans. In Mexican men, they saw only drunkenness, crudeness, brutality, and tyranny over women. In Mexican women, they saw only persecution and subjugation by men or surrender to vice: they saw women downtrodden or fallen but in either case, low. This white women's sense of their own greater claim to respect is one of the contradictions of colonialism, an irony that could be found throughout Africa, in much of Asia, and in Latin America: the irony that the Anglo-colonial lament about Mexican-"native" women's victimization then justified a second victimization that the Anglo women imposed themselves. In their discourse about Mexican women's immorality, the Anglo women did not consider the poverty that forced women into jobs in the bars and into sex work, not to mention Anglo responsibility for that poverty. In their attack on mixed-race relationships, the Anglo women did not discuss the exploitative and even abusive behavior of the white men in forming and maintaining those relationships.

This is not to say that the Anglo women were entirely wrong in their observations of Mexican women's ill-treatment. One did not have to look far to find examples of injustices to women in Clifton-Morenci. Certainly the Mexican women were more domestically confined, more overworked, more often ill, than the Anglo women. Yet these Anglo perceptions were distorted. Protestants assumed that Catholicism was ipso facto worse for women. Anglos considered Mexican women entirely lacking in autonomy. They considered Mexican women more obedient to their husbands, a presumption based on a circumscribed and culture-bound reading of how husbands and wives negotiate and dicker about power. Anglos believed Mexican men were more violent toward their wives, and that may have been the case, but Clifton-Morenci's court records do not show it. All these judgments rested on rumor and impression; as the trial would show, one could not find an Anglo woman who had ever entered a Mexican home. Tragically, their own restiveness against male dominance led Anglo women to even greater disregard for another group of women.

October 2, 1904, Night

Clifton Hotel

As THE MEN BROUGHT THE ORPHANS IN, the women were waiting in the private parlor of Mrs. Jake Abraham, at the hotel Jake
managed for his brother Sam.[1] Besides her, five others had spent most
of the evening there, anxiously chatting: her sister-in-law Laura Abraham, Mrs. Pascoe, Etta Reed, May Simpson, and Muriel Wright. But
they were not idle. In addition to stitching the needlework that several
of them had brought along, they were reviewing the situation, re-
confirming their community's understanding of why what was being
done had to be done, and elaborating the arguments they would put
before the court a few months later.

"They are very illiterate people," Muriel Wright testified, "and they
are not a cleanly class of people, and spend nearly all their earnings in
drinking and gambling. And those that earn anything at all, of course, it
is just a mere pittance; not enough to clothe their own children." Asked
if she knew any of the Mexican women, she said, "I know of one that I
have heard of, the one that Mrs. Jake Abraham's little baby was given
to . . . she has been a very bad woman, and she keeps a boarding-house
now, and her house is visited by the worst class of people in town; in
fact, she boards them." She was talking about Angela Flores, alleging
that Flores was a prostitute. Mrs. Wright couldn't bring herself to say the
word but everyone knew what she meant. Her Victorian propriety
overlaid by racism branded lower-class Mexican women as sexually
loose, and Anglo women were just as implicated as Anglo men in the
spread of this attitude, if not more so. The women gathered at the hotel

that night might well have adored Teresa de Cabora, and lined up for her healing services, but that double standard—welcoming the light-complexioned upper-class Mexican women and ostracizing the poor—was the core of this titillating talk. The fact that Flores was married to Juan Maxwell, himself the son of a mixed marriage, was part of what made her seem immoral to these Anglo women. Intermarriage, once common, was dwindling thanks to women like Mrs. Wright: because Anglo men now had women of their own kind to marry, and because Anglo women were redefining these mixed relationships as disreputable. Women are often the masters in setting familial rules of racial intercourse. It is possible that Mrs. Wright had some "evidence" of Juan Maxwell's alleged immorality: It generally was not easy for Anglo men to meet Mexican women, chaperoned and secluded as they usually were, and so Juan might have met Angela in a bar or restaurant where she worked; some women might well have considered such a public job ipso facto disreputable. But Muriel Wright? whose husband owned a saloon? where she herself sometimes served food and drink? whose friend Laura Abraham had been a singer and entertainer and who still occasionally performed in her hotel bar? the Laura Abraham who had a diamond set in one of her front teeth?[2]

Etta Reed said that during the day she had gone to see two of the children in a Mexican home, although she did not know which one. "It is just like all other Mexican homes; it is very rude; I wasn't inside the dwelling [but] . . . It appeared very coarse—they brought the children outside for me to see; but the outside surroundings were very coarse . . . [built of] Lumber, as well as I remember; it might partly be made of adobe." She did not know whether it had a floor. They all knew that the Mexican women's and children's clothing was hopelessly shabby and dirty, that they were personally dirty, and that their housekeeping was poor, although Mrs. Pascoe made an exception for the woman who cleaned her own house, including the room where her husband worked at his undertaking business. (The others also had Mexican maids, but they did not seem to catch the irony of their denunciations.)

It might seem surprising that they did not much cite Mexican lack of fluency in English as evidence of their unsuitability as parents. (At the trial only Neville Leggatt made a point of this, thereby underscoring the flimsiness of his own sense of superiority.) The silence about English suggests the Anglos' unconscious acceptance of Clifton-Morenci as a bilingual community, and in fact most Anglos learned to speak some Spanish. The Anglos were accustomed to European immigrants whose

English was far from perfect, and assumed that these newcomers were nevertheless citizens, Americans, Anglos. Mexicans were different, not just another ethnic group; their deficiencies were unredeemable.

The women had gathered blankets and used them to make pallets for the babies on the carpeted floor. Most of the children were chilled and soaked, having been carried through the rain for a good while, so the women kept busy warming, quieting, and fussing over them. One little girl, Josephine Corcoran,[3] arrived coughing but also, strangely, singing wildly and for a long time. She was the liveliest of all the kids, and Mrs. Jake Abraham was enchanted with her. It was 2 A.M. before all sixteen were asleep on that parlor floor.

The women were exhausted by the evening's adventure but so exhilarated few could sleep. They were heady with the responsibility for the children, their own confidence that they knew what to do for the children, the importance they felt about the rescue, and their own power in effecting it. They did not commonly stay up so late or stay out with their women friends. Perhaps Louisa Gatti wasn't the only one who hadn't managed to cook her husband's supper that night.

Mixed with the exhilaration was anger. The pitiful condition of the children confirmed—no, magnified—the Anglo women's fury about how crude the Mexicans were and how callous the nuns who had set up this situation. In her key testimony at the trial, Laura Abraham told a story of illness, thus building the evidence of acute endangerment of the children. When they first got off the train, she said,

> what attracted us so towards the children, they were so neatly and so cleanly dressed, and their hair was curled . . . [Now] Their clothing, of course, was very scanty because it was, well, 10 or perhaps a half-past at night, but their hair was matted, and their faces were dirty, and their clothing, what little they had, was dirty . . . and they were all very, very ill. I had medicine and a doctor for most all of the perhaps 14 little children that came into the Clifton hotel.
>
> Q. In what respect were they ill, if you know?
> A. Well, the only way a child has of being ill is perhaps stomach trouble, and they all vomited.
> Q. What did they vomit?
> A. Well, I could tell you that.
> Q. Tell the Court?
> A. Well, chili and beans and tortillas, and watermelon, and Mexican beans.
> Q. Was there any peculiar odor on the breath of any . . . ?
> A. Some of them had a very strong odor of whiskey and beer . . . I

nursed every one of those crying babies the night through until the next morning, with the assistance of two or three friends . . .

The citizens were quite sure that the Mexicans had given the kids liquor, and Eugene Fountin, a copper company engineer, said he had seen them doing it:

> I was going home for dinner, and I had to pass Mr. John Maxwell's place; and three or four of these prostitutes were in the house drinking beer—I guess they were celebrating the welcome of the children; and the little girl Mrs. Maxwell had was running about in the yard, and she come out and I stopped there to see the child; and she called the child in Mexican, and she begun crying, and she kept telling it to stop; and finally she came outside and grabbed the child—I guess she was full of beer; I could see a lot of beer on the table . . . and dragged her inside.

Well, he had not actually seen the woman feed beer to the girl, but perhaps he just knew that this was something that Mexicans did. As to the vomiting, it would not be surprising, if it were true, since the children may have just drunk Clifton water and eaten beans for the first time. They may have had a version of "Montezuma's revenge." Everyone knew the water was terrible. The townspeople had complained to the mines, mills, and smelters about the wastes they dumped into the San Francisco River, but they did not worry as much about the human or cattle wastes, percolating down into the river and wells from the pastures and outhouses, and few of them were well-informed about germ theory.

The next morning the Anglo women discovered that the children's heads were filled with "vermin," that is, lice. Etta Reed said that she saw little Raymond Spencer clawing at his head with both hands, and Mrs. Pascoe said it took six weeks to clear her Jerome's head of nits. And they were sure that the lice had been transmitted from the Mexicans. Yet several of the children arrived at the hotel that evening with their hair cut short or virtually shaved—Mrs. Jake Abraham lamented the loss of their pretty long curls and damned the Mexicans for this atrocity—which was a standard antilice measure of the age. Could the Anglo women have had no experience with lice and the laborious means of getting rid of them, especially in homes without running water, let alone hot water? Probably they had no experience with large children's institutions like the Foundling Hospital, where lice were endemic (and trivial compared to its larger health problems, such as smallpox).[4] And possibly, too, they did not understand that it would

have been impossible for the children to acquire such massive infesta-
tions in the twenty-four hours since they had gotten off the train.

Despite the retching and the lice, the Anglo women bonded with the
children intensely. The fact that the children arrived soaking wet and
shivering became the visual sign that they needed rescuing—although
it was, of course, the Anglo rescuers who were responsible for their
exposure to the elements—and above all it was precisely their need to
be rescued that was so captivating. There was simply no way that these
Anglo mothers could have lived with themselves had they allowed the
orphans to remain in such disgusting homes. As Louisa Gatti put it, "it
looked like its little heart was broken." Olive Freeman said, "And I put
out my hands to the child and it cried to come to me." It even
happened to Mr. Pascoe: "The night he was brought in there was a
little girl handed him to Mr. Pascoe, and he put up his hands and said,
'Papa,' and from that time until 2 o'clock in the morning Mr. Pascoe
couldn't get him out of his arms."

A metamorphosis had transpired among these children, although
they were themselves unaware of it. As the orphan train chugged across
the Mississippi and the great plains, the children were bleached, as the
Mexicans say, as they went. This transformation made their placements
"interracial," or, as the Clifton Anglos said, "half-breed."[5]

Oddly, the children's whiteness also rubbed off some of Louisa
Gatti's remaining swarthiness. Catholic, Italian, uneducated, Louisa
and her husband had been Euro-Latins despite their wealth. John
Gatti's leadership in organizing the community after the terrible 1903
flood had definitely raised his status, but Louisa was not a member of
the network of leading townswomen, and she was not at the hotel that
evening, not a member of the Presbyterian Church or of the women's
clubs. But in the days after the orphans' "rescue," after she took in
three-year-old William Norton, and as she rehearsed with the Anglo
group the reasons that drastic action had been necessary, she found
herself more and more a part of the group. Then her forceful husband
took the lead in getting a lawyer to help them file for legal custody and
defend the Anglos' guardianship against the Foundling Hospital. Consequently, John Gatti was the first listed defendant and the name by
which the case became known: *New York Foundling Hospital v. Gatti*. By
the beginning of 1905 the Gattis were unquestionably Anglos.

Toward the end of the bringing in of the children, Dunagan and
Simpson arrived back in Clifton with Swayne and Mandin in hand.
The Catholic men learned with alarm that the children had not only

been forcibly taken from Catholic homes but kidnapped: the Anglos had them, planned to keep them, and would not return them to the nuns. And the "people" not only remained unapologetic but accused the Foundling representatives of unspeakable crimes. Collecting the children had not calmed but intensified the Anglo wrath. Now the Anglos were screaming for blood. A crowd of 350–400 were in and outside Library Hall, and they surrounded Swayne and Mandin in an extraordinarily threatening manner. They would not allow Swayne to be heard, called him and the padre "all the names in the calendar, made us all kinds of threats . . . and they had all the preparations; they had the tar, they had the rope, and they had the feathers. Those men, the greater number, were loaded with pistols in full view." Some in the crowd expressed fear that if the orphans were returned to the sisters they would be horribly disposed of, and Swayne tried to correct them. "One of the parties there–I forget his name; he was an ex-constable–was particularly boisterous and threatening, and he was about 3/4 drunk; he led the meeting, and he says, 'You'll take them into Mexico and give them to the Mexicans.' I said, 'No, I have told you we will take them back to New York.' He says, 'Will you give us a bond?' I says, 'We'll give you a bond for any amount, a million dollars, if you want it.'" But that was not really what the crowd wanted. When Swayne argued that he did not have the authority to leave the children in Clifton, the crowd demanded that he telegraph the Foundling to get the authority, and Swayne said, "No I will not telegraph." Finally the meeting was "adjourned" until 1 P.M. the next day, Monday, when Sheriff Parks and Probate Judge P. C. Little were to come to Clifton.

When Dunagan and Simpson with help from a few others finally got the New Yorkers away from the crowd, they tried to register at the hotel, but Jake Abraham refused them so they had to find a room in a Mexican boardinghouse. They had to share a single room. Dunagan and Simpson stayed next door to protect them, alternating sleeping and keeping watch.

While the lynch mob was still churning at the library, the Anglo women at the hotel already knew they would never give up these children. They felt as if a precious gift had somehow come to them. If a passing anxiety crossed their minds that they were thieves in relation to the Foundling Hospital, perhaps they compared themselves to Robin Hood or to those who steal from large, faceless owners such as corporations; they never thought of themselves as stealing anything from the

Mexicans. They not only felt entitled but also believed that the "rescue" should have earned them gratitude.

The children on the hotel carpet did not sleep long, and the women had dozed a few hours at most. By morning they had decided to distribute the children as quickly as possible to individual homes. The intention to keep the children permanently grew so imperceptibly that the women themselves had not been aware of when they began to take it for granted. On this Monday morning they may still have been thinking of these as temporary homes. But now they could not maintain the calm of the late night. Clifton's Anglos poured into the hotel that morning eager to see and hear everything. In this tumult, the women could not quite control the distribution process. People began literally fighting for children. Laura Abraham described the scene cautiously at the trial: "All of our friends came into the hotel, friends that know me in Clifton; and of course, knowing that the children were there . . . and of course they were very much infatuated with these little children, and each one of the ladies took one of these children home with them." But another witness saw it differently. One Foundling Hospital nurse, Marian Taylor, had stayed behind in Clifton, and had been fast asleep in this very hotel all night. In the morning she came downstairs to a literally incredible scene: a discount sale of children, with hotel owner Sam Abraham arbitrating conflicts among the overexcited Anglo women. The children were being dickered over as if at a bazaar.

All of the women who had spent the night at the hotel claimed a child before the crowd arrived: four took girls and two took boys. Mrs. Jake Abraham took Josephine Corcoran, the child who had been hysterically singing; Laura Abraham took the youngest, Elizabeth Kane; May Simpson took Anna Doherty; Muriel Wright took Katherine Fitzpatrick; Mrs. Pascoe took Jerome Shanley, who had called her husband papa; and Etta Reed took Joseph Ryan, the little José who had promised to lessen Baleria Balles's loneliness. The Anglos who arrived in the morning had to choose from what was left over. George Frazer and his wife took Hannah Kane, Elizabeth's older sister; the Gattis took William Norton. Mr. and Mrs. Tyler took the oldest, Marie Mack, who was over six—she had been with Roja Guerra, the woman who ran a large boardinghouse. Rose Hill, wife of the richest Clifton resident, took Raymond Spencer, even though her husband was away on business in Solomonville—it was the county seat, and he was a member of the County Board of Supervisors. (Did she telephone to discuss this with him or simply act on her own? He did not return to see his new child for two weeks.) Rebecca Tong, wife of a machinist who worked for Arizona Copper in Metcalf, heard about the availability of the orphans from a friend's phone call; childless, she had been already seeking a child to take in and had asked her friend to look out for children. She knew Lee Windham and went to see the child who had been placed with him, then showed up at the hotel at 10 A.M., just in time to get one.

At this point the Anglo women did not know all the names or ages of their children correctly, because in several cases the possemen had not asked or requested the paperwork. May Simpson immediately and unapologetically hunted up the Mexican woman who had earlier received Anna to get the information ("she'll be four on October 21"). Getting the information was important to the new Anglo mothers, and no one except Rebecca Tong and Olive Freeman changed the first name of her child: Gabriella Welsh became Gabriella Quinn, Edward Gibson became Edward Hargis, and so on, except that Violet Lanwick became Helen Tong, and Sadie Green became Gladys Freeman. Although the orphans were not, after all, infants, and all could speak, many of them may not have known their birthdays, and their new parents may not have trusted the information of those who did. Perhaps the new mothers thought they would need the information to adopt the children legally.

If the adults' intentions were still somewhat unformed on Monday morning, by the evening they had firmed up. The possemen had already summoned the closest judge, P. C. Little of the Graham County Probate Court, and now they determined to ask him to write up adoption papers or the like. They were taking their first step toward *ex post facto* legalization of their vigilantism. The judge, originally expected at mid-day, could not come until evening, so there was a little time to take their new children home and introduce them to relatives and neighbors. The women had time to reconfigure their emotions: once rescuers and jealous would-be mothers, they were rapidly becoming mothers, each with a mother's intensity in refusing to give up her child. And already the men had stepped forward as spokespeople and decision makers. They too were affected by and participated in the women's transformation: fatherhood too had its imperatives, among them defending one's child and its mother. The women had accomplished a great rescue, elevating their own status and authority in the process. Now they looked to their men to defend the coup they had effected, and the men turned to the law.

The Coronado Incline, located in a remote mountainous desert in southeastern Arizona, where profitable copper mining accelerated in the late 1880s and by the 1890s had produced two boom towns, Clifton and Morenci. (Courtesy anonymous donor.)

A Catholic orphanage in New York City arranged to place forty of its foundlings in Clifton-Morenci in 1904, accompanied by several nuns from the Sisters of Charity. One group of the New York Foundling Hospital orphans
(above) was gathered in the parlor of the Clifton Hotel. An unidentified nun
(facing page), dressed like those who arrived in Arizona. (Above: from *Leslie's
Weekly;* facing page: courtesy Sisters of Charity Archives, Mount St. Vincent College.)

Clifton-Morenci was the epitome of the wild west, with saloons its largest and most numerous commercial establishments, gunfire heard nightly, and the hangings of desperadoes public events. Chase Creek (*top*) was Clifton's main street in 1903; the gamblers (*bottom*) are playing faro in a Morenci saloon in 1895. (Courtesy Arizona Historical Society, #20780 [top] and #2819 [bottom]).

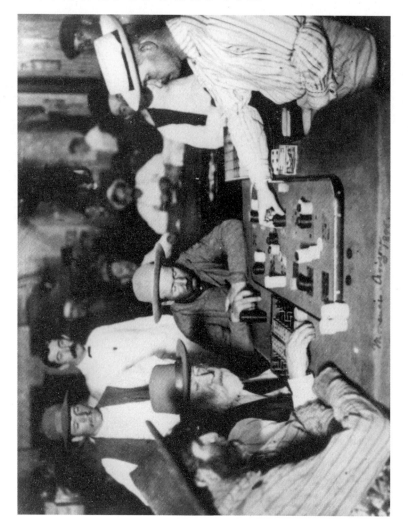

The majority of Clifton-Morenci's mineworkers were Mexicans. Most were immigrants from Mexico, and some were longtime residents of the area, but all were paid 50 percent to 75 percent of the wages Anglos earned, and the towns were increasingly segregated, with Mexicans excluded from better jobs and better neighborhoods. The miner drilling *(above)* worked one mile underground; the Morenci street in "Mexican town" *(facing page)* is shown in 1903. (Courtesy Arizona Historical Society, #20692 [above] and #74468 [facing page].)

A Mexican miner rides a supply car down the Metcalf Incline while Anglo managers watch. (Courtesy Arizona Historical Society, #B91351.)

The 1903 mineworkers' strike *(above)* was ultimately defeated by a paralyzing flood *(facing page)* that killed thirty-nine people and wiped out scores of homes. (Above: courtesy Arizona Historical Society, #58785; facing page: courtesy Greenlee County Historical Society.)

The orphans were received by the local priest, Constant Mandin *(above)*, and his devoted assistant, female church leader and teacher Margarita Chacón *(facing page)*. (Above: courtesy Diocese of Tucson Archives; facing page: courtesy Margarita Hinojos.)

The foster mothers were Mexican mineworkers' wives, perhaps like the woman in this photograph, who had probably come to deliver lunch to her husband on the Longfellow Incline. (Courtesy Arizona Historical Society, #BD91357.)

Some Anglo women, observing the placements, charged that the Mexican foster parents were unworthy. The press published this picture to "demonstrate" the poverty and "shiftlessness" of the Mexicans. (From *Leslie's Weekly*.)

But Clifton-Morenci Mexican families also looked like this. (Courtesy Arizona Historical Society, #51148.)

The Anglo copper company executives and prosperous businessmen had developed a lavish lifestyle in Clifton-Morenci. They shopped at a company store that imported and sold luxury goods, lived in elegant bungalows, and lounged at an opulent private club. The Morenci Hotel *(top)* is where much of the action took place; members of the whites-only Morenci Club *(bottom)* relax on its veranda. (Courtesy Arizona Historical Society, #24455 [top] and #45114 [bottom].)

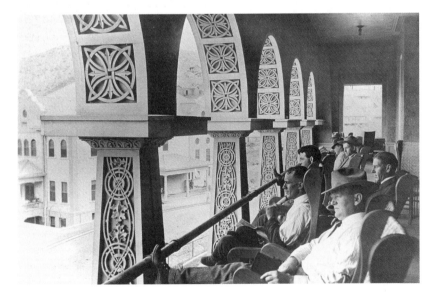

Most of the Anglos, however, were at best middle class. Many belonged to fraternal lodges, such as the Sons of Herman, a German lodge where the boots and furniture were those of workingmen. (Courtesy Greenlee County Historical Society.)

This Christmas concert choir was typical of the activities of the lodges and auxiliaries organized by Anglo women; they not only sponsored dances but also worked to create schools, end violence, and control drunkenness in the copper camp. (Courtesy Arizona Historical Society, #51134.)

Women in Clifton-Morenci did not have easy lives, and even the more privileged Anglos performed heavy physical labor and put up with difficult conditions, like this woman doing her laundry with a washboard in 1902. (Courtesy Arizona Historical Society, #62407.)

Anglo observers sometimes tended to view all Mexicans as lower class, ignoring their own experience with Mexican businessmen or legendary Mexican healer Teresa de Cabora (shown with her father, Don Tomás Urrea), who lived and cured the sick in Clifton. Her charm and charisma attracted Anglos as well as Mexicans, who called her Santa Teresa. (Courtesy Southwest Collection, Texas Tech University, William Curry Holden Papers.)

Even the poor working-class Mexicans of Clifton-Morenci were mainly responsible citizens, contrary to Anglo claims. Like Anglos, Mexicans belonged to fraternal lodges, of which the most important was the Alianza Hispano Americana, shown here in parade *(top)* and in a studio portrait *(bottom)*. Note the light-skinned beauty queens. (Courtesy Greenlee County Historical Society.)

Except for lodge dances, most formal Mexican social occasions centered around the church, where large sectors of the community assembled to celebrate masses, communions, and marriages, as in these portraits from Clifton's Sacred Heart parish. (Courtesy Arizona Historical Society, #51123 [top] and #51154 [bottom].)

The community also came together in sadness, to mark the all too frequent funerals, particularly of young men killed in mining accidents and of babies who died of infectious diseases.   (Courtesy Arizona Historical Society, #51169 [top] and #51117 [bottom].)

The Mexican parents had not sought adoptive children for their labor, for children rarely worked in the mines. But most children did domestic, often arduous labor, such as carrying water up steep hills. (Courtesy Arizona Historical Society, #61556.)

The schools enrolled primarily Anglos and kept the few Mexican children in segregated classes. Morenci's 1905 senior class, pictured here, consisted only of Anglos. (Courtesy Greenlee County Historical Society.)

Mexican parents sent their children to school when they could. In the school shown here (in Metcalf, part of the Clifton-Morenci mining camp) one teacher, Sofie Farnsworth, taught all the children herself. Other Mexican children attended private classes like those Margarita Chacón taught in her home. (Courtesy Greenlee County Historical Society.)

Anglo women stirred up a townwide hysteria against the placing of "white" children in Mexican families and pushed the Anglo men to form armed vigilante squads, which kidnapped the "orphans." Among the vigilantes who kept children they had seized were Harry Wright, saloon owner *(top)*, shown behind his bar, and Jake Abraham *(bottom)*, standing at far left with his banjo in a Clifton orchestra. (Courtesy Arizona Historical Society, #1277 [top] and #2298 [bottom].)

The only extant photo of an orphan (the smallest child, in white, standing on a chair) in her or his original foster family calls into question the Anglo contention that the Mexicans were unfit to be parents. (From *Leslie's Weekly*.)

The Anglos' elite vision of what created a proper upbringing is expressed in this studio portrait of five of the orphans, posed with whips for goat carts. They are *(left to right)* Anna Simpson, Leah Abraham, Raymond Hill, Gladys Freeman, and Katherine Wright. (Courtesy Greenlee County Historical Society, O. A. Risdon Collection.)

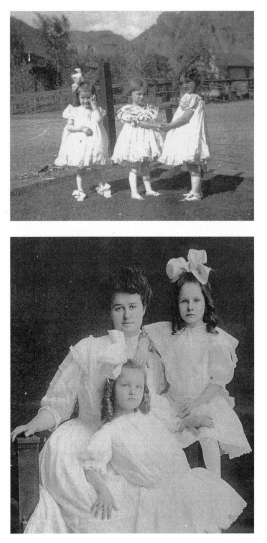

Anna Simpson's fifth birthday party, October 21, 1905, Clifton, attended by *(left to right)* Anna, Leah Abraham, and Katherine Wright. (Courtesy Greenlee County Historical Society, Mary Milo Collection.)

The New York Foundling Hospital sued to get its charges back, but three courts, ending with the U.S. Supreme Court, upheld the vigilantes, who kept the children permanently. Pictured here are Mae Wright Simpson, wife of one of the vigilante leaders, with two of the orphans in 1906: her own adopted daughter, Anna Louise (Doherty) Simpson *(top),* and her niece Katherine (Fitzpatrick) Wright, adopted by Harry and Muriel Wright. This studio portrait captures the vision of a proper childhood that spurred the Anglos to "rescue" the orphans from their assigned Mexican parents. (Courtesy Greenlee County Historical Society, Mary Milo Collection.)

6

The Strike

EVERYONE IN CLIFTON-MORENCI saw the orphan incident through memories of the 1903 strike. It amounted to a further episode in the strike: an act of revenge, perhaps, or at least of restoration, a next step in the return to order, not just the economic but also the civil and familial order. The moment the posse took its rifles in hand and went to the Mexican homes, 1903 was back.

For some this was literally true: for men like James and John Parks, Gus and Lee Hobbs, John Gatti, Charles Mills, who participated both in restraining the strike and in capturing the orphans; for Cornelio and Margarita Chacón, Abigai and Andrés Villescas, Rafael and Josefa Holguín, Francisco and Trancita Alvidrez, John Maxwell and Angela Flores, who had been on strike and who had taken in orphans. But virtually everyone in these small towns felt the reverberations of 1903 in the mob scenes ignited by the orphans.

The orphan-seizing posse executed an act of revenge, perhaps, or at least of restoration, a next step in the return to order, not just the economic but also the civil and familial order. But restorations can never exactly replicate the past. The strike and the orphan incident together changed Clifton-Morenci. They changed the race categories and the class struggle; they even shifted slightly the balance of power between the sexes. Some have asked me, of what importance is the impact of these local events given that other Arizona towns or southwestern mining towns developed virtually identical race, class, and gender relations? Every town has its unique stories, its personalities and local politics–why are they significant? But that's just the point, I an-swer: it is through these local particularities that social systems get constructed. Besides, Clifton-Morenci wasn't just anytown, USA. It was on its way to becoming the most important mine of the most powerful corporation in the most vigorous and vital aspect of the Arizona and regional economy. The 1903 strike was the biggest labor conflict so far in the region and, like its 1983 great-grandchild, it changed the way Phelps Dodge, the other copper barons, and other giant hard-rock mining corporations did business. New York financiers might not have understood this immediately, but the Gattis, the Chacóns, and Father Timmermans did.

The orphan story could not be told without including the 1903 strike. That strike derived, of course, from the conditions and relations of producing copper–in mines, mills, and smelters. Copper work shaped the daily mood of Clifton-Morenci. The posse that kidnapped the orphans also derived from the social and political power structure maintained by copper production. So did Anglo impressions of Mexican character. Consider the irony that the Mexican workers' griev-ances underlying the strike–poverty, illness, dirtiness–formed also the Anglos' justification for the kidnapping. So we need to understand, first, these grievances. Then we need to see how the labor conflict was intersected by other Arizona protocols: independent sheriff standing firm, posses chasing desperadoes and rustlers, fearless Arizona Rangers and Indian-fighting cavalry riding in to rescue the townspeople, the guns in every home. These codes, invoked in 1903, were at the ready again in 1904. Finally, we need to understand the lingering wounds of the strike.

MINERS ARE THE PARAMOUNT WORKING-CLASS HEROES, pro-tagonists in romance or tragedy, the genre dependent on the time, place, and point of view. Yet most men in Clifton-Morenci who worked for the mining companies were not miners exactly. Arizona Copper employed 1,900–2,000 in 1903, only 900 of them in its Metcalf mines; the rest worked in the smelter and mill, and in the myriad other auxiliary works that made the operation go–as carpenters, pipe fitters, boiler makers, machinists, timbermen, welders, trainmen, hoist engineers, skimmers. But the essence of the place, the job that put Clifton-Morenci on the map, and the largest single occupation was underground mining.

It was a round-the-clock operation.[1] Night and day looked the same underground, but they didn't feel the same. Social and family life were continuously disrupted by swinging shifts, typically switched every few weeks. If the men were often marginally undernourished, they were almost continually sleep-deprived. Especially in winter, a worker might well have to cut wood for the day's needs before setting out. Gulping quick breakfasts, they put on their shoes (not hard-toe boots, not yet required), grabbed their candles and soft-brimmed hats or sombreros (not safety helmets, not yet required or supplied), and walked to the mine entrance—a walk that might well add an hour or more to the working day. (Lacking locker rooms, the miners had to carry equipment home and back.) The companies usually measured the shift from the moment the miner reached his underground station, adding still more to the length of the day. Some carried lunch boxes, others were lucky enough to get hot food delivered by a wife or children.

They descended in metal cages, sometimes with several layered platforms so as to move more men at once, attached by rope or wire cable to hoisting machinery. Underground men talked to hoist operators with bell signals. No matter how many times you rode the cage, you dreaded the descent. The fall of 800 feet per minute or faster, down as far as 4,000 feet underground, knotted your stomach. The drop into the dark shaft was intersected only by muted sounds, the smell of damp, rushes of air, glimpses of timbers that seemed to be darting upward. When they reached their station, the miners headed off on foot along the drifts and crosscuts to the veins they had been working. Not everyone underground actually drilled for ore. Lower-paid muckers shoveled up and carted off waste rock after a blast, and had to have the expertise to distinguish ore from waste; trammers, still lower paid, pushed or pulled the heavy ore-loaded cars on tracks (or lifted them back on to the track when they derailed); nippers or "pick boys" hauled water to the miners and picked up dull drill bits and picks and took them to the blacksmith for sharpening. Among the better paid were timbermen, who wrestled huge logs with which to build the supports that held up the tunnels, and upon whose care everyone's life and limbs depended, and the miners who drilled and blasted. Drilling could be single-jacking, one man holding a drill in one hand and wielding a hammer in the other, or double-jacking, less tiring because two men took turns holding the drill and swinging the hammer with both hands. Either way, an average miner was expected to strike twenty blows a minute, and from every position and in all directions—up, down, at an angle, to the side. Long experience with rock and careful scrutiny before drilling allowed skilled miners to get the maximum effect from each swing of the hammer. Machine drills and jackhammers created new kinds of demands: extremely heavy, they had to be braced against the body even when mounted on a tripod, and the noise and vibrations rattled every bone and organ. Using power drills required even more control and knowledge of the rock, precisely because they operated faster than the human arm. Loading and detonating blasts required, of course, equal knowledge and caution.

The mine climate was not easy to bear. Depending on the season and the altitude of the mine, the temperature could be so cold that miners had to light fires to thaw the rock or so hot (well over 100 degrees Fahrenheit) that prostration and dehydration were chronic threats. In the heat the miners often worked nearly naked and consumed great quantities of ice. Water dripped from the walls and roofs of the drifts, and the men frequently stood in deep pools; if the water dripped on bare skin it often burned and left sores. The tunnels and stopes filled with the smells of Giant Powder (the brand name by which most miners knew dynamite), decaying lumber, human excrement (no toilets were provided until about a decade later), sweat, and dangerous gases. The residual vapor of unburned nitroglycerine caused headaches, nausea, and vomiting. Yet these stenches, along with the flickering of the candles and the behavior of the mice used in lieu of canaries,[2] were vital to the detection of danger.

In these conditions the working day in the mines was sometimes a tug of war between foremen and workers sneaking off to rest, drink, or breath fresh air by moving closer to the shaft. Al Fernandez described one foreman, Jim Killsby, whose Spanish was limited to *ándale, hombre* (get going, man), which he repeated many times a day.[3] How miners took breaks depended on their working arrangements, which varied. Only some received wages calculated according to hours of work at rates set directly by the company. Many Mexican miners worked for subcontractors, *contratistas,* who had sold the labor of a group of men to the company. These labor brokers, usually bilingual, controlled communication between workers and bosses, who often did not speak each other's language accurately. Miners might have been given subcontractors' names while still in Mexico and sought them out immediately upon arriving in Clifton-Morenci. Subcontractors could be harder and less forgiving than foremen in squeezing maximum work out of their men, mine managers realized.[4] When labor was short, subcontractors were especially useful: "a native, recognized by his countrymen as a leader, can daily bring a hundred men to work where the alien shift boss can collect but half that number with any regularity."[5] Mine foremen often invited good Mexican miners to become subcontractors, in the hopes that they would drive their workers harder than the company man could.[6] Yet in other cases the miners used these subcontracts to create more cooperative, egalitarian work groups. Mine managers recommended that "all contracts should be terminated at the end of every week . . . contracts running for a fortnight or longer [are] liable to frequent abuses, as in many cases under this system, the contractor is such in name only, every man with him sharing equally in the profits or losses, and the contract becomes practically a small benevolent association with the company paying the bills."[7]

Questions of control influenced contract preferences among both workers and managers. Those miners hired directly by the company could be paid by the task or by the day, or the task could define what counted as a day's work: for example, drilling three and a half meters. (Sometimes the men were not allowed to leave work until they had accomplished their assignment.) This system encouraged workers' speed, but it also gave them an incentive to carelessness: they had nothing to gain from slowing down to make sure the angles of the holes were correct, for example, and they could drill where the rock was softest, rather than where the dynamite would be most productively placed or where the hole could be blown with the smallest effective blast. Mine managers particularly complained that miners wasted expensive explosives. On the other hand, if the work was straight digging, "pick work," without blasting, the per-meter contract would be advantageous to the company.[8] Company bosses might prefer to retain supervisory prerogatives even if the men worked somewhat more slowly, and workers might prefer to control their own labor even if they had to work harder. Such considerations meant that for both employer and worker, what arrangement was advantageous depended on the task of the moment, and preferences shifted. Often the differences were not negotiated but imposed, depending on the labor supply at the time. One worker at the Coronado mine was offered a contract that would pay a fifty-cent bonus for every "set of ground" he broke, provided he broke three in a day; he refused this contract so the company fired him.[9] Bitterness about the control issue shows in the seventh of the "Miners' Ten Commandments":

> Thou shalt not have an opinion concerning thy place of work, for thy employer payeth a fat salary to a school-of-mines expert for constructing in his mind bonanzas that don't exist, so thou shalt refrain from theorizing, and concentrate thy efforts on drilling and the blasting of an abundance of powder.[10]

Add to these divergent bases of contract the lack of universal principle in fixing wages and the varying individual rates of pay among men doing the same work, and the result is a bewildering variety of wage rates (as revealed by a glance at a mine payroll ledger from this period). It would seem the more surprising that such a high proportion of Clifton-Morenci workers could unite in a strike if it were not for the one consistency in the wage structure: racial inequality. Not only were the Mexicans paid much less, but white workers had been able to win wage increases over the copper-mining era, doubling their average wages from $2 to $4 per day between the 1870s and 1910, while Mexican workers had increased their wages from approximately $1.50 to $2.50 at most.[11] The existence of the Mexican wage is not a conclusion that had to be inferred from analyzing wage discrepancies; it was frequently inscribed in the payroll ledgers. In this wage, all "Mexicans" were grouped together, whether immigrants or citizens. The separate "Italian" category seems to be unique to Clifton-Morenci, but the Mexican wage prevailed throughout the Southwest. In some mining camps, the gap between Mexicans and Anglos was wider than in Clifton-Morenci, because there the Mexican wage so predominated that it forced all wages downward, just as it made Arizona mining wages altogether lower than those in states to the north.[12] As with so much wage discrimination, the discrepancy derived also from the exclusion of Mexicans from most of the skilled or supervisory jobs. Among smelter workers in 1911, for example, 97.5 percent of Mexicans were "laborers," and only 2.5 percent were foremen, engineers, or mechanics; Anglos, by contrast, were distributed half and half. Although the Anglo workers may have had little influence on wages, with regard to jobs they weighed in heavily, harassing Mexicans or even refusing to work alongside them. Anglo preferences moved upward through foremen to shape personnel policy.[13]

The mill and smelter jobs may have a less heroic reputation than mining, but the workers knew they were at least equally difficult and demanding. A quick narrative of the refining processes shows the range of jobs: The ore went first to a mill, and then a concentrator, both of which crushed or ground the ore and separated the metal-bearing from the non–metal-bearing elements, taking advantage of the fact that the metal was heavier than other components of the ore and could be made to settle through the openings in mesh screen.[14] Railroad cars dumped the ore into a hopper that emptied onto conveyors carrying the ore through increasingly fine crushers and screens. Water in vast quantity was required at later stages of the process to move the ore along and send the final waste to its depository. Smelting applied heat and chemicals to retrieve the pure copper from the concentrated ore emerging from the mill. The concentrate was conveyed from the filters to roasters, operating at about 1,200 degrees Fahrenheit, which released sulfur, giving off sulfur dioxide, and turning the concentrate into a powder, calcine. The calcine then traveled to blast furnaces, which reduced the ore through the action of carbon monoxide, which yielded copper sulfide, and/or to reverberatory furnaces, which used reflected heat to achieve temperatures around 2,600 degrees Fahrenheit to burn off still more waste and induce the heavier copper to settle to the bottom. The resulting copper matte, tapped off the bottom of the furnaces into ladles, went into converters that used blasts of air to release yet more sulfur dioxide to create 99 percent pure blister copper. In the final casting department, workers poured the blister copper from ladles into pouring spoons, which emptied into molds.

Mill jobs were usually preferable because they were not as hot and because crushing the ore did not create as much dust and smoke as smelting did. The hierarchy of jobs in smelters and mills was determined less by skill and more by decreasing degree of misery. The newcomers got the dirtiest, dustiest, hottest jobs and hoped to work up to more bearable jobs.[15]

Perhaps the most unifying aspect of the copper work experience was its danger. Everyone in Clifton-Morenci knew someone lost to the mines. Whatever pride miners derived from staring at death, they paid a high price in accidents, stress, and disease, while the mill and smelter workers faced equal dangers without the thrills.

Death and injury from mining accidents occurred weekly, often daily. When experts finally began to look at hard-rock mining, they learned that its fatality rate was higher than that of any other work, including coal mining. In 1912, when keeping records of mine accidents became mandatory in Arizona, 214 involving death or injury were reported at Arizona Copper's Longfellow group of mines alone. (Records are missing, but one would expect the Coronado group of mines to have produced a comparable number. And how many accidents never got reported? The miners charged: most.) Approximately half the victims were married men, and their average age was twenty-eight. The average time lost to an injury was twenty-two days; these were not minor bruises. The overall annual accident rate was 272 per 1,000–in other words, 27 percent of the workers were injured each year. Of the nonfatal accidents reported, 43 percent were from falling rock, 19 percent from collisions with trams, and 13 percent from falling timbers.[16] There was always, inevitably, loose rock. Whether it was overhead or under foot, even relatively small rocks could scrape, cut, break, or crush the unprotected body. A slip of the foot off a board, onto a track, down an ore chute, could kill or maim. Conditions that forced miners to operate with little light, their hearing acuity reduced by the blasting and their alertness reduced by exhaustion and pressure to work fast, contributed to the accident rate. These accident reports did not count the bruising and battering that came from drilling; the loss of hearing due to blasting; or the strained muscles and repetitive strain injuries.[17]

The most deadly sort of accidents–due to explosions and gas–were fewer but took many lives. Dynamite could be mishandled, misplaced, overloaded. The worst danger was from misfired holes: ten charges might be lit but only nine exploded; then the next group of miners into the area could be blown up. A close second was the constant danger of mine gas, which could overcome miners before they could escape or reach help. The hoisting cages produced many fatalities: cables broke or were overwound; a miner sometimes became dizzy from the rapid motion and change in temperature and if he slipped or staggered a leg could be caught in the shaft and crushed or he could be pulled off or fall off. Rapid technological change meant that miners were frequently using new and unfamiliar machinery. These advances allowed mines to descend ever deeper and put men farther from help.[18] In 1912, 17 men died from such accidents in Arizona Copper's mines: in the company's categories, there were 5 Mexican miners, 1 Spanish miner, 1 Mexican mucker, 1 American electrician, and 9 unenumerated men killed in a single accident.[19] (This number would appear to be somewhat higher than the national average among metal miners, about 3.8 per 1,000 workers per three-hundred-day year, while the Arizona Copper figure in 1912 was about 8.5 per 1,000. It seems probable that both rates are underestimates.)[20] The company wanted, of course, to place responsibility for the accidents on the men themselves whenever possible, and it attributed the fatalities thus: 2 to "carelessness," 2 to "inexperience," 13 to "pure accident."

Sacred Heart's burial records show the community impact.[21] In 1900–1902, 45 percent of male deaths were due to mine accidents. If we eliminate the old-age deaths, the proportion go up to 47 percent; add violence, and 60 percent of male deaths sprang from "unnatural" causes. These are underestimates because they reflect only Catholics in good standing in Clifton, while Morenci and Metcalf had higher accident and violence death rates, and because churchgoers were more likely to be married men who were more cautious and less violent.[22]

For the mills and smelters there is no count, because no labor legislation required reporting. Fatalities were probably fewer than in the mines, but injuries were equally common: from getting caught in the moving belts, gears, and pulleys; from converters that "blew," sending out hot metal; from flying sparks that hit the face, even the eyes, of the men working without protective glasses; from anodes and other heavy pieces of metal or machinery falling from hoists; from arsenic and acid burns, often right through clothing and even through leather-soled shoes; from inhaling sulfur dioxide and arsenic fumes; from electric shocks; from falling into the crushers. Molten metal caused the most spectacular accidents, unbearable even to describe.[23]

If we could add to the deaths and accidental injuries the mine-, mill-, and smelter-induced illnesses, the proportion of men hurt by the copper industry would probably be well over 75 percent in a camp with as young a population as Clifton-Morenci. Exposure to acids, chlorine, cyanide, mercury, arsenic dust, and a variety of other chemicals, often unrecognized, ate away at skin and internal organs, despite the workers' resourcefulness in devising protective clothing. Most men in the industry suffered hearing damage from the extreme noise, although they stuffed cotton in their ears. (The noise also made it harder for injured workers shouting for help to be heard.) Occupational health and safety pioneer Alice Hamilton found that more than a quarter of smelter and refinery workers suffered from lead poisoning (not just in lead plants).[24]

The biggest killer, what the miners called consumption, miners' con, miners' puff, dusted lungs, or *consunción,* was silicosis. Yet few of its victims died in Clifton-Morenci. Although silicosis began quickly—its onset most commonly occurred within two years of work as a miner—it was a slow executioner; those sick with it had to quit work long before they died, and many returned home to Mexico. As silicosis began to be studied in the second decade of the twentieth century, most of the research focused on mines in the northern Rockies, ignoring, as these studies typically did, the Mexican miners. A 1912 study found silicosis responsible for 56 percent of the deaths of western miners, and in Butte in 1921, well after preventive measures began to be used, 42 percent of the active miners had the disease. (Presumably the rate among retired miners would have been higher.) Moreover, dust in the lungs made miners more susceptible to other lung diseases such as emphysema, pleurisy, and tuberculosis. Concentrations of silica dust in mine air were often one hundred times the federal limit set in 1988. Miners in high-silicosis areas commonly died between the ages of thirty-five and forty-five, while miners in low-dust mines survived thirty years longer.[25]

The history of the identification of silicosis offers a glimpse of a scientific advance that did not at first benefit humanity. In medicine, germ theory and the subsequent identification of the tuberculosis bacillus (TB) in the 1880s led researchers to categorize most pulmonary disease as TB. They concluded, therefore, that where there were higher rates of consumption, as among miners, the cause had to be sought in unsanitary living and working conditions. Until this time there had been accumulating knowledge of the effect of dust on lungs, but now that line of study came to a halt. Where studies of miners were done, mine managers naturally supported the germ theory to explain the coughing, wheezing, wasting ailment. The miners, however, knew better, as did the mill workers, stonecutters, grinders, and other workers whose jobs produced dust. They also knew that the new power drills, used in 86 percent of mines by 1902, the "widow makers" or "orphanizers" as some called them, drastically worsened the dust. Power drills not only generated more dust, they pulverized it finer and spread it further, thus affecting nearby muckers and trammers as well as miners. At the same time, speed-ups meant that workers were moving faster, breathing harder, and inhaling more dust.[26]

The copper companies assumed no responsibility for killed or injured workers or their dependents. A decade later, as pressure for workmen's compensation arose, the companies began a systematic approach, compensating men at 50 percent of pay for days lost due to injury, and making one-time payments to widows and children. But in 1903 workers had no entitlement. The companies did usually offer something to widows, and in 1905 PD President James Douglas thought its payment of $150 to a miner's widow—perhaps two months' pay—more than generous. In 1910, the earliest date for which we have such records, the widow of Filiberto Vásquez collected $750 from an Arizona Copper insurance program, but the company then sued her to get back what she owed: a total of $266.80 for funeral expenses, rent, and company store debt; as well as $408.20 advanced by the Mexican consul for train fare for sending the children back to Mexico, board, lodging, and clothing for the children.[27] The copper companies' power in Arizona politics was such that few workers ever won a suit against them, and it was even harder for a Mexican to do so.[28]

Despite all this, these copper workers were proud. They had high status among the people they cared about. The copper workers were a labor aristocracy (or plutocracy) to the Mexican peasantry and proletariat, and the fact that their high wages were offset by a high cost of living was not readily apparent to outsiders. In Mexico miners earned 3 pesos ($1.50) a day in the best-paid mines, surviving in shacks when they did not succumb to the rampant pneumonia, influenza, typhoid, malaria, and smallpox.[29] The fact that these *norteños* worked so hard and took such risks for their relative prosperity only made them prouder of themselves and the vast industrial enterprise to which they belonged. Their families were proud also. The pride came no longer just from the gifts they could send and bring home to Mexico, the pleasure of making their families' lives easier, the swagger they could indulge in. It was also now about sending their children to school, offering bread and meat to wives, owning a new suit—that is, about aspirations. Their wives inhaled this pride and status too, and it added a sense of responsibility to their generosity in offering their homes to motherless orphans. They too lifted their aspirations and believed they could raise their children, natural and adoptive, to a high standard.

The copper workers' desires were at once old (things they would have always wished for if only they had known them) and quintessentially new, that is, American. Hardship, danger, sweat had to them a variety of meanings, some positive, some angry. Their resentment arose not directly from their experience at work but from the intersection between their raised aspirations and their sense of exploitation and powerlessness. When they organized and struck, they did so out of pride and confidence.

THE STRIKE OF 1903 WAS AN UPRISING, a massive threat to "American" arrangements of power. It had not begun that way, but that is how it ended. The mines, mills, and smelters stopped, a heart attack shutting down Clifton-Morenci's supply of blood and oxygen. It was a small general strike, a protest directed at Detroit Copper that soon spread to the other local operators. Perhaps as many as 3,500 men, 80–90 percent of the mining labor force, walked out and stopped most everyone else from working for three weeks.[30] They did not head back to Mexico, and only some hung out in the saloons. Instead 1,500–2,000 armed strikers and some women gathered daily on the hills, while down in the towns "nearly every white man carried a gun."[31] In fact, the strikers offered no violence—not one person was hurt in the strike—but their presence terrified Anglos nevertheless. PD's man, Charles Mills, fled, leaving his flock. Sheriff Parks became a hero to the Anglos but only after a calculated tactical retreat while waiting for the U.S. Army, in its biggest deployment since the Indian wars. Meanwhile the "citizens," the Anglo nonstrikers, endured two weeks of fear.

At the outbreak of the strike, opinion in Clifton-Morenci did not neatly separate Anglos from Mexicans or strikers from ranchers and small businesspeople. A new territory law, effective June 1, 1903, limited the working day to eight hours for underground miners.[32] In other mining camps, which employed only Anglos in the mines, the eight-hour day was already in practice. Clifton-Morenci townspeople understood that the legislation aimed specifically to remove what some saw as the unfair advantage of mine operators who exploited Mexican labor and what others saw as a force that depressed wages. Since Arizona and Detroit Copper were the only large companies still scheduling ten-hour shifts, the law was like a bill of attainder directed particularly against this Mexican camp. The split followed partisan politics: the Republican press, like Clifton's *Copper Era,* denounced the law's interference with free enterprise and blamed the strike on it: "Until the politicians interfered they [workers] were content and happy." The Democratic press, like the Anglo miners' union, applauded the law as a step to drive cheaper "foreign" labor out of the mines.[33] Most miners, Mexicans included, believed that their success in driving the Chinese out of the mines in the period 1870–1890 was responsible for the improvements in their wages;[34] now whites hoped to do the same with the Mexicans. The Western Federation of Miners (WFM) used and at times fomented this racial strategy for working-class progress, attempting to win Anglo members by excluding and denouncing Mexicans. A small antiexclusion faction could not persuade WFM leadership otherwise. Perhaps the most bizarre application of this WFM policy was its anti-Mexican agitation among Anglo miners *in Mexico*.[35]

The WFM claimed that "experience" lay behind its hostility to Mexicans, some of whom had been strikebreakers in Cananea in 1902 and would be used that way again in the Colorado coal fields in 1903–1904. But "experience" reaches us only through the lens of existing attitudes and ideologies; after all, whites had also been scabs (as in 1900 in Ray, Arizona); and the WFM attitude predated these strike episodes anyway.[36] I do not invoke "racism" as a fixed and "given" attribute of white workers and unionists, or attribute to racism an irresistible force, but I want to show how it got constructed.

The mine labor movement in Arizona from this moment until World War II would develop along segregated tracks. The WFM recognized and occasionally cooperated with a Mexican workers' movement, but its guiding attitude was hostility. For example, although the WFM supported a "Mexican strike" in Clifton-Morenci in 1915–16, it continued to lobby for legislation that would exclude Mexicans from jobs and from the franchise.[37] The relationship was colonial, not so different from that of white and African unions in South Africa.

When the eight-hour law was passed, the majority of mineworkers of all racial and ethnic groups welcomed it. Apparently no one expected the copper companies to respond to the eight-hour day by cutting the daily wage (or its equivalent in task pay), which averaged $2.50 a day for Mexicans. From the owners' point of view, not to cut the daily wage would have represented a 20 percent increase in the hourly wage, from 25¢ to 31¢. The operators, pleading a falling price of copper,[38] offered to compromise by paying $2.25 a day, splitting the difference with the workers.[39] The workers saw it differently: They were accustomed to conceiving of the wage as daily rather than hourly, a holdover from an era before labor was a commodity; and they cherished a moral-economy notion of what constituted a good day's work, maintaining that the added rest would make it possible for them to accomplish in eight hours what they had previously done in ten. It was no small matter, besides, that most did not believe they and their families could live on less money. They may not have known that when white miners at Prescott complained, they immediately got an upward adjustment in wages, or that miners in Globe were simultaneously agitating for the $4 day, but they knew perfectly that Anglos always got more money somehow.[40]

As the copper workers discussed this pay cut in groups small and large, they began also to articulate additional demands. This is typical of social movements: once the aggrieved come together, they begin to "speak bitterness," and to transform other deprivations into new wants. These included:

> The established wage, $2.50, for 8 hours work; no cuts in daily pay.
> Locker rooms in which they could shower and change out of their filthy and often soaking wet work clothes before going home.
> Companies to pay hospitalization costs and insurance for death or injury.
> Companies not to fire men without good reason.
> Companies not to employ men who would not join their new organization—this is what we today call a union shop.
> No price increases at company stores except to meet wholesale price increases.

This was probably the order of importance to the strikers. The workers' awareness of the illness and injury risks involved in mining, and the economic threat to families' welfare as a consequence, made them see medical insurance as urgent.[41] The union-shop and no-firing demands were directed against corrupt labor brokers as well as against management—an effort to transfer the power of these subcontractors to an organization representing workers collectively.

The owners considered these demands impossible. Operating in Clifton-Morenci was expensive because the ore was thin, and they argued that a pay raise would make the works unprofitable—in other words, they were threatening the community with capital flight. Managers Mills and Colquhoun considered the Clifton-Morenci labor organization a proxy for the militant WFM, to which a pay raise would be a dangerous concession, and this fear strengthened their resolve.[42]

When first enunciated, the demands seemed reasonable to many townspeople and to "American" as well as Mexican workers, although most Anglo workers were unaffected by the pay cut since they were more likely to work above ground and their wages were higher anyway. The sheriff and several deputies were sympathetic; Sheriff Parks's sister wrote that "existing conditions were deplorable enough, for the company had no change rooms. After the men came off shift in the mines, they had to walk over the hills to their homes in their wet working clothes, even during the cold winter weather." Even the captain of the Arizona Rangers thought the miners' refusal to accept a pay cut was justifiable.[43] Several newspapers, including a few English-language ones, condemned the operators and supported the strikers. One charged that the owners exaggerated the costs of production to justify the low wages—"they buck and snort around like they were in the last throes of poverty."[44]

As in all mining strikes, had community unity remained stable, the strikers might have won. But the labor organization that planned, disciplined, and invigorated the strike, strengthening itself through the strike, became increasingly identified as Mexican, in a spiraling process: Anglos dropped out because the strike demands were of particular benefit to Mexicans and because they would suffer if they were too associated with the Mexicans; the copper companies wooed the white workers; Mexicans consecrated their class solidarity through assertions of *mexicandidad;* and the more the Mexicans stuck and the whites left, the more both sides saw it as a Mexican strike.

Newspapers at first identified Italians as the strike leaders, skeptical that Mexicans could have organized such a massive event, and many of them always blamed outside agitators.[45] Contrary to the owners' fears, the organization was not connected to the WFM, and in fact its independence resulted directly from the racial policies of the WFM. These were not merely policies of exclusion; they were matters of fundamental identity. Racial identity and pride were at the core of much nineteenth-century unionism; the WFM's class analysis *was* a race analysis. Just as manliness was sometimes the basis of the rights workers claimed, so was whiteness. And this whiteness became a property that could gain or lose value according to the market, so that sharing one's union and class position with nonwhites could dilute and thus reduce its value.[46] But still at issue was who would be white, and nothing was yet settled when the strike broke out. In Clifton-Morenci Italians formed an in-between group, a buffer that made the whites and Mexicans more distinct. Just as PD recognized Italians as a separate wage group, so did the observers in this strike. No one called them white or Anglo. The hostile press frequently referred to "Mexicans, Italians and other foreigners"; the Irish, Cornish, Scottish, and German workers were as likely to be immigrants, but they were not "foreigners."[47]

Consider the leaders, as best we can identify them—from a list of those arrested, who most likely consisted of those who spoke publicly and those named by company spies. The top thirteen were

A. C. Cruz, miner, age thirty-one, born in Chihuahua, in United States four years.

Juan De La O, miner, born in Zacatecas, in United States thirteen years.

Francisco Figuerroa, age nineteen, born Mexico City, in United States four years.

Manuel L. Flores, age thirty-one, miner, born in Chihuahua, in United States six years.

Francisco Gonzalez, declined to give any personal information.

Weneslado H. Laustaunau, would not talk to the press.

F. E. Montoya, miner, born in New Mexico, in Morenci since 1895.

Rafael Murillo, miner, born in Chihuahua, in United States three years.

Gaetano Parianni, miner, age forty-one, born in Italy, in United States eight years.

Frank Polombo (elsewhere called Colombo), miner, age twenty-six, born in Italy, in United States three years.

José Porepe (elsewhere Joe or Guiseppi Purpi), miner, age twenty-six, born in Italy, in United States three years.

Abrán F. Salcido, miner, age twenty-nine, born in Chihuahua, in United States seven years.

Frank Serlini, miner, age twenty-three, born in Italy, in United States five years, naturalized.[48]

Of these thirteen men, mostly miners (not mill or smelter men), there were four Italians, eight Mexicans (presuming from the names and including a New Mexican), and a Euro-Latin of ambiguous origin (Laustaunau—some called him Rumanian, some French, some Spanish, one just described him as "some kind of Bohunk"),[49] who was usually identified by the press as the "real" leader. In fact, the most experienced organizer was probably Abrán Salcido, who had recently arrived in Clifton-Morenci to help the men organize, and to test their interest in an anti-Díaz movement; he went on to play a leadership role in the influential strike at the Cananea mines in Mexico in 1906.[50] At one point an injunction cited two hundred leaders, and ultimately ten, four Italians and six Mexicans, were tried, convicted of "riot," and sentenced to one- or two-year terms.[51] The smaller group of leaders was pretty well off, more skilled and higher paid than most non-Anglos, as was typical of labor insurgents, who often rose from among the elite within the class.

The strike temporarily united Euro-Latins and Mexicans,[52] but it alienated Anglos from Mexicans. There were exceptions, of course: at the trial Stella Welsh, Tom Clark, and W. J. Arthur appeared as witnesses for the strikers, facing an all-Anglo jury. But among the Clifton-Morenci copper companies' employees in general, the eight-hour law and the companies' response to it intensified awareness of how differently situated were Mexicans and whites, a difference that made the whites less invested in a strike. Many of the white workers aspired to leave the mines. Although they lived on the "wageworkers' frontier," not the cowboy frontier and no longer the prospectors' frontier, mine-workers who saw themselves as white usually believed that "getting ahead" meant becoming independent. As the Mexicans were saving to send or bring money home, the whites saved to move on and up, to self-employment or away from manual labor. These aspirations were shaped and could be reshaped by local conditions: in some of the white camps, the largely immigrant workers were as persistent in their union struggles as the Mexicans were here. But in this camp the whites were an elite. For workers here to object to the pay cut they virtually had to challenge wage discrimination, which meant challenging a white privilege.

The Clifton-Morenci copper operators were caught in a vice: dependent on Mexican labor, they could not afford to alienate white skilled workers and foremen, who wielded substantial autonomy.[53] So PD led the way to resolve this contradiction by hardening racial stratification among its employees. The copper companies worked to define the strike as a Mexican revolt rather than a class conflict.

But the Mexican workers also contributed to the strike's being labeled a Mexican uprising. Their antidiscrimination consciousness was joined by a uniquely *national* Mexican political influence in the workers' organization they were developing. When the strike was in its second week, the Mexican consul in Washington sent a vice consul, Arturo Elías, to Clifton-Morenci to mediate. One newspaper reported that the strikers had threatened that the government of Mexico would intervene on their behalf.[54] Before the walkout the miners called in a Señor Alvarez from Nacozari, a mining town in Sonora, as an adviser, and it was only after his arrival that a strike was called.[55] Alvarez was most likely an experienced miners' union organizer. The labor movement in Mexico, at this time more developed than that in the U.S. Southwest, had grown jointly with the development of mutual benefit societies, *mutualistas*. By 1870 a number of these *mutualistas* had formed a national central labor union, with twenty-eight branches in twelve states by 1875. Including artisans as well as industrial workers, the organization divided over ideology and strategy: moderates advocated legislative reform rather than strikes; militants, influenced by European anarchism and early socialism, conducted major strikes in the 1870s. In the 1880s repression and internal differences caused a split between mutualism and unionism.[56]

In Clifton-Morenci, the mine workers seemed to be recapitulating their Mexican past, developing a labor organization within the womb of the *mutualistas*. "The Mexicans belong to numerous societies and through these exert some sort of organization to stand together," wrote a local newspaper reporter bewildered by the apparently sudden appearance of a labor organization.[57] Three of the strike's most public leaders were *mutualista* officers (along with Cornelio Chacón): Abrán Salcido was president of the Alianza chapter, and Laustaunau was vice president; the Sociedad Juárez met at the home of Juan de la O.[58] Laustaunau's position exemplified the Mexican–Euro-Latin unity and suggests that the Alianza had a non-nationalist perspective at this time. (So did the fact that men named Modesti, Peluci, Massoletti, Gamboa, and Baroldi–not Mexican names–were Alianza officers, although Clifton also had an Italian mutual benefit society, the Società Fratellanza Italiana di Mutuo Soccorso.)[59] Such leadership positions constituted important character as well as status references, since mutual aid societies operated on the basis of rigorous moral and behavioral standards for membership. To join, one had to be voted in. A committee would normally investigate a prospective member's local reputation for responsibility and honesty before admitting him; this was part of the actuarial calculations that minimized risk. Meetings ran on the basis of strict rules of propriety, mutual respect, and procedure. Rituals included an initiation rite, mottoes, and ceremonial pageants. To be an officer was a great honor.[60]

Still, the *Alianza* was not a front for a union.[61] The Clifton-Morenci workers started a new and distinctly labor organization in 1903. They would not have been able to rely only on the *mutualistas* because they had to bring together members of different lodges, and they would not risk the stability of the insurance they depended on by introducing controversy into the *mutualistas*.[62] They were dependent on the *mutualistas* for communication and meeting places. As late as 1917 PD in Morenci and Metcalf would not allow the union to build, buy, or rent a hall for meetings, and so the workers used Alianza spaces.[63]

But the relation between *mutualista* and union ran deeper than the tactics of organizing. Not only were the members the same people, but the organizations shared the same worldview, emphasizing honor, morality, loyalty, self-improvement, and fraternity. The Alianza's motto was *Protección, Moralidad, Instrucción*. Alianza leaders delivered formal speeches in slightly antique language about brotherly bonds, uplift, and individual self-denigration. This society is "our incomparable source of sustenance for progress and civilization."[64] Another society dedicated itself to "wiping the tears from the eyes of the anguished worker."[65] Union discourse was similar:[66]

> We the representatives of the various assemblies of the order of united workers . . . assembled in convention, declare our principles as set forth in the following resolutions.
>
> Whereas this society sees fit to foster,
>
> First, Fraternal love of one for another, and mutual support in all just things.
>
> Second, Morality, Respect, and Kindness; toward oneself and toward others.
>
> Third, that this whole society will be seen as a single family . . .
>
> Be it further resolved that as representatives of the working people we extend a vote of gratitude: First, to the supreme being, for his great goodness in bestowing the idea of organizing such a society. And in second place, to the Organization and its early members who deserve great credit for undertaking so large and difficult a task and it is our fondest wish to see this society organized throughout the territory, with our slogan of unity, Fraternity and true Christian Charity, as as a stronghold and reliable supporter of every working man . . .
>
> We declare our position that every worker's salary whether by the day

the month or the week be valued in such a way that the worker shall profit from his work and be able to live decently and that capital should pay out [wages] with pleasure and without criticism.

This style affords a clue to another stream in Mexican working-class sensibility: concern for respectful treatment by managers and foremen. Management literature on how to "handle" Mexican workers repeatedly observed that the men took great offense at familiarity, obscenity, or peremptory language. One manager suggested that "a smile and a cigarette will go further with them than a substantial raise in wages, if accompanied with sourness."[67] Another opined, "It sometimes seems that more tact is necessary to handle the peon than is required with higher class labor."[68] Workers disliked stereotypical insults, such as references to Mexican drunkenness, laziness, dumbness. The fact that there *was* a lot of drunkenness among poor Mexicans only strengthened resentment at the implication that all Mexicans were drunkards, especially as workers' organizations were engaged in a temperance campaign.[69] The literary language of the fraternal organizations proclaimed a style of formality, dignity, grace, and civility that contrasted sharply with the vulgar slang so many men used with their familiars in mines and bars. Yet the familiarity that licensed rough language was itself formalized, echoed in the distinction between *usted* and *tú*. Knowing when intimacy had been established and made appropriate was essential to the culture. The juxtaposition of ceremony and casualness, fineness and roughness, defined the range of Mexican working-class manliness. Unions and benefit societies produced both, creating formal, ritualized occasions and intimate let-it-all-hang-out relaxation. Both were modes of male bonding, both strengthened fraternity, and nowhere was fraternity more important than in the mines where one's life depended on brothers.

Formality did not exclude radicalism. Mexican workers' radicalism, like that of all the hard-rock miners, had both ideological and spontaneous dimensions. Revolutionary socialism and, even more, anarchism were influential in the Mexican labor movement—two of the three principal labor organizations in 1900 were run by anarchists, and anarchist propaganda appeared in numerous Mexican mining strikes starting in the 1880s. The anarchist ideology rests on the assumption that human beings have natural capacities, even predilections, for order and cooperation that can prevail under the right structural conditions. Most anarchists, like Marxists, shared a class analysis and supported union organization. Mexican anarchism overlapped with Mexican liberalism and anticlericalism—in short, it was by no means an isolated sectarian ideology. Anarchist ideological influence probably came to Clifton-Morenci not only with Mexicans but also with Italians and Spaniards.[70]

Mexican American unions maintained an explicitly antiracialist policy. Their organizations emphasized the unity of the working class, as if the workers could erase racism by the sheer force of their ideology. As one such union maintained in 1904, "the question of race or religion will be entirely eliminated and unknown as part of our Society."[71] A decade later about a thousand Mexican Americans were members of socialist party locals. Many Clifton men voted socialist in 1904: 15 percent of the vote for congressman, 23 percent for Graham County Council, 28 percent for Territorial Assembly.[72] We have no way of knowing how much support came from Mexicans, but we do know that Mexican men constituted 22 percent of Clifton-Morenci registered voters in 1902.[73]

We have to assume that most Clifton-Morenci workers had no direct book knowledge of anarchist, socialist, or trade-unionist thought. Many were illiterate and few read. But some did. In nearby west Texas, the closest region for which we have information and the region through which most immigrant miners came up from Mexico, 35 percent of Mexican adults were literate in 1900, and the zeal for education was striking, especially among immigrants: 31 percent of their children were attending school in 1900, in contrast to 25 percent of native Tejano children.[74] It seems likely that literacy among miners was higher than among peasants or other workers.[75] Clifton a decade later had the highest per capita school attendance rate in Arizona—the vast majority of the pupils Mexican—and the labor union offered English and literacy classes to its members.[76] A Morenci correspondent writing for a New Mexico Spanish-language labor newspaper claimed that "there is almost not a man among those who know how to read [in Morenci] who is not a subscriber to some newspaper."[77] Later observers were impressed by the Mexican unionists' knowledge, not only about political ideology but also about the American labor movement.[78] Even those who did not or could not read absorbed some of this book knowledge, as reading aloud was a common practice in working-class mutual aid societies.[79] Judging from what was sold at a Mexican bookstore in El

Paso—the capital of Mexican politics in the United States—readings might have been from the works of Poe, Spencer, Darwin, Kropotkin, and Marx. A visiting Industrial Workers of the World (IWW) organizer remarked, "It is the Mexican in blue overalls, the labor leader, as you call him, that supports these libraries of world-wide knowledge and passes all that he learns to his brothers who may not be able to read."[80] There may be some Wobbly romanticism here, but the Mexican working-class political culture was substantial and only gained in importance in the next years, as Mexicans in the United States were drawn into the developing revolutionary movement.

The Partido Liberal Mexicano (PLM), an early anti-Díaz organization, influenced by anarchism and Marxism, became the dominant force in the Mexican labor movement in the first decade of the twentieth century and developed a strong rank and file in the United States after 1900. Like the Clifton-Morenci strikes, the PLM was an example of transnational social activism.[81] Its leader, Ricardo Flores Magón, began the newspaper *Regeneración,* which moved its headquarters first to San Antonio, then to Chicago, and then to St. Louis in 1904 to escape Mexican repression. In the United States he built connections with radical activists such as Emma Goldman. PLM Liberal clubs drew their largest membership from the Arizona-Sonora mining triangle, and they showed particular strength in Arizona mining towns. Money and subscriptions poured into St. Louis from the United States. By 1905 there was a Liberal club in Clifton-Morenci. At the 1906 Cinco de Mayo celebration, Abrán Salcido, having served his three-year term in jail, spoke in Clifton against the Porfirian dictatorship; his revolutionary rhetoric got him literally deported from Clifton-Morenci, and a reported 75–100 armed men left with him to join the guerrilla forces in Mexico. Praxedis G. Guerrero, a guerrilla fighter in Mexico, came up to establish the Obreros Libres of Morenci.[82]

At the same time these Clifton-Morenci Mexican activists also identified themselves as Americans, when it was in their interest to do so. Moreover, their ideology encompassed liberal notions—indeed, in their political culture anarchism was the true expression of individual freedom and rights. (The dominant Mexican miners' union at this time was the Unión Liberal Humanidad.)[83] When the army occupied Morenci and banned workers' meetings, the strikers protested that they were being denied their rights as American citizens.[84] Most of them probably were not citizens, but everyone knew what they meant, just as when the

Anglos referred to them as foreigners, lack of naturalization was not what *they* meant. Working in a mining camp where most of the whites were immigrants had clearly revised the Mexicans' concept of national identity to mean something that could be altered and admitted newcomers.

The anarchist view of unions differed considerably from that of the American Federation of Labor (AFL) and may help to explain the tenacity of the Clifton-Morenci strikes. Mexican anarchists were revolutionaries who wanted unions to subvert and destabilize economic and political domination and prefigure a governmental form based on decentralized, local, democratic control. Anarchists adopted an artisanal tradition of workplace organizing, which subordinated collective bargaining over wages and hours to struggles for workers' control of their working conditions and design. Thus the importance to them of the closed shop. Tradition, ideology, and self-interest all affected Mexican workers' politics. One of the reasons some Mexican workers preferred the task system of contracts is that they liked the control over work processes and the schedule it gave them, and some managers thought they were even willing to sacrifice income in order to get this control. One Anglo newspaper close to the strike complained that the "Mexicans, Italians and other foreigners [were] ignorant and susceptible to the influence of the agitators who . . . led the strikers to believe that they had as much right to say what should be done in Morenci regarding the operation of the mines and works as the companies who owned them."[85] Occupational-health-and-safety reformer Alice Hamilton visited the Clifton-Morenci mines in 1919 and reported exactly the same attitude; paraphrasing the owners, she wrote: "You say the men want more self-government . . . That is impossible–they don't know anything about the management of a business . . . what did the men do but come and say they wanted to be in on the profits, fifty-fifty, when they hadn't done a thing but mine ore?"[86] This attitude, conceived as stubborn and insolent by management, appeared particularly prominent in mining, where risk was so high and skill and experience mattered so much.

In many places the anarchist tradition, like most programs for workers' control, tended to appeal most to skilled workers. Some Clifton-Morenci workers fit this category. Experienced miners, timbermen, smelters, blasters, blacksmiths, bricklayers, and boilermakers, for example, had much to gain from the ability to control their own work strategy and pace. Mexican workers were stratified, a readily apparent fact that was nevertheless often missed by Anglo observers. Even managers who subcontracted with labor brokers and team leaders would then generalize about "the Mexicans" as if they were homogeneous.[87] The 1904 vigilantes would show the same blindness. The 1903 antistrike posse similarly denied Mexican social stratification by projecting a different kind of hierarchy onto that population: outside agitators and passive, innocent followers.[88]

But the Mexican working-class political culture was by no means limited to an elite. Later, when the WFM had been dragged into organizing Mexican miners by the workers' own militancy, the workers' desire for control also pitted them against union leaders. The Clifton-Morenci workers became notorious for their wildcat strikes, which became so frequent that a new Spanglish word arose: *strikitos*.[89] They have a mistaken idea of unions, one witness testified to a federal commission a decade later; they strike without consulting their leaders and they believe that "the moment they joined the union that the card of that union gave them the right to work, and that the company was compelled to give them work." Another witness complained that the Mexicans always "pick the most radical man" as their leader.[90] These wildcat strikes were the collectivized transformation of the individual responses that had prevailed in the 1880s and 1890s: quitting or simply leaving. For many workers throughout the United States at this time, the answer to the abusive boss or the speed-up was to walk out; miners hit the road for another mining town. This behavior characterized Anglo and Mexican workers equally. But by 1903, when the great majority of workers had their families with them, that response was no longer a possibility. What was most remarkable about the 1903 strike was that thousands of idled workers stayed in the Clifton-Morenci camp, made do for weeks without any pay, and showed up repeatedly at the sites of their demonstrations.

COPPER WORKERS' LEADERS had been discussing how to respond to a possible pay cut for weeks before the new law took effect June 1. Mills knew about this planning and secured a detective agency, which supplied Italian and Mexican operatives, placed into the Detroit Company works as informers (the first known use of detectives here). Upon hearing rumors of a threatened strike, PD's top man in Arizona, James Douglas from the Copper Queen mine in Bisbee, convened a meeting in Clifton of all the operators of the district, which agreed to hold firm on wages.[91] Perhaps their spies communicated the need for concerted action. On Sunday May 31, the operators posted notice of the shorter hours and reduced pay, and on Monday the miners walked out.[92] By Tuesday morning the miners had refused to allow trainmen to draw ore out of the bins, forcing smelters and mills to shut down, and on Wednesday the Morenci smelter men called an eight-hour sympathy strike, which soon spread to other plants, even those where workers had been offered their previous (ten-hour) rate of pay. In Clifton they prevented the transfer of ore to the mill. In Morenci they blocked the Detroit concentrator. By the end of the week "not a wheel was turning."[93]

The 10–20 percent of the original strikers who were Anglos probably expected, as the companies did, a quick compromise after the workers' vivid show of strength; faced with a choice of standing with the militant Mexicans or defying the strike, many began to leave the camp to look for work elsewhere. By contrast, the Mexicans, Italians, and other strike supporters exhibited considerable discipline. Few crossed the lines or left. Lacking a building in which to meet, they gathered two or three times a day in an old lime pit quarried out of a Morenci hillside and listened to "speeches from the leaders [standing on big boulders] who are very industrious in their efforts to hold the men together." (The hostile press called them "harangues.")[94] Laustaunau appeared often. Called *el negro* because he was dark, and "Three-fingered Jack" (which he hated because it was the nickname of a brutal killer) or *mocho* (mutilated) or *el mojo* (which might be a misunderstanding of *el cojo,* crippled) because he was missing two (or was it three?) fingers, he had a charismatic or repellent presence, depending on who was talking. He was probably a blacksmith, not a miner, and evidently had a passionate, stubborn streak: imprisoned after the strike was suppressed, he served numerous stints in solitary for being incorrigible and died of heat prostration while in such a cell in 1906.[95]

Others spoke too, but there is no record of their words. The Anglo press reported that they "used harsh language concerning the 'gringos.'" The men soon began to challenge the dual wage system. Nevertheless, Anglo union men from other mining towns came and spoke, notably WFM men from Globe. "Big Bill" Haywood of the WFM sent a telegram of support, the beginning of the union's belated recognition of Mexicans as workers and potential allies—a recognition that, one suspects, met some cynicism as well as gratification from the Clifton-Morenci workers, since the union provided no material help.

As the strike went on, the frequent gatherings–or nonstop meetings–produced a camp within a camp. A brass band played between speeches. The mood was festive as well as indignant, and the men drank from barrels of "Dago red," which they carried up the hills suspended from poles.[96] At other times they sat in small groups, a few men with guitars singing *corridos*. From Morenci Square you could sometimes see them massed up there, occasionally joined by a few women and children who lugged food and water up. The women spent most of their time scrounging, trying to feed children on no wages. As always in strikes, women's attitudes could be critical: if positive, they could not only support but even lead the men in militancy; if hostile, they could severely erode determination.

"The mining company bosses got pretty much excited," one Arizona Ranger later recalled, and "didn't lose much time [before] hollering for the law to protect them."[97] Sheriff Parks deputized a group of men, eventually to number sixty, to help him–do what? Phrases like "control the strike" and "curb the situation" are often used as euphemisms in labor struggles,[98] as double-talk for protecting scabs or breaking up demonstrations and pickets. But Parks was not simply a company man, and he tried to create an independent and somewhat more neutral role for local law enforcement. Ranchers with large land and cattle holdings, Jim Parks and his brothers, George and Deputy Sheriff John, embodied the only significant economic interest that could challenge mining. He said his deputies were largely "cattlemen, cowboys and ranchers," and the first group may have been. Of the twenty-three members of the posse that could be identified, fourteen were likely independent of the mining companies because they were cattle raisers, "cowboys," or shopkeepers or had already been serving as deputy sheriffs for some time.[99] Many ranchers resented the power and arrogance of the mine owners, especially the absentee owners, who grabbed land and water with seemingly limitless supplies of capital. Jim became a deputy sheriff in 1888, before he was even twenty-one, so he had experienced authority in the old days when prospectors worked with their own muscles and picks, before the mines were owned by men behind desks.

Adding to the mining companies' distrust of Parks was the fact that his possemen were a motley crew, "armed with every kind of an old gun you could think of, and a lot of them had ammunition that didn't fit

their guns."[100] So Mills and Colquhoun got the governor to call out the
Arizona Rangers. Created in 1901 by Governor Nathan O. Murphy,
himself a mine owner, their original purpose was to patrol the border
against smuggling and cattle rustling. They were now returning as
heroes to Clifton-Morenci, having captured the most-wanted bandit
Augustín Chacón in November 1902. But this 1903 Morenci expedition
would transform their reputation, identifying them primarily as a mine
owners' weapon against strikes. The squad of twenty-four was only
partly professional; poorly paid, they had no uniforms and were required to supply their own pistols, rifles, horses, saddles, and pack
mules. Many had been Texas Rangers before, however, and they were
used to life as itinerant, unsupervised law officers.[101] They arrived on
Sunday June 7, bringing three cases of rifles loaned to Detroit Copper
by the Copper Queen. The rangers believed that the strikers also had a
small arsenal: "double barrelled guns, revolvers with four barrels that
the barrels revolved, guns with brass barrels, and a lot of other kinds—all
of foreign manufacture, and . . . some of them homemade." Yet the
streets of Clifton-Morenci were peaceful: about 3,500 strikers from all
the camps, a ranger recalled, "walked up and down the streets and
milled around, but didn't form any big crowds and didn't make any
trouble."[102] (The trial of strike leaders provided evidence of their non-
violence: one Mexican man, Manuel Relles, was indicted for assault
with a deadly weapon, but the only charge that could be thrown at the
others was incitement to riot, the kind of conspiracy charge that allowed
prosecution for their words without any evidence about acts.)[103]

Parks did not like the rangers' interference in his work and challenge
to his authority. (Later hostilities between the rangers and the sheriff's
office would break out into a public dispute.)[104] But as the strike
progressed, Parks needed more men. He had to guard the railroad
bridges to prevent the strikers from dynamiting them or attacking the
train that would carry the rangers. He decided to occupy the top of
Longfellow Hill, a vantage point from which to watch the strikers'
activities.

This was the rangers' first strike-breaking assignment, and some of
them did not like it: preferring to imagine themselves as gunfighters
going after rustlers, "standing guard over striking miners who toiled for
half the monthly pay of a Ranger held little appeal for such men."[105]
But despite their hesitations, violence seemed imminent. Following PD
orders, on Monday June 8 they deployed across the roads from Metcalf

(where many miners lived) to keep the strikers from entering Morenci. The strikers, however, surprised them, by heading down the Chase Creek canyon toward Clifton and up to the West Yankee mine from the east. Attempting to follow them, the rangers climbed up a steep mountain "in our high-heel boots, for we didn't have any horses," to try to reopen West Yankee. Rangers captain Tom Rynning recalled,

> we see about a hundred and fifty Mexicans, wild-looking hombres in their Old Mexico clothes, formed in a semicircle round Sheriff Jim Parks and his thirty-two deputies. They had their guns leveled on the sheriff and his posse there in the rincon [narrow valley] between the little peaks; had them captured, it looked like. I see there wasn't noways any use all of us going down there and starting an all-round killing . . . Got . . . [the rangers] arranged so the Mexicans would be enfiladed from the other side if they tried to get away in that direction after things busted loose . . . A deputy of Parks', Little Dave, come up where I was and says Jim Parks had 'laid them down,' meaning he'd quit.[106]

(This is the way many Anglo old-timers spoke, an early Spanglish, or English larded with Spanish words.) The *Copper Era* reported that the rangers and sheriff's posse together were "inadequate to cope with the strikers, who had stationed themselves on the surrounding hills, and by their long range rifles commanded the situation. At one time they had it in their power to capture or kill all the deputies and Rangers, as they were surrounded by twelve hundred armed miners, who jeered the officers and laughed at them, then defied them to advance further."[107]

Sheriff Parks tried to mediate. He told Mills, his sister recalled, "that the strikers' demands were not unreasonable, that the miners were underpaid and that their working conditions were deplorable. So, rather than have any loss of life or destruction of property, the officers advised Mills to grant the men's demands. But Mills, who was an obstinate man and much disliked by the employees, refused to grant anything."[108] After this refusal the strikers' speeches became more incendiary, and they threatened to take Mills and Parks as hostages. Mills, presumably terrified, fled Morenci at night. The sheriff also tried to talk to Laustaunau, asking him to maintain the peace and stay off company property. Laustaunau grew insolent, but Parks declined to arrest him.[109]

Around Parks's and Rynning's retreats and Mills's flight arose a competitive discourse about bravery and cowardice, honor and shame. Strikers jeered at Mills's lack of *cojones,* although the supposedly cowardly Mills had volunteered to join Roosevelt's Rough Riders in the Spanish-American War, refusing an officer's commission and fighting as a private.[110] Rynning claimed that Parks surrendered when the rangers would have stood down the strikers; Parks's supporters praised him for good judgment, and Ranger Bassett claimed that Rynning was the yellow-belly, spending his time in Clifton-Morenci hobnobbing with politicians while his deputy Jack Foster actually commanded the rangers. Rynning and Parks had established a command center in the Morenci Hotel, and Rynning rarely left the hotel, charged another memoirist of the rangers.[111] There were other kinds of accusations against Parks—that he and his men were corrupt in collecting gambling license fees from the saloons and claiming expenses for deputies that did not exist—suggesting that he, too, knew how to throw his weight around.[112] We can guess that the strikers attached gendered meanings to their tactical disagreements. All the men wanted to be macho, an exclusively laudatory adjective at the time.

The balance of power shifted on June 9. The strikers interpreted Mills's departure to mean that he would not negotiate, and they tried to raise the cost of the strike for PD by preventing its use of scab labor. In the early morning they moved to stop the ore cars that ran on the Longfellow incline. They surrounded and disarmed the white tram men and the deputies guarding them, then made their way to the Longfellow company store, apparently seeking food and provisions. This time the sheriff's brother John Parks tried to mediate. He got help from the Longfellow store manager, Paul Nicholas, respected by the miners, who promised to use his influence on behalf of the men. In return Laustaunau agreed to ask the strikers to back off, and he returned the deputies' guns, but it was evident to John Parks that Laustaunau was losing control over the men. Several more confrontations at PD works ensued. Despite a pouring rain, groups totaling several thousand strikers—by now almost exclusively Mexican and Euro-Latin—swirled around the mine and plant entrances. Then, returning to Morenci, they spread out over the hills, stationing themselves behind big rocks, with their rifles leveled at the rangers and deputies. The sheriff, restrained as usual, ordered his men to withdraw, forcing Mills, who had returned, to order the stoppage of all his works. The strikers seemed to be in charge. They "held all of the commanding positions in the hills . . . cut all of the telegraph and telephone lines," PD managers charged; "they are intending to make themselves complete masters of the town . . . threatening the lives of prominent citizens, most of whom are officers of or managers of departments of the copper company."[113]

Sheriff Parks no longer could or would promise to contain the strikers, and Anglo townspeople were badly frightened—although not a shot had been fired—so he and the rangers, no doubt persuaded by Mills, called on the governor to send troops.[114] (Mills was a personal friend of the governor—they had been Rough Riders together.) Six companies from Forts Grant and Huachuca, including the entire Territorial Militia and 200 soldiers of the regular army, arrived in Morenci the evening of June 10, and a cavalry troop from Fort Apache arrived the next day, bringing the total of law-enforcement men to about 800.

Had the army arrived on June 8, there might indeed have been a bloodbath. Instead, an act of God, as some religious and antistrike people said, defeated the strikers: the biggest flood yet known in Clifton-Morenci. On June 9 the rain came down with great force, as if driven by a policeman's power hose, soon followed by walnut-sized hail. Thunder reverberated off the walls of the narrow canyons. The very earth seemed to shake. The strikers ducked beneath rock overhangs. The rangers, ordered to hold their positions, were soon standing in water over their boot tops. The water rushing down from Morenci broke through Arizona Copper's tailings dam. In Clifton, alas, the townspeople mostly did the wrong thing—they sought shelter inside their homes. So when an enormous wall of water came down Chase Creek many were trapped as houses collapsed around them.

> The flood waters struck the upper end of town with a breast of from six to eight feet, carrying houses, horses, wagons and human beings on to the Frisco river with a speed and fury indescribable . . . Houses were picked up and jammed against others only to break into a thousand pieces, carrying their helpless occupants for a few hundred feet, when they sank beneath the murky waters . . . Wreckage and debris would pile against a building or block up the narrow street, causing the water to pile up until its force swept everything before it, crushing strong buildings like egg shells, and hurling the debris with still greater violence against another building.[115]

Thirty-nine people were killed, mostly women, children, and old people. The first seven bodies to be recovered were those of Juanita

Cuateres, 70; Juan Vega, 53; Louis Jacques, 37; Sun Su Yen, 35; Jas. Nash, 35; Gay Midlin, 16; and Alvina Norte, 12. It took a while to get to the other dead as they were buried under debris. Chase Creek was a predominantly Mexican neighborhood, and so the dead were disproportionately Mexican. The many small businesses on this street were severely damaged, some losing all their stock and some losing even their buildings. The strikers scrambled down into Clifton to try to save whoever and whatever they could, but theirs became mainly a cleanup operation. Many of Clifton's striking families now had not only no wages, but also no homes, clothing, water, or food. Damage was estimated at $100,000.

This "act of God" was largely man-made. Harvesting the trees for coke and fuel had stripped the hillsides of the juniper, oak, and mesquite that held down the soil. What was not taken by the axe was snuffed out by smelter smoke.[116] And if Arizona Copper's tailings dam had been stronger? The townspeople considered the company's dam failure responsible for most of the damage, and citizens called a meeting at Library Hall at which $100,000 was asked of Arizona and Detroit Copper. John Gatti chaired a committee that approached the two mine bosses, Mills in Morenci and Colquhoun in Clifton, and both hung tough: they expressed sympathy and made noncommittal offers to help but vowed to resist to the end should the citizens take their demand to court. No Mexicans were on this committee; as an afterthought Father Timmermans was added, presumably to represent them. The companies and their bank eventually paid $10,000.[117]

The flood did not completely quell the strike, which continued on, fragmented, for a few days; but the anguish, demoralization, and distraction created by the flood allowed the soldiers to take control. As mineworkers searched for bodies, attempted to salvage belongings, and mourned, the army was establishing martial law. Commanding Colonel McClintock prohibited all assemblies, used his bayonets to round up "unruly subjects," and began searching Mexican homes. To everyone's surprise, he found few weapons in these searches, suggesting that they had been hidden or that the strikers were not as heavily armed as had been thought. The army arrested those they considered strike leaders.[118] Most strikers capitulated on Friday June 12. Some leaders and men continued the walkout, but whenever the strikers tried to meet at the lime pit or elsewhere, they were dispersed by the army. The Arizona Territory Superior Court issued an injunction against four leaders and two hundred others, prohibiting interference with Detroit Copper's operations such as congregating on or near its premises, inciting its employees to quit, and making inflammatory speeches. (Judge Fletcher Doan, who issued the injunction and presided over the trial of strike leaders, also deliberated on the New York Foundling Hospital's suit to get the orphans back.) On July 1, a cavalry troop was still in Morenci.[119] The worried Anglos proposed that Morenci establish its own cavalry, and A. M. Tuthill, Detroit Copper company physician, Masonic leader, and member of the posse that kidnapped the orphans, was elected captain: "The boys expect to commence drilling at once."[120] If this unit actually materialized, it never functioned against strikers.

THE MARKS LEFT BY JUNE 1903 were indelible. Short-term consequences included some PD concessions, notably changing rooms and a small raise after a few months. But PD also concluded that intransigence paid. Mills announced that those "who had not made themselves objectionable" could return to work,[121] establishing a blacklist. The threat of the blacklist made workers less likely to complain, of course; and it licensed corruption, often forcing miners to pay kickbacks, sometimes as much as $5–$15 per month, to foremen and managers to acquire and keep jobs.[122] Many Mexican workers quit, but others came. At the cost of increased turnover, the racial segmentation of the labor force had proved effective at limiting the workers' power by cutting them off from most white sympathy. The Mexican workers' own national identity also contributed to that division. Moreover, from its 1903 struggle PD had learned several tactics it would apply in the future: the use of spies, the army, and private enforcers.

The mineworkers drew a parallel conclusion: that workers' organization could move, if not defeat, the copper companies. A WFM left wing, against racial exclusion, sent organizers. By 1907 the WFM listed locals in both Clifton and Metcalf (PD always retained greater control in Morenci), and the workers struck again later that year. They failed then, but in 1915 the union brought PD to the table and forced it to recognize the WFM and engage in collective bargaining. But racial division kept the Arizona miners' unions weak until the National Labor Relations Act and World War II provided an opportunity for a new, insistently multiracial union. Subsequently the Clifton-Morenci camp experienced four decades of relative prosperity until, exactly eighty years after the 1903 strike, PD was able to return to its fundamental principles and, thanks to the Reagan National Labor Relations Board and courts, drive the mineworkers' union out of Clifton-Morenci.

The WFM as a whole never saw the obvious lesson of the 1903 strike. It continued to seek to maintain a standard of living for workers it considered racially "white" or "American," and to restore a labor sellers' market by driving out an allegedly wage-lowering, unorganizable competition. The evidence, however, showed once again that "experience" can never explain racist thought. Miners' experience could have yielded antiracist conclusions. Mexicans were at this time easily as militant, solidaristic, and committed to unionism as any other group in the United States, and in Arizona they were the leaders. Of the five major strikes in Arizona between 1896 and 1915, Mexican workers led four of them. (In the fifth, white workers tried to drive Mexicans out of the camp and failed.)[123] Moreover, previous Clifton-Morenci strikes in which Mexicans were prominent already provided ample evidence of their organizability: In 1887 smelter workers went out in response to a wage reduction. In 1885 and 1889 workers had won holidays on Mexican Independence Day and Good Friday.[124] But the Arizona WFM not only continued its exclusionist strategy, but also entered a powerful Democratic coalition and fought to restrict "alien" labor, arguing once again that Mexican workers were unorganizable. The WFM not only lost this fight but stimulated PD and other copper companies into greater political activity to defend their antiunion interests. The WFM succeeded only in getting a literacy requirement for voting, which further disfranchised Mexicans.[125]

In Clifton-Morenci the 1903 strike altered racial meanings, firmed up amorphous categories, and redrew boundaries. The walls between whites and Mexicans rose higher. Mexicans gained a new reputation among whites: dangerous, radical, and capable of violent surprises, qualities in some tension with earlier stereotypes of them as placid, lethargic, unambitious.[126] Mexicans became even more fixed in the white mind as aliens, not "Americans." Whites strengthened their reputation among Mexicans as ruthless, money-grubbing, only out for themselves. Race had been superimposed more neatly than previously onto class categories. What changed was less the actual occupations and wealth of various "racial" groups, more the class meanings of racial identity and, of course, the racial meanings of class identity.

Although Clifton-Morenci's racial demography remained complex, it simplified considerably, moving toward an Anglo-Mexican binary. Pressure on the Euro-Latins grew. At one point it seemed that Italian miners might bear the worst of PD's blacklist: it was announced that they would no longer be given preferential treatment and would be categorized either as Mexicans or as "Americans."[127] They were being punished for their loyalty to the Mexicans in the strike and ordered to choose sides. This is similar to what Sheriff Parks and his deputies experienced, as their attempts to hew to an independent, neutral tactic failed. Parks's experience in turn resembled that of Sheriff Harry Wheeler in the much more famous Bisbee strike and deportation of 1917; Wheeler, a former captain of the Arizona Rangers, tried first to cool the conflict and to remain neutral between strikers and PD, but was forced by the company to legitimate and oversee the "deputization" of several thousand men into a vigilante army that illegally captured and deported several thousand strikers, dumping them in the New Mexican desert without food or water in the blazing heat of mid-July.[128]

For those Clifton-Morenci dwellers who tried not to take sides, like Parks, there was no substantial option for neutrality, given the accumulation of economic and political power by the copper companies. The independents were becoming fewer, the copper company employees more numerous. Father Timmermans, his church dependent on copper-company gifts, urged the strikers back to work.[129] It is not happenstance that the labor song "Which Side Are You On," denying the possibility of a middle position, comes from a mining town. As the strike ended, the identification of the Euro-Latins with an in-between race and class position was symbolized by John Gatti's chairing the town committee to get the copper companies to pay for the flood damage. A year later he was the chief spokesman for the Anglo vigilantes' denunciation of the "half-breed," "degenerate" Mexicans as he fought to keep the child he had kidnapped.

Racial constructions have many builders, but Clifton-Morenci's big daddy, Phelps Dodge, held the frame together. It asserted, in its insistence on the 1903 pay cut, that the Mexican wage was vital to its ability to work a mine with low-concentration copper. (It did not address the reasons wages were higher in low-concentration "white men's camps.") It used the threat of capital flight against Clifton-Morenci residents, but it combined that threat with the bribe of better treatment for the whites. PD would not tolerate any support for the strikers. (It was alleged that PD, owner of the only available telegraph line during the strike, was censoring news reports going out, but there is no corroboration available for this charge.) When the combined force of its own detectives, the Arizona Rangers, and the deputies could not stop the strike, it demonstrated its ability to wield the ultimate force in the American polity, the U.S. Army. With its weak tailings dam, it even created a flood, some might argue—a bit hyperbolically but no more so than those claiming that the flood was God's punishment.

But not even PD was powerful enough to impose an arbitrary racial policy; it merely used and strengthened racial structures it found. Even when the citizens were offered a fresh opportunity for cooperation against PD, in trying to get recompense for the flood, they wasted their chance because the Anglos could not conceive of a citizenship in which Mexicans could participate. Neither political party offered an alternative to racism; in fact they offered two versions of it. PD's strong influence in the Republican party solidified political support for its racial policy of hiring "aliens" at lower wages, blaming the Democratic Party's eight-hour law for causing the "trouble." The Democrats tried to exclude "aliens" and denounced the manipulation of "ignorant Mexicans and Italians . . . to vote the Republican ticket."[130]

Mexicans' lack of political power—notable in their lack of influence over the sheriff's office, the Arizona Rangers, and the army—contributed to the outcome of the strike. The strike further defined them as noncitizens, in the moral as well as legal sense, in the minds of those who controlled the operational borders of citizenship. Not a single Hispanic or Italian name appeared on the list from which the jury in the strike leaders' trials was drawn.[131] In fact, Mexican political power was declining throughout this period, as indicated by a shrinking share of voter registration. In 1894, 44.5 percent of Clifton-Morenci voters were apparently Mexican; in 1902, 22 percent; in 1910, just after the literacy law, 11 percent; in 1922, 8 percent.[132] As if compensating for, and possibly adding to, their exclusion from U.S. politics, Mexican Americans became increasingly drawn into Mexican politics, as an anti-Díaz movement built. The PLM became a magnet, attracting the most politicized Mexicans away from U.S. political involvement.[133]

In contrast to racial and class politics, when it came to gender the strike changed little. Women, fundamental to the working-class economy, seemed inactive in the strike. Strikes often seem to marginalize women: the solidarity engendered among strikers can be an intensely male cohesion, its celebration of brotherhood and condemnation of weakness, frailty, inconstancy expressed as abhorrence of femininity. The strikers, so many of whom would have said they were struggling for their women and children, found the strike an occasion for extra-familial male bonding. Clifton-Morenci's Mexican women, at home, were usually out of hearing of the men's gossip and talk of rights, humiliations, and inequities, a separation not conducive to the development of political knowledge. Yet the support of women—particularly wives and older daughters or sisters—became more vital than ever to the strikers. The striking men were ipso facto failing in their breadwinning responsibilities and could not wield that crucial source of power, the pay envelope. Whenever men are unemployed, wives and children tend to gain power at male expense. Women sometimes seize these opportunities to exert more autonomy, perhaps even unconsciously as they respond to men's increased vulnerability. In the next big strike, in 1915, Mexican women and girls marched through Morenci, cheering for the strikers and jeering PD, and strikers endorsed this unconventional and assertive behavior.[134] In 1903 Mexican women and children limited their political expression to taking care of the strikers as they always took care of workers: bringing lunches and drinks, for example, but now hauling them up the Morenci hillside to the lime pit instead of to the mine and mill entrances. Their less visible forms of help were no doubt more vital: spending less money, making goods from scratch that they might have purchased, giving food to families more impoverished than their own, resisting desires to return home to Mexico, bucking up tired and pessimistic strikers. Was there also an underside, a cost to women's exclusion? Did they dread or even oppose the strike's continuation and counsel a realistic, defeatist capitulation? Did these devout Mexican women take from the flood a message of God's or the Virgin's disapproval?

"Must have," "perhaps," "can be," question marks—these are the historians' codes for lack of evidence. Not a single newspaper account, reminiscence, or legal document of the 1903 strike mentioned any women. But we must ask the questions nevertheless, because not to ask them is to perpetuate the blotting out of historical subjects and of elemental aspects of life. It is better to realize what we don't know than to oversimplify the picture. In 1904 several groups of women, Mexican and white, initiated dramatic events, and in so doing demonstrated substantially more agency than had been customary among them.

What were the roots of this initiative? The strike left many people with motives for revenge: strikers against scabs, possemen, and others who had sided with the companies; nonstriking townspeople against the strikers who had taken up arms against the local order and menaced private property and leaders of the community; and women who had borne the sufferings and hardships of the strike and flood without acknowledgment. However buried, subconscious, or repressed these vengeful emotions, the orphans reactivated them.

October 3–4, 1904

Clifton Drugstore and Library Hall, Morenci Hotel

EXPECTING SHERIFF PARKS AND JUDGE LITTLE to arrive at 1 P.M. on Monday, several of the sisters had hired a hack to bring them to Clifton. When the meeting was postponed until evening, it was decided that the road would be unsafe then, so great was the hostility they evoked, and they returned to the children in the Morenci Hotel. That's why, once again, only George Swayne and Father Mandin represented the Foundling Hospital. Although a crowd of several hundred was waiting restlessly at Library Hall for this second "citizens' meeting," a group met the train from Solomonville at about 8:00 and took the judge and sheriff first to a small, private meeting of thirty to forty of the town's leading citizens at the drugstore. The town's elite knew or sensed that they had to orchestrate the large open meeting by creating a plan and arranging a consensus in advance. The drugstore meeting was a premeeting leadership caucus. Dunagan and Simpson were asked to bring the New Yorkers—although never under arrest, Swayne and Mandin did not dare move away from the deputy sheriff—because the leading citizens wanted to cut a deal. With the children now in their possession, they wanted the judge's help in figuring out how to use the law, not to defy it. They thought he might help them negotiate an agreement with Swayne without the sisters, perhaps suspecting that the nuns would remain immovable because they were more committed to the children and to the Foundling's procedures.

But their group was already too big to conduct a negotiation. In fact, they were making demands, not negotiating; and what they wanted of the judge was unlawful. They asked the judge to issue them adoption papers. Little told them that the law did not allow him to do so without the consent of the children's legal guardian. They tried to get Swayne to give that consent, but he would not. Swayne, on his side, hoped that the judge would inform the townspeople that the only legal guardian of the orphans was the Foundling Hospital and its agents, that Arizona Territory was bound to recognize the New York State laws that gave the sisters and Swayne exclusive custody of the children, and that the sheriff had to enforce the law and return the children. But Judge Little would not do this either. A typical vigilante judge, perhaps, he would neither exceed his authority by granting the Anglos adoption papers, nor demand respect for the legal or peaceable procedures due the Mexicans. As the citizens at this small meeting began to get belligerent, he made no attempt to calm or control them.

Although Judge Little would not oblige them, these community leaders had, by calling him to Clifton, begun a legal journey vital to their interests. The path would lead them beyond their imagining: not only to Phoenix to the Arizona Territory Supreme Court, but also to the United States Supreme Court, only eighteen months from this night.

Right now, however, these "citizens" were running scared. Sensing their fear, I wondered: what would have happened had the judge ordered them to return the children to the sisters? Or if, compromising, he had ordered the children to be held by the sisters remaining in Clifton pending a trial? Would the citizens have backed down? Would the sheriff have ordered them to back down? It seems unlikely, considering the balance of forces. On the one side were several hundred assembled Anglos, most with rifles nearby if not on their person. On the other side were seven New York Catholic women; an Irish man who was himself a bit of a loose cannon; a young French priest; and an assortment of Mexican families, also with rifles at home, but never having come together as a community to discuss these events, the men possibly without commitment to these orphans taken in by women. Had the Mexicans been able to know how uncertain the Anglo leaders were at this moment, there might have been a different outcome—quite possibly a more violent one.

The Anglos, lacking confidence that the court system would decide in their favor, turned their focus from Judge Little to George Swayne. They tried to coax and to coerce Swayne's consent to a fait accompli, announcing repeatedly that they would never release the children. But Swayne let them know again, vociferously, that he would never back down. As before, Swayne's obstinate stand soon provoked threats, even from within this select group. Mandin evoked what was to become his one-note motif throughout the whole affair: he was new and a foreigner and had not understood that there was a difference between Americans and Mexicans, but it did him little good. He had nothing the group wanted anyway, and it quickly drowned him out with hoots and insults.

The negotiation having failed, the citizens reaffirmed that they would keep the children and demanded that Swayne and Mandin leave town. They threatened Swayne by announcing their inability to control the hoi polloi waiting at Library Hall, enunciating a passive view of their own responsibility: "the people [in this case the "leading citizens" positioned themselves as separate from the "people"] had become so enthused over it [the situation] that they didn't think it advisable for him to attempt to take the children."[1] Dunagan, it now became clear, was playing a double role: while he was supposedly calming the crowd, he was simultaneously threatening Swayne that the crowd was uncontrollable in order to get the agent to concede.

The larger "indignation" meeting at the Library Hall, to which they proceeded after the stalemate of the drugstore meeting, followed rules of order no more than the earlier mob gatherings at Morenci and Clifton. As one newspaper reported, "Free speech was denied. Any attempt at explanation was met with jeers, and abuse was rained on both the strangers."[2] Did categorizing the padre as a stranger refer only to the fact that he had been in town just eight months? Or did it refer to some deeper way in which they considered him an outsider? Having worked themselves up with accusations and bravado, the Anglos present were not pleased to hear the judge's refusal to provide them with post facto legality, so once again there was talk of tar, feathers, rope. The least threatening of their suggestions was that Swayne and Mandin should get out of town immediately, but when the Catholic men reluctantly began to do this, others in the crowd found this option unsatisfactory and began chasing them. Dunagan gathered up his charges, eluded the pursuers, and shepherded Swayne and Mandin into the back of a saloon, where they hid for a few hours. Dunagan was not sorry that they could hear the continuous uproar outside.

It was long past midnight by the time the deputy and his two charges got back to Morenci. No sooner had they got out of the hack than another deputy sheriff, Gus Hobbs, who had been awaiting their arrival, informed them that the people of Morenci also planned to take the remaining orphans from the nuns and distribute them among the Anglos. The Morencians made clear that they would bridge no opposition and that the New York group had better be on the 7 A.M. train out of town, or else.

Monday had been a day from hell for the sisters. Anna Michaella and one other sister, hoping to meet with Judge Little, had traveled by hack to Clifton at midday, enduring again the dusty and terrifying ride down the road with horseshoe turns and several-hundred-foot drop-offs just feet from the wheels of the wagon. From the judge they expected to get law reinstated and the children returned to their rightful guardians. But then the judge was late, and they saw just enough of the crowd milling around Library Hall to have to make the scary trip back up to Morenci in a mood of intensified apprehension. There they waited with the children, virtual prisoners, afraid to leave the hotel rooms. At 11:45 P.M., having heard nothing from Clifton, the sisters asked the Morenci Hotel clerk what was happening and he, of course, knew—the judge had decided that the children should remain where they were. Sister Anna Michaella felt a bolt of anxiety followed by a rush of adrenaline as she realized that the sisters had to protect the twenty-four children with them from a likely second kidnapping attempt. She had barely fallen asleep when she was awakened by Swayne, returning from the Clifton meeting in the wee hours of Tuesday morning. Swayne reported that his life had been on the line and that the judge had offered no help. Now it was Anna Michaella's turn to be tested, and she rose to the occasion. She declared that the sisters had decided that they would never leave the children behind but would sacrifice their lives here in Morenci first. Swayne then had no choice but to go along with her position. But he seemed relieved when Dunagan suggested that the sisters could stay—Dunagan thought they would be safe—but that Swayne and the priest go; Dunagan was no longer able to protect them, he said. Sister Anna Michaella let Swayne off the hook by noting that he had a wife and children to think about. So leave they did: Mandin for Tucson (never to return to Clifton!) and Swayne to New York.[3] The seven women were to face the mob alone.

One must assume that the Mexicans were becoming alarmed. There were neighborhoods in which Mexicans and Anglos lived near each other, and everyone shopped in the same stores. It must have smelled like a race riot, an embryonic lynching, an attack that could easily spread: the race riot by proxy—focusing on white Catholics—could have become an actual race riot. Men and women who had seemed honorable, with whom they had exchanged friendly greetings, whose stores they had patronized, with whom they had rubbed shoulders in the mines and smelters were now part of an armed mob shouting anti-Mexican slurs. A mob that seemed to believe the most ludicrous lies. A mob that was, incredibly, threatening the sisters. Such a mob could easily turn on the Mexican people. They knew that vigilante attacks on Mexicans had happened before. When the Mexicans heard that their priest had run, they knew they no longer had an Anglo ally. No doubt they were cleaning their rifles.

Meanwhile Dunagan had been maneuvering to get the sisters alone. Despite their death-defying declarations, he calculated that without Swayne he could manage them peacefully. At 8 A.M. he went back to their rooms and informed them that they had to turn over the children to the "citizens" of Morenci. Furthermore, he reported, if they tried to leave with the children, the engineer had vowed not to run the train. They were trapped.

For a few minutes they were alone with the children in their rooms. The kids were showing the effects of the chaos, some agitated and others unusually silent. Talking with one another, the seven women were too realistic to return to their our-children-or-die declarations of the night before, but they could not imagine what they would say to the children. Theirs was not an age in which honesty to children was thought best. They tried to reassure themselves that the Anglo families would take good care of the children, that once the frenzy abated, these strange Arizona women would again be governed by what they considered normal maternal instincts, as opposed to this most unwomanly rage. But there was no comfort for their deepest dread, for the souls of these Catholic children would be lost forever.

Their agonizing decision making was postponed when at 9 A.M. there was another knock on the door; Anna Michaella wondered what worse news they could expect. It was Jeff Dunagan once more, and now she learned for the first time about a deal that he had struck with Swayne, sometime during the previous twenty-four hours, when the badly frightened New Yorker had felt particularly vulnerable. In return for protection, Swayne had agreed, Dunagan alleged, to give Dunagan two children. The bartering for children begun in the Clifton Hotel now extended to Morenci. Anna Michaella was so numb in mind and emotion that she might not have been able to articulate an objection even if she had not been so frightened and so resigned that she was literally speechless. She wondered if it were really true that Swayne had agreed to this, but it did not matter, and there was no logic to protesting: since her authority over the children had ended anyway, they were all already lost.

In his way Dunagan followed the same logic—since the children were staying here anyway, why shouldn't he get to choose some? This is how he later explained it:

> Mr. Swayne thanked me for what I had done and said he should remember me; and he said if it was in his power to accommodate me in anything he would be more than pleased to do it. I told him he didn't owe me anything for what I had done for him, but I says, "I will suggest one thing, that I may place two of these children at Morenci." He says, "I am perfectly willing you shall do it, but," he says, "I may not have any more to say about them than I have about these [referring to the Clifton orphans]." But he says, "You have my permission" . . . after we got to Morenci he made the same statement to the sisters that just testified; that if it was agreeable with the people of Morenci, that I should have my pick of two children . . . The sister says, "We will only be too glad."

A newspaper put it differently: "Tuesday morning the sisters were obliged to forcibly Surrender three more of the best [*sic*] children to the deputies who took them to Clifton to . . . people of high standing."[4] Jeff Dunagan did not want the children himself. He gave them as a "gift" to George Frazer and J. T. Kelly. We can only assume that these men and their wives were among the Clifton crowd who had been unable to get one of the original sixteen; perhaps they had even charged Dunagan with the task of getting them orphans, or perhaps they were an unsolicited gift. The deputy chose Hannah Kane, three and a half, and Edward Cummiskey, four and a half, and gave the girl to the Frazers and the boy to the Kellys. The boy had a scar on his neck from an abscess, and at Sister Anna Michaella's instruction, as the children were being dressed, the nurses pointed it out to Dunagan and explained its origin, so that there would be no accusations that it resulted from mistreatment at the Foundling Hospital.[5] And off went the two, to parents unknown to the sisters.

Shortly afterward Charles Mills knocked and he too asked for and took a child, also not for himself. His friend Dr. W. F. Davis, a former

Morenci physician now living in Los Angeles, was visiting in Clifton, had heard about the orphans, and wanted a child.[6] The sisters presumably knew by now that Mills was the boss, and they didn't even bother to protest.

None of the Anglos seemed to think these arrangements strange: after all, the children were orphans, they needed homes, and the Anglos could provide good ones; and if the Mexicans thought it unseemly to market children in this way, if it seemed to them that the New York Catholics and the padre were not people of their word, the Anglos did not hear it. No criticisms of the Anglos' methods of acquiring children were raised at the trial. By contrast, Swayne and the sisters stood to be embarrassed about these transactions at the trial because the attorneys for the Clifton Anglos argued that since Swayne was willing to give them to Dunagan, he might as well have agreed to give them to the other Anglos; and that since he appeared to be giving them to Dunagan as payment for his kindness, he was, by implication, selling them. Swayne defended himself by saying only that the children had been taken away from them anyway and that he wanted to repay Dunagan's kindness.

The Morenci crowd, as if to avoid being outdone by the Clifton crowd, turned its fury on the sisters, and Tuesday became the most terrifying day of all. First a throng assembled outside to watch Swayne and Mandin depart, after which, instead of dispersing, the mob flowed into the hotel, and not just into the lobby but upstairs and actually into the nuns' five rooms, and refused to leave.

> Q. Now as to the people—I think you mentioned that your rooms were invaded or something of that nature? Who came in there and did they come by invitation . . .?
> A. They seemed to have free access to our rooms; we had no privacy whatsoever until Mr. Mills had spoken to the authorities at the hotel.

There were so many people entering their five rooms that the sisters could not estimate a number. They refused to leave when asked. Several times the deputies pushed the crowd out, but each time it returned. As always the men were armed. Women were in the majority, but this fact did not seem to make the crowd less aggressive. The angry men and women accused the nuns of being slave dealers and child sellers. They shouted vile insults and called the nuns vulgar names: "they treated us with scorn; so much so I cannot remember what they said because I was not looking for any redress for myself at all; it was only to have the little ones left to our care." The twenty-one children in the rooms were terrified.

Sensing that the deputies could not or would not control the crowd, the resourceful Sister Anna Michaella sought help from the only source remaining. She managed to sneak out of the hotel, find Charles Mills, and plead her case. As before, he came to the rescue (although only after he had taken the child he was after). He not only kept the crowd out of their rooms thereafter, ordering the hotel to let no one in and placing guards at the doors, but he gave the sisters "permission" to leave with the twenty-one remaining children and arranged to have guards accompany them from the hotel to the station and into the railroad car on Wednesday morning. Thank goodness for a company town, one might say!

So the four sisters and three nurses, shaken and unnerved, took their twenty-one remaining foundlings back to their New York home. Of the forty who had first disembarked in Arizona, sixteen remained with the Anglo parents who had originally seized them in Clifton, two more had been claimed the next day by Dunagan and given to two other Anglo families in the area, and one, appropriated by Charles Mills, was on his way to the home of Dr. Davis in Los Angeles. But these placements were by no means a fait accompli as far as the sisters were concerned. The situation was to them, literally, unacceptable. To have done as well as they could was not enough: their duty was to save these children, and saved they would be. Anna Michaella had already wired the Foundling Hospital and knew that Head Sister Teresa would call upon every powerful connection at her disposal to bring back the children into the church.

7

Vigilantism

THE ARMED MEN WHO SEIZED THE ORPHANS were classic western vigilantes. Their purpose was unusual, for child saving was not a typical vigilante goal, but the posse's composition, and its members' understanding that what they were doing was honorable, were standard. Including deputy sheriffs Dunagan, Parks, and Hobbs, local businessmen Sam and Jake Abraham, Mike Riordan, and Harry Wright, company manager George Frazer, and company doctor A. M. Tuthill, the posse represented the town leadership just as hundreds of other western posses did. That skilled worker Tom Simpson and unskilled laborer Neville Leggatt were also among its proudest and most pugnacious members typified the democratic ethos often found among western vigilante groups. These armed kidnappers were hysterical bullies, so why should their racist delusions of honor concern us? The answer is that their simultaneously self-righteous, self-heroizing, and vindictive spirit was, perversely, part of our democracy, of the very essence of the democratic spirit to which Americans owe so much. They represent a flaw in the democracy, but one so close to its center that we need to understand how it affected the whole if we are ever to remove it.

The concept of vigilantism comes not just from the word *vigilance,* watchfulness, but more specifically from vigilance committees created to watch out for, spread the word about, prevent, and subdue attacks on the community. These had a venerable tradition in the United States, used, for example, to guard against British attack in the earliest days of the nation. Vigilance committees reappeared throughout the early nineteenth century, among abolitionists who organized to prevent pursuers of runaway slaves from entering free states and among slaveowners who organized against abolitionists. Redolent of militias, the notion of vigilance was closely identified with popular sovereignty and democracy in early America.[1] In 1858 Indiana "regulators"–an early term for vigilantes–declared "that the people of this country are the real sovereigns, and that whenever the laws . . . are found inadequate to their protection, it is the right of the people to take the protection of their property into their own hands."[2] Opponents of vigilantism in the early nineteenth century tended to be conservatives critical of the principle of popular sovereignty.[3]

Vigilantism not only suffused but even symbolized early American democracy. And this is just the problem we face, as interpreters of the Clifton-Morenci orphan kidnapping and as citizens in a society with expanding vigilantism at the end of the twentieth century. For the last 150 years vigilantes pursued primarily conservative ends, antiliberal and often antidemocratic as well. The quintessential vigilantisms of the late nineteenth and early twentieth centuries were lynching parties, and their most common ideology was racism. No doubt most readers would put that label on the Clifton-Morenci vigilantes, as I would, and would condemn them, as I would. But even the most barbaric lynchers often legitimated their activity by calling on a democratic ideology of popular direct action. This legitimation underlay their remarkably unambivalent self-righteousness. If we are to understand vigilantism, rather than simply condemn it, and to grasp its revived appeal today, we need to examine vigilantes' own sense of the warrant for their activism, in the connections between democratic and conservative vigilante ideologies. Vigilantes who executed some of the most vicious and ignoble acts of lawless brutality in U.S. history nevertheless considered those very acts to be the work of citizenship and in many cases elicited wide popular approval.

The boundaries of vigilantism are not, after all, perfectly clear. It can be difficult to distinguish it from rebellion, social banditry, even feuds; "one man's mob is another man's militia."[4] Vigilantism generally means bypassing the legal procedures of the state and substituting direct, usually punitive and coercive action by self-appointed groups of citizens. Yet not even those most committed to the rule of law will necessarily condemn vigilantism universally. There have been times when legal procedures are so unjust that they must be defied, and places where law does not operate. Was not the French Resistance's execution of Nazi occupiers a form of vigilantism? One common impression is that vigilantism occurred primarily on frontiers where law-enforcement institutions had no reach, but such situations accounted for only a minority of cases. Most occurred after a criminal justice system was well established.[5] Vigilantism usually expressed citizens' distrust of established law enforcement or desire to participate directly in legal prosecutions. The notion of the absence or inadequacy of law functioned most powerfully as a metaphor for grievances against the law's bias or leniency and as a justification for popular participation in violence. Many cases of vigilantism were legalized after the fact—sometimes by judges and juries who refused to indict or convict, sometimes, as in the orphan incident, by formal decisions that the vigilantes were right in their exercise of citizenship.[6] Some vigilante actions seemed to be the extension of personal or family feuds. At the other extreme, vigilante actions became rebellions or coups, overthrowing established authorities and substituting others. The San Francisco vigilance committee of 1856, with a membership of 6,000–8,000 men who trained in pistol, rifle, artillery, and cavalry units, constructed an army and a countergovernment, overthrowing the Democratic Party's popularly elected municipal government. There is little evidence for the committee's claim to have been driven to action by high levels of crime and disorder in San Francisco.[7] Montana's territory-wide vigilante organization lasted from the 1860s through the 1880s. Nor was it the only case in which vigilantism drew close to becoming a popular rebellion: Richard Maxwell Brown, the primary chronicler of American violence, counted nine movements in U.S. history ranging in size from 700 to 8,000 members.

Vigilantes can call upon a rich vein of democratic thought to defend themselves: the right of self-preservation, the right of revolution, popular sovereignty, participatory democracy. The concept of vigilantism arose only after democracy became a dominant ideology in the United States.[8] But at the same time vigilantism raises significant political challenges to the nature of legitimation in a liberal polity, by exposing the fissures between the idea that the people are the source of all political authority and the idea that conformity to official, legal procedures is the minimum condition for freedom. In other words, vigilantism points to the seemingly endless conflict between liberal and republican, passive and active, individual and collective emphases in democratic political theory. Vigilantism emphasizes, of course, active participation over mere voting, majority rule over minority rights, the commonweal over the individual. Its version of republicanism conceives of the citizens as a group capable of forming consensus decisions, usually through instantaneous collective common sense. Vigilantes implicitly reject the liberal version of representative government, in which individuals come to the group with preexisting "interests" and in which democratic decisions arise from compromise among competing individual preferences. In its emphasis on participation, vigilante political rhetoric frequently takes us back to the source of authority, and more specifically to the vigilantes' conviction that the popular will transcends the law. They do not despise the law but only supersede it, overrule it, when it has deviated from its duty to express the popular will.[9]

Whereas vigilante justifications emphasize a nonindividualist version of democracy, popular thinking about vigilantes often treats them as an expression of individualism. "The frontier placed a premium on independent action and individual reliance," wrote one historian in explaining the West's proliferation of vigilante activity.[10] But in most vigilante stories, even when fictionalized, the individual hero is one who stands against the lynching. The vigilante group represents the opposite of individual independence; it is a pliant agglomeration of men who have lost their individual rationality to a process that at best rests its case on simple majority rule without protection of minorities and at worst sets in motion a ganglike following of powerful leaders. Vigilantes characteristically speak of "the people" as a collective identity, an indissoluble integer. In their references to the "people" or the "citizens," as in Clifton-Morenci, they deny difference of opinion and rarely name individuals; the people is a "single sovereign."[11] In their discomfort with difference of opinion and their suppression of dissent, vigilantes typically invoke an assumption, however inarticulate, that the political contract rests on a preexisting, immanent morality, inherent in nature and prior to the existence of government, discernible by all.

This set of natural moral principles not only supersedes the law of governments but is superior in its ability to know and to mete out justice. The superiority of this ultimate, unwritten law might derive from a higher power—"The voice of the people is indeed the voice of God," wrote a Wyoming defender of lynching in 1902[12]—or it might derive from a concept of self-evident natural justice. In either case the imperative of justice overrides that of law, and the two are often deemed mutually antagonistic. "More justice, less law."[13] This stance puts vigilantes within a grand tradition, a tradition particularly honored in liberal societies when it rests on a commitment to peaceful disobedience, the tradition of Thoreau, Gandhi, and Martin Luther King, Jr. But it is a tradition also claimed by violent groups such as the Ku Klux Klan and the neo-Nazis, in their reliance on the natural law of Aryan superiority. In the "pioneer" West it was the tradition of those white settlers who thought themselves entitled, also by natural law, to dominion over the land.

With their view of justice and right as self-evident, vigilantes tended to assume that those who did not share their moral vision were blind, incapable of joint membership in a moral community. They regarded those they attacked as outside the implicit "people." They conceived their targets in premodern terms as permanently alienated men who, by choosing evil, had made themselves unredeemably bad, like a vicious dog.[14] One reason that lynch mobs tended to care little whether their victims had in fact committed the crimes alleged is that the victims were defined as immutably and continuously bad, not as the perpetrators of specific bad actions. Legalities might have had a stronger claim if particular actions were at issue, but legal procedures often seemed to vigilantes to be incapable of getting at the core evilness of these bad men. In addition to the frustration and seemingly unbearable bitterness vigilantes felt when accused miscreants were acquitted or inadequately punished, vigilantes were frequently convinced that the protections for individual rights imbedded in liberal legal procedures prevented courts from "seeing" true evil. Such Manichaean thought fit neatly into the racial universe vigilantes often inhabited, to the point that white-supremacist groups took (and still take) people of color to be fixedly morally inferior. Similar views characterized the attitudes of vigilantes whose targets were alleged communists or unionists.

Vigilantism has had a special affinity for the persecution of minorities, including ideological dissenters but particularly often racially subordinated groups. This leaning derives, in part, from its rejection of the liberal, civil libertarian aspects of the democratic tradition. The notion of participatory democracy, for example, as referenced and symbolized by vigilantes, did not in its liberal (as opposed to authoritarian) forms usually recommend mass participation in matters of criminal justice. As one historian put it sixty years ago, describing a New Orleans vigilante episode in which a mob of thousands killed eleven Italians (thereby generating America's enduring fixation on the Mafia), "the judicial power was deliberately and openly taken back by those who . . . conferred it in the first place."[15] The bureaucratization of state criminal procedures, of which vigilantes were so often contemptuous, was, of course, the guarantee of civil liberties, minority rights, and presumption of innocence. Ironically, vigilantes frequently seized victims even from courts that would have sided with the vigilantes' point of view—for example, they abducted black men from prison and lynched them, although the racist courts of their region usually convicted and hanged black defendants anyway. Yet vigilantism's impatience with courts was by no means entirely irrational, for its direct-action punishments delivered messages to criminal justice officers as well as to potential miscreants, disciplining the courts, so to speak, forcing them to conform to vigilante sentiment.

Vigilantism has also secured the masculinity of participation in government. It is activity that calls upon the definition of the citizenry as armed and battle-ready and serves to revive that standard when it seems to be giving way to nonviolent means of defending the polity. Vigilantism affirms that the armed citizens assembled on a field carry a greater legitimacy than, say, twelve men in a jury box. Women's participation did little to alter that masculinity, and often reaffirmed the analogy between male responsibility for the physical protection of women and children and male responsibility for the state.

These fundamental tensions around vigilantism—that it is both a participatory enactment of citizenship arising from the democratic state and a violation of the rule of law on which the democratic state depends—cannot be resolved or erased.[16] Moreover, precisely its construction as a sovereign committee of citizens has allowed vigilantes to justify, even ennoble, persecution and murder of those they wish to exclude from citizenship, on racial, ethnic, religious, or ideological grounds.

To MANY AMERICANS, vigilantism is strongly identified with the West—with frontiers, open land, open opportunity, cowboys, cattle rustling, the cattlemen's war against the sheepmen. And with Western virility: "The timid never gathered the riches, the polite nearly never," writes a vigilantism expert. The frontier promised "the spice of danger," which "carries its own dignity."[17] The imagined West, the West that dominated popular and scholarly discussion until recently, was implicitly male, and its vigilantism evokes places real and imagined such as Tombstone, Dodge City, or Deadwood, cow towns or mining camps, where there weren't many women and male camaraderie was the common form of sociability. Presumably women civilized not only private and social life but also criminal justice, and it is a fact that Western vigilantism declined as the proportion of women rose. "The church bell has superseded the click of the pistol," a Colorado mining-camp newspaper reported.[18] Before the women, there was little to discipline men's propensity to violence except more violence. Such is the folkloric description of Clifton in the 1880s, when gunfighter Kid Louis lived by robbery and intimidated even the judge and jury that tried him; and after him there was Tex Yorkey and his gang, who used their hold-up loot to open a saloon.[19] Against such outlaws there was no law except that of other armed men. A common Anglo Western trope expressed disdain for priggish, effeminate easterners who objected to vigilante actions: "Eastern sanctity is horrified in every fibre of its creased pants . . . Yankeedom, the civilized government of the American republic, and that Atlantic patriotism which hates the west."[20] Frontiersmen had no "sympathy for the man who made his decisions on paper."[21] In some ways Western vigilante activity itself represented a repudiation of what its participants considered eastern values—formal, bureaucratized state procedures that adopted a pose of moral neutrality, insisted on following procedural rules, and resulted in coddling dangerous criminals.[22] And these legal procedures were too slow: in 1902 some Wyoming vigilantes pinned this jingle to the body of someone they hanged:

> Process of law is a little slow,
> So this is the road you'll have to go.[23]

In fact the association of vigilantism with the West is misleading. Although vigilantism in the West has been popularized and romanticized, it has been a national phenomenon. Significant vigilante movements developed throughout the United States, extending from 1767 to the 1960s, in virtually every region except New England, Wisconsin, Utah, and Oregon (and today's militias are making up for previous absence). From the eighteenth-century South Carolina regulators' roundups of horse thieves and bandits, vigilantism moved west, first to the lower South, then to the Midwest, then to the Far West.[24]

Vigilantism not only spread westward but circled back to the east and transformed itself several times. Early vigilantes tended to whip or drive out the bad guys they caught, but before long the customary punishment became killing, usually by hanging. And in the West vigilantism increasingly targeted enemies defined by ethnic, racial, religious, ideological, or political difference rather than criminality.[25] Even the gunfight at the O.K. Corral in Tombstone in 1881 involved a political conflict between Democrats and Republicans.[26] Because of its increasing partisanship, vigilantism declined in prestige after about 1850, and public response more often condemned "mob" actions.[27] But new forms countered that trend, as antiunion posses became a standard, even genteel practice.

It would appear that protracted vigilante episodes, when vigilance committees replaced established authority, also declined. These were the actions in which it was hard to distinguish vigilantism from rebellion. Both the Montana and San Francisco vigilantes, like the regulators before them, had not only conducted their activities for periods of over a year, but also relied on formal and often military-style organization and leadership, and wrote constitutions or manifestos to which members agreed. Some such groups conducted "trials" of their victims, using procedural rules that matched or mimicked those in the official courts–like the criminals' trial of the child molester in the movie *M*. These popular tribunals or "people's courts" grew less frequent in the second half of the nineteenth century."[28] Instead, the West and the South in the late nineteenth century became the sites of what appear as "instant vigilantism," one-shot, impulsive attacks. Yet even these "instant" actions were continuous at a deeper level: in a self-perpetuating feedback, the political culture of the participants came to normalize vigilantism and to expect it.[29] Vigilante rituals, rhetoric, networks of communication, leadership hierarchy, weapons, and even locations were often familiar enough that some participants brought into each episode memories of the organization of a previous one. Just as in Paris's repeated revolutionary street warfare citizens erected barricades in the same places from decade to decade, so in vigilantism men knew the drill–whom to notify, where to meet, and so on.

Even lynching, a fairly distinct subtype of vigilantism, can lose its distinctiveness amid the general category of vigilantism.[30] Lynching was not necessarily more violent—many vigilante actions not called lynchings led to hangings—although lynchings more often involved tortures and vicious celebrations. The separation between lynching and vigilantism in scholarship and popular thought has been constructed partly by different historiographical traditions. What has been written about lynching has been, in the last half century, focused almost exclusively on southern white killings of blacks and primarily denunciatory, reacting to the horror and brutality of this form of terrorism. By contrast, western vigilantism, which was commonly also racial in its direction and purpose, was written about primarily with respect and romance until recently. The most common standard for evaluating a vigilante episode was whether the perpetrators hanged the "wrong" man; if the chronicler concluded that the victim was actually an evildoer, the vigilantism became ipso facto justified, even honored.[31] Only the new antiracist western history of the last several decades has reexamined this provigilante attitude. But lynchers believed they were doing citizenly work, preventing blacks or other subordinated people from leaving their "natural" social place and creating disorder; lynchers proudly acknowledged that they were punishing miscreants in such a way as to terrorize others. The fact that lynching served other purposes—keeping labor cheap and fearful, performing sadistic and often sexualized rituals of desire—does not diminish its political meanings but adds to our understanding of the variety of political processes.

Many lynchings were performances directed at an immediate audience, often of considerable size. Lynching's racial and other political content was aimed as much at spectators as at victims, making the truth of specific criminal allegations usually insignificant. Lynchers did little if any detective work. Since lynchings were so often spectacles they required advance planning and publicity. They might be announced days in advance to attract the large crowds, sometimes reaching the thousands, that were essential to the event and its impact. Lynchings were frequently drawn out over hours so as to intensify the torture and terror and to make the spectacle satisfying to its participants. Often the bodies were literally cut up so that observers might take away pieces of flesh as souvenirs. Most western vigilante actions did not share these ferocious patterns. There were, however, many lynchings in the West in the mid-nineteenth century—between 1849 and 1853, more than two hundred documented cases in California alone. These too were largely racial: the lynchers were usually all white, the alleged victims for whom vengeance was sought were 90 percent white, but the accused were about half nonwhite, with Hispanics the overwhelming majority.[32] One of the few cases that has been studied suggests that we may have underestimated the sadism in these episodes: In 1910 in south central Texas a mob of several thousand Anglos dragged a Mexican accused of murder out of a jail and burned him at the stake.[33]

What happened in Clifton-Morenci was not a lynching and, fortunately, no one was physically injured (with the exception of an orphan who died shortly thereafter from illness, possibly from catching a chill when being carried through the rain at night). But one common aspect of lynching helps us understand what happened in Clifton-Morenci: The importance of spectators calls attention to the participation of women, who have been mainly ignored in studies of vigilantism. Lynchers often acted with the rationalization that they were avenging and protecting white women's chastity and honor. The same ideology of white female delicacy and purity might prevent (or excuse) elite women from watching lynchings, but many women were enthusiastic participants, as much involved in egging on the torture and dismemberment as the men.[34] In the West, vigilante hangings were frequently executed in the countryside out of the public gaze. But there were public hangings with female witnesses, like that of Augustín Chacón, for which formal invitations were mailed to prominent citizens: "Miss Minnie Ringgold, you are invited to be present and witness the execution of Augustín Chacón, in the jail yard." At these occasions the cheering crowds did not censor their language because of the presence of ladies. Women also probably participated in the discussions that gave rise to the indignation meetings and posses more often than has been noted.[35] Occasionally women were vigilantes themselves: in Nebraska in 1893, for example, several women were prosecuted for their activity in a group related to the KKK.[36] A key Montana vigilante episode of 1863–64 involved several women who first rescued two men from hanging by their assertive weeping and pleas for pity and then, becoming convinced of the men's guilt, egged on their executioners. Their participation was contested, to be sure: the memoirist who described this episode thought that women did not belong near this "rough and masculine business."[37]

Women were occasionally vigilante victims, mainly lynching victims, and these were disproportionately women of color.[38] Women were attacked particularly, it seems, if they were accused of violations of the sexual, gender, or family order. Lynchings stimulated by such infractions, especially when they intersected property quarrels, were common among early KKK actions but numerous in the West as well. Elizabeth Taylor was lynched for a bad reputation of this sort: She and her husband homesteaded in Nebraska in 1885; either he was passive or she was ambitious or both, because she believed he was not defending their property adequately, so she had him transfer the property to her name, taking advantage of the Nebraska Married Women's Property Act. After he died, with her neighbors already suspicious, Elizabeth spurned a neighbor's marriage proposal, and this man was so humiliated that he further maligned her. When she quarreled with neighbors over alleged fence cuttings, cattle stealing, and the burning of a barn, she was lynched. "Cattle Kate" and her husband were lynched for alleged rustling in Wyoming in 1889, but her community notoriety was built on a previous divorce, a possible stint as a prostitute as she ran from her abusive husband, and her ownership of individual property.[39] Although differently constructed, the Clifton-Morenci vigilante action also arose from alleged transgressions of family and moral standards.

The presence of women on either side of the noose, so to speak, did not dilute the intense fraternalism within the vigilante group. Just as fraternal societies had their auxiliaries, so did vigilantes. Vigilantism's climax was, of course, the actual capture and punishment of victims, and at these moments women became secondary but not necessarily absent. In paradigm cases of lynching, the iconic woman-as-victim was ever present, and actual women often constructed these attacks through their allegations of rape, or, in the Clifton-Morenci case, accusations of child abuse.

Fraternalism remained, however, as fundamental to vigilantism as it was to the citizenship and popular sovereignty that vigilantes were enacting. Posse members shared as brothers the intense experiences of hunting down a bad man, capturing him, and punishing him. The communal responsibility for killing exuded its own cement. In lynching, some scholars have seen homoerotic performance, even a communal rape, as so many lynchings involved mutilating, cutting off, displaying, and defiling victims' genitalia.[40] The racialization of the victims—along with sexual fantasies about the victims' alleged crimes—further increased the lynchers' thrills, because white racism, male and female alike, was saturated with anxious, exaggerated sexual fantasies about black men, fantasies that included both fear and desire. The racism allowed the lynchers to disguise their sadistic sexual indulgence and its homoerotic content. Western vigilantism may have been less sexualized and less fiendishly sadistic than southern lynching, its fraternity constructed less out of torture and more in the posse and the chase.[41] But hangings, legal or illegal, and the trials, formal or kangaroo, represented nevertheless the ultimate enactment of bonding through the exile of another from the community or from life itself.

Intense fraternal bonds were visible in the play between pride and secrecy in the attitude and behavior of the participants. In a majority of cases of large-scale vigilantism, the leaders were prominent men whose presence gave prestige to the actions, typically merchants but often lawyers.[42] A posse member of lower-class background might well brag about inclusion, as Neville Leggatt did. But most vigilantism, especially the smaller episodes, was intensely secret, and men often swore blood oaths against revealing membership. Although members usually knew that punishment or even embarrassment as a result of exposure was highly unlikely, they also knew how to cooperate in keeping it that way, and their clandestinity became as much a matter of honor as their participation itself. This explains the many contradictory statements of witnesses who can describe actions in detail but deny all knowledge of the participants. The silence was often organized through secret fraternal societies, notably Masonic orders, which were implicated in a wide variety of vigilante actions, including that in Clifton-Morenci. In San Francisco the symbol of the vigilance committee was the all-seeing eye, a Masonic emblem. In the notorious Montana vigilantism, the posse first organized itself at the funeral of a Mason; since many Masonic groups kept their membership confidential, men saw for the first time at this funeral how many others were Masons. Trusting their mutual oaths of silence, they were able to risk soliciting participation, which they would not have been able to do at a public meeting or by asking relative strangers.[43]

Yet the obsessive, rarely violated secrecy points to the possibility of a suppressed truth: that communities were by no means so unanimous in their support of vigilante actions as is usually alleged by their champions. Hints of misgivings or even disapproval, and allegations that the vigilantes got the wrong men, raise questions about the silencing of objectors. Membership in posses was sometimes virtually compulsory, owing to social pressure and, typically, the powerful positions of vigilante organizers.[44] Just as with lynchings, vigilantism not only affected victims but also communicated fearsome messages to witnesses or anyone within hearsay distance. But despite the likelihood of such intimidation, vigilantism grew more secret over the second half of the nineteenth century as condemnation of it grew.[45]

Vigilantism's secrecy is yet more ambiguous because of the prominent roles so often taken by law-enforcement officers. Collusion and even open cooperation between vigilantes and public officials were more the norm than the exception. In the West the legendary gunfighters—Wild Bill Hickok, Judge Roy Bean, Wyatt Earp—straddled both sides of the law. Arizona Territory Sheriff John Slaughter killed twelve men in isolated places, and no journalist or authority asked any questions. Western sheriffs were notoriously corrupt, using their responsibility for collecting taxes, licensing fees, and stipends for prisoners in their jails to enrich themselves.[46] Sheriffs, police chiefs, justices of the peace, marshals, judges, and even governors supported and joined in vigilantism. Their participation indicates not only vigilantism's legitimacy but also the fact that it did not so much disregard as defy the law, deliberately and with conviction. Vigilantism did not arise in the heat of the moment nearly as often as its apologists claimed; it was often thoughtful and planned. Often it amounted to an extremely aggressive reverse form of jury nullification.

In some instances vigilantism was entirely official. The first prominent Western official vigilantes were the Texas Rangers, initially a privately financed group established in the 1820s, then publicly funded in the 1840s by the Republic of Texas until their subordination by the Confederacy. At first the Rangers fought Indians, chased runaway slaves, rounded up thieves, and attempted to subvert Mexican rule. After the Mexican War they regularly harassed Tejanos and Indians, illegally invaded Mexico, tortured and lynched "bad men," and shot "escaping" prisoners with impunity, their strong conviction of righteousness surrounding all these activities.[47] The Arizona Rangers were patterned after their Texas heroes. Territorial governors had been requesting "vigilant mounted border patrols" since the 1880s.[48] When the Arizona Rangers were created by statute in 1901, their membership was secret, just like that of unpaid vigilantes. When they helped suppress the 1903 strike, were they vigilantes? The fact that the rangers were paid by the territorial government does not automatically prove the negative.

If the rangers blurred the boundaries of vigilantism, posses virtually erased the boundary. A "posse" usually meant a vigilante group whose members had been formally deputized by the local sheriff, but these deputies were not consistently more law-abiding than self-appointed enforcers. Clifton-Morenci's posses of 1903 and 1904 represented different meanings of the term: that of 1903 was appointed by the sheriff; that of 1904 was a collection of angry residents without official status, although it included several deputy sheriffs. The notion of a posse comes from the legal concept, *posse comitatus,* literally, power of the county, a tradition authorizing magistrates and peace officers to summon aid. Arizona legislated this authority explicitly in 1901.[49] The same powers underlay Sheriff Parks's assembling a posse and calling upon the National Guard to put down the strike. That many Cliftonians regarded the two posses as fundamentally similar in their source of authority and legitimacy resulted not only from their assumptions about popular sovereignty but also from the similarity in practices between formal and informal "law enforcement." The procedures and punishments of formal courts were not necessarily less biased or sadistic than those of vigilante groups; the distinction was more likely to focus on bureaucratic requirements of formal law enforcement that produced delays and paperwork.[50] Legal hangings were more likely to take place on a scaffold, vigilante hangings on trees–but the Montana vigilantes built a scaffold and used the same one repeatedly, and the audiences at legal and extralegal hangings were similar.

So why the secrecy? There seem to have been two opposing constraints on candor: one, the fear that not everyone would accept vigilante legitimacy and coercion; two, the function of secrecy to intensify the fraternal bonding. For vigilante fraternalism, like that of the Masons, was almost always nonuniversal. Unfortunately for the cause of universal brotherhood, it seems that those solidarities which exclude some outsiders are the most gripping. Vigilantism by definition is about guarding against or punishing those who are outside and seem to threaten the brotherhood.

The vigor and magnetism of racism particularly aroused vigilante fervor. Despite the greater scholarly attention paid to the major California and Montana vigilante episodes, the enduring structures of western vigilantism developed from attacks on Indians, the Chinese, and Mexicans. People of color were rarely vigilantes themselves but were disproportionately vigilante victims. These were the attacks that most closely resembled southern lynchings of African Americans. There is no way to distinguish military from vigilante actions in the Indian wars. The terror used against the Chinese in the mining camps created mob race riots—such as the one in Wyoming when white coal miners in 1885 set fire to Chinese dwellings and, when the Chinese tried to escape, captured them and threw them back into the burning buildings.[51] Vigilantism against Mexicans in Los Angeles was so wide-spread during the 1850s that it produced open warfare, turning Mexican "banditry" into "social banditry," a kind of bottom-up vigilantism.[52] In fact, some of these western attacks on minorities resemble attacks that in other places have been called race riots, which in turn raises the question whether some of the notorious urban race riots in New York, East St. Louis, Chicago, and Tulsa should not be categorized as vigilante actions.[53]

Individual Mexicans were lynched so frequently that some nineteenth-century southwesterners seemed to hold a racial double standard about punishment—white bad men got trials, Mexicans just got hanged. In 1873 in Tucson, a city once controlled by a Mexican elite and where Mexicans still possessed more power than elsewhere, protestors tried to stop the lynching of several white accused murderers, claiming, "You can hang a Mexican, and you can hang a Jew, and you can hang a nigger, but you can't hang an American Citizen!"[54] As some scholars of southern lynchings have argued, it was as if there were a racial social contract that authorized whites to punish nonwhite transgressions.[55] But the legal executions were not less racialized. Of Graham County's five legal hangings in the decade before the orphans came, the victims included one Indian, one black man, and three Mexicans.[56]

The prevalence of racism in vigilantism does not mean that people of color never developed their own vigilantism. The most prominent example, the Gorras Blancas, or White Caps, of New Mexico, serves to illustrate, however, the exceptionalness of this practice. Although these White Caps dressed like other masked vigilantes, such as the KKK, their goals and methods differed. Protesting the seizure and enclosure by Anglo ranchers and railroad developers of land that had traditionally belonged to New Mexican Hispanics, groups of riders disguised in white fought back during the years 1889–1892 by cutting and destroying fences.[57] When captured and tried, alleged White Caps were acquitted by juries, which at this time included Hispanics, the majority of the population. The White Caps and their supporters then formed a political party, El Partido del Pueblo Unido, which won all the county offices, gained four seats in the Territorial Legislature, and elected a congressman in 1890. Later they affiliated with the People's Party. Compare these New Mexican White Caps to the White Caps of Oklahoma who, five years later, hunted down and hanged alleged wrongdoers, burned houses and barns, and drove off homesteaders in order to appropriate their land. Both groups of White Caps operated in secrecy and performed illegal acts intended to coerce. But the Oklahoma group were exemplary classic vigilantes, aiming to punish and intimidate enemies or would-be challengers, while the New Mexico group attacked not individuals but property and then turned to politics to change the power structure. The Gorras Blancas were more like a labor union committed to sabotage—they were in fact connected to the labor organization known as the Knights of Labor—than like vigilantes, and its members soon concluded they could accomplish more through politics. By contrast, Anglo vigilantism against the Hispanic majority continued in New Mexico. Sometimes aroused by the refusal of Hispanic-dominated juries to convict accused Mexicans, they functioned just like southern lynch mobs: to intimidate and thus make it easier to expropriate Hispanics.[58]

Vigilante racism had a particularly close relationship to vigilante fraternalism. In turning upon people of other ethnic or racial groups and excluding them from the citizenry, the vigilantes made their own racial identity the irreducible basis of unity. Many eager posse members were veterans of the Indian wars, often rootless, womanless men who had enjoyed the male camaraderie of the hunt and chase.[59] Particularly attractive in those western communities where an ideal of democratic polity and open opportunity prevailed, vigilante groups practiced a deformed democracy—a *herrenvolk* democracy that united men across class lines through their racial identity. Celebratory accounts, like Thomas Dimsdale's 1866 chronicle of the Montana vigilance committee, announced the composition of the posses like a chorus: "Merchants, miners, mechanics and professional men, alike . . ."[60] Vigilantism intensified and solidified racial definitions of citizenship in ways that denied or mystified other power inequalities.

Yet even within the white male population, vigilante groups were typically far from democratic. Virtually all who have studied western vigilantism have been impressed with its elite membership and leadership. The San Francisco committee of vigilance was orchestrated by Republican elites and, proportionately to their numbers, large merchants were most likely to join, followed by petty proprietors; the membership inverted a graph of the class structure, with those on the bottom the least likely to join. Leland Stanford, California governor, later U.S. senator, and one of the "big four" builders of the Southern and Central Pacific railroads was a member.[61] In Tombstone, Arizona, the "town builders," the "best class of citizens," were most active in vigilante campaigns. In the ranching West vigilantism was part of a "Western Civil War of Incorporation" (Marx would have called it primitive accumulation), practiced primarily on behalf of powerful ranchers securing their private property against rustlers, poachers, or simply those who clung to an open-land view of the West and tried to graze their animals on what had become private land. Far from trying to suppress vigilantism, the business elite argued that it demonstrated community spirit and attracted investment. The Masonic orders so prominent in vigilantism were the most elite of the fraternal groups.[62] Many of the most prominent Americans, not only merchants but also professionals and men in high political office, have been enthusiastic participants and supporters of vigilantism. Brown counted two presidents, five U.S. senators, and eight governors in the vigilante movements he compiled. Eminent scholars, including historians, not only justified the movements but participated, even as they often also blamed vigilantism on the rough lower classes.[63]

This elite participation would seem to confound vigilantism's foundational legitimation in terms of popular sovereignty. Sometimes the elites supplied their own alternative justifications. George Parsons, a Tombstone merchant and vigilante, argued that "Peculiar organizations of a certain character are very necessary at times under certain circumstances for the maintenance of right and paving the way to the highest order of civilization. Might should never triumph over right."[64] His understanding of vigilantism emphasized a hierarchy of values over popular rule, an attitude that expressed the widespread notions that a limited number of town leaders constituted the "best men of the town" or, as in Clifton-Morenci, that the "citizens" formed a kind of republican aristocracy.

Then why did elites resort to vigilantism? Surely they were able to organize legal means of enacting their justice. The answer requires us to dispense with functionalist explanations or at least with literal under-

standings of vigilantes' claims about the need for extraordinary measures to secure their will. Instead we must look to the symbolic meanings
of vigilantism for victims, participants, and observers and the cultural
work vigilantism performed. The willingness of the elites to serve side
by side with (white) common men in these popular militias constituted
democratic public pronouncements and helped negotiate contradictions between democratic and undemocratic arrangements of power.
Posses provided a venue for widespread participation far more control-
lable than other arenas. Through posses and lynchings, elites could
suppress conflicts among whites and elicit the loyalty of white subordinates. The gendered brotherhood of the posses served equally to reassure plebeian white men of social respect, to head off feelings of exclusion or powerlessness among nonelites, and to give them instead a sense
of investment in the existing order. Elites not only used common men
but needed them: since vigilantism served to deliver terrorist messages
far and wide, elites needed the participation of plebian posse members
to send these signals. Moreover, participation in a posse was deeply
satisfying—diverting, entertaining, thrilling—even when it was troubling.
But the ultimate meanings and the most significant consequences of this
inclusiveness often perpetuated or even enlarged class inequality: elites
accommodated to and used the "racial contract" for controlling popular
challenges, whether consciously or unconsciously.

Nothing illustrates the class politics of vigilantism better than its use
in the hands of large employers, notably mine operators. What the
white miners first used against the Chinese and the Mexicans was then
turned against them by mine management. The boundary between
vigilantism and class warfare in the West was often fuzzy, and in the
armed conflict between large and small ranchers, miners and employers, many participants on both sides had been members of posses.
Large employers began in the 1870s to hire professional enforcers of
private law, such as the Pinkertons and other "detective" agencies, but
in the context of western class struggle these were not clearly distinguished from vigilantes. These private, paid armed forces first worked
for the railroads in hunting down robbers but soon became specialized
in union-busting work for a variety of industrialists, notably mine
operators. Pinkertons regularly kidnapped witnesses, bribed juries,
coerced confessions. Except for their work as incognito spies, they
engaged more in beatings and threats of violence than in detection,
and they were many times accused of functioning as assassins for hire.

One Arizona deputy reportedly killed seventeen men on orders from the Pinkerton Agency; although these and many similar allegations were not usually proved, working men and women believed them, and the Pinkertons became identified as mercenaries in the class war.[65] On other occasions employers resorted to the language and traditions of vigilantism in their battles with unions, as in the case of the San Francisco Law and Order Committee organized in 1916 by structural steel companies, or the Phelps Dodge deportation of Bisbee unionists in 1917.

Although Pinkertons and similar hired thugs often threatened and attacked strikers directly, their greatest successes came through separating strikers from their potential supporters among the middle classes. Particularly in mining camps, many businessmen and professionals not only socialized with miners but also depended on them economically, and knew it. As in Clifton-Morenci, the middle class often had its own grievances against the mine operators, the more so as the mines grew larger and ownership consolidated. Forming vigilante groups, such as the 1903 Citizens' Alliance of Cripple Creek, Colorado, against striking miners, the operators drew in middle-class people with patriotism, red-baiting, and threats of capital flight, and with a rhetoric that blamed outside agitators and treated rank-and-file miners as dupes, but also with the vigilante experience itself.[66] Mine managers, their allies, and their employees called indignation meetings at which they used or even created identities such as "the citizenry," which joined independent businessmen to the company. They made participation in these posses an honor. A tactic that was to be used several times in mining conflicts—rounding up union supporters and deporting them from the town with orders never to return—expressed the essence of popular-sovereignty vigilantism, in claiming a statelike authority. A vigilante leader of the Cripple Creek deportation, a man who was the head both of a mine and of the First National Bank, pronounced, "it is good law for us citizens [to act] . . . Don't do anything unlawful, but we can't have bad citizens among good ones, and we must get rid of them."[67]

Vigilantism could also embody small-scale class (or caste) friction. Not only big corporations but also small businessmen, middle-class people, and even poor workers and farmers used violence to drive out competition and prevent those on the bottom from moving up. Lynchings enforced caste most nakedly and brutally. Southern lynchers disproportionately struck ambitious and hard-working southern blacks—men who sought to increase their land holdings or build up businesses, or politically assertive blacks who challenged Jim Crow. Lynchings not only punished such aspirations but also notified others not to try it. So little western vigilantism has been studied that we do not know to what extent the same patterns applied to it, but the Arizona situation probably came closer to the southern model than did, say, the New Mexican, where Mexicans held on to more political and economic power.[68] Certainly the evidence of the Clifton-Morenci episode suggests that the Mexican adoptive parents were more upwardly mobile than average. Could this fact have increased the white rage?

The Clifton-Morenci vigilantes of 1904 had direct experience with the 1903 antistrike posse, whether as members or close observers. They were all in a position to understand the vital importance of a tractable Mexican labor force to their personal welfare. And they understood that the leading citizens had to take responsibility. Consider Harry Wright, a young capitalist at age twenty-nine. His business career had had a head start: His father, Arthur, a veteran Indian fighter, was a Clifton justice of the peace for four successive terms; "No character was ever so tough, if brought before him for evil doing, whom 'Dad' Wright did not give all he needed." Young Harry was already a principal owner of the Keystone mine with its thirty-four copper claims and, for recreation, had inherited three of the most valuable mineral and coin collections in the United States.[69] The posse involved a good proportion of the town's businessmen. Recall that Frazer worked for Arizona Copper; and the Abrahams, Riordan, and Dunagan owned hotels, saloons, and a liquor store; although Simpson was a locomotive engineer, he, like all the rest, had invested in mines, which were every man's dream in Arizona. They were not just individual leading citizens but possessed a group consciousness and many personal ties: Riordan and Simpson were brothers-in-law, three of them were deputies for the powerful sheriff, and all the businessmen saw one another at least several times a week.

Clifton-Morenci's citizens knew of many precedents for their posse, even beyond that of 1903. The mining camps of the Rocky Mountains and the Southwest had a half-century tradition of vigilantism, since the mass lynchings of Chinese miners and the miners' courts of the 1860s. William Zeckendorf, a German Jew like the Clifton Abrahams, had been a pillar of a Tucson committee of public safety in the 1870s.[70] Lynchings, or "necktie parties," as they were fondly called, continued in Arizona through the 1880s, and Mexicans were particularly victimized. These actions had been for the most part directed at individuals accused of crimes, but the mechanisms could easily be turned to perform a "rescue mission."

And theirs was no instant vigilantism. They were well practiced and knew just who was reliable and decisive, where the key people lived, where and when to hold a meeting, where to find the deputies and the sheriff and judge. In Clifton-Morenci, as throughout the western towns, a dense weaving of white fraternal societies provided lines of trust, patterns of solidarity, and means for assembling men—and women— quickly. So did the interactions that took place in stores and saloons. In such a small town no one had far to go; and it was Sunday so men were closer to home. The women who spread the word and explained the seriousness of the problem did not find it difficult to get together the Library Hall meeting in just twenty-four hours.

At this point, no secrecy was required. In fact, from the point of view of the organizers, "everyone" was invited. The exclusion of Mexicans was to them so natural it would only have become an issue if some of the borderline people had turned up—one of the Euro-Latins or an upscale Mexican like physician Jesús Martinez or saloon owner David Arzate. Why didn't they? Perhaps they had not heard the news. Perhaps they did not feel comfortable, or did not approve. Although some were included in more formal occasions, such as the copper company dances, they were outside the innermost nucleus of political leadership. And it was to this innermost core that the town leaders turned when formal law would not be quick enough and firm enough. Like so many vigilant citizens before and after them, the town elites were not only stirred up and angry but certain that it was their duty to act resolutely.

January 1905

Courtroom of the Arizona
Territorial Supreme Court, Phoenix

COURTROOM DRAMAS are our national soap operas. Ever since the "penny press" of the 1830s discovered that it could sell newspapers on the basis of suspenseful trials, courtroom spectacles have gripped a mass public. As the hype expanded, so did the list of "trials of the century," performances that provided entertainment, the chance to be outraged at the behavior of others, and vicarious thrills, all in a public arena that created unifying national conversation. They generated the tension of a serial that leaves us on edge at the end of each episode, a living melodrama with its outcome unknown. The orphan trial was such an event for many Arizona residents and others, too. Although the trial was not quite as widely covered in the national press as was the kidnapping of the orphans, for Arizona papers it was a daily front-page spread and it was covered in most newspapers throughout the country.[1] Had the orphan trial been telecast, it would have won top ratings. For those lucky or influential enough to get into the packed courtroom, the show was a thrilling entertainment. It became the only topic of conversation: "Never in its history was Phoenix so stirred up." At least one newspaper thought feelings ran so high that there was danger of violence.

Like the O. J. Simpson case and Louise Woodward's "nanny trial," the orphan litigation was not just entertainment but also serious political discourse. These recent trials not only diverted us but also served as crystals through which spectators viewed moral lessons. Some saw the central issue in the O. J. case as domestic violence, others as police racism and lying. Some saw Louise Woodward as an innocent used as a scapegoat for parents—specifically, mothers—too busy with their careers to notice their children's ailments; others saw the sympathy for Woodward as an emanation of hostility to mixed marriages, working mothers, and (in England) American arrogance. Spectators were so certain of their interpretations that they frequently expressed wonderment at how other people could be so blind as to not "get it."

The orphan trial was different because the audience was unanimous. The trial's spectators thought the issue was child welfare: the Foundling Hospital's astounding callousness toward the children and the posse's gallant, citizenly rescue. John Gatti, the named respondent who stood for them all against the Foundling Hospital's effort to reclaim its children, received offers of financial support from numerous "prominent people" in his fight to retain the orphans; he asked newspapers to report "that as a matter of sentiment the people of Clifton and Morenci prefer to bear the expense themselves."[2] (This statement was, of course, also part of his publicity campaign to win the case.) The chief local attorney for the Foundling Hospital, Eugene Ives, a wealthy and prominent Anglo Catholic who was at this time president of the upper house of the Territorial Assembly, complained bitterly that he became unpopular throughout the territory because of this case.[3] In the press and on downtown streets of Phoenix there were no audible or visible dissenters.[4] All seemed to agree that the central issue of the case was the best interests of the children. So the trial appeared to grip the public not because of its contentiousness but by its very illusion of unanimity, providing a fervent experience of consensus and common purpose.

There was a background leitmotif of regional conflict, between Arizona and the East. The bad publicity, especially in the Hearst press, which had blamed the Anglo Arizonans for "mob rule," only got their backs up and further consolidated local opinion against the Foundling Hospital.[5] Arizona pride was at stake. The episode demonstrated, once again, that outsiders did not understand life in Arizona, where sometimes direct action by the citizens was required to create justice.

All other controversy was exiled. The courtroom, downtown Phoenix, and the press operated like a gated, guarded community. The trial and the scene around it excluded entirely the opinions of a large sector of the public, Arizona's Mexicans. This erasure was breathtaking in its audacity: Throughout the trial not one Mexican voice was heard. No Mexican witness was called, no affidavit from a Mexican was introduced, no Mexican sat in the audience, no Mexican was interviewed by a journalist. Since both sides of the case were Anglo, the effect was not only to reinforce the white line encircling citizenship in Arizona but also to place the Mexicans so far outside the circle as to be of, literally, no account.

I would like to write that the silenced Mexican public opinion was a covert presence in the courtroom, a shadow which reminded the Anglo spectators, witnesses, and defendants, however unconsciously, that they were at most coowners of and cocitizens in this land of Arizona. But that was not how it felt. Mexicans were powerfully present, but only as an Anglo chimera, as a principle of inferiority, an image moored with few actual observations. It was an Anglo courtroom in its personnel and equally in its definitions of non-Anglo people.

To a lesser extent, it was a female-dominated courtroom. Of course the men ran it. Probably no one envisioned that a woman might be a judge or a lawyer. The only female professional was a court reporter, Mrs. Henderson, whose transcript made this book possible. But the spectacle was entirely constructed by Anglo women, and its impact was so powerful that one cannot imagine the bank of judges ruling against the women even had they been so inclined. Here is what the courtroom was like: Crowds waiting to get in well before the hearings opened each morning. Governor Brodie, Territorial Secretary Nichols, and other notables sitting at the front just behind the lawyers' tables. All the Anglo foster mothers, the orphans, and most of the foster fathers in attendance, along with some of their other children, the women and children "dressed up" for the occasion. Frequent noise and bustle when the mothers occasionally left the courtroom to quiet the children and then reentered; more noise and disturbance as the female spectators expressed their emotions—crying, laughing, openly disapproving. Three black-robed nuns from the Sisters of Charity, silent.

The journalists seized the opportunity for producing purple prose, looking forward to extraordinary street sales. Yet their professional tropes also revealed that they joined the audience in projecting intense albeit conventional moral tales onto the story:

> One woman, the possessor of a beautiful little girl sat at lunch in a restaurant and cried when she thought of the possibility of an adverse decision. "I would rather," said she, "give up my right arm than lose her."

One little boy stopping with his foster father and mother at a hotel grew sleepy yesterday and when his father told him to go to sleep he said: "Won't you watch me so the Mexicans can't get me?"

There was one little red-headed fellow with freckles in a foster papa's arms. He would not take a prize at a beauty show but he looked manly, little as he was, and bless his heart, let it be hoped he will be given the chance with all of the boys to be a manly man.[6]

This kind of discourse manipulated the emotions of the entire audience (except perhaps the nuns, who had seen many mothers leave and regain their children and were thus more experienced with the peaks and valleys of maternal passion). Women spectators frequently begged, and were allowed, to hold the children. There was a great deal of weeping, even "the eyes of many strong men filled with tears."[7] Frequently the lawyers for the Anglo parents asked that a child be displayed, to demonstrate his or her current well-being, and a mother or father would hold the child up, to the oohs and ahs of the crowd; "perhaps such an aggregation of beauty was never before gotten together in such a haphazard manner."[8] "The little children who have so commonly been called foundlings have become great favorites about the courtroom and the hotels. Their cherry [sic] little faces and ever willingness to be friendly with every kindly hand makes them the post [sic] of the crowd among which they have now begun to move about freely during the interims of the court. They run from 'mother' to 'mother' and from 'father' to 'father' [and] entertain the crowd." At one point Katherine Fitzpatrick, now in the possession of Muriel and Harry Wright, was brought forward and placed on top of a desk. "She turned her attention to the justices, laughed and waved her little hand at the court en banc." She was credited with inducing the judges to quit trying to maintain silence in the courtroom.[9]

What is genuine emotion and what is sentimentality? Everything everyone did in and around this courtroom was strategic, and even the children must have understood that they were being asked to perform for the crowd and to summon up their cutest gestures. But it is also true that by now the Anglo parents had lived with their new children three and a half months, and bonds had formed. Any judge would have faced one of the classic dilemmas of child custody contestation: a conflict between the legality of *how* an adult became a child's de facto guardian and the value of subsequently developed bonds with the child. Arguments for the best interests of the child could, in the extreme, benefit anyone who kidnapped a child and managed to evade capture or legal action for an extended period of time.

As soon as Swayne, Mandin, and the sisters had left town, Clifton's townspeople began their campaign to keep the children. In an implicit sexual division of labor, the men turned to the law and several women turned to informal persuasion.

Three women—Laura (Mrs. Sam) Abraham and two other Anglos—wrote passionate, personal letters to the head sister of the Foundling Hospital (Teresa Vincent, who had not come to Arizona). These appeals, from women who identified themselves as Catholic, show the racial and religious boundaries that mattered to them. Laura Abraham wrote in the militant, unbending, denunciatory style that she would exhibit at the trial, devoting most of her fourteen-page letter to damning the Mexican families and the priest. She charged that Mandin turned to "the very lowest, vilest, cruelest, most poverty stricken, most ignorant," and forced them to take children. Why? "Because the more ignorant the more he could impose on them." It gets worse: the women were "the blackest ugliest" of women, "as black as Indians and more inhuman," the only exceptions (to the ugliness) being three prostitutes. Laura Abraham did not seem to grasp that the sisters had already acquiesced to the charge that they should not have given the children to Mexicans, and that their purposes now were to defend the Foundling's guardianship rights and the Catholicism of its charges. Or perhaps she understood this quite well but in her letter was rehearsing her trial testimony, which, she certainly knew, had to focus on the shortcomings of the Mexicans. Her slurs on the priest as well as the Mexicans seem the more bewildering when, later in the letter, Mrs. Abraham reveals herself to be Catholic: "I . . . wish to say that I went to a convent in Silver City New Mexico and the Sisters of Mercy for seven years and when she [the orphan Elizabeth Kane] is old enough to go to school she will have the same advantage & be sent to the same school . . . and will be raised a Catholic as well not mentioning that she can have every thing else she may wish for or ask for." She offered two personal references for her Catholic standing: Rev. Mother Paul at the convent and E. M. Williams of Arizona Copper. But Catholicism quickly gave way to affluence as her claim to the child, an affluence rendered as "white": "they [the Clifton orphans] all sleep tonight in their very own little snow white beds with good nourishing food fresh air & the best physician in town in attendance & in god fearing educated *English* speaking [her emphasis] families." She could not stop herself from attacking Swayne and the priest repeatedly, as if unaware that this strategy might antagonize the sisters. At the trial it came out that, from the church's point of view, she was no Catholic, since she never attended mass or took Communion. But the sisters at the Foundling did not know this when they received her letter, and perhaps they would have responded positively to a truly Catholic appeal. Mrs. Abraham's letter shows how her sense of the rightness of what she had done was so racialized that she could not effectively plead her case on religious grounds.[10]

A second plea came from Mrs. F. H. Kane, the next-door neighbor of the George Frazers, who now parented three-and-a-half-year-old Hannah Kane. Mrs. Kane—she must have noticed their identical names— asked nothing for herself but wrote to support her friends and neighbors. She started her letter more sympathetically than Mrs. Abraham, offering, "I knew how your heart would ache when the three Sisters who left Morenci yesterday morning related to you the experience they had," but quickly veered into a repetition of Laura Abraham's themes: "how those little ones was forced upon poor ignorant Mexicans who were unwilling to take them. I speak the language and they tell me—I didn't want them but father told me I must take them I have 2 and I gave him 40.00 other say I gave $8.00 and next pay day I pay $10.00 more. They are a class of people even lower than the negro of the south and almost as dark." But Mrs. Kane distanced herself from the mob. Like Dunagan and Mills, she used the mob to threaten while claiming moderation and heroism for others: "I never want to see people in such white heat again. The agent has cause to thank the few cool headed men who were here, or he would not be in the land of the living." She too offered affluence as the strongest case for leaving the orphans where they were; she knew the women who now mothered nine of the orphans and knew that eight of them would be the only child and seven would have everything money could buy: "In mining camps people make money quite easily and spend it freely." Mrs. Kane also interjected her own Catholicism, by suggesting that the mother superior contact Sister St. Peter at the Orphans Home in Tucson, who visited Clifton a few months ago and would know how wretched the Mexicans were.[11]

A Morenci woman, Mrs. A. Le. Burge, articulated yet further the racial and religious bind for an Anglo Catholic. She wrote asking for an orphan—not just any orphan but a particular child. She had picked up a baby girl, Catharine Lane, eighteen months old, as the baby was being returned by Mexican parents to the Morenci Hotel, but had returned the girl, upon request, to a sister. In that moment Mrs. Burge experienced the same powerful emotion as had the Clifton Anglos who were lucky enough to be able to keep the children: "Dear Mother, My Heart went out to the little one I showed her to My Husband and said if we get her I will think God has sent us a little angel through the Dear Sisters . . . I know I could not love my own any more." Moreover, "all of the citizens are anxious for me to have her because they say she looks just like me." She pleaded her religious case: although she was born a Catholic, her mother had died leaving her father with six small children, so they were placed out with Protestants; she apologized for "not [having] lived up to the church as I should" and for having a non-Catholic husband. She even apologized for the treatment of the sisters (and was the only white person who did so): "I fear you may be so disgusted with us here . . . [for] the awful trouble . . . and shame on me I was among them." She promised to raise the child Catholic. But, she wrote frankly, "I can not promise to attend the Church here as I understand white people or Americans do not attend here only as they are obliged to do. But if the priest will call on me here . . ."[12] It was not her personal prejudice but the racial system trapping her, as it did most others, that prevented her from going to mass. Mrs. Burge was not part of Morenci's elite: her husband was a skilled worker, manager of the boiler shops, earning $120–$130 a month, perhaps $4 a day, and her spelling was poor. But she was white and could not, therefore, be a practicing Catholic in Clifton-Morenci.

Two other appeals reached the New York Sisters of Charity, from Morenci Protestant men. These letters marked another division of labor—with their Clifton compatriots busy with legal proceedings, the Morenci leaders felt that they should contribute in some way. Three prominent citizens of Morenci, including Detroit Copper doctor A. M. Tuthill, addressed themselves, rather comically, to "New York Foundling Society . . . Gentlemen": Their tone, like Laura Abraham's, was furious but more anti-Catholic: Swayne had been insolent, the Mexicans were unable to support families, the Foundling had committed a "criminal mistake," and they demanded, "as American citizens . . . some reasonable explanation of your action to the people of Morenci, who at the present time are filled with disgust and loathing towards an institution which can so carelessly consign children by wholesale to a life of moral degeneracy."[13] A Protestant minister in Morenci tried a different tack, writing to the New York Charity Organization Society—the influential Protestant-dominated federation of charities—which forwarded excerpts to the Foundling. This minister quoted Tuthill, who "gave it as his opinion that half of the children would be dead in six months" if they had been left with the Mexicans, and pleaded, "what ought these people to have done?" But the minister, somewhat more wisely, tried to distinguish this particular action from the general policy of the church: "The great charitable institutions have been a mighty power for good in the world."[14]

On its side, the Foundling Hospital leadership had begun to campaign for the return of the children even before the sisters returned with the full story. They believed their legal position was irrefutable: The citizens of Arizona were obliged to honor, and the Arizona courts to defend, the New York State charter that gave guardianship of the children only to the Foundling Hospital. Politically experienced New Yorkers that they were, however, the sisters never relied on the courts to see things their way but embarked on a publicity campaign as well. The *New York Daily News* conducted a petition drive in its pages, gathering signatures on an appeal to President Roosevelt to take back the children from a kidnapping "aided or connived at by United States Deputy Marshals." The Ancient Order of Hibernians denounced the outrage in a letter to President Roosevelt. The head of a prominent Humane Society, the physicians on the Medical Board of the Foundling, and even the mayor of New York City wrote Arizona Governor Brodie to request return of the orphans to their rightful guardians.[15] Responding to this pressure, Governor Brodie personally went to Clifton to "investigate," but once there he was taken in hand by the Anglos and shown how terrible were the Mexican homes (the newspaper described them as "Mexican 'homes,'" using quotation marks). Threateningly the "citizens" asked him, "How would you like to be the man, governor, who would come here to take them away?" Not surprisingly, Brodie hedged, announcing later that there had been two mistakes: the initial placement of the children and then the citizens' refusal to return them to the Foundling. The governor's primary commitment was to staying out of this hornets' nest. But at the bishop's urging the governor wrote about the case to President Roosevelt, who told the attorney general, who instructed Phoenix U.S. District Attorney Frederick S. Nave to enter an *amicus curiae* brief on behalf of the Foundling against the awarding of custody to the Anglos. This victory for the Sisters of Charity never impressed Ives, perhaps because he knew Arizona better.[16]

Another part of the sisters' strategy was, of course, to publicize the extreme disrespect and fear to which they had been subjected in Arizona. They also wanted, perhaps without conscious calculation, to keep themselves in the spotlight and thereby to keep the case focused on religious intolerance. Shortly before the trial started, one of their lawyers telegraphed Governor Brodie that the sisters "apprehended discourtesy" when they arrived to testify. This wire induced a return wire and letter from the governor guaranteeing their courteous treatment.[17]

To the Clifton-Morenci Anglos, despite their varying views of Catholicism, there could be no doubt that race was the greater issue. The Sisters of Charity could not afford to acknowledge the race issue. They had failed in their primary objective, an objective protected by law in New York—to place Catholic orphans in Catholic homes. Now their strategic impulses were intersected by those of a few prominent Anglo Catholics elsewhere in the territory. In preparing for the trial, several groups wrangled for control—the sisters; the New York Roman Catholic hierarchy; the church's New York attorney, Charles E. Miller; and Tucson Bishop Granjon and his Arizona supporters. Fragments of this struggle for control lie scattered throughout several caches of papers. Miller made it clear that he took his ultimate orders from the archbishop, not the sisters.[18] Granjon criticized the New York hierarchy's choice of a young and inexperienced Arizona attorney, Thomas D. Bennett, to try the case, and when Ives came into the picture, he made it clear that he thought Bennett and the New York lawyers were handling the case incompetently.[19] Moreover, Granjon and Father Timmermans, who returned to Clifton to resume his duties after Mandin fled, feared that New York was advising the lawyers to drop the case. Granjon had already been angry that the sisters had not consulted him before delivering children to Clifton, and now it seemed to him that they were using Mandin as the fall guy. He believed that they did not understand the kidnapping's implications for Arizona Roman Catholics. To him, the very fact that the vast majority of his flock were Mexicans—a stigmatized, impoverished people who could not defend themselves—made it all the more important for Anglo Catholics to protect the faith against Protestant incursion. "The Asylum must fight for their rights to a finish," he wrote. "It is a test case and one where most elemental and vital rights of the church are involved. The question of expense should not be considered a moment."[20]

Luckily for Granjon, the "question of expense" had a local solution. Granjon had close relations with several wealthy Catholics in Arizona. His best friend was William Henry Brophy, manager of the PD company store in Bisbee and a prominent banker. Born in Ireland, Brophy was later to become manager of the entire PD Mercantile Company, the umbrella corporation that ran all the company stores, and a confidante of PD boss Douglas.[21] At his death in 1922, Brophy left a fortune to establish Brophy College Prep in Phoenix, now the most prestigious Catholic school in the state. Brophy invested Granjon's (and we assume the diocese's) money and gave the bishop expensive gifts and vacations.[22] Immediately after the news of the orphans' kidnapping, Brophy got the Bisbee Knights of Columbus (which he had founded) to send their deputy grand knight to Clifton to investigate. His report identified anti-Catholicism as a major factor in the conflict. It also raised questions about the fitness of some of the Anglo parents, disputing the claims of some to be Catholic and calling special attention to those who were saloon keepers.[23] Brophy paid for a good deal of the local costs of the litigation, arranged for Father Mandin to speak to the Bisbee Knights of Columbus about the incident, and raised contributions from Catholics.[24] Brophy also mobilized support from a network of Anglo Catholics throughout the Southwest.[25]

Together Brophy and Granjon had recommended attorney Eugene Ives to the sisters at the Foundling. No one could have brought more clout to the Foundling's side. Educated at Georgetown University and Columbia Law School, as well as in Austria and France, Eugene Semme Ives practiced in New York until he was thirty-seven and then came to Tucson; there he became possibly the most prominent lawyer in the territory and certainly the most prominent Catholic lawyer. He had represented big copper companies and would later represent the Southern Pacific Railroad. Nevertheless, he was a Democrat (like most Catholics at this time) who had supported the eight-hour law in 1903. When he appeared in Morenci speaking against H. R. Rice, a PD man from Morenci and a fellow member of the Territorial Council (the upper house of the legislature), the newspaper derided him as "he of the eight hour jaw."[26] (Rice would become Ives's antagonist again because of the orphan affair.) He was also an extremely expensive lawyer and later quarreled with the sisters' New York attorney, Miller, about his bill, which he set at $5,000, though he ended up accepting much less and considered "the balance of what I believe a proper charge as 'bread cast upon the waters.'"[27] He became the chief Arizona strategist for the Foundling, using T. D. Bennett as an assistant.

So THE LEGAL BATTLE BEGAN. Despite his high status in the territory, Ives knew he was fighting an unpopular cause. Long before the first formal motion was filed, virtually every law officer in the county weighed in to defend the kidnapping of the children; Graham County District Attorney Rawlins even managed to get his pronouncement picked up by the Associated Press and thus published throughout the country.[28] On October 16 the Anglo parents petitioned Probate Judge Little for guardianship of the sixteen orphans in Clifton, on the grounds that these children of "persons unknown" to the petitioners had "no guardian[s] legally appointed: but were abandoned." Judge Little held a hearing November 16, without the presence of Foundling Hospital attorney Bennett, and awarded guardianship to the Clifton Anglos on grounds of the "best interest of said minor in respect to its temporal and its mental and moral welfare."[29] When the Foundling complained to him, Bennett rationalized his absence with the claim that his efforts would have been useless, since Judge Little had taken "an active part in the kidnapping . . . by his advice and counsel, if not by direct personal activity." Bennett's and the Foundling's plan at this time was to appeal the guardianship to the Graham County District Court, but soon they decided instead to go directly to the Territorial Supreme Court so that the decision would "be taken as final and save time and expense in appeals."[30]

But Ives believed that the New York sisters and lawyers were overconfident,[31] perhaps because he knew Arizona, perhaps because he knew the supreme court justices. Chief Justice Kent and Associates Davis, Doan, and Sloan could be said to represent the new, not the old, Anglo Arizona: all came from northern, antislavery families (three of the four from Ohio), unlike the southerners who were overrepresented in early southern Arizona. All four were Republicans, Protestants, and partisans of Arizona's economic development, very much imbued with respect for Anglo pioneers and risk takers, by no means in the pocket of particular corporations but certain that maintaining an environment hospitable to business was essential to the state's future. Their rulings supported big-business interests but not without exception, and in cases of corporate-state conflict they tried to compromise. In 1903 the four upheld United Verde Copper in taking timber from federal lands (without payment) on the grounds that fuel for roasting and smelting was necessary to mining, and therefore authorized under an act of 1878. In an appeal against Arizona's 1891 law exempting the railroads from taxation, the court went with the railroads. In several complaints brought by PD that it was being overtaxed, the court found that, although the county tax board had meant no unfairness, it had not been systematic or uniform in its assessments or collection and so reduced the company's debt. The court ruled against the Southern Pacific Railroad and a big copper company, requiring them to pay compensation for wrongful death and breach of contract, but refused to find the same company responsible when its open water flume caused the death of a three-year-old. These were men who cared very much for the sanctity of contracts, large or small, and were not at all sympathetic to the populism that had spread through Arizona in the 1890s. Regarding racial matters, the court's values were clear: it dismissed a case in which a black convicted murderer charged bias in the all-white composition of the jury and the racist remarks of the district attorney; it held a railroad construction company liable for violating the law against recruiting Mexican workers in Mexico. And it was Doan who issued the 1903 injunction against the strikers at PD's request.[32]

As the legal battle developed, three aspects of law were in play: conflict of laws, best interests of the child, and habeas corpus. "Conflict of laws" refers to inconsistencies or clashes between the laws of different countries or states; since in the United States so many areas of law, including that of child guardianship, are state rather than federal, such conflicts are common occurrences. In the orphan incident, the conflict arose around the matter of Arizona's obligation to honor the New York State charter that made the Foundling Hospital the legal guardian of its children. The "best interests of the child" doctrine had been developing in the United States since the 1830s, as a rule of thumb for adjudicating child custody disputes which broke with patriarchal assumptions that children belonged to their father.[33] Ranking a child's welfare as more sacred than a father's right was simultaneously an ideological extension of the republican view of the family as a collection of individuals with rights and needs, and a measure of the influence of organized women's campaigns for motherhood and child saving. "Habeas corpus" refers to a variety of writs used to bring a person before a court, and their main function is to release someone from unlawful imprisonment.

Equally important were the aspects of law not in play: criminal charges of kidnapping, threat with a deadly weapon, and riot. The law-enforcement officials of Graham County and Arizona never considered bringing criminal charges against the vigilantes.[34] And Ives, despite his claim that the vigilantes took the children unlawfully and with force and violence, did not accuse them of kidnapping. His silence in this regard is a good measure of the allowable discourse: he knew it to be entirely futile to argue that the Anglo citizens had acted criminally.

Ives had to develop a *civil* suit that would break the children free from their kidnappers, and to this end he prepared writs of habeas corpus. He simply ignored the best-interests claim and countered with the claim that Gatti, "his servants and employees, unlawfully and with force and violence, entered into the house of the said person where at the time of said unlawful entrance the said child" was located and took the child forcibly. In other words, he tried to translate a crime—kidnapping—into a civil wrong, that of holding the children away from their lawful guardians. The writ thus insisted that William Norton, John Gatti's orphan, was at that time a resident of the state of New York, never at any time abandoned by his legal guardian, the New York Foundling Hospital. On these grounds—the wrongful taking of children belonging to an agency legally chartered by the state of New York—Ives wired to Sheriff Parks seventeen habeas corpus writs[35] and four witness subpoenas to be served. Aggressively, Ives pointed out that the law required the sheriff to serve these but nevertheless offered to pay him to do so.[36] Parks was presumably too smart to take the money; he served the writs on January 6, along with "show-cause" orders requiring Gatti and the others to appear at the Phoenix Court on January 9. They responded to the writs with several arguments: that the Foundling was a "foreign corporation" with no rights recognized in Arizona; that its rights of guardianship gave it no authority to dispose of children in Arizona; that the relevant authority, Graham County Probate Court, had issued letters of guardianship; and that the Foundling had abandoned the children to unfit people who then voluntarily surrendered them.[37]

Meanwhile the number of children at issue had shrunk: The child delivered via Jeff Dunagan to Dr. Davis had been severed from the Foundling's claim since Davis was in California. And Josephine Corcoran, the two-year-old taken in the rain from Juan Maxwell and Angela Flores and then claimed by Jake Abraham, died of pneumonia.[38]

The Foundling's attorneys led off the trial because they represented the "petitioners" in this civil, nonjury trial. They put eight witnesses on the stand: five people from the Foundling Hospital—three sisters, a nurse, and Swayne—plus Dunagan, Leggatt, and Gatti. Ives and T. D. Bennett aimed, first, to establish the carefulness of the standard procedures at the Foundling Hospital and, second, to document the threats and intimidation used against the Foundling group. The Foundling people described their outrageous treatment and fear of attack, although the defense attorneys managed to get some of their characterizations of the mob stricken from the record. Sister Anna Michaella made a point of her dismay that the majority of the threatening crowds were women. But the character of the Mexican homes was never at issue. No witness or lawyer questioned whether all these families were equally degraded. Instead, the petitioners at once conceded that these homes were as bad as the Anglos claimed. One sister was now characterizing her first encounter with the Mexicans thus: "As we came to Arizona we saw dark skinned ragged people about depots and living in adobes. They were the first Mexicans we had seen, and a destitute uninviting lot they were . . . Mexicans pounced on our car, came inside and swarmed around like a horde of savages."[39] This description does not fit the witnesses' testimony about the sisters' first encounter with the adoptive parents they had chosen, and the last allegation that Mexicans entered the train was contradicted by all the trial witnesses. It reveals, rather, the sisters' participation in the spiraling racial attack on Mexicans.

The Foundling's attorneys tried occasionally to cast doubt on anti-Mexican testimony. Some of the most questionable claims, on both sides, derived from the fact that no one on the stand could speak Spanish, yet all communication regarding the children's original placements took place in that language. Swayne insisted that he could understand the goings-on because he knew Latin, and John Gatti claimed to be able to talk to the padre in French. The Foundling attorneys tried to introduce into the record some skepticism about these translations and about the condemnations of the Mexicans for drinking. Ives got Leggatt to agree that several of the Anglo parents not only drank but ran saloons, although Leggatt insisted that it was different because the Anglos could afford it. T. D. Bennett went to Clifton before the trial and visited some of the Mexican homes. Having done that, he was able to show, on cross-examination, that Tom Simpson—one of the most threatening members of the posse and a vociferously anti-Mexican witness—knew nothing of Mexican life in Clifton or of the alleged payments to the priest.

But these points ultimately amounted just to quibbles. Ives's objections were like the yips of a small dog, circling round and barking at a horse who barely noticed. No one challenged the fundamental propositions: the Mexicans were too poor, uneducated, and uncivilized to parent Anglo children; the whiteness of the New York Catholics did not make the Mexicans white.

One witness who did not show might have offered a serious challenge. Ives subpoenaed Margarita Chacón. Because of her looks, her English, and her education, Bennett thought her a potentially effective witness. But she would not come. Clifton's Dr. Burtch wrote back certifying that she was "in a delicate condition" and that he forbade her to travel.[40] "In a delicate condition" meant, at that time, pregnant. This might possibly have been true because Mrs. Chacón later told a census taker that she had lost a number of children, but it seems unlikely, since she had just been trying to take in two foster children. But she, her husband, and her community were not foolish enough to step into this explosive cauldron. More striking, the ignorance that allowed Ives and Bennett to think that one lone Mexican woman could be induced to testify in this Anglo Supreme Court tells us how impoverished was the Anglo ability to imagine what it was like not to be white. Why should she have participated in this conflict? She could expect brutal treatment in court and retaliation afterward in Clifton. And neither she nor her family (nor her community) had anything to gain. Even her devotion to her faith and respect for the sisters could not induce her to comply. With her history and her deep religiosity, she must have identified strongly with their work at the orphanage; their habits were familiar to her, she knew what it was to devote one's life to the Lord.

Yet they had proved themselves false: they had turned their backs on the Catholic people of Clifton-Morenci and disrespected the priest.

Mrs. Chacón was entirely correct about the trial. The Foundling made only one claim that differed with the Clifton Protestants' version of events: that within a few days after the original placements the sisters would have seen their mistakes and regathered the children. Ives induced his witnesses to blame the priest and plead understandable ignorance on the part of the Foundling people. There was a fascinating twist in the multiple power struggles here: The sisters claimed that they had had to defer to Father Mandin's priestly, male judgment when they first came to Clifton-Morenci. Three months later, they vilified him. I have to suspect that their motives (conscious or not) included not only trying to save their own skins but striking back at the church hierarchy's disrespect for women religious. Bishop Granjon was furious at them for their betrayal of his protégé, Mandin.

Both parties to the suit agreed in anointing Charles Mills, Sheriff Parks, and Dr. Tuthill as heroes for preventing violence. Ives got Sister Anna Michaella virtually to thank Mills for his intervention and to condemn the absence of such a town boss in Clifton.

In cross-examination, the respondents' attorneys, Walter Bennett and W. C. McFarland, challenged the Foundling's procedures on a number of points: (1) that the sisters had not inquired into the qualifications of the priest for judging foster families; (2) that the sisters could and did readily see that the Mexicans were unfit but declined to act on this perception; (3) that the Foundling would have gotten the orphans back had Swayne immediately agreed to recall them from the Mexicans; (4) that no threats of force were used against the Foundling people; (5) that the Mexicans paid the priest or the sexton for the children; (6) that the sisters freely, without coercion, "gave" three children to Dunagan in Morenci; (7) that since the only purpose of the Foundling was to find good homes for its children, there should be no objection to their current placements. Ives introduced testimony that contradicted or raised doubts about each of these claims, but ultimately the only claim that mattered was not argued because it was assumed by all parties: that the Mexican families were unfit to parent Anglo children. To a contemporary, antiracist consciousness this Anglo belief appears circular in the context of Clifton-Morenci: the Anglos believed that Mexicans could survive on lower wages because Mexicans did not require an Anglo standard of living, with accoutrements such as bathrooms; the Anglos then criticized the Mexicans for their low living standards. But to the Anglos this approach was not circular because it rested on a view of racial hierarchy as fixed, biological: Mexicans thrived on an uncivilized way of living but Anglo children did not.

Ives had decided to "concede" the bad character of the Mexican homes because he hoped thereby to exclude negative testimony about the Mexicans from the trial. He left unchallenged the sisters' statement that Mandin's communication had specifically asked for fair, light-complexioned children. He preferred to argue that the nuns were in the process of discovering a problem but were not allowed to rectify it. Thus in responding to one of the allegations—that the child William Norton was "abandoned to the keeping of a Mexican Indian whose name is unknown to the respondent and who was unable properly to feed, clothe, shelter, maintain and educate said children, and who was otherwise, by reason of his race, mode of living, habits and education, entirely unfit to have the care, control, custody and education of said minor"—Ives challenged only one word, "abandoned." He would accept the statement if "abandoned" was changed to "placed temporarily." But respondents' attorney Bennett insisted on introducing the testimony about how nasty the Mexicans were because "the respondents are directly and indirectly charged with raising an indignation meeting, and we desire to show . . . the foundation for that natural indignation which was raised in the breasts of the people of Clifton and Morenci."

Legally, the value of the anti-Mexican testimony to Walter Bennett was in supporting an interpretation of the vigilante action as a kind of citizen's arrest, an emergency exercise of the state's *parens patriae* power to intervene in a case of child abuse, because the Foundling's placement of the children constituted abuse.[41] Although this might logically have been an argument against indicting the vigilantes for kidnapping, it could not defend their refusal to surrender the children to the Foundling, for no claims of child mistreatment were ever leveled at that institution. No matter, because Walter Bennett's main strategy was to arouse racism and to raise the political cost to the judges of ruling for the Foundling, should they have been so tempted.

The judges sided with Walter Bennett, who called nineteen witnesses, eleven of whom devoted significant parts of their testimony to disparaging the Mexicans' standards of living and morality. Indeed, this chorus was the greater part of the defense's case; over the three days of testimonies the damnation of Mexicans echoed continually, one allegation more scurrilous than another. Several Anglo witnesses were permitted to vilify Mexican foster parents who had not, in fact, taken in orphans. For example, Eugene Fountin complained about Mercedes (no surname–the Anglos rarely knew Mexican names properly), who was ragged, lived with a man not her husband, took in washing (presumably, not suitable work for the mother of Anglo children), and got drunk: "Mr. Dunagan has her in jail now; he has had her about three times in the last month."

The lesser part of Bennett's strategy–demonstrating the Anglo mothers' devotion to their new toddlers–perfectly complemented the anti-Mexican testimony, creating a whole made up of bad and good parenting. To demonstrate good parenting, few words were needed, for the mere presence of beautifully dressed mothers and toddlers in the courtroom did most of the work. The fact that the children fussed occasionally and had to be temporarily removed from the courtroom only drew more press and audience attention to these fair (in both meanings of the word) mother-child pairs. When not in the courtroom, they were surrounded by admiring crowds outside the building.[42]

Thus Ives's maneuver to concede the inferiority of the Mexicans failed miserably. A maneuver by the respondents, to claim that some of the Anglo parents were Catholic, also failed, but it did not matter. Respondents' attorney Bennett's witnesses Laura Abraham, Henry Hill, Grace Laskey, Mary Quinn, and J. T. Kelly each claimed to be Catholics. (Louisa Gatti had already testified that her husband was Catholic but she was not.) Ives promptly recalled Sister Anna Michaella and asked her the requirements of being a Catholic; he then recalled each of these parents and asked when they had last gone to confession or Communion; none had been in over a year (most longer), which meant they were ipso facto not Catholics. The importance of religion can be gauged by the offers that several Anglo mothers made in the midst of the trial to convert to Catholicism. Mrs. Sam Abraham said, "My husband also intends to become a convert . . . We have been receiving religious instruction from the good father at Clifton, and hope soon to be baptized."[43] Given Father Timmermans's insistence to the bishop that the children must be returned to the Foundling, this claim about his offering religious instruction is dubious. But none of this testimony reverberated. Religion just wasn't the issue.

In fact, Ives barely mentioned Catholicism in his closing statement.

Walter Bennett's summation emphasized the best interests of the children almost to the exclusion of all other issues; he cited precedents for weighing this concern above others. Ives's statement won high marks for eloquence, even from the Arizona press, which was aligned against him. He conceded more fully than ever, not only the baseness of the Mexicans and the guilt of the priest in placing children with them, but also the poor judgment of the sisters. And he defended the Clifton-Morenci citizens with a remarkable mea culpa: "God forfend that I should ever again speak of them as a mob as I did at the beginning of the trial. I now believe that the exercise of their sympathy, which rescued the little ones from the hands into which they had fallen was a mark of good American citizenship."[44] His words indicated his appraisal of the power of this racial steamroller clearing the way for the vigilante parents.

Perhaps judging that questions of legal guardianship could not outweigh the best-interests issues, especially with this kind of public pressure on four judges, Ives tried to make his own best-interests argument. He was indeed ingenious. The children were all born, he said,

> branded with a scarlet scar and it is one of the functions of the hospital to remove that from the eyes of the world. The Sisters recognize in this scar a fatal handicap and in placing the innocents always had in mind getting them where the facts of a sinister birth would not be known. If the children were now allowed to grow up in the custody of the families who have them, after the limelight of publicity has been thrown so scorchingly upon them, the hateful cicatrice [*sic*] will be forever visible and the disgrace inherited from their parents will be remembered in the community and will haunt them until the scar and the memory are buried in the earth.[45]

It is true that adoption still carried stigma in 1904, because in the past century most adopted children had been "rescued" from poverty, neglect, abuse, illegitimacy, even delinquency. But Ives's argument suggests that perhaps he did not understand Arizona very well after all. Pollution of the child by the immorality of its parents, a traditional approach to protecting inheritance and morality that had been revitalized by Victorian culture, had less purchase here than in the East.[46] This was the land of opportunity, a more democratic place than New York, whence these foundlings had come. Just as the posse's membership had signified the inclusion of all the "citizens," regardless of the modesty of their social position, so these new families would bring the children into a full citizenship, unqualified by their parents' economic or moral failings.

But Ives was right about one thing: "best interests" was the ground on which the court would stand. Entirely ignoring the use of force, Judge Kent's opinion referred to the mob as "committee meetings" and the kidnapping as "volunteer" actions. In his opinion, the conflict in Clifton-Morenci took place between "Americans" and "half-breed Mexican Indians . . . impecunious, illiterate . . . vicious." He ruled that "the existence of a legal right [to the children] on either side, while properly a factor to be taken into consideration in determining the welfare of the children, is not conclusive upon the court, the welfare of the children being the controlling, vital, and determinative fact." The court noted that a further reason New York law need not apply was that the sisters brought the children to Arizona with the intention of leaving them here permanently. Finding that neither party had an overwhelming legal claim to the children, the court found it obvious which party could best provide for them: not the "degraded half-breed Indians" but the "good women of the place." There was not one word about religion. Nor was there any reference to the unclean-hands doctrine, that is, the principle that someone who has behaved wrongly should not be able to claim an equity right to that which has been gotten from wrongdoing. Instead, the Foundling people were the wrongdoers: The sisters were guilty of an "unintentional blunder," the priest of ignorance, and Swayne of "tactless stubbornness." The present foster parents, by contrast,

> with humanitarian impulse, and actuated by motives of sympathy for their pitiful condition . . . assisted in the rescue of these little children from the evil into which they had fallen, down to the time of their attendance at this trial, at cost of much time and money, in their loving care and attention, have shown that more than ordinary ties of affection bind them to these children, and that in no other homes that can be found for them are they so likely to fare as well. We feel that it is for their best interests that no change be made in their custody.[47]

Playing to the audience, Judge Kent concluded with a paean to individual opportunity in the West. The spectators clapped and stomped their feet. Mrs. Gatti, ever the most expressive, burst into tears.[48]

Commenting on his plans for appeal that night, Ives returned to his conflict-of-laws strategy. He did not differ one iota with the racial assessment offered by the court.

> The statement of facts was absolutely fair and just. The proposition left to be determined by the supreme court of the United States is a clear cut matter of law as to how far a court can extend the principle that the welfare of the child shall be the controlling element. In my opinion the court in this case extended such principle beyond all limits recognized by the authorities. They virtually decided that if a guardian passing through Arizona with his ward should temporarily pass his ward to a bystander . . . and the bystander should kidnap the ward the guardian would be compelled in order to regain possession of the child, to prove that the welfare of the child would be better in his hands than in those of the kidnapper.[49]

Ives vented his frustration, privately, on U.S. Attorney Nave, whose entrance into the case had antagonized the judges and, worse, enraged the Arizona public; Nave's presence meant that a decision for the Foundling Hospital would have been interpreted, Ives believed, as succumbing to presidential pressure. He also pointed out that a decision against the Anglo parents would have had high political costs for the judges.[50]

The families' return to Clifton was a festival. Hundreds gathered at the train station, and when their train came into sight, a brass band struck up "America." The crowd screamed as the first mother and child alighted, and the cheers grew louder as each successive family appeared. The Mexican people probably stayed close to home that day, but it is hard to imagine whether they laughed or cursed or did both.

But the Clifton foster parents remained nervous about what the U.S. Supreme Court would do. A month after the Arizona court decision state legislator H. R. Rice, assistant manager of the Detroit Copper company store, introduced a bill to change the territorial law of custody and guardianship so as to give probate judges more discretionary power to dispose of children—the power that Judge Little had lacked. Rice drafted this bill to make it retroactive! Ives got wind of this move early, saw its implications for the Gatti case, and pledged, "I shall do my utmost to defeat it." (As president of the legislature's upper house, Ives had just led a successful maneuver to block joint statehood with New Mexico.) He did not succeed, but he did manage to make the law explicitly nonretroactive, thus without power to affect pending litigation.[51]

As Ives prepared his brief to the U.S. Supreme Court, it became clear that his praise for the Arizona Supreme Court's fairness had been tactical and momentary. The Statement of Facts from the Arizona Court had been riddled with prejudicial errors and omissions, many of which Ives tried, to no avail, to get amended. To argue the case the Foundling hired Judge D. Cady Herrick, former New York district attorney, Appellate Division judge, and Democratic candidate for governor in 1904. His fee was $1,500. The case was heard in April 1906, with two Anglo foster fathers in attendance (Gatti and Hill), and no transcript was made. The Court delayed its decision until December 1906, when it dismissed the appeal for want of jurisdiction.[52] William R. Day, the newest and youngest justice, delivered the opinion on strictly legal logic: Habeas corpus rights against unlawful imprisonment did not apply to children.[53] Children have no right to freedom, only to care and custody. Thus the Arizona Supreme Court had adjudicated between rival adult claimants to custody, not about the children's right of personal freedom, and thus an appeal was not allowed. Yet the high court's racial logic was not hard to find in its brief since it incorporated verbatim the claim of the vigilantes: "the child in question is a white, Caucasian child . . . abandoned . . . to the keeping of a Mexican Indian, whose name is unknown to the respondent, but one . . . by reason of his race, mode of living, habits and education, unfit to have the custody, care and education of the child."[54]

The Arizona and U.S. Supreme Courts were adjudicating whiteness nearly as explicitly as South African courts did. It is an example not only of regional variation in racial categories but also of contradictions within the state that while the courts were saying that white children did not belong with Mexicans, the U.S. census categorized Mexicans as white.

Ives's habeas corpus case had failed, and he had no other. It is not clear that he made mistakes; he may have had no other available strategy. Once criminal charges were ruled out, the vigilantes could become heroes instead of felons, and the court could easily decide that the best interests of the children should outweigh the legal and religious claims of the Foundling Hospital.

THE IMPERFECT FIT BETWEEN ARIZONA'S RACIAL SYSTEM and that of the whole country is vividly illustrated in a clippings scrapbook assembled by the Sisters of Charity in New York. In the West, press coverage defined the racial politics of the trial as a battle between Arizona Anglos and New York Catholics, the latter not understanding—even subverting–the necessary struggle of western whites to defend their civilization against the low Mexicans. Most Arizona white newspapers exulted at both the Anglos' seizure of the children and their court victories, interpreting them as patriotic victories for the would-be state. Anglo Arizona was in the midst of a struggle for statehood in which its Mexican population represented a danger. (Indeed, to some the foundling conflict suggested just why Arizona–New Mexico jointure would be a mistake: "The recent incident . . . indicates how such a feud [between races and religions] would be waged.")[55] Just as Mexicans were being excluded from citizenship, the Anglo press exiled them from Arizona altogether, with headlines such as "Arizonans Win Decision Famous Foundling Case," or "Arizona Mothers Wept for Joy." The battle for statehood reinforced the drive among Arizona's whites to suppress Mexican ambitions.

The same racial divide sometimes colored the Arizonan understanding of New York. From the Anglo Arizonan side of this opposition, New York was not just another state, and its defeat carried moral and cultural messages. The meaning of New York to Anglo westerners then was perhaps not so different from what it is to many today: a city of iniquity, corruption, immigrants, and Catholicism. This was both a racial and a gendered story. New York was a city losing not only its whiteness but also its masculinity. Its effete residents lacked the manliness to face danger and wilderness and were by the same token ignorant of life's most rewarding challenges. Its crooked politicians were in hock to a party machine and manipulated by Romanist bishops. "Arizona's" victory was an assertion not only of the independence of the state and its citizens, but also of republican civic virtue, a white attribute. Arizona was a community whose men and women would not tolerate child abuse.

Southwestern press coverage included wild exaggeration and sensationalist extremes. "Mexican Purchasers of New York Orphans Surrender Slave Holdings in Terror as the Vigilantes Appear . . . Sale to Mexican peons of a consignment of white orphans"; "Mexicans clamoring for children were denied them if they had nothing to pay"; "Inflamed citizens swept the Mexicans from the City"; "Arizona Vigilantes Rescue 40 Infants Sold at Auction."[56] At a certain point it becomes difficult to distinguish ordinary, quotidian racism from incredible rumors, as in "Save Orphans from Bondage"—a kind of spil-lover in which denunciations of Mexican peonage blamed the victims as well as the owners.[57] The bondage theme was also applied widely to the sisters, as in "Slave Dealers Driven Out of Camp: Human Traffic Agents . . ."[58] The journalists did not make this up, but they reported unverified rumors and allegations. No doubt the Foundling Hospital had its enemies. Earlier accusations against it reappeared, including a charge by a correspondent in Colorado, dating from three months before the orphans arrived, that the sisters had delivered eleven young-sters into the hands of Mexicans there.[59] Some of the grudges against the Foundling had some basis in fact. For example, a Boston justice of the peace wrote to the Morenci chief of police that this "notorious institution" sold and shipped out poor unfortunate children and re-fused to tell where the children were—a reference to policies that did make it difficult if not impossible for natural parents to track down their children.[60]

Outside Arizona, the press gave the story some different meanings and was by no means so universally positive about the foundling affair's outcome. Criticism included some East Coast clichés about the lawless, uncivilized West—"Arizona Mob Law" ran one such headline. The degree of criticism was a gauge of Catholic influence. Throughout the country Democratic newspapers, especially Hearst papers in cities with Catholic power, and a few other New York area papers, empha-sized the violence against the sisters and the priest. Several used the word "lynching." "Children Held Prisoners," headlined the New York Hearst *Journal.* Others used leads like "Sisters of Charity Persecuted: Armed Men Aroused Them at Night, Invaded Their Rooms, and Drove Them Away—Children Stolen by Mob"; "Mob of Americans Tried to Lynch Prelate"; "Dregs of the Nation Now Holding Infants"; "Armed Ruffians Forcibly Seize 19 Foundlings"; "Bigotry in Arizona." Clifton-Morenci Anglos in response berated the Hearst press, whose "Yellow Balloons Libel Good People . . . The Hearst papers . . . have not only suppressed the truth . . . but in their usual yellow style they have maligned, vilified and abused the entire community."[61]

The pro-Foundling reports also exaggerated and misinformed, as in a story headlined "Little Waifs from a New York Asylum Held Prisoners in a New Mexican Hotel by the Whites."[62] In November there had been widespread erroneous reporting that Governor Brodie had convinced President Roosevelt to order the orphans returned to the Foundling. At least two newspapers reported that the rangers or the army had been called out, while another reported that U.S. marshals had been ordered to take the children and leave them with sisters in El Paso.[63]

Some papers spoke of "bigotry," but most meant by that anti-Catholicism, not racism. After all, the politics involved was twisted: the Democratic Party held the allegiance of most Catholics but was also the party most associated with racism. So it is not surprising that most papers that defended the nuns ignored or even condemned the Mexicans as well as the vigilantes. Only a few writers gestured toward antiracism. "Objected to 'Greasers,'" one story began. "There is a big Mexican population, but the 'whites'–the born Americans–look upon a Mexican in these parts as a Georgia Democrat looks upon George Washington Jones, colored, or a Californian looks upon a Chinaman."[64] Hardly a ringing denunciation of racism. And some of the eastern Republican papers did not have their racial categories any straighter than the sisters, as in "Arizonians Objected to Spaniards as Parents." The few articles that defended the original placements of the children ignored race; for example, "we fail to see the crime of the Sisters in placing certain of their charges in humble Catholic homes."[65] The only wholly condemnatory comments came from southwestern papers with Mexican and Catholic readerships. The *Dallas Times Herald*, Democratic, opined that "a Mexican has as much of the milk of human kindness in his breast as an American. There are brutes in all countries and among all races and nationalities."

In their effort to unify whites on their side, the Arizona defense attorneys wanted to keep the trial's focus on race, not religion. They actively denied religious division and fostered news stories like one that described how among "the decent citizens of Clifton and Morenci, Catholics stood shoulder to shoulder with Protestants." The Foundling's attorneys, by contrast, directed attention to religion, not race, which they accomplished through silencing the Mexicans and harping on the threats from the Clifton-Morenci mob to the priest, Swayne, and the Foundling sisters. Since the journalists who were even slightly sympathetic tended to be Catholic, they followed the interpretation of the sisters and the hierarchy in presenting the conflict strictly through a religious lens. Head Sister Teresa Vincent insisted that "the prejudice animating the mob was religious rather than racial. Such an incident recalls to the older people some of the stormy days of long ago before enlightenment had dispelled the clouds of anti-Catholic hatred . . . It is scarcely a half century since a Knownothing mob marched to the cathedral of New York for the purpose of burning it."[66] But as the Sisters of Charity emphasized religious persecution they denied the racism of the Clifton-Morenci vigilantes to which they had acceded. Tucson's Bishop Granjon, in defending his Mexican followers, reversed the aspersions but also followed a racialist line of thought: "how hollow are the claims of superiority of the so-called Americans who objected to the children being placed in Mexican families . . . A girl was given to a divorced Jew, another to a saloon keeper and gambler; a man and wife, both Mormons, obtained a little girl."[67]

One New York Catholic paper went so far as to extend its critique of the Clifton-Morenci vigilantes to the entire Anglo-Protestant child-saving establishment, adopting the same romance about Latinos that the Tucson bishop indulged:

> Americans have some right to regard our form of civilization as superior . . . to that of Latin, including Spanish-American countries, but in one important, indeed essential, feature of humanity and Christianity those countries are immeasurably superior to us. That is the treatment of the innocent and helpless foundling, and of those of the weaker sex who are more sinned against than sinning. Here, under our harsh and inhuman system of public so-called charity the doom of the foundling is, or generally has been, death . . . in no homes in the world are the morals of the young more safeguarded than among Spanish-Americans.

This romanticism was also accompanied by the typical eastern ignorance of the Southwest, by which all Mexicans are assumed to be agrarian, organized into haciendas, and divided among landowners and peasants: "The upper class are large land owners and cattle owners . . . The lower class are, as a rule, small cultivators, under the protecting care of their superiors."[68]

The Spanish-language southwestern press, which might have been expected to offer an antiracist take on the case, was silent. Papers that had covered the 1903 strike intensively, papers with Clifton-Morenci subscribers, ignored the foundling episode. Excluded from the trial, Mexicans seemed to exclude it from their world of concern. I suspect many tried to wash their hands of this affair, just as they had chosen not to fight for the foundlings, putting it down to the barbarity of the Anglos and their racism. But surely the case confirmed their cynicism about American law.

Even the critical press applauded the "rescue" of the children while condemning the mob threats to the sisters and Swayne and, sometimes, the refusal to return the children to the Foundling. Typical was the even-handed "Waifs in Mexican Hovels: Arizona Mob Threatens to Lynch New York Agent and Nurses."[69] The *New York Times* took a fittingly stately position: "As between the Anglo-Saxon hoodlum and the Mexican 'greaser' who to so large an extent compose the citizenship of Arizona, and contend between themselves for the control of its destinies when it is admitted to the Statehood . . . we should dislike to be forced to a choice . . . Since no bones were broken their experience is not to be deplored if it has taught them [the Sisters of Charity] to abstain in future from handing over American foundlings to be reared in Mexican homes."[70] The country's leading progressive social-work periodical, *Charities,* published the Arizona court's opinion in full and editorialized in its favor: "The local communities of Arizona . . . must be acquitted of any charge of having resorted to mob violence . . . The indignation which followed the action of the representatives of the hospital . . . was as natural and as creditable . . . neither Catholic nor Protestant sentiment will justify carrying this principle [of placing children in homes of the same religious faith as their parents] to the extent of giving a preference to homes of the religious faith desired when such homes are degraded and unfit."[71] The vigilante action and court decision meshed perfectly with the racialized agenda of social work agencies on the East Coast, for whom protecting children often meant struggling to raise up immigrants–regarded by the agencies as racially nonwhite–out of their old-world culture to the level of Americans. This child-saving work, furthermore, frequently meant removing children from homes unfit due to poverty, degradation, and presumed immorality, and the social work agencies' knowledge of these immigrants' homes was not always superior to the Clifton Anglos' knowledge of Mexican homes.

There was plenty of religious content in the conflict and plenty of anti-Catholicism in the mining camps. Even such a wealthy and well-connected man as Brophy felt it, right there in Bisbee. The American Protective Association had followed the church as it expanded westward, promoting anti-Catholicism in the mining camps as well as the cities, and its successes imbued significant sectors of the western Republican Party with anti-Catholicism. Brophy recounted his personal melodrama of temptation and affirmation: he nearly succumbed to the many inducements to leave the faith, created by the prejudice he encountered and by his own yearning for a place among Bisbee's and PD's elite; he was saved by a letter from his sister, a missionary in Spain, who invited him to visit her; he was able to do so thanks to financial help from none other than James Douglas of PD's New York headquarters, and Brophy never wavered again.[72] Brophy won for himself a place as an exception, an active Catholic amid the Protestant elite, as Catholicism in the mining camps became increasingly associated with Mexicans and pro-union immigrants. Although many Clifton-Morenci Anglos held anti-Catholic sentiments, they knew it was in their interest to suppress those. They refused to define any part of the issue as Protestant against Catholic but returned always to race and to the defense of Arizona against outsiders, a category that, if applied accurately, took in a majority of Anglo as well as Mexican Clifton-Morenci residents.

So it was never an either/or question, religion or race. To ask the question this way is to assume something fixed and fundamental about prejudice and about categories such as religion, race, and ethnicity, when they were in fact varying, fluid, and easily reshaped. Those who insisted that religion was primary were either easterners whose interests lay in assimilating foreigners of different racial "stock" or Catholic leaders who knew that the Mexican flock was vital to their religious empire. Denying religious prejudice was relatively easy for Clifton Anglos, who experienced little religious fervor in this period. The Catholic clergy would defend its parishioners when necessary, as Granjon did, but doing so did not include promoting racial equality, given the church's own policy of segregation: in Phoenix just after the Arizona Supreme Court's decision, Granjon was conducting separate confirmation services, one for "Americans" on Sunday and one for Mexicans on Saturday.[73]

The Foundling's attempt to spin the conflict in exclusively religious terms fooled no one in the Southwest and few elsewhere. For Arizonans there was little ambiguity in the courts' message. To Anglos, the decision confirmed that this was American country, that its citizens would not allow Mexicans to subject white people to their low standards, and that the protective umbrella of American standards would cover children as well as adults. Such guarantees helped make Arizona safe for statehood and added to the Anglo Arizonans' conviction that merger with New Mexico, with its Mexican majority population, was unacceptable. To Mexicans—and despite the exclusion of Mexicans, the

trial was a proclamation directed mainly to Mexicans—the courts confirmed that they could not be Americans no matter where they were
born or what their citizenship status, that they had few rights that
Anglos had to respect. Worse, the decision advanced Anglo dominance in a painful and humiliating way, asserting that direct Anglo
power over Mexicans need not stop at the front door but extended into
the heart of Mexican families.

OVER THE YEARS THE ORPHAN INCIDENT came to be rewritten
in the memories and tellings of Clifton-Morenci residents. When I
began to interview people in Clifton, I learned that most knew the
orphan story, and most knew it wrong, as is typical when historical
events are preserved primarily as folklore. Their errors and misrecol-
lections, however, do not obscure their political and racial perspective
on the events. The best artifact of the Anglo version is this oral history
collected by a Federal Writers Project interviewer during the 1930s:

> In the spring of 1905, two men posing as Catholic Priests appeared in
> Clifton-Morenci districts . . . they spent several weeks amongst the Mexi-
> can-Catholics and disappeared.
>
> In November, a train bearing 300 white children appeared in Clifton;
> the children were accompanied by several Sisters and the same two
> priests. They were taken to the Morenci Hotel, but no suspicion was
> aroused, until it was noticed that the Priests were taking them away, two
> and three at a time and were leaving them at the homes of Mexicans.
>
> W. C. Crawford, deputy sheriff, happened to drop-in at the hotel, and
> noticed that the children were "tagged" with a number and the name of
> some Mexican resident of the district; the tags aroused his curiosity and
> he began to ask questions; one of the Sisters broke down and began to
> cry, but would say nothing, the others were evasive.
>
> Crawford reported the matter to the Sheriff in Clifton and the local
> Priest, Father Swain, was questioned; little was gained from Father Swain;
> the news spread like "wild fire" and the white citizens began to "boil." An
> investigation committee was sent out; the first place they called they were
> denied permission to see the white child that the priest had left there, in
> fact, the Mexican, tried to deny that there was such a child there; the
> committee searched the place by force, and found the tiny blond girl,
> wrapped in a blanket, under the bed; the child had cried until she could
> make only a sobbing sound, and was scared within an inch of her life.
>
> The committee went from house to house, taking the children, by

force; some two hundred of them had already been delivered, guards were stationed at the hotel to see that no more were taken away.

The Mexicans, unwilling, gave them up, stating that they had paid good money for them, away last spring, and they wanted either the children or the money—preferably, the children. The prices ranged from $25.00 to $150.00.

The resentment of the citizens soon amounted to "mobbery"; they didn't hesitate to go "gunning" for the Priests, and tar and feathers were prepared for Father Swain, but somehow, all three Priests managed to escape . . .

The matter was taken up with the Governor, and the children were returned to the New York Foundling Home. About twenty were left for adoption.[74]

Mexican versions of the story have not been preserved in writing—few of the Federal Writers Project interviewers talked to Mexicans, for example. Several Cliftonians of Mexican descent believe that the vigilantes never got all the foundlings, that some of the orphans remained with Mexican families, and that this fact explains the presence of some light-skinned and even red-haired members of their families. This version of the outcome serves the function of reducing the Anglo victory slightly, affording the Mexicans a chance to savor some private laughs at Anglo expense, and reminding the listener of the frequent transgression of racial boundaries in Clifton-Morenci.

Whatever potential the trials held to unite Anglo and Mexican Catholics was not fulfilled: an alliance of Anglos across religious lines grew, while no alliance of Catholics across racial lines emerged. Brophy and his allies remained loyal to PD and accepted by Arizona's Protestant elite. Exiled by the Anglos from the Clifton-Morenci parish, Mandin was sent first to Prescott and then in 1913 to Bisbee, where he and Brophy formed a long-lasting partnership. There Mandin displayed again his skill with women, spurring them to outstanding fund-raising efforts, and he reenergized men through the Knights of Columbus; together the men and women raised $40,000. With this money he built a new church—called Saint Patrick's, perhaps in deference to Brophy's Irish roots—rather grand for the price because the miners did most of the construction work themselves. In Bisbee Mandin soon found himself on the other side of a posse, perhaps as helplessly as before: Mandin and Brophy cooperated with PD in the notorious Bisbee deportation of striking miners in 1917 and later defended the action.[75]

Racism and anti-Catholicism infused western anti-Mexicanism, although not necessarily in equal parts, and the fused bigotry in Clifton-Morenci proceeded from strength to strength for the next three decades or so. In the 1910s and 1920s the Arizona Ku Klux Klan grew, attacking Mexicans and other "aliens." The KKK created a chapter in Clifton-Morenci, where one old-timer remembers at least three cross burnings. One gigantic cross was erected on the chalk cliffs in South Clifton and burned for hours; this Anglo witness remembered it as "awe inspiring and made our spines tingle," so one can imagine how Mexican Catholics felt.[76] Prejudice could not always be distinguished from ideology. In the summer of 1913 the Morenci home of Father Colle, suspected by Anglos of sympathy for politically radical Mexican miners, was bombed at midnight, and he only escaped death only because he had just that evening changed his sleeping room to another part of the house; twice that fall his church was dynamited while he was sleeping there, and each time he narrowly escaped.[77]

Such terrorism was only the most conspicuous aspect of the racial segregation installed in Clifton-Morenci in the first decades of this century. PD and its wholly owned town, Morenci, established segregation in jobs, housing, recreation, and locker rooms. Mexicans were allowed in the swimming pool only in the late afternoons, not in the morning when the water was fresh. In Clifton, an incorporated township with its own municipal government, segregation was more informal, but Mexican Americans were effectively shut out of politics and denied equal opportunity in business, education, and employment. Clifton-Morenci's apartheid was dismantled, haltingly, only decades later, starting in the 1950s, after World War II's demand for huge quantities of copper gave workers the leverage to win recognition of a union with a commitment to racial equality.

ABOUT A DECADE AFTER THE KIDNAPPING two of the orphans experienced further serious traumas, about which I have only fragmentary information. The orphan known to the Sisters of Charity as Sadie Green had been adopted by Olive and Charles Freeman, renamed Gladys, and taken to Los Angeles. There in June 1914 Mrs. Freeman brought charges against a grocer for raping Gladys and making her pregnant. As is common among so many sexually abused girls, Gladys had not "told on" the grocer, so the assault was not discovered until she was in advanced pregnancy. Other parents in the neighborhood had previously complained about the man's "mistreatment" of young girls. In the typical, and brutal, double standard of the time, Gladys was said to have "got in trouble" in a communication to the Foundling sisters.[78]

The second orphan's experience, reported in the Foundling archives, is as unverifiable as the Anglo rumors about the depravities of the Mexican parents, although more specific and significantly more serious. At some point prior to 1914, foster father George High was tried and convicted for attempted rape of his foster daughter. A local man reported that he was "nearly lynched" in Duncan (a "suburb" of Clifton), "where the outrage was attempted."[79] This is a confusing piece of information, because the Foundling Hospital and court records showed that High had taken a boy, George Webber. So perhaps the victim was not his foster daughter. Or perhaps the records were not correct. Or perhaps he had another daughter.

Do not, then, convict George High without more evidence. But even a rumor can remind us of a vital truth: It is difficult to be sure who will be a good parent, and heaven knows that prosperity, white skin, and political power do not guarantee it.

8

Family and Race

THE ECHOES OF THE ORPHAN STORY reach far from Clifton-Morenci. It is not only an Arizonan but also an American story, simultaneously an allegory that symbolizes our legacy of race hatred and a parable that offers lessons for reducing that hatred. Like Blake's grain of sand in which one can see the world, the story allows us to learn something big by studying a very small story.[1]

Most prominently, the orphan story makes visible the often unacknowledged force that women have exerted in constructing and defending race lines. The conflict arose from initiatives taken by women—the Mexicans and Anglos of Clifton-Morenci (not to mention the Sisters of Charity). Their initiatives were constrained by powerful structures not mainly of the women's own making: by gender, by sexual divisions of labor, by racial formations, by the labor market, all of which shaped their feelings about motherhood and children. The Mexican women's motives were formed also by their church and their faith. Yet both groups caused these events to happen by choices they made, the Mexicans in volunteering to take in orphans, the Anglos in leading their community to seize the orphans through violent intimidation.

The passions and hierarchies of race gave both Mexican and Anglo women opportunities to improve their families and communities, and they carried out these responsibilities as diligently as did men. *Mexicanas* managed to influence not only their homes and church but also their communities, and were beginning to use the Anglo law courts in their own interest. The antidemocratic racial practices of white women, in Clifton-Morenci as everywhere, were inseparable from their progressive reform practices, such as organizing schools, cleaning up the towns, protecting children. The Clifton-Morenci Anglo women were as certain that they were acting in the best interests of the children as were East Coast big-city reformers who "Americanized" immigrants by teaching them the errors of their traditional practices. The foundling affair functions as a unique but graphic example of the racialization of child welfare policy.

It also illustrates how women, even those for whom public appearances and activities were limited, could exert power in public as well as in private affairs. What could be more private than adoption? A family-building strategy that could overcome infertility, comfort and console women far from home, and very possibly provide a means of increasing the family income in the future. Yet at the same time taking in the orphans represented a public matter for the Mexicans of Clifton-Morenci, a community-building strategy, applying Mexican principles of upward mobility through lighter skin color to a new American context. And what activity could be more public and political than organizing and directing an armed posse? The story reminds us that even women who defined themselves as housewives, brought by husbands and fathers to a remote mining camp that offered almost no opportunity for employment and limited opportunity for female leadership, could find ways of becoming citizens. Indeed, they could instigate and manage male citizenly activity. Citizenship, like child welfare, has long been a racialized practice, intimately connected to whiteness.

That women were fighting over children is hardly unfamiliar or unusual, given the intensity of motherhood among women's experiences. As custody disputes become more common, we see how parental conflicts can escalate. Less often noticed is the influence of such maternal concerns in constructing community antagonism, in this case along race and class lines. The intensity of these conflicts resulted, ironically, from women's shared experience, across race lines, of motherhood and community-betterment work. The Clifton-Morenci women's clash could be called a tragic encounter because both groups were motivated in large part by the truly charitable impulse to mother an orphan, an impulse defiled by racism but visible nevertheless. Both groups of women took pride in mothering.

The Anglo passion for the orphans demonstrates a vital generaliza-
tion about race: that one of the sites most fertile for the bloom of racism
seems to be family. The evil flower is perhaps more familiar in the form
of anxiety about whatever relationships are locally considered "interracial," and to prevent these the states erected anti-"miscegenation"
walls. But interracial parenting can produce equal or greater fury. It
does not necessarily matter whether this parenthood is adoptive or
biological. Part of the tenaciousness and adaptability of the idea of race
is that it harmonizes so well with the emotional secret gardens we
construct around family relations.[2] It is not surprising that a women's
story leads to that awareness, since women's emotions about children
are so violent, certainly violent enough that Anglo women could bring
Anglo men into their sense of duty to "rescue" the orphans. Most
parents know that parent-child relations can be easily as passionate as
romantic bonds. As adoption became more common, it became a site
where racial difference seemed to many a violation of the "natural"
intimacy of family. On a larger scale, "interracial" adoption reproduced white panic about "miscegenation."

Today the rapidly expanding number of "mixed-race" couples and
adoptions may be reducing the anxiety about "race mixing" in the
present. But mixed-race adoptions, even more than mixed-race couples, occur only in one direction: there is debate about whether whites
should adopt children of color, but adoptions of white children by
parents of color are so rare they are not even debated. This dimension
of racial policy in child welfare suggests something of the degree to
which race is about hierarchy, not difference.

Understanding this, we are better able to comprehend other historical cases of child stealing in which dominant groups have felt entitled
to seize the children of subordinate groups. The century-old movement
against child abuse and neglect has protected many children but also
made many poor mothers vulnerable to professional and government
decisions–typically without the right of appeal–that their mothering
was not adequate. Child-saving agencies removed children from parents on the basis of culturally biased standards of child raising.[3] Even
when the agencies committed themselves to not removing children
"for poverty alone," they could not keep this promise because poverty
is never alone; rather, it often comes packaged with depression and
anger, poor nutrition and housekeeping, lack of education and medical
care, leaving children alone, exposing children to improper influences.

The judges who ruled for the vigilantes believed they were upholding the best interests of the children, and they might have pointed out that with Anglo parents the children got better clothes, medical care, education, for example. How would they have confronted, then, the logical conclusion that the poor have weaker claims to their children than the prosperous? Did they believe that equality of opportunity, the premise of the American political system, meant that all children should be raised by those who have the money to provide for them well?

This remains a troubling question today. And the Clifton-Morenci incident, from that perspective, resembles many other instances of child stealing in the name of the best interests of the child. Between 1910 and 1975, white Australians stole 100,000 children from aboriginal women, giving the light-skinned children to white couples to adopt and the dark-skinned to orphanages. Inuit and Native American children were forcibly removed from their families by both U.S. and Canadian government action. The Swiss government took Romany children. In Israel, Ashkenazi (European) Jewish women, with the help of doctors, stole babies born to Sephardic Yemeni Jewish mothers from the hospitals; the mothers were told that the babies had died.[4] Here is a phenomenon that is racist yet lacks even the kind of racial justification evident in 1904 Arizona: in these large-scale child stealings there was no claim that parents and children should "match," only the confidence and entitlement that come from a group sense of superiority.

The racial motives for adoption among the Mexican and Anglo women in Clifton-Morenci afford a sense of the breadth and depth of racial thought a century ago. Most Americans at this time understood human groups and differences by dividing people into categories, described phenotypically but infused with characterological meanings and comparisons. They called these categories races. Although racial talk and thought probably develop only in the context of hostility, exclusion, subordination, and invidious comparison, it is nevertheless analytically useful to distinguish race from racism. Scholarly and popular conversation at the turn of the century was thick with attempts to root human differences in notions of differentiated "stocks"; the "scientific" race talk of the period tried to describe these categories physically and to explain them in terms of biogenetic origin. Although the Mexican racial system was different than the American, both groups in Clifton-Morenci frequently discussed racial difference, and Mexicans like Anglos infused it with hierarchical notions of superiority/inferiority, civilization/primitivism. The familial dimensions of their racial feelings make evident how different motives, influenced by power or lack of power, translate and manipulate racial categories into justifications for discrimination or even persecution. The Mexican parents' motives for adoption included their awareness that white was respected while brown was not; they were trying, perhaps, to expand the circle of whiteness (although they did not wish to include Indians, blacks, and Chinese). The Anglo parents shared the same awareness, but it gave them an interest in defending the circle's boundary, keeping Mexicans excluded from the privileges of whiteness. One group succeeded, the other lost.

The perimeters of the circles of whiteness wavered in 1904 Clifton-Morenci. Individuals and groups could occasionally erase and move the lines, although they believed that they were merely trying to discern boundaries drawn by nature. The Euro-Latins, Santa Teresa and her family, some of the Mexican businessmen were functionally or partially "white," defined by their inclusion in Anglo social occasions and by their resources. But already the vast majority of Clifton-Morenci residents were fixed as members of a "race" without the power to change their own or their family members' position (with the exception of those in mixed-race relationships—once Mexican women had been able to move upward, become "white," in this way, but by 1904, more commonly, white men with Mexican women moved downward, "gone Mexican").

These racial fences became even more sturdy as the new political and economic relations of statehood and large-scale industry reinforced the barbed wire. Just as voting came to matter more, Mexican Americans were increasingly disfranchised. The struggle over statehood, a battle primarily fought over race issues, in turn further intensified the racial divide by legitimating white power as a political goal. As wage labor in the mines, mills, and smelters became the dominant means of earning a living, racial barriers were maintained primarily by the copper companies. No Mexican mineworker, slotted into his job by the copper companies, could shed his race, no matter how skillful or respectable he was, just as no white mineworker or manager could lose his race, not matter how badly he worked and behaved. The development of company-town Morenci with its manicured segregation completed the construction of apartheid. The mineworkers' 1903 effort to get better pay and working conditions, an effort that began as a racially integrated one, became in the popular understanding a Mexican campaign, one that directly threatened Anglo control over law and order. What an irony, that workers engaged in what they saw as a class struggle, with an integrationist and nonracialist ideology, ended up contributing to racial segregation, their strike used by whites as a justification for discrimination.

The labor market equally affected the political aspects of racial formation. The copper companies drew in Mexican workers and their families, and then used their migrations to define all of them as foreigners, while itinerancy among the Anglos had no such effect. Men seemed to divide, increasingly, between white citizens and Mexican noncitizens, regardless of their legal citizenship, as indicated in the sharp decline in Mexican voters in the area. The Mexican immigration had a contradictory effect on southwestern race: On the one hand, the racial difference of the Mexicans became marked, by Anglos, as a difference between immigrants and "Americans." Seeing all Mexicans as foreigners then justified and intensified Anglo fear that Mexicans would steal jobs and drive wages down, thus deflecting Anglo workers' anger from mining companies to Mexican workers. On the other hand, partly in response to exclusion from American politics, Mexican Americans plunged into Mexican politics in the era of the Mexican revolution, and their national pride kept alive an antidiscrimination consciousness. This consciousness nurtured understandable anger against Anglo mineworkers and their unions.

Yet already in these early decades of the twentieth century political and economic developments along the border were challenging older national and racial identities. The rise of a border economy and a border politics, which drew U.S. Mexicans into the Mexican revolutionary movement, complicated identities. Copper mining and smelting generated border people as the *maquiladoras*[5] do today. But this was hardly a border between equals. The U.S. economy not only pulled workers in and pushed them out cyclically, but the U.S. government acted for the employers, alternatively as labor recruiter and deportation agency. Anti-Mexican discrimination thus operated on both sides of the border from the beginning of this century, in a fashion that continuously reinforced the fusion of racism with anti-alien sentiment and the identity of Mexicans, in the dominant Anglo mind set, with low-wage, unskilled laborers.

If we look back from the end of the twentieth century, the orphan affair seems a tragedy because the very social values that produced conflict might, in another context, have evoked solidarity. The women shared a similar desire to civilize the frontier and discipline men's unruliness. They all wanted churches, schools, sanitation, clean water, flood control, beautification. Their common willingness to put themselves out to care for another city's orphans could have yielded a common interest in child welfare. The orphans who became tokens of racial transgression and objects of revenge could have been seen as representing a transcendence of racial suspicion and hierarchy. The Mexican border people were envisioning, partly out of necessity, perhaps largely unconsciously, a more beneficial version of binational, Mexican and American society. In the Mexican women's desire for these New York Irish babies, were they not claiming simultaneously an American ambition for social mobility and an identity as border people? In their working lives, they had a vision, however humble, of a transnational economy that could benefit both countries. Not as academic outsiders but as daily participants they imagined a border of mutual fascination instead of a border "where the Third World grates against the first and bleeds."[6] Instead, the Anglo women's passions for children gave rise to a race riot, a vigilante action that served to reinforce their dominance. Such is the force of racial identity, however shifting and recently constructed, that even the guileless orphans became its pawns.

Epilogue

WHETHER HISTORIES HAVE A HAPPY ENDING or not depends on when the chronicler ends the tale. Two years after the orphan incident, the U.S. Supreme Court had ratified a terrible injustice, and the Clifton-Morenci Anglos were on their way to establishing thoroughgoing racial segregation. Forty years after the orphan incident, the future shone with industrial and political promise in Clifton-Morenci: World War II had sent copper production into a boom, a successful union drive was generating an upward trajectory in the workers' standard of living, and a new civil rights consciousness was beginning to challenge the color line. Eighty years after the orphan incident, life in Clifton-Morenci could hardly have been worse: In the midst of a two-and-a-half-year strike, the people were bitterly and violently divided, another flood had devastated virtually all of Clifton, and PD had permanently fired the strikers who were subsisting on meager strike pay and contributions from out-of-town supporters. Today, at the end of the century, PD operates union-free in its wholly owned company town Morenci. Because it drove out the 1983 strikers, and because of the transformation of mining into a largely technical, white-collar operation, Anglos now outnumber Mexican Americans two to one in Morenci. Economically depressed Clifton, by contrast, remains predominantly Mexican American, poorer (although with less racial differential in wealth than in Morenci), and older, because younger people often have to leave to find work.[1] Clifton townspeople are hoping to stimulate tourism to revitalize the economy.

The orphan story could be told without any reference to what came after, but the after-events change the resonance of the story. Because several of my Clifton-Morenci informants perceived the orphan story through the lens of the defeated 1983 strike, I had to explore that perspective myself. Like the visual gaze, historical perception originates from a particular vantage point, creating a line of sight from present to past. However complete the evidence we compile, we cannot escape subjecting the evidence to questions that the present stimulates us to ask. Part of the historian's job is to resist this presentism, to break free of the sticky web of today's categories, and to do that one begins by becoming conscious of and trying to root out the present lurking in the phrases, the emphases, the scripts through which we hear about the past. But we also learn more about the past by interrogating it from the present.

When I began interviewing old-timers about life in old Clifton-Morenci, I was surprised that the 1983 labor conflict colored their stories. Several said they did not wish to speak to me because they did not want to think about the strike of 1983 again—although I had told them I was writing about the orphan incident of 1904. The 1983 strike, covered in the national press primarily as a major setback to union strength, had additional meaning for Clifton-Morenci, where it tore open the healing gash of racism in the area. So it was from contemporary Clifton-Morenci people that I learned to see the influence of PD's labor policies on the racial system that gave rise to the vigilante kidnapping.

After their defeated attempt in 1903, Clifton-Morenci workers tried repeatedly to organize a union but were regularly frustrated until the 1940s.[2] By that time the National Labor Relations Act of 1935 had guaranteed workers the right to unionize, and World War II's demand for copper gave the workers leverage. A militant industry-wide strike in 1946, spurred on by World War II veterans—returning, with their medals and their memories of fallen brothers, to the same old segregation—forced PD to recognize the union. Until 1967 this was the Mine, Mill, and Smelter Workers, an industrial union distinguished by its commitment to organizing Mexican workers and combating racism. Although Mine, Mill was thrown out of the CIO[3] in 1950 for alleged communist infiltration, Clifton-Morenci workers stuck with it, and in 1967 it merged with the United Steelworkers. In Clifton-Morenci, the union's substantial gains for workers transformed the whole community. Workers got higher wages, health benefits, a grievance procedure with which to resist arbitrary and driving foremen, and greatly improved health and safety conditions at work. The union struggled to desegregate jobs and end wage discrimination (although it did not do much for the growing number of women working in the industry). Union strength spilled out into the whole region: increased Mexican political assertiveness and voting power in particular got Mexicans elected to local offices and chipped away at segregated schools, housing, and commercial and public facilities. In 1983 pro-union men Tommy Aguilar and Eduardo Marquez were mayor and vice mayor of Clifton, while Morenci remained, of course, a private PD-owned estate.

PD never fully reconciled to bargaining with a union but remained the antiunion diehard among the Big Four copper producers (Ana-. conda, ASARCO, Kennecott, PD). PD waited for the right moment to hit back, a moment that came when the Reagan administration put in place a more pro-employer National Labor Relations Board (NLRB). In 1983, empowered by Reagan's dismissal of the striking air traffic controllers, PD provoked a strike, then hired permanent replacements for the strikers.[4]

The 1983 strike bore an uncanny resemblance to the 1903 strike. Even the forces of nature seemed determined to show that you can't escape your history: After three months on the picket line, the strikers were weakened by a particularly severe flood, which demolished more than a third of Clifton's 1,800 homes (disproportionately those of the strikers), left most of its 4,200 people without clean water, sewers, electricity, or natural gas for days, and put everyone at risk of infectious disease. As if to demonstrate its control over the entire community, PD chose the week after the flood, with sanitary conditions at their worst, to announce that it was cutting off medical coverage for the strikers. As in the 1903 strike, PD's political clout got the governor to call in the National Guard to protect "order," which meant PD's right to bring in its replacement workers, but this time the army arrived in tanks and helicopters. Up Route 666 came a convoy of "gamma goats" and armored personnel carriers, with a fleet of Hueys overhead, carrying troops armed with M16s.[5] As in any occupied country, the entire community was pulled into the fight, and neutrality was not an option. Just as eighty years previously, a strike that began with overwhelming and interracial majority support quickly became racially divided. Structures of interracial respect built with decades of painstaking and demanding work came tumbling down. As the strike dragged on for two and a half years, the great majority of Mexican workers and family members (80 percent) continued to walk the picket lines or refuse to cross them while a much higher proportion of Anglos did not. Symbolic of the Mexican strikers' transnational consciousness, speakers like the formidable Fina Roman identified their struggle with that of Emiliano Zapata. Symbolic of the racial meaning of PD's victory over the union, in the midst of the strike in July 1984 the PD store posted a policy forbidding employees to speak Spanish while working.[6]

But in the eighty years that separated the two strikes much had changed—especially the women. The few women who were now mine-workers had been among the most zealous strikers from the beginning, but when PD got injunctions preventing strikers from picketing, women family members took over. Women "manned" the picket lines and attacked scabs with songs, poetry, and epithets as well as occasional sabotage. The women's fervor gave the strikers their best publicity. In the process women transformed the strike, expanding it from its political and economic core into an epic drama, a test of community loyalty and morality, a fight of David against Goliath to defend a democratic way of life. Theirs was a thoroughgoing vision of democracy, challenging male as well as corporate and white power.

The strike naturally got personal, not just dividing workers from management but, as people were forced to choose sides, setting neighbors and coworkers against one another, sometimes even brother against brother, father against son, sister against sister. As gripping as the anger and sorrow of the defeated strikers were the distress and conflictedness of some Anglo PD employees, decent people who felt constrained to cross picket lines walked by longtime coworkers, even friends; who had to see these colleagues lose their jobs forever; who had to hear themselves called scabs and worse; who had to feel like *gringos*.

PD's total victory in driving out the union was an ending, probably the final ending, of a way of life. Consequently, for some Cliftonians, especially those of Mexican background and working-class identity, the orphan incident became an artifact of the conflict between PD and its workers, which in turn encapsulated the Mexican American experience of racism. The specific connections between the orphans and the copper companies have been lost in the evolving folklore: the legacy of the 1903 strike, the leading role of PD's manager Charles

Mills, the companies' wage policy, the actual status in the community of the Mexican adoptive parents in contrast to how the mine supervisors viewed them. But those in Clifton who tell the story their way are not wrong to associate the orphan incident with racism, and racism with Phelps Dodge. In fact, their construction of the case offers a corrective to discursive interpretations of racism, which slight the responsibility of powerful institutions like corporations and governments.

Still, the mining companies did not invent the racial system. They took what they found locally, like the mesquite for making charcoal, and used it industriously in order to make copper as profitably as possible. Indeed, mine managers may have felt powerless to resist the evolving racial hierarchy, although there is no evidence that they tried. In the same way, everyone in Clifton-Morenci found race, used it, experienced it as irresistible and, by not resisting, reproduced it and, in reproducing it, sometimes changed it. These everyday human practices of race happened everywhere, in kitchens and bedrooms, in churches and stores, at fiestas as well as board meetings. Nowhere were they practiced more zealously than in parenthood, motivated, tragically, by parents' very love for their children.

Notes
Acknowledgments
Index

Notes

October 2, 1904, Night

1. Throughout this book, all quotations, unless otherwise noted, come from the transcript of the trial before the Arizona Territory Supreme Court, New York Foundling Hospital v. John C. Gatti, 9 Arizona 1905, State of Arizona Department of Library, Archives, and Public Records, Phoenix.

September 25, 1904

1. This composite description of a Foundling Hospital orphan train send-off comes from miscellaneous clippings in the New York Foundling Hospital (NYFH) Archives, New York, Clippings Scrapbook.
2. The term "foster" was not then in use; the children were said to be "placed out." But since legal adoption was not then widely practiced—indeed, until 1900 the Foundling did not permit legal adoption of its charges—I am using the contemporary term that most accurately conveys the meaning of what was happening.
3. Letter in NYFH Archives; *New York Herald*, December 11, 1918, NYFH Archives.
4. Thanks to Sisters Rita King and Anne Courtney of the Sisters of Charity Archives at the College of Mount St. Vincent for digging up this biographical material on the nuns.
5. NYFH could find no biographical information about Swayne.
6. Virginia A. Metaxas Quiroga, *Poor Mothers and Babies: A Social History of Childbirth and Child Care Hospitals in Nineteenth-Century New York City* (New York: Garland, 1989), chap. 5.

7. List of the orphans and their origins in NYFH Archives; and Harold Speert, *The Sloane Hospital Chronicle* (Philadelphia: F. A. Davis, 1963). Thanks to Judith Walzer Leavitt for explaining the Sloane Hospital to me.

8. Letters quoted by Sister Marie de Lourdes Walsh, *The Sisters of Charity of New York, 1809–1959,* vol. 3 (New York: Fordham University Press, 1960), 79–80.

9. Throughout this chapter I am particularly indebted to Maureen Fitzgerald's "Brigit's Profession: Irish-Catholic Nuns, Cultural Resistance, and Charity, New York City, 1830–1917," forthcoming, especially chap. 5, and her "Charity, Poverty and Child Welfare," *Harvard Divinity Bulletin* 25, no. 4 (1996). I am also grateful to Professor Fitzgerald for reading and correcting some mistakes in this chapter; she is of course not responsible for errors or misinterpretations that may remain.

10. Carolee R. Inskeep, ed., *The New York Foundling Hospital: An Index to Its Federal, State, and Local Census Records (1870–1925)* (Baltimore: Genealogical Publishing, 1995), pp. ii–vii; and Quiroga, *Poor Mothers.*

11. Walsh, *Sisters of Charity,* 3: 79–80.

12. 1881 Report, NYFH Archives.

13. Linda Gordon and Sara McLanahan, "Single Parenthood in 1900," *Journal of Family History,* 16, no. 2 (1991).

14. Linda Gordon, "Single Mothers and Child Neglect, Boston 1880–1920," *American Quarterly,* 37, no. 2 (Summer 1985).

15. Charles L. Brace, "What Is the Best Method for the Care of Poor and Vicious Children?" *Journal of Social Science,* 2 (1880), quoted in Robert H. Bremner, *Childrn and Youth in America: A Documentary History* (Cambridge, Mass.: Harvard University Press, 1971), pp. 291–292; Brace, *The Dangerous Classes of New York and Twenty Years' Work among Them* (New York: Wynkoop and Hallenbeck, 1880).

16. Quoted in Jeanne F. Cook, "A History of Placing-out: The Orphan Trains," *Child Welfare,* 74, no. 1 (January–February 1995), p. 186.

17. Miriam Z. Langsam, *Children West: A History of the Placing-out System of the New York Children's Aid Society, 1853–1890* (Madison: State Historical Society of Wisconsin, 1964), p. 27.

18. Lonnie R. Speer, "When Orphan Trains Rolled West," *Wild West,* February 1995, p. 56; Donald Dale Jackson, "It Took Trains to Put Street Kids on the Right Track out of the Slums," *Smithsonian,* August 1986, pp. 95–103.

19. Recollection of Noah Lawyer of his placement at age seven in 1907, in Jackson, "It Took Trains," p. 95.

20. Joan Gittens, *Poor Relations: The Children of the State of Illinois, 1818–1990* (Urbana: University of Illinois Press, 1994), p. 32; Cook, "A History of Placing-out," pp. 188–189.

21. Linda Gordon, *Heroes of Their Own Lives: The Politics and History of Family Violence, Boston 1880–1960* (New York: Viking Penguin, 1988).

22. Cook, "A History of Placing-out," summarizing various evaluations, pp. 188–192. In some locations parents were required to surrender their children for adoption before they could enter a poorhouse; Gittens, *Poor Relations,* p. 25.

23. My estimate comes from the U.S. Census, 1900; U.S. Census of Religious Bodies, 1906; *The Official Catholic Directory* (New York: P. J. Kenedy and Sons, 1912), p. 158; Kennedy T. Jackson, ed., *The Encyclopedia of New York City* (New York and New Haven: New York Historical Society and Yale University Press, 1995), p. 920. Thanks to historians Tom Archdeacon, Mary Brown, Laura McEnaney, and Lydio Tomasi for guidance; the final estimate, and hence any inaccuracy, is mine.

24. Langsam, *Children West,* p. 14; Marilyn Irvin Holt, *The Orphan Trains: Placing Out in America* (Lincoln: University of Nebraska Press, 1992), p. 135.

25. Quotation, 1876, in Fitzgerald, "Brigit's Profession," p. 490; Langsam, *Children West,* pp. 45–46 and chap. 5 passim; Holt, *Orphan Trains,* pp. 134–136.

26. U.S. Immigration Commission, *Dictionary of Races and Peoples* (Washington: GPO, 1911).

27. *New York Evening World,* October 13, 1904, and NYFH papers, passim.

28. David C. Hammack, *Power and Society: Greater New York at the Turn of the Century* (New York: Columbia University Press, 1987), chap. 3.

29. Dorothy M. Brown and Elizabeth McKeown, *The Poor Belong to Us: Catholic Charities and American Welfare* (Cambridge: Harvard University Press, 1997), p. 87.

30. Walsh, *Sisters of Charity,* 3:69–70.

31. It later moved to today's location on Sixth Avenue. In 1875 New York City passed the Children's Law, which stipulated that each dependent child would be housed in an institution of its own religion and that the city would pay maintenance to these institutions. While this law related to children who were unsupported (or delinquent) rather than foundlings who had been surrendered by their parents, it strengthened the premise that children should be placed where they could keep the religion of their birth. Fitzgerald, "Brigit's Profession"; Inskeep, *The New York Foundling Hospital,* pp. ii–vii.

32. "A Car-load of Babies," *Milwaukee Sentinel,* September 26, 1891, p. 3; "Sister Irene's Noble Work," *The World* (New York), August 24, 1896, clipping in NYFH Archives; Fitzgerald, "Brigit's Profession," chap. 5; Brown and McKeown, p. 90.

33. Donald L. Kinzer, *An Episode in Anti-Catholicism: The American Protective Association* (Seattle: University of Washington Press, 1964), pp. 14–15. This American group directed its efforts particularly against the St. Louis–based French clergy, who, as we shall see, dominated the Catholic clergy in the Southwest.

34. *New York Evening World,* n.d., December 1918, clipping in NYFH Archives. This comes from an NYFH press release, indicated by the fact that an identical article appeared in several newspapers.

35. Today the Foundling's children are mainly Puerto Rican, African American, and Central American.
36. "The South Calls for Northern Babies," *New York Times,* March 18, 1910, p. 1.
37. Walsh, *Sisters of Charity,* 3:81.
38. "A Car-load of Babies," p. 3.
39. *New York Times,* March 18, 1910, p. 1.
40. Although the sisters mainly publicized their orphans' availability through priests, they also used regional agents, who included members of branches of the Sisters in six western states by 1906: Kansas, Nebraska, Colorado, New Mexico, Wyoming, and Montana. Holt, *Orphan Trains,* p. 110.
41. George Whitney Swayne to Hon. M. J. Scanlan, State Board of Charities, Albany, N.Y., n.d., copy in NYFH Archives.
42. Constant Mandin, letter to the *Southern Messenger,* n.p., December 24, 1904, in NYFH Archives.
43. Swayne to Scanlan, as cited in n. 41.
44. See illustrations in Holt, *Orphan Trains;* "A Car-load of Babies," p. 3; *New York Times,* December 18, 1910, p. 20; Ruthena Hill Kittson, *Orphan Voyage* (Tavernier, Fla.: Arvin Publications, 1980), p. 171. After placement, agents were to visit each home once a year; Walsh, *Sisters of Charity,* vol. 3, chap. 5.

1. King Copper

1. Tailings are waste from the milling of ore, usually silt suspended in liquid; when discharged, they create vast ponds which then dry out and settle, forming flat hard surfaces.
2. Information from a Phelps Dodge guide on the mine tour and from Kevin Franklin, "Really Big Show," *Weekly Wire,* November 9–15, 1995, website http://www.desert.net/disk$ebony/tw/www/tw/11–09–95/outthere.htm.
3. James Colquhoun, *The Early History of the Clifton-Morenci District* (London: William Clowes and Sons, 1924), p. 27, quoting Henry Lesinsky.
4. Copper Development Association, "Copper Facts" (brochure), n.d. but acquired 1996; Phelps Dodge Morenci Inc. brochure, n.d.; Phelps Dodge Morenci Fact Sheet, November 1994; Ira B. Joralemon, *Romantic Copper: Its Lure and Lore* (New York: D. Appleton-Century, 1934), p. 198; Jonathan D. Rosenblum, *Copper Crucible: How the Arizona Miners' Strike of 1983 Recast Labor-Management Relations in America* (Ithaca, N.Y.: ILR Press, 1995), p. 15. Recently the use of aluminum and then fiber optics has reduced demand for expensive copper wire.
5. Copper Development Association, *Copper through the Ages* (Radlett, Hertsfordshire: Kendals Hall, 1934).
6. Joralemon, *Romantic Copper,* pp. 198–203.
7. Colquhoun, *Early History,* p. 24.

8. David M. Pletcher, *Rails, Mines, and Progress: Seven American Promoters in Mexico, 1867–1911* (Ithaca, N.Y.: Cornell University Press, 1958).

9. The Spanish capital of Sonora, San Juan Bautista, shipped out quantities of silver and gold. Had they cared about copper, they might have noticed Papago Indians producing copper near Ajo, in today's Arizona, when the Spanish arrived. By 1800 there was a copper mine in that area with six hundred employees; mule or donkey pack trains took the ores to smelters further south in Mexico. C. W. Pritchett, "Ancient Copper Smelting in Mexico," *Engineering and Mining Journal*, February 15, 1902, p. 246; Dan Rose, *The Ancient Mines of Ajo* (Tucson: Mission Publishing, 1936), chaps. 1–4; Robert G. Raymer, "Early Copper Mining in Arizona," *Pacific Historical Review*, 4, no. 2 (June 1935), pp. 123–130; Carey McWilliams, *North from Mexico: The Spanish-speaking People of the United States* (Philadelphia: J. B. Lippincott, 1949), p. 142.

10. Quoted in W. Dirk Raat, *Revoltosos: Mexico's Rebels in the United States, 1903–1923* (College Station: Texas A & M University Press, 1981), pp. 68–69.

11. D. W. Meinig, *Southwest: Three Peoples in Geographical Change, 1600–1970* (New York: Oxford University Press, 1971), pp. 31–32. Some claim that Tucson is the oldest city in the United States, established in 1555 by the order of Charles I of Spain and V of Germany, the successor to Ferdinand and Isabella, the patrons of Columbus; see John George Hilzinger, *Treasure Land: A Story* (Tucson: Arizona Advancement Company, 1897), p. 110.

12. Joseph F. Park, "The History of Mexican Labor in Arizona during the Territorial Period" (Master's thesis, University of Arizona, 1961), p. 187.

13. Apache raids were so regular and unstoppable that one observer compared them to the ocean tides; another called Sonora "the great Apache rancho, where they went when they needed cattle or horses." Miguel Tinker Salas, *In the Shadow of the Eagles: Sonora and the Transformation of the Border during the Porfiriato* (Berkeley: University of California Press, 1997), pp. 60–62, quotation p. 64. Civilization was the mother of barbarism, as Ana María Alonso put it, because the disruption and displacement of the Apaches turned them into specialists in violence, uncontrollable by U.S. or Mexican armies. There were no more than a thousand people of all ethnic groups in the Tucson, Tubac, and San Xavier area at that time. Alonso, *Thread of Blood: Colonialism, Revolution, and Gender on Mexico's Northern Frontier* (Tucson: University of Arizona Press, 1995), pp. 24–30; Meinig, *Southwest*, esp. pp. 31–32; George F. Leaming, *Labor and Copper in Arizona* (Tucson: University of Arizona, College of Business and Public Administration pamphlet, 1973); Raymond J. Flores, "The Socio-Economic Status Trends of the Mexican People Residing in Arizona" (Master's. thesis, Arizona State College at Tempe, 1951), p. 12; Rose, *Ancient Mines;* McWilliams, *North from Mexico*.

14. Quotation from Sister M. Colette Standart, O.P., "The Sonora Migration to California, 1848–1856: A Study in Prejudice," *Southern California Quarterly*, 58

(1976), pp. 333–357, reprinted in Antoinette Sedillo Lopez, ed., *Latinos in the United States,* Volume 1, *History, Law, and Perspective* (New York: Garland, 1995), pp. 123–47; see also Richard H. Peterson, "Anti-Mexican Nativism in California, 1848–1853: A Study of Cultural Conflict," *Southern California Quarterly,* 62 (1980), pp. 309–327, reprinted in Sedillo Lopez, *Latinos,* pp. 181–199; John R. Chavez, *The Lost Land: The Chicano Image of the Southwest* (Albuquerque: University of New Mexico Press, 1984), p. 47; Joseph Henry Jackson, Introduction, in John Rollin Ridge (Yellow Bird), *Joaquín Murieta* (Norman: University of Oklahoma Press, 1986); María Herrera-Sobek, *Northward Bound: The Mexican Immigrant Experience in Ballad and Song* (Bloomington: Indiana University Press, 1993), p. 15; Leonard Pitt, *The Decline of the Californios: A Social History of the Spanish-speaking Californians, 1846–1890* (Berkeley: University of California Press, 1966), pp. 70–74; Raat, *Revoltosos,* pp. 28–29; W. P. Morrell, *The Gold Rushes* (New York: Macmillan, 1941), chaps. 4–6; Malcolm J. Rohrbough, *Days of Gold: The California Gold Rush and the American Nation* (Berkeley: University of California Press, 1997), chap. 14.

15. William Kelly, writing in 1851, quoted in Peterson, "Anti-Mexican Nativism," p. 310.

16. Norbert Finzsch, "Anti-Mexican 'Nativism' in the California Gold Mines, 1848–1856," *Jahrbuch für Geschichte von Staat, Wirtschaft und Gesellschaft Lateinamerikas,* 21 (1984), pp. 283–302; Manuel P. Servín and Robert L. Spude, "Historical Conditions of Early Mexican Labor in the United States: Arizona—A Neglected Story," *Journal of Mexican American History,* 5 (1975), pp. 43–56.

17. This great Sonoran migration was not entirely a failure because it brought back over $2 million in gold; Peterson, "Anti-Mexican Nativism," p. 186. Meinig, *Southwest,* p. 42; McWilliams, *North from Mexico,* pp. 127, 144; Richard Lingenfelter, *The Hardrock Miners: A History of the Mining Labor Movement in the American West, 1863–1893* (Berkeley: University of California Press, 1974), p. 5.

18. Carlos A. Schwantes, "The Concept of the Wageworkers' Frontier: A Framework for Future Research," *Western Historical Quarterly,* 18, no. 1 (January 1987), pp. 39–55; William H. Lyon, "The Corporate Frontier in Arizona," *Journal of Arizona History,* 9, no. 1 (Spring 1968), pp. 1–17.

19. Quotation from Lyon, "The Corporate Frontier," p. 16. Information on Mills is from Larry Schweikart, *A History of Banking in Arizona* (Tucson: University of Arizona Press, 1982), pp. 46–47; Ernest J. Hopkins, *Financing the Frontier: A Fifty Year History of the Valley National Bank* (Phoenix: Arizona Printers, 1950), pp. 7–10, 80–82; obituary in the *Tucson Citizen,* 1/17/1929; James B. Allen, *The Company Town in the American West* (Norman: University of Oklahoma Press, 1966), pp. 44–45; Blaine Peterson Lamb, "Jewish Pioneers in Arizona, 1850–1920" (Ph.D. diss., Arizona State University, 1982), pp. 228–233; obituary in *Arizona Historical Review,* 2, no. 1 (April 1929), pp. 7–9.

20. Charles Herner, *The Arizona Rough Riders* (Tucson: University of Arizona Press, 1970), pp. 43, 56, 170–171.

21. Ajo, Arizona, in midcentury was an example of "plain diggings." The miners cut horizontally into the base of the hills and dug underground only when surface veins were exhausted. They dug wide-mouthed shafts with no pillars or timbers to protect against cave-ins (although such reinforcement had been required by a 1584 mining ordinance in New Spain!), often tunneling 60 feet deep on a 60-degree incline. To climb out they built a sort of ladder laid along the floor of the tunnel. They used hand drills to make holes for blasting, often requiring three or four men to drive the drill 8–10 feet into the hard rock. Into the holes they packed powdered lime, wet it, and sealed the top; the water made the lime hot and the resultant steam exploded outward. Then men carried out 50–60 pounds of ore in rawhide buckets attached to a broad band of rawhide that went under the armpits and over the head of the bearer, resting on his forehead. The ore was at first freighted out by ox team, to San Diego or to Guaymas, and then shipped to Swansea, Wales, for smelting. The company tried to smelt its own ore but the cost of making or importing coke or charcoal was prohibitive. (Ultimately the scarcity of water, the remote location, and the decreasingly rich ore made the whole enterprise unprofitable, and it closed in 1859.) Rose, *Ancient Mines,* pp. 16–17; Robert C. West, *The Mining Community in Northern New Spain: The Parral Mining District* (Berkeley: University of California Press, 1949); Michael N. Greeley, "The Early Influence of Mining in Arizona," in J. Michael Canty and Michael N. Greeley, eds., *History of Mining in Arizona,* 2 vols. (Tucson: American Institute of Mining Engineers, 1987–88), 1:15; Joralemon, *Romantic Copper,* chap. 7; Servín and Spude, "Historical Conditions"; Raymer, "Early Copper Mining," p. 125.

22. Alonso, *Thread of Blood;* Thomas E. Sheridan, *Arizona: A History* (Tucson: University of Arizona Press, 1995).

23. John Rowe, *The Hard-Rock Men: Cornish Immigrants and the North American Mining Frontier* (n.p.: Barnes and Noble Import Division, 1974), pp. 224–225.

24. Howard Roberts Lamar, *The Far Southwest, 1846–1912: A Territorial History* (New Haven: Yale University Press, 1966), pp. 416–444, quotation pp. 436–437; James W. Byrkit, *Forging the Copper Collar: Arizona's Labor-Management War of 1901–21* (Tucson: University of Arizona Press, 1982), pp. 13–14; Lesinsky refers to "mining fever" in Lesinsky, *Letters,* p. 47.

25. Quotation from Park, "History of Mexican Labor," pp. 185–187; Henry Lesinsky, *Letters Written by Henry Lesinsky to His Son* (New York, 1924); Lyon, "The Corporate Frontier"; Works Progress Administration (WPA) interview with Frank Ramsey, by Frances E. Totty, April 7–April 11, 1938, WPA Life Histories Collection (Archives, State of Arizona Department of Library, Archives, and Public Records, Phoenix). Subsequent references to WPA interviews are to this collection.

26. Jay J. Wagoner, *Arizona Territory, 1863–1912: A Political History* (Tucson: University of Arizona Press, 1970), p. 148; Lamar, *The Far Southwest,* p. 462; Meinig, *Southwest,* pp. 38ff.

27. Prospectors from Silver City, New Mexico, then found "beautiful green copper carbonate near the top of the limestone cliffs two thousand feet above the bed of Chase Creek." They staked out claims in 1872–on the Apache reservation–but needed more capital. Joralemon, *Romantic Copper,* p. 204.

28. Colquhoun, *Early History,* chaps. 5–6; Lesinsky, *Letters;* Floyd S. Fierman, *Roots and Boots: From Crypto-Jew in New Spain to Community Leader in the American Southwest* (Hoboken, N.J.: Ktav Publishing House, 1987), chap. 4; Servín and Spude, "Historical Conditions"; Charles H. Dunning, *Rock to Riches: The Story of American Mining . . . Past, Present, and Future . . . as Reflected in the Colorful History of Mining in Arizona–The Nation's Greatest Bonanza* (Phoenix: Southwest Publishing, 1959), p. 75; "Phelps Dodge: A Copper Centennial, 1881–1891," supplement to *Arizona Pay Dirt* and *New Mexico Pay Dirt* (Bisbee: Copper Queen Publishing, 1981), pp. 4–11, 36–50.

29. Lesinsky, *Letters,* pp. 48–50; Wagoner, *Arizona Territory,* pp. 148–149.

30. As James Colquhoun, the first manager of the operation for the Scottish corporate owners put it, "When the Spaniards invaded Mexico . . . [they were] the most skilled metallurgists in Europe . . . many improvements . . . [were] made by the Mexican people who thus acquired not only a great knowledge of the manufacturing of metals, but a remarkable skill in . . . mining." Colquhoun, *Early History,* pp. 36–37; see also Jane Eppinga, "Ethnic Diversity in Arizona's Early Mining Camps," in Canty and Greeley, *History of Mining in Arizona,* vol. 2.

31. The following account of the early history of the Clifton-Morenci mines comes from Colquhoun, *Early History,* chaps. 7–8; and idem, *The History of the Clifton-Morenci Mining District* (London: William Clowes and Sons, 1924); Harriet Sweeting, "Greenlee County," in *Arizona: The Grand Canyon State,* vol. 2 (Westminster County: Western States Historical Publishers, 1975), pp. 577–581; McWilliams, *North from Mexico,* pp. 143–144; James M. Patton, *History of Clifton* (orig. Master's thesis, Univ. of Arizona, 1942–1944) (Clifton: Greenlee County Chamber of Commerce, 1977), pp. 7–11; Joralemon, *Romantic Copper,* pp. 205–206; "Phelps Dodge: A Copper Centennial 1881 to 1981," pp. 4–7, 36–41; "The Clifton District, Arizona," *Engineering and Mining Journal,* April 28, 1904, pp. 679–681; Park, "History of Mexican Labor"; interview with Mrs. Louis Abrahams *(sic),* taped 1952, Arizona Historical Society, Tucson.

32. The smelters' appetite for charcoal was so great that virtually all the trees, and other plants that depended on trees, were destroyed in the Sonoran highlands mining areas, and what was left was poisoned by the smelter fumes; today no one knows the original array of vegetation. When Colquhoun first arrived he

found the country rich in cedar and stunted pine, with mesquite on the mesas; "grass grew thick and deep, affording feed in plenty for the wild game which abounded." Colquhoun, *Early History.* Today the hills are mostly barren of trees; the smelter fumes also prevented regrowth. West, *The Mining Community,* pp. 39–46.

33. Lesinsky, *Letters,* pp. 50–53.

34. The cost was high, and the Lesinskys tried to compensate with a return load; the team brought supplies in and Henry put his brother Charles Lesinsky in charge of a company store that sold them to the workers for a profit.

35. Hauled across the desert by mule team, it was so light that if it jumped the track it hardly made a dent in the ties, and the crew could lift it back onto the tracks. Its engineer, Hank Arbuckle, was a prominent early Cliftonian, and today some Clifton residents claim that he was the father of movie star "Fatty" Arbuckle. Biographies of Fatty claim different, however.

36. Colquhoun, *Early History,* chap. 9; Roberta Watt, "History of Morenci, Arizona" (Master's thesis, University of Arizona, 1956), pp. 1–17; Edward Holland Spicer, *Cycles of Conquest: The Impact of Spain, Mexico, and the United States on the Indians of the Southwest* (Tucson: University of Arizona Press, 1962), pp. 253–255; Tinker Salas, p. 225.

37. The miners took their furniture apart, making rafts of it, and managed to cross the raging torrent. Colquhoun, *Early History,* pp. 63–64.

38. On the exact location of Geronimo's forces see *Arizona Bulletin,* 1903, special souvenir edition; *Arizona Weekly Star,* April 27, 1882; Colquhoun, *Early History,* p. 73; George H. Kelly, "How Geronimo Was Finally Overcome and Deported from Arizona" (a reminiscence), *Arizona Historical Review,* 1, no. 3 (October 1928), pp. 36–44; Phelps Dodge Corporation, *Ajo, Bisbee, Morenci,* from the manuscript of Arthur Train, Jr., 1941 (n.p., 1941), Special Collections, University of Arizona Library, Tucson.

39. There was also a Clifton in Michigan's copper-mining district, but no one seems to think that Clifton, Arizona, got its name from that source. See *Copper Country Journal: The Diary of Schoolmaster Henry Hobart, 1863–1864,* ed. and intro. Philip P. Mason (Detroit: Wayne State University Press, 1991).

40. Sweeting, "Greenlee County."

41. Watt, "History of Morenci."

42. Other accounts give the figure as $1.2 or $1.5 million.

43. James Clifton Colquhoun, *James Colquhoun, 1857–1954: The Man and His Work* (Perth, Scotland: privately printed for Colquhoun, 1970); Colquhoun, *Early History.*

44. This ore could not be smelted directly, so he devised a system of first putting the finely crushed ore over shaking tables once used for gold and smelting the resulting concentrate—a method that twenty years later became the industry's norm.

45. "Phelps Dodge: A Copper Centennial, 1881–1981," pp. 36–50; Joralemon, *Romantic Copper,* pp. 206–207; Park, "History of Mexican Labor," p. 207.

46. A third booming mining camp, Metcalf, never developed a thriving township and remained a "suburb" of Morenci.

47. Geo. H. Kelly, state historian, compiler, *Legislative History of Arizona, 1864–1912* (Phoenix, 1926), p. 217; Glenn S. Dumke, "Douglas, Border Town," *Pacific Historical Review,* 17, no. 3 (August 1948), pp. 285–286; "Prices Likely to Resume Uptrend," Standard and Poor's *Industry Surveys,* October 1995, pp. M81–86;

48. Throughout Arizona mining, Mexicans became a larger proportion of the mining labor force as Anglo mine, mill, and smelter engineers appropriated the skilled jobs and management, and deskilled the labor of miners. See A. Yvette Huginnie, "A New Hero Comes to Town: The Anglo Mining Engineer and 'Mexican Labor' as Contested Terrain in Southeastern Arizona, 1880–1920," *New Mexico Historical Review,* 69 (October 1994); and idem, "*Strikitos:* Race, Class, and Work in the Arizona Copper Industry, 1870–1920" (Ph.D. diss., Yale University, 1991).

49. Detroit Copper also operated a concentrator, smelter, and short railroad line connecting to that of Arizona Copper. This data and more can be found in Horace J. Stevens, *The Copper Handbook,* vol. 4 (Houghton, Mich.: Horace Stevens, 1904), pp. 98–101, 193–194, 350; vol. 8 (1908), pp. 326–329, 627–628; L. S. Austin, "Progress in the Metallurgy of Copper in 1903," *Mineral Industry,* 12 (New York and London: Engineering and Mining Journal, 1904), p. 93; D. H. Newland, "Copper," in Mineral Industry, 12, pp. 74–76; and unsigned, "Copper," in *Mineral Industry,* 13 (1904), pp. 104–107; *Engineering and Mining Journal,* April 28, 1904, pp. 679–681.

October 1, 1904, 6:30 P.M.

1. George Whitney Swayne to Hon. M. J. Scanlan, State Board of Charities, Albany, N.Y., n.d., copy in NYFH Archives.

2. *Arizona Bulletin,* 1903, special souvenir edition.

3. Harold T. Shortridge, *Childhood Memories of a Fabulous Mining Camp, Clifton, Arizona, 1915–1926* (Cottonwood, Ariz.: Harold Shortridge, 1990), p. 4; quotation from James W. Byrkit, *Forging the Copper Collar: Arizona's Labor-Management War of 1901–1921* (Tucson: University of Arizona Press, 1982), quoting from an article in *Scribner's,* p. 20.

4. Bishop Granjon, letter published in several papers, October 22, 1904; Father Mandin, letter to *Southern Messenger,* October 24, 1904; both in NYFH Clippings Scrapbook.

5. Mr. and Mrs. Chacón were listed in both the 1900 and the 1910 Clifton census but with different information. In the 1900 census she is said to have been

born in New Mexico in 1877 of German and Spanish parents and he in Mexico in 1872. They are listed as married two years; she has had no births; he is a smelter hand; they house one nineteen-year-old lodger. In 1910 she is said to have been born in 1880 in Florida of German and French parents; "Cornelius" is given a birth date of 1872. She is said to have given birth to seven children, of whom only one was alive, a son, seven months. They are listed as married twelve years; he is a liner at the smelter and came to the United States in 1885. In 1900 they were both categorized as white, in 1910 both as Mexican (although that was not an official race category at the time). He is not a citizen.

6. My interpretation is based on conversations with Raquel Rubio-Goldsmith and Caroline Walker Bynum, and on Bynum's *Holy Feast and Holy Fast: The Religious Significance of Food to Medieval Women* (Berkeley: University of California Press, 1987), pp. 17–18.

7. Interview with her grandson, John Chacón, May 6, 1997.

8. I am indebted to Raquel Rubio-Goldsmith and Francisco Scarano for explaining this religious position to me. See also Socorro Félix Delgado in Patricia Preciado Martin, *Songs My Mother Sang to Me: An Oral History of Mexican American Women* (Tucson: University of Arizona Press, 1992), pp. 67–72.

9. The Sacred Heart Church interment records say he died in 1928 at age 69, which would have put his birth date at 1859, making him 39 when he married Margarita. The Clifton census says, however, that he was born in 1872, making him 26 at marriage.

10. *El Labrador* (Las Cruces), January 6, 1905, p. 2. I used the term "Latino" here because the sources are contradictory about Arzate's ethnic origin, labeling him both Mexican and Italian. The historical record is confused as to Arzate's nationality. A discussion of Arizona sheriffs labels him, in the same volume, once as Italian and once as "Hispano"; Larry D. Ball, *Desert Lawmen: The High Sheriffs of New Mexico and Arizona, 1846–1912* (Albuquerque: University of New Mexico Press, 1992), pp. 32 and 408. But Ball, like Arzate's boss Sheriff Parks, probably lumped "Hispanos" and Italians together, as did Parks's daughter Jennie Parks Ringgold in her *Frontier Days in the Southwest* (San Antonio: Naylor Company, 1952).

11. Emilio Zamora, Jr., *The World of the Mexican Worker in Texas* (College Station: Texas A & M Press, 1993), pp. 104–105; idem, "Chicano Socialist Labor Activity in Texas, 1900–1920," *Aztlán*, 6, no. 2 (September 1975), pp. 221–236; Leonor Villegas de Magnón (Clara Lomas, ed. and intro.), *The Rebel* (Houston: Arte Público Press, 1994), p. xii; Salvador Guerrero, *Memorias: A West Texas Life*, ed. Arnoldo De León (Lubbock: Texas Tech University Press, 1991), p. 10; Vicki L. Ruiz, *Comadres, Cowgirls, and Curanderas: Women of the Borderlands, 1540–1900* (Albuquerque: University of New Mexico Press, forthcoming).

12. Laura Abraham, deposition taken by NYFH lawyer, n.d., lawyer's notes, NYFH Archives.

2. Mexicans Come to the Mines

1. Some verses from the *corrido* "Despedida de un norteño," from Paul S. Taylor, "Songs of the Mexican Migration," in J. Frank Dobie, ed., *Puro Mexicano* (Austin: Texas Folk-lore Society, 1935), pp. 222–223; and in María Herrera-Sobek, *Northward Bound: The Mexican Immigrant Experience in Ballad and Song* (Bloomington: Indiana University Press, 1993), pp. 68–70.

2. That is the distance on highways today; by burro or train in 1904, it was further.

3. Miguel Tinker Salas, "Sonora: The Making of a Border Society, 1880–1910," *Journal of the Southwest,* 34, no. 4 (Winter 1992), repr. in Oscar J. Martínez, ed., *U.S.-Mexico Borderlands: Historical and Contemporary Perspectives* (Wilmington, Del.: Jaguar Books on Latin America, Scholarly Resources, 1996), p. 87; Charles D. Poston, *Building a State in Apache Land,* articles originally serialized in *Overland Monthly,* 1894 (repr. Tempe: Aztec Press, 1963), pp. 72–78; Howard Roberts Lamar, *The Far Southwest, 1846–1912: A Territorial History* (New Haven: Yale University Press, 1966), p. 424.

4. The claim that there was a border culture has been made by several scholars. I am primarily indebted to Josiah McC. Heyman, *Life and Labor on the Border: Working People of Northeastern Sonora, Mexico, 1886–1986* (Tucson: University of Arizona Press, 1991); and to Ana María Alonso, *Thread of Blood: Colonialism, Revolution, and Gender on Mexico's Northern Frontier* (Tucson: University of Arizona Press, 1995). See also Mario García, *Desert Immigrants: The Mexicans of El Paso, 1880–1920* (New Haven: Yale University Press, 1981), p. 231.

5. Josiah Heyman interviewed residents of the twin towns Douglas, Arizona, and Agua Prieta, Sonora. The Hoyos, Aguirre, and Córdoba stories are in Heyman, *Life and Labor,* pp. 65ff. and 93ff.

6. *Report of the Governor of Arizona Made to the Secretary of the Interior* (Washington, D.C.: GPO, 1907), p. 5; Ramón Eduardo Ruíz, *The People of Sonora and Yankee Capitalists* (Tucson: University of Arizona Press, 1988), p. 183.

7. James D. Cockcroft, *Outlaws in the Promised Land: Mexican Immigrant Workers and America's Future* (New York: Grove Press, 1986), p. 49; Manuel García y Griego and Leobardo F. Estrada, "Research on the Magnitude of Mexican Undocumented Immigration to the U.S.: A Summary," in Antonio Ríos-Bustamante, ed., *Mexican Immigrant Workers in the U.S.* (Los Angeles: UCLA Chicano Studies Research Center, 1981); Raymond J. Flores, "The Socio-Economic Status Trends of the Mexican People Residing in Arizona" (Master's thesis, Arizona State University, Tempe, 1951), p. 13; *Bisbee Daily Review* quoted

in Richard Griswold del Castillo, *La Familia: Chicano Families in the Urban Southwest, 1848 to the Present* (Notre Dame, Ind.: University of Notre Dame Press, 1984), p. 58; Manuel Gamio, *Mexican Immigration to the United States: A Study of Human Migration and Adjustment* (Chicago: University of Chicago, 1930; repr. Arno and New York Times, 1969), chaps. 1–2; Lawrence A. Cardoso, *Mexican Emigration to the United States, 1897–1931: Socio-Economic Patterns* (Tucson: University of Arizona Press, 1980), pp. 34–35.

8. The push-pull connections manifested themselves several times over: The U.S. promise to Mexico given in the Treaty of Guadalupe Hidalgo to control Apache raids, withdrawn in the Gadsden Purchase treaty for the good reason that it couldn't be done, would have promoted earlier economic growth in Sonora and Chihuahua had it been accomplished; when the promise was finally made good forty years later through the force of the U.S. Army, the American wage-labor market was already pulling Mexicans over the border with irresistible force. Miguel Tinker Salas, *In the Shadow of the Eagles: Sonora and the Transformation of the Border during the Porfiriato* (Berkeley: University of California Press, 1997), p. 99.

9. In one of the classic ironies of modernization, the destruction of the Mexican peasantry was accomplished simultaneously with the "Porfirian peace" that finally subdued and thus rescued the peasants from incessant warfare among northern Mexican *caudillos.* Alonso, *Thread of Blood,* p. 127; Cardoso, *Mexican Emigration,* chap. 1; George Sanchez, *Becoming Mexican American: Ethnicity, Culture, and Identity in Chicano Los Angeles, 1900–1945* (New York: Oxford University Press, 1993), chap. 1; John R. Chavez, *The Lost Land: The Chicano Image of the Southwest* (Albuquerque: University of New Mexico Press, 1984), pp. 70–76; Thomas E. Sheridan, *Where the Dove Calls: The Political Ecology of a Peasant Corporate Community in Northwestern Mexico* (Tucson: University of Arizona Press, 1988), pp. 17–22; Arthur F. Corwin and Lawrence A. Cardoso, "Vamos al Norte: Causes of Mass Mexican Migration to the United States," in Arthur F. Corwin, ed., *Immigrants—and Immigrants: Perspectives on Mexican Labor Migration to the United States* (Westport, Conn.: Greenwood Press, 1978), pp. 38–43; Roger C. Owen, *Marobavi: A Study of an Assimilated Group in Northern Sonora* (Tucson: University of Arizona, Anthropological Papers no. 3, 1959), pp. 11–14; Frank Tannenbaum, *The Mexican Agrarian Revolution* (New York: Macmillan, 1929).

10. Tinker Salas, *In the Shadow,* pp. 56–57, 90, points out that even American employers sometimes treated Mexican workers as unfree labor, chasing them down like runaway slaves when they left. Because of in-migration, the Sonoran urban population increased 40 percent between 1895 and 1910; the annual urban growth rate in the north was 2 percent as opposed to 1.2 percent nationwide. Barry Carr, "The Peculiarities of the Mexican North, 1880–1928: An Essay in Interpretation" (University of Glasgow Institute of Latin Ameri-

can Studies, occasional paper no. 4, 1971), p. 6; Oscar Martínez, *Border Boom Town: Ciudad Juárez since 1848* (Austin: University of Texas Press, 1978), p. 20; Sanchez, *Becoming Mexican American,* p. 44; Victor S. Clark, *Mexican Labor in the United States,* U.S. Deptartment of Commerce Bulletin no. 78 (Washington, D.C.: GPO, 1908); Cardoso, *Mexican Emigration;* Devra Weber, *Dark Sweat, White Gold: California Farm Workers, Cotton, and the New Deal* (Berkeley: University of California Press, 1994), pp. 49–50.

11. Heyman, *Life and Labor;* Tinker Salas, *In the Shadow,* pp. 53, 230–233.

12. Sanchez, *Becoming Mexican American,* p. 23; Sheridan, *Where the Dove Calls,* p. 22.

13. In 1909 the nine western U.S. railroads alone employed six thousand Mexicans just in their "maintenance of way" departments; this amounted to more than half the track crew. James E. Officer, "Arizona's Hispanic Perspective," Research Report of University of Arizona, May 17–20, 1981 (Phoenix: Arizona Academy, 1981), p. 13; Mark Reisler, *By the Sweat of Their Brow: Mexican Immigrant Labor in the United States, 1900–1940* (Westport, Conn.: Greenwood Press, 1976), p. 3; Cardoso, *Mexican Emigration,* p. 27.

14. Charles C. Cumberland, *Mexico: The Struggle for Modernity* (New York: Oxford University Press, 1968), p. 215; Cardoso, *Mexican Emigration,* p. 28; Corwin and Cardoso, "Vamos al Norte," p. 43.

15. Lines from "Los reenganchados a Kansas," in Herrera-Sobek, *Northward Bound,* pp. 41–43.

16. George F. Leaming, *Labor and Copper in Arizona* (Tucson: University of Arizona, College of Business and Public Administration pamphlet, 1973), p. 1; Mark Wyman, *Hard Rock Epic: Western Miners and the Industrial Revolution, 1860–1910* (Berkeley: University of California Press, 1979), pp. 37–41; Richard E. Lingenfelter, *The Hardrock Miners: A History of the Mining Labor Movement in the American West, 1863–1893* (Berkeley: University of California Press, 1974), pp. 3–5 and passim; quotation from James M. Patton, *History of Clifton* (Clifton: Greenlee County Chamber of Commerce, 1977), p. 35; Carlos A. Schwantes, *Bisbee: Urban Outpost on the Frontier* (Tucson: University of Arizona Press, 1992), p. 53; Elizabeth Jameson, *All That Glitters: Class, Conflict, and Community in Cripple Creek.* (Urbana: University of Illinois Press, 1998), chap. 7. The same importation and then exclusion of the Chinese occurred in Sonoran mines; Tinker Salas, *In the Shadow,* pp. 224–229.

17. Sylvester Mowry, *Arizona and Sonora: The Geography, History, and Resources of the Silver Region of North America* (New York: Harper and Brothers, 1864), pp. 93–95; repeated by federal investigator Victor Clark, *Mexican Labor,* p. 477.

18. Matias Romero, *Mexico and the United States: A Study of Subjects Affecting Their Political, Commercial, and Social Relations, Made with a View to Their Promotion* (compiling Mexican government statistics) (New York: G. P. Putnam's Sons,

1898), pp. 513–521 and Appendix 1; Martínez, *Border Boom Town,* p. 20; Ruíz, *The People of Sonora,* p. 102.

19. In Chihuahua alone U.S. mining investment totaled $100 million. Paul J. Vanderwood, *Disorder and Progress: Bandits, Police, and Mexican Development,* rev. ed. (Wilmington, Del.: Scholarly Resources, 1992), p. 76; Corwin and Cardoso, "Vamos al Norte," pp. 41, 46–47; Tinker Salas, *In the Shadow,* p. 10; Tinker Salas, "Sonora," pp. 86–87; Michael J. Gonzales, "U.S. Copper Companies, the Mine Workers' Movement, and the Mexican Revolution, 1910–1920," *Hispanic American Historical Review,* 76, no. 3, (August 1996), pp. 503–534.

20. Lingenfelter, *Hardrock Miners,* p. 5; Patton, *History of Clifton,* p. 35; Corwin and Cardoso, "Vamos al Norte"; Juan Gómez-Quiñones, *Mexican American Labor, 1790–1990* (Albuquerque: University of New Mexico Press, 1994), p. 73; Clark, *Mexican Labor,* p. 470.

21. James Colquhoun, *The Early History of the Clifton-Morenci District* (London: William Clowes and Sons, 1924), chap. 9; Roberta Watt, "History of Morenci, Arizona" (Master's thesis, University of Arizona, 1956), pp. 1–17; Joseph F. Park, "The History of Mexican Labor in Arizona during the Territorial Period" (Master's thesis, University of Arizona, 1961), p. 126; Sanchez, *Becoming Mexican American,* chap. 1, "Farewell Homeland," esp. pp. 19, 39–40, 44–45; Park, "History of Mexican Labor," p. 217.

22. Some *enganchadores* were paid by mining or railroad companies, while others were free-lance recruiters who sold crews they had collected to an employer or even to another agent, sometimes holding them back and retaining them on subsistence allotments to fetch a higher price. Clark, *Mexican Labor,* pp. 470–476. The continuing use of subcontractors (or *padrones*) both to recruit and to "rent" workers to mine operators, although "a seemingly archaic form of labor recruitment," was common in western mining; see Gunther Peck, "Divided Loyalties: Immigrant Padrones and the Evolution of Industrial Paternalism in North America," *International Labor and Working-class History,* 53 (Spring 1998), pp. 49–68.

23. Paul S. Taylor, *A Spanish-Mexican Community: Arandas in Jalisco, Mexico* (Berkeley: University of California Press, 1933; repr. Arno Press, 1976), p. 47; Ana María Alonso, "Work and *Gusto:* Gender and Re-Creation in a North Mexican Pueblo," in John Calagione, Doris Francis, and Daniel Nugent, eds., *Workers' Expressions: Beyond Accommodation and Resistance* (Albany: SUNY Press, 1992), p. 179. The Mexican saying is a modern version of a sentiment that prevailed during the Porfiriat. One example: a bourgeois lady describes her home, "Isn't it beautiful! . . . There is nothing Mexican in it!" Lesley Byrd Simpson, *Many Mexicos* (Berkeley: University of California Press, 1941), p. 290.

24. Heyman, *Life and Labor,* pp. 53, 58–59; Sanchez, *Becoming Mexican American,* p. 41; Alonso, "Work and *Gusto,*" p. 179; Corwin and Cardoso, "Vamos al Norte," p. 53.

25. J. Blaine Gwin (of El Paso Associated Charities), "Immigration along Our Southwest Border," *Annals of the American Academy of Political and Social Science*, 93 (January 1921), pp. 126–127.

26. Sanchez, *Becoming Mexican American*, p. 23; Park, "History of Mexican Labor," p. 223; Ruíz, *The People of Sonora*, pp. 195–196.

27. Alonso, *Thread of Blood*, part 1; Alonso, "Work and *Gusto*"; Miguel Léon-Portilla, "The Norteño Variety of Mexican Culture: An Ethnohistorical Approach," pp. 77–114, in Edward H. Spicer and Raymond H. Thompson, ed., *Plural Society in the Southwest* (New York: Weatherhead Foundation, 1972); Owen, *Marobavi;* Sheridan, *Where the Dove Calls;* Carr, "Peculiarities of the Mexican North"; Ramón A. Gutiérrez, *When Jesus Came, the Corn Mothers Went Away: Marriage, Sexuality, and Power in New Mexico, 1500–1846* (Stanford: Stanford University Press, 1991). An excellent although much later illustration of the greater reasonableness and calculation attributed to *norteños* can be found in the character of Luis in Victor Villaseñor's novel *Macho!* (Houston: Arte Publico Press, 1991). Mexican *norteños* reminded me of the Russian cossacks I wrote about in a previous work, for just as the cossacks had cohered into a brotherhood consecrated to holding the border against the Tatar barbarians, so the *norteños* defended their civilization; Gordon, *Cossack Rebellions: Social Turmoil in the Sixteenth-Century Ukraine* (Albany: SUNY Press, 1983).

28. Tinker Salas, *In the Shadow*, p. 53.

29. The *norteños* were scorned by Mexicans of the central plateau: To them the northern border was the *poso del mundo,* the lowest hole in the world, because of its sinfulness, lawlessness, secularness, and immorality. Martínez, *Border Boom Town,* p. xv.

30. Alonso, *Thread of Blood,* pp. 15–16, 65–68; John Michael Nieto-Phillips, "'No Other Blood': History, Language, and Spanish American Ethnic Identity in New Mexico, 1880s–1920s" (Ph.D. diss., UCLA, 1997).

31. Alonso, *Thread of Blood,* pp. 84–90, 96; Alonso, "Work and *Gusto,*" p. 179.

32. Alonso, *Thread of Blood,* p. 67. Historian Steve J. Stern has showed how men in the eighteenth century had fought against commercial milling, to keep women grinding their own corn, out of a finely tuned sense for what insubordination might ensue were women able to reduce their food preparation time. Stern, *The Secret History of Gender: Women, Men, and Power in Late Colonial Mexico* (Chapel Hill: University of North Carolina Press, 1995), pp. 332–335.

33. Heyman, *Life and Labor,* p. 84.

34. Clifton itself had two sewing-machine representatives at this time: L. Baroldy from White Sewing Machine Company and E. D. Wilson from Singer. *Arizona Business Directory,* 1905–1906, p. 145. Also see Heyman, *Life and Labor,* pp. 58, 70, 88, and passim; ads in regional newspapers.

35. Sanchez, *Becoming Mexican American*, p. 51.

36. Taylor, *A Spanish-Mexican Community,* p. 55.

37. The ensuing discussion of migrant labor relies on Michael J. Piore, *Birds of Passage: Migrant Labor and Industrial Societies* (Cambridge: Cambridge University Press, 1979); Heyman, *Life and Labor.*

38. Manuel Gamio, *The Life Story of the Mexican Immigrant: Autobiographic Documents* (Chicago: University of Chicago Press, 1931), testimony of Nivardo del Río, for example, pp. 153–159; Heyman, *Life and Labor.*

39. The pursuit of Mexican dreams in the United States is also confirmed by John Milton Armstrong, "A Mexican Community: A Study of the Cultural Determinants of Migration" (Ph.D. diss., Yale University, Department of Anthropology, 1949), p. 473.

40. Piore, *Birds of Passage,* pp. 54–55, quotation p. 54.

41. Gamio, *Mexican Immigration,* pp. 4–5; see also Clark, *Mexican Labor,* pp. 494, 497.

42. Clark, *Mexican Labor,* p. 488.

43. Armstrong, "A Mexican Community," p. 503; Piore, *Birds of Passage,* p. 54.

44. For a powerful early critique of this view, see Octavio I. Romano-V., "The Anthropology and Sociology of the Mexican-Americans: The Distortion of Mexican-American History," in idem., ed., *Voices: Readings from El Grito* (Berkeley: Quinto Sol, 1973), pp. 43–56.

45. The following discussion is primarily influenced by Michael Burawoy, "The Functions and Reproduction of Migrant Labor: Comparative Material from Southern Africa and the United States," *American Journal of Sociology,* 81, no. 5 (1976), pp. 1050–1087. Of course, employers could gain the advantage of low wages only when they used labor defined as unskilled; if skilled labor was required, workers had more bargaining power and migrants might be of little value. But changes in the management and division of labor in copper-mining processes in the late nineteenth century were greatly increasing the demand for "unskilled" labor.

46. Sylvester Mowry made this the core of his appeal: "the immense advantage Sonora and Arizona have over California or Nevada for the development of mineral wealth is the low price of labor . . . fifty cents to one dollar per day, paid in great part in merchandise at large profits." Mowry, *Arizona and Sonora,* pp. 93–95. Similar opinions can be found in Raphael Pumpelly, *Across America and Asia* (New York: Laypoldt and Holt, 1870), e.g., p. 6; Phoecian Way, "Overland via 'Jackass Mail' in 1858: The Diary of Phoecian Way," ed. William A. Duffen, *Arizona and the West,* 2 (Autumn 1960), pp. 279–292.

47. Phillip J. Mellinger, *Race and Labor in Western Copper: The Fight for Equality, 1896–1918* (Tucson: University of Arizona Press, 1995), p. 36. After World War I, when anti-immigration sentiment heated up, those with interests in Mexican cheap labor used this migratory practice to argue that the open

border was thus benign: "The majority of them will return to their country again this winter, no matter how much work there is. Those who do not go back so soon will do so as soon as they have earned or saved up a sufficient sum of money." J. Blaine Gwin, "The New Mexican Immigration," *The Survey,* 40, no. 18 (August 3, 1918), p. 492.

48. Federal investigator Victor Clark found that "when the rains begin, usually about May, he must be at home to plant his crop. After that he is willing to work during the growing period, leaving his family to attend to irrigation and weeding; but he must be home for harvest. From that time until the fiestas ending with the December holidays are over, the labor market in Mexico is tight; from January to May the workman is willing to go anywhere providing it is not too cold." Clark, *Mexican Labor,* pp. 473–474. See also Allen H. Rogers, "Character and Habits of the Mexican Miner," *Engineering and Mining Journal,* 85, no. 14 (April 4, 1908), p. 701.

49. Fred Roberts of Corpus Christi, representing the South Texas Cotton Growers' Association, House Committee on Immigration and Naturalization, *Hearings on H.J. Res. 271,* 66th Cong., 2d sess., 1920, p. 62.

50. Ibid.

51. Ibid., pp. 92–93.

52. Morris J. Elsing, "Mining Methods Employed at Cananea, Mexico," *Engineering and Mining Journal-Press,* 90, no. 19 (November 5, 1910), pp. 914–917.

53. The ensuing discussion relies heavily on Pierrette Hondagneu-Sotelo, *Gendered Transitions: Mexican Experiences of Immigration* (Berkeley: University of California Press, 1994), and Burawoy, "Functions and Reproduction of Migrant Labor."

54. Victor Clark, quoted in Neil Foley, *The White Scourge: Mexicans, Blacks, and Poor Whites in Texas Cotton Culture* (Berkeley: University of California Press, 1997), p. 43.

55. Herrera-Sobek, *Northward Bound,* p. 56.

56. This finding by Hondagneu-Sotelo is confirmed by data in Armstrong, "A Mexican Community," p. 367; and in Owen, *Marobavi,* p. 17.

57. Cardoso, *Mexican Emigration,* p. 82.

58. Hondagneu-Sotelo, *Gendered Transitions,* pp. 56–62, 83–86; Erich Fromm and Michael Maccoby, *Social Character in a Mexican Village: A Sociopsychoanalytic Study* (Englewood Cliffs, N.J.: Prentice-Hall, 1970), p. 153. This and similar analyses have been criticized as demeaning and falsifying Mexican family life, no doubt with some merit, but the criticisms also reflect an unwillingness to recognize the male dominance and, often, cruel treatment of women, which Mexican and Mexican American feminists are bringing to light.

59. The quotation comes from a discussion of masculinity among Chilean copper miners in Thomas Miller Klubock, "Mortality and Good Habits: The Construction of Gender and Class in the Chilean Copper Mines, 1904–1951," pp.

232–263 in John D. French and Daniel James, eds., *The Gendered Worlds of Latin American Women Workers: From Household and Factory to the Union Hall and Ballot Box* (Durham, N.C.: Duke University Press, 1997).

60. Sanchez, *Becoming Mexican American,* pp. 35, 41.
61. Interviewed by Vicki Ruiz and discussed in her *From Out of the Shadows: Mexican Women in Twentieth-Century America* (New York: Oxford University Press, 1998), pp. 3ff.
62. Heyman, *Life and Labor,* p. 49.
63. Gamio, *The Life Story,* testimony of Juana de Hidalgo, p. 162.
64. Recent studies of Mexican migratory communities show that village people tended to divide into the fortunate, with a foothold in the U.S. job market, and the unfortunate, without; those who settled in the United States retained that high status on return visits. The fortunate ones were further subdivided between those who did unskilled work in the United States and sharecropping in the village, and those who did semiskilled work or became entrepreneurs in the United States and who returned to the village for recreation and visiting. Richard Mines, *Developing a Community Tradition of Migration: A Field Study in Rural Zacatecas, Mexico, and California Settlement Areas* (La Jolla, Calif.: UCSD Program in US-Mexican Studies, monograph no. 3, 1981), pp. 116–119. I suspect that these patterns were arising even early in the century.
65. Mines, *Developing a Community Tradition,* pp. 123–124.
66. According to the manuscript census, Clifton had 2,150 residents and Morenci 2,558 in 1900, and they had 4,874 and 5,010, respectively, in 1910. But it takes only one look at the towns to know that these were undercounts: there is no way the census enumerators could have found all the shacks clinging to the hillsides.
67. The following discussion comes from the 1900 manuscript census. The Clifton data come from a 100 percent sample, the Morenci data from a 20 percent sample, chosen by selecting particular manuscript census pages to provide the proper proportions of Mexicans and Anglos. I got a great deal of help on some of these tallies–including the very hard work of reading the poor microfilm copies–from Ellen Baker, Laura McEnaney, Jules Unsel, Susan Wirka, and Kerry Woodward, and I am grateful.
68. In Clifton in 1900 there were 1,410 adults (one-third of the population was children). For simplicity in this summary discussion of Mexican migration and settlement, I have eliminated from my computations 17 blacks, 65 Chinese, and 5 Japanese adults who lived in Clifton and 15 blacks in Morenci. Of the remaining adults, 713 were Mexicans (54 percent) of whom 42 percent were women, and 610 were Anglos, of whom 27 percent were women. In Morenci, the total adult population was 1,745, of which 69 percent was Mexican, and only 16 percent of the Anglos were women, as opposed to 35 percent of the Mexicans. By contrast, in Arizona's largest white mining camp of the time,

Jerome, which was 14 percent Mexican, only 22 percent of residents were female; and other western mining camps reached a ratio of men to women as high as 5:1. On Jerome see Nancy Lee Pritchard, "Paradise Found? Opportunity for Mexican, Irish, Italian, and Chinese born Individuals in Jerome Copper Mining District" (Ph.D. diss., University of Colorado, 1992), tables 4 and 5, pp. 295–296. On sex ratios in other mining camps see Jeremy Mouat, *Roaring Days: Rossland's Mines and the History of British Columbia* (Vancouver: University of British Columbia Press, 1995), p. 110; Laurie Kay Mercier, "Smelter City: Labor, Gender, and Cultural Politics in Anaconda, Montana, 1934–1980" (Ph.D. diss., University of Oregon, Department of History 1995), p. 575, table 1; Paula Petrik, *No Step Backward: Women and Family on the Rocky Mountain Mining Frontier, Helena, Montana, 1865–1900* (Helena: Montana Historical Society Press, 1987), p. 21; Susan Johnson, "'A Memory Sweet to Soldiers': The Significance of Gender in the History of the 'American West,'" *Western Historical Quarterly,* 24 (November 1993), pp. 495–517.

69. In Clifton there were 206 Mexican heterosexual couples and 133 Anglo, in Morenci 255 and 80. There were a few "interracial" couples, to be discussed later.

70. Elliott West, "Heathens and Angels: Childhood in the Rocky Mountain Mining Towns," *Western Historical Quarterly,* 14 (1983), pp. 145–164.

71. On this measure, the proportions were the same in Clifton and Morenci.

72. Female-headed households numbered 53 in Clifton, or 9 percent of all households, and 85 in Morenci, or 13 percent of the total.

73. Several studies of im/migrant labor show that the presence of a nuclear family is usually associated with settlement rather than with back-and-forth migration: Leo R. Chavez, "Households, Migration, and Labor Market Participation: The Adaptation of Mexicans to Life in the United States," *Urban Anthropology,* 14, no. 4 (Winter 1985), pp. 301–346; idem., "Settlers and Sojourners: The Case of Mexicans in the United States," *Human Organization,* 47, no. 2 (Summer 1988), pp. 95–108. In general, the further from the Mexican border, the more men outnumbered women; thus when El Paso had a male-to-female ratio of 86:100, Chicago's ratio was 170:100; José Hernández Alvarez, "A Demographic Profile of the Mexican Immigration to the United States, 1910–1950," *Journal of Inter-American Studies,* 8, no. 3 (July 1966), pp. 471–496. But I would hypothesize that steady income might have been as important a factor as distance from the border.

74. In Clifton, 171 Mexican men (41 percent) and 189 Anglo men (42 percent) did not head households; many lived as lodgers. This is the population we would expect to find most transient. A few of these men were working sons living with their mothers: 18 Mexicans and 11 Anglos. That leaves, of course, lots of single male lodgers—more Anglo than Mexican—but they were not the norm. Morenci had a more transient population but not more so among Mexicans than among Anglos. Only about one-third of Morenci men headed

households, suggesting that two-thirds lived as lodgers or as working sons
with their parents, a proportion virtually identical among Mexicans and
Anglos. The miners mainly lived in Morenci, while the mill and smelter
hands were in Clifton, but the major difference was Clifton's larger population of small businessmen and workers in enterprises only indirectly part of
the mining industry.

75. Pritchard, "Paradise Found?" p. 92; Clifton 1900 census, family #888. This
kind of information is hard to come by because the census taker usually spoke
only to the male head of household and left many columns blank for the
woman—including, usually, citizenship and "number of years in the US." This
male-only interviewing policy was a result perhaps of the enumerator's laziness but more likely of the Mexican discomfort with women's speaking with
strange Anglo men.

76. Clifton 1900 census, family #909; Clifton 1900 census, #1046. Unfortunately
the census taker did not list the surnames of wives, although Mexican women
did not lose their birth names upon marriage. Santa Cruz Lara died in a mine
accident a year later; see Sacred Heart Church, Record of Interments, p. 2.
Learning this was one of several eerie serendipitous research events I experienced: First I picked Lara out of the 1900 census, in the fall of 1996, to
illustrate the exceptional case of someone who'd married a Clifton woman;
then in February 1997 I picked at random a page of the Sacred Heart burial
register that contained his name.

77. Morenci 1900 census, ##112 and 126.

78. Heyman, *Life and Labor,* e.g., pp. 65ff; Hondagneu-Sotelo, *Gendered Transitions;* Armstrong, "A Mexican Community"; interview with Ernesto Ochoa,
Tucson, February 13, 1997.

79. *El Labrador,* December 23, 1904, editorial, p. 3.

October 1, 1904, around 7:30 P.M.

1. George Whitney Swayne to Hon. M. J. Scanlan, State Board of Charities,
Albany, N.Y., n.d., copy in NYFH Archives.

2. Mandin on his part immediately began to blame the nuns. By Wednesday he
had fled to Tucson and was closeted with Bishop Granjon. In an interview he
granted, through an interpreter, with the *Tucson Citizen,* Mandin claimed that
he had written to New York doubting "the wisdom of granting thse American
children to the Mexican families." *Citizen,* October 5, 1904, p. 1.

3. Contemporary Chicana feminist critics might interpret their duality as arising
from the energy of both of their country's female goddesses: the Virgin of
Guadalupe, who fused in her being the spirit of Mexico and of womanly purity,
and Malintzin, who betrayed the Aztec empire to the Spanish conquerors. The
mythic Malintzin, or *la Malinche,* was Cortés's whore-mistress and his translator. She not only slept with the enemy but made possible communication

between the enemy and her own people—she translated, mediated, crossed boundaries, violated the integrity of her nation. She became known as *la lengua,* the tongue, language, or interpreter, the position occupied both literally and symbolically by Clifton-Morenci's Mexican foster mothers. In a culture as religious (and anticlerical) as Mexico's, such Manichaean oppositions structured values, and the oppositions here delineated national as well as gender virtue. The literature on the gendered symbolic meanings of the Virgin of Guadalupe and Malintzin is by now quite extensive. I have been influenced by Norma Alarcón, "Traddutor, Traditora: A Paradigmatic Figure of Chicana Feminism," *Cultural Critique,* 13 (Fall 1989), pp. 57–87; Cordelia Candelaria, "La Malinche, Feminist Prototype," *Frontiers,* 5, no. 2 (1980), pp. 1–6; Gloria Anzaldúa, *Borderlands/La Frontera* (San Francisco: Spinsters, 1987); Cherríe Moraga, *Loving in the War Years: lo que nunca paso por sus labios* (Boston, Mass.: South End Press, 1983); Vicki Ruiz, *From Out of the Shadows: Mexican Women in Twentieth-Century American* (New York: Oxford University Press, 1998); Tzvetan Todorov, *The Conquest of America: The Question of the Other,* translated from the French by Richard Howard (New York: Harper and Row, 1984), p. 101; and, with several grains of salt, Octavio Paz, *The Labyrinth of Solitude: Life and Thought in Mexico,* trans. Lysander Kemp (New York: Grove Press, 1961), esp. chap. 4.

4. On *compadrazgo* in general, see Sidney W. Mintz and Eric R. Wolf, "An Analysis of Ritual Co-parenthood (Compadrazgo)," *Southwestern Journal of Anthropology,* 6, no. 4 (Winter 1950), pp. 341–368; Edward P. Dozier, "Peasant Culture and Urbanization: Mexican Americans in the Southwest," pp. 140–158 in Philip K. Bock, ed., *Peasants in the Modern World* (Albuquerque: University of New Mexico Press, 1969); Lola Romanucci-Ross, *Conflict, Violence and Morality in a Mexican Village* (Chicago: University of Chicago, 1973), pp. 79–85; Paul Ming-chang Lin, "Voluntary Kinship and Voluntary Association in a Mexican-American Community" (Master's thesis, Department of Sociology and Anthropology, University of Kansas, 1963). On its practice in Clifton, evidence in baptism records of the Sacred Heart Church and interviews is abundant.

5. Why and when these six children died we do not know: in infancy, most likely; is it possible that she counted miscarriages in reporting this number? Eventually she had a second son. Census data and interview with grandson John Chacón, May 6, 1997.

6. Clifton 1900 manuscript census (see n. 66 to Chapter 2), #949; *Arizona Business Directory,* 1905; interviews with Al Fernandez and Charles Spezia, Clifton, February 15, 1996, and February 9, 1997.

7. Interview with Andrés Padilla, Clifton, February 15, 1996; Clifton High School Yearbook, 1910, Austin Grimes Collection, MS 315, Arizona Historical Society, Tucson.

8. "Report on Families from Whom Children Were Taken," prepared by

Thomas D. Bennett for NYFH, n.d., NYFH Archives. She is identified by NYFH lawyer Eugene Ives in the trial transcript, pp. 195–198, but I was unable to find her in any census. There is, however, a Guerra, first name illegible, thirty-nine years old (in 1900), female head of household, boarding-house keeper, with four children ages ten through twenty-two and a fifty-three-year-old mother; only one lodger is listed; 1900 census, #916/926. "Roja" would be a nickname anyway.

9. On the Villescases, in addition to census information, there are references in Charles Spezia's brochure for a walking tour of Clifton, Greenlee County Historical Society pamphlet, n.d.; Al Fernandez, "The Destitute Philanthropist," from a typescript collection of his newspaper columns written for *The Copper Era* and compiled by Richard Fernández, his nephew; unless otherwise noted, all references to Fernandez's columns are to this collection.

10. The NYFH record says that Sadie Green went to Josefa Villescas; the court record says that she went to the Windhams. Windham is spelled "Windom" in the trial transcript.

11. Jennie Parks Ringgold, *Frontier Days in the Southwest* (San Antonio: Naylor Company, 1952), 40; "Report on Families from Whom Children Were Taken"; Thomas D. Bennett to Charles E. Miller, "Report on matters . . .," November 7, 1904, in NYFH Archives. Franking *(sic)* Lee Windham and Mariam Refugio *(sic)* Olanis [illegible] married on January 18, 1904, according to the Sacred Heart Church records. He is Lee Windham, age thirty-six, in the 1902 Great Register of Graham County (list of registered voters), Archives, State of Arizona Department of Library, Archives, and Public Records, Phoenix, hereafter ADLAPR.

12. Clifton 1910 manuscript census; "Report on Families from Whom Children Were Taken."

13. Balles to NYFH, November 3, 1904, NYFH Archives; James M. Patton, *History of Clifton* (Clifton: Greenlee County Chamber of Commerce, 1977), p. 128.

14. The name was misspelled "Alvidras" in the trial transcript; see pp. 200–201, 219. Although no such family is listed in the Foundling Hospital records, three posse members testified at the trial that they went to this house to take two foundlings.

15. Interview with Ernesto Ochoa, Tucson, February 13, 1997; Padilla, Fernandez, and Spezia interviews.

16. Padilla interview.

17. Sacred Heart baptismal records.

18. Al Fernandez, "Foundling Home."

19. Fernandez and Spezia interviews.

20. Fernandez, "Foundling Home." The information on his age is not reliable since it is not confirmed by NYFH records.

21. Fernandez, interviews and "Foundling Home."

22. "The Innocents," *Weekly Arizona Republican,* January 19, 1905.

23. George Whitney Swayne to Hon. M. J. Scanlan, State Board of Charities, Albany, N.Y., n.d., copy in NYFH Archives; Father Mandin letter to *Southern Messenger,* October 24, 1904, in NYFH Clippings Scrapbook.

24. Most evidence of the rumors comes from later newspaper articles, but it seems safe to assume that the papers reported what was being said on the street.

25. *Bisbee Daily Review,* October 6, 1904, p. 1.

26. *Copper Era,* October 20, 1904, p. 2.

27. Letter from George C. Sturges, March 21, 1996, author's possession.

28. Quotation from Almeron Newman, "Sad Story of the New York Orphans," *Leslie's Weekly,* 99, no. 2564 (October 27, 1904), p. 386. Other rumors reported in "BABIES GIVEN AWAY AND SOLD! Forty White Orphans Doled Out to Mexican Cholos," *Arizona Bulletin,* October 7, 1904, p. 1; Lowell Parker, "'The Baby Train,'" *Arizona Republic,* February 5, 1974. See also below, "January 1905."

29. Deposition of Charles Bull, taken by NYFH lawyer, December 7, 1904, NYFH Archives.

30. Deposition of Laura Abraham, taken by NYFH lawyer, November 29, 1904, NYFH Archives.

31. *Tucson Citizen,* October 5, 1904.

32. Anthony Blake Brophy, *Foundlings on the Frontier: Racial and Religious Conflict in Arizona Territory, 1904–1905* (Tucson: University of Arizona Press, 1974), p. 37, from *Arizona Bulletin* October 7, 1904.

33. *Leslie's Weekly,* October 27, 1904, p. 386.

34. I thank Dionne Espinoza for pointing this out to me.

35. I am indebted to Professor Robert Orsi for referring me to such tales.

36. Edward Kent, Arizona Territory Supreme Court Justice, statement of facts, in NYFH Archives. This is repeated by Raymond A. Mulligan, "New York Foundlings at Clifton-Morenci: Social Justice in Arizona Territory," *Arizona and the West: A Quarterly Journal of History,* 6 no. 2 (Summer 1964), p. 107; and by Brophy, *Foundlings on the Frontier,* p. 28, based on the allegation by Sister Anna Michaella at the trial.

37. Mrs. Sam Abraham is Laura; I was never able to learn Mrs. Jake Abraham's first name. The Abraham and Riordan names are spelled variously: the latter sometimes as Reardon, and former as Abrahams, Abram, Abrams. I am unable to determine a single correct version. I even have advertisements for the hotel, presumably placed by the Abrahams, in which their name is spelled two different ways.

38. Telephones were new here, but affluent Cliftonians were among the most eager customers of such new devices. Already at the beginning of 1900, Clifton had the largest number of subscribers to the new Gila Valley tele-

phone system: thirty-one, as opposed to only sixteen in the county seat, Solomonville. *Copper Era,* January 25, 1900.

3. The Priest in the Mexican Camp

1. American visitors, Catholic and non-Catholic, believed the priests they found in the newly acquired American Southwest to be scandalously immoral— "there was hardly a priest in the country who did not rear a family of illegitimate children," observed W. W. H. Davis, U.S. attorney to the Territory of New Mexico, in his *El Gringo, or, New Mexico and Her People,* 1857, p. 96. See also Paul Horgan, *Lamy of Santa Fe: His Life and Times* (New York: Farrar, Straus and Giroux, 1975), pp. 125–131. Communities tolerated these practices without much anxiety; Ramón A. Gutiérrez, e-mail communication, August 3, 1998.

2. In the entire period 1880–1921, only three priests in the Tucson diocese had Spanish surnames. Paul Horgan, *Lamy of Santa Fe,* esp. part 2, chap. 12; Lawrence J. Mosqueda, "Twentieth Century Arizona, Hispanics, and the Catholic Church," *U.S. Catholic Historian,* 9 (Spring/Winter 1990), p. 90; Ramón A. Gutiérrez, *When Jesus Came, the Corn Mothers Went Away: Marriage, Sexuality, and Power in New Mexico, 1500–1846* (Stanford: Stanford University Press, 1991); interview with Ramón A. Gutiérrez, April 9, 1997.

3. Bishop Granjon, "State of the Church in Arizona in November, 1900," typescript, November 27, 1900, trans. Msgr. Louis J. McCarthy; and 1902 annual report, trans. Marcel G. Langlois; both in Diocese of Tucson Archives, Granjon Collection.

4. Monsignor Henry Granjon, Bishop of Tucson, *Along the Rio Grande: A Pastoral Visit to Southwest New Mexico in 1902,* ed. Michael Romero Taylor, trans. Mary W. de López (Albuquerque: University of New Mexico Press, 1986), p. 17; Ralph Gibson, *A Social History of French Catholicism, 1789–1914* (London: Routledge, 1989); Granjon to Paris Central Council, typescript, n.d., in Granjon Papers, Diocese of Tucson Archives.

5. Gilberto M. Hinojosa, "Mexican-American Faith Communities in Texas and the Southwest," in Jay P. Dolan and Gilberto M. Hinojosa, *Mexican Americans and the Catholic Church, 1900–1965* (Notre Dame, Ind.: University of Notre Dame Press, 1994), p. 27. See also Moises Sandoval, *On the Move: A History of the Hispanic Church in the United States* (Maryknoll, N.Y.: Orbis Books, 1990); Sandoval, ed., *Fronteras: A History of the Latin American Church in the USA since 1513* (San Antonio, Tex.: Mexican American Cultural Center, 1983).

6. Most Rev. John Baptist Salpointe, *Soldier of the Cross: Notes on the Ecclesiastical History of New-Mexico, Arizona, and Colorado,* ed. Odie B. Faulk (Banning, Calif.: St. Boniface's Industrial School, 1898; repr. Tucson: Diocese of Tucson, 1966), p. 15; Horgan, *Lamy of Santa Fe,* p. 125.

7. A *retablo* is a religious painting on tin, typically about seven-by-ten inches, usually either a *santo,* an image of a saint, Christ, or the Virgin, or an ex-voto, an image painted as a token of payment for a divine favor received.

8. Since the Franciscans did not want to create ambiguity or heresy around the celebration of the sacraments, they focused their energies instead on paraliturgies. Franciscans introduced the cult of the Virgin of Guadalupe, for example. Ramón A. Gutiérrez, e-mail communication, August 3, 1998. Horgan, *Lamy of Santa Fe,* part 4, chap. 6, quotation p. 151; Sandoval, *On the Move,* pp. 36–37; Hinojosa, "Faith Communities," p. 20; Eric Wolf, "The Virgin of Guadalupe," *Journal of American Folklore,* 71, no. 279 (1958), pp. 34–39; William B Taylor, "The Virgin of Guadalupe," *American Ethnologist,* 14, no. 1 (1987), pp. 9–33; Lawrence J. Mosqueda, *Chicanos, Catholicism, and Political Ideology* (Lanham, Md.: University Press of America, 1986); Mosqueda, "Twentieth Century Arizona," pp. 87–103; Gutiérrez, *When Jesus Came,* pp. 165–166; Raquel Rubio-Goldsmith, "Seasons, Seeds, and Souls: Mexican Women Gardening in the American Mesilla, 1900–1940," pp. 140–156 in Heather Fowler-Salamini and Mary Kay Vaughan, eds., *Women of the Mexican Countryside, 1850–1990* (Tucson: University of Arizona Press, 1994), p. 148; Miguel Tinker Salas, *In the Shadow of the Eagles: Sonora and the Transformation of the Border during the Porfiriato* (Berkeley: University of California Press, 1997), pp. 36–38.

9. My narrative about Teresa comes from William Curry Holden, *Teresita* (Owings Mills, Md.: Stemmer House, 1978); Paul Vanderwood, *The Power of God against the Guns of Government: Religious Upheaval in Mexico at the Turn of the Nineteenth Century* (Stanford: Stanford University Press, 1998); Brianda Domecq de Rodríguez, "Teresa Urrea: La Santa de Cabora," in *Temas sonorenses: A través de los simposios de historia* (Hermosillo, 1984); Mario Gill, "Teresa Urrea, la santa de Cabora," in *Historia Mexicana,* 6 (April–June 1957), pp. 626–644; Frank Bishop Putnam, "Teresa Urrea, 'The Saint of Cabora,'" *Southern California Quarterly,* 45, no. 2 (June 1963), pp. 245–264; James M. Patton, *History of Clifton* (Clifton: Greenlee County Chamber of Commerce, 1977); Al Fernandez, "Santa Teresa"; Helen Dare, "Santa Teresa," *San Francisco Examiner,* July 27, 1900; Jay J. Wagoner, *Arizona Territory, 1863–1912: A Political History* (Tucson: University of Arizona Press, 1970). Additional work on Teresa will soon appear in the dissertation of Marian Perales. One historical documentary video features a section on Teresa: "Nobody's Girls: Five Women of the West" (PDR Productions, n.d.).

10. In the following interpretation of Santa Teresa de Cabora I am indebted to conversation with Caroline Bynum and to her published work, notably *Jesus as Mother: Studies in the Spirituality in the High Middle Ages* (Berkeley: University of California Press, 1982), esp. part 5; *Holy Feast and Holy Fast: The Religious Significance of Food to Medieval Women* (Berkeley: University of California Press, 1987); "The Female Body and Religious Practice in the Later Middle Ages," in *Fragmentation and Redemption* (New York: Zone, 1992), pp. 181–238. I have also

learned from comments by Robert A. Orsi and from his *Thank You, St. Jude: Women's Devotion to the Patron Saint of Hopeless Causes* (New Haven, Conn.: Yale University Press, 1996). See also William A. Christian, Jr., *Visionaries: The Spanish Republic and the Reign of Christ* (Berkeley: University of California Press, 1996); and Christian, *Moving Crucifixes in Modern Spain* (Princeton: Princeton University Press, 1992). If I have made interpretive mistakes, which would not be surprising given my own religious culture, these scholars are not responsible.

11. One Mexican historian, Mario Gill, implies that he profited, in *Episodios Mexicanos: Mexico en la Hoguera* (Mexico: Editorial Azteca, 1960), p. 13, while Holden denies it, *Teresita,* p. 229.

12. As interviewed by Dare, "Santa Teresa."

13. Nogales was too close to Mexico, and the sick, the crippled, and the rebellious continued to seek her out and leave her thus vulnerable to Porfirian repression. Clifton seemed ideal because it combined a large Mexican population with enough distance from the Mexican border to reduce the influx of adorers and followers. On Porfirian fear of Mexican oppositional activity within the United States, see Juan Gómez-Quiñones, "Piedras contra la Luna, México en Aztlán y Aztlán en México: Chicano-Mexican Relations and the Mexican Consulates, 1900–1920," pp. 494–527 in James W. Wilkie et al., *Contemporary Mexico,* Fourth International Congress of Mexican History (Berkeley: University of California Press and Mexico City: El Colegio de Mexico, 1976).

14. One group of Yaquis used a banner reading "Teresa, la Reina de los Yaquis," not a particularly spiritual usage; Holden, *Teresita,* p. 230.

15. Dare, "Santa Teresa."

16. Since her powers seem to have outlasted her first brief marriage, one wonders if it was "unconsummated."

17. Clifton was made a mission in 1882 with the visit of Rev. Antonio Jouvanceau and then Bishop John B. Salpointe from Tucson; there were visits again in 1884 and 1885. At some point Rev. Julio Gheldof built a frame church in North Clifton, which was destroyed by fire in 1891. Typescript on history of the Sacred Heart Parish, Clifton folder, Diocese of Tucson Archives.

18. "Memoirs of Msgr. P. Timmerman [sid]," mimeographed typescript, n.d., prepared from his handwritten notes after his death; a biographical form apparently filled out by each priest in the diocese; clippings from *Tucson Citizen,* June 4, 1937, and May 5, 1941; "History of the Sacred Heart Parish, Clifton, Arizona, Golden Jubilee Celebration, 1899–1949," pamphlet; all in Clifton folder, Diocese of Tucson Archives.

19. Patton, *History of Clifton,* p. 26. The same claims were made by other copper barons, as by William Clark in Butte; see Mary Murphy, *Mining Cultures: Men, Women, and Leisure in Butte, 1914–41* (Urbana: University of Illinois Press, 1997), p. 4; and Donald Mac Millan, "A History of the Struggle to Abate Air

Pollution from Copper Smelters of the Far West, 1885–1933" (Ph.D. diss., University of Montana, 1973), pp. 20–21.

20. *Bisbee Daily Review,* March 3, 1929, clipping in Clifton folder, Diocese of Tucson Archives.

21. Granjon, *Along the Rio Grande,* p. 19.

22. First quotation from George B. Gamble, "Clifton and Old Graham County," typescript, 1932, Arizona Historical Society, Tucson; second quotation from WPA interview with Ralph E. Bates, by Kathlyn M. Lathrop, WPA Life Histories Collection, trans. p. 5.

23. Crimes reported in *Arizona Bulletin,* April 15, 1904, p. 1. On mining camp violence elsewhere, see Murphy, *Mining Cultures,* chap. 2 and 4.

24. On Chacón's toughness: He "could watch the building of that scaffold from his cell, but it had no more effect on him than if he had been watching the building of a chicken coop. Of course, according to Law, we had to grant him one last request, and he asked for a pot of coffee to be made over a camp fire. Well, John Eppley, the official hangman, made the coffee and then Chacón refused to drink it, he said, 'Better let the sheriff and his brave posse drink that coffee, they need it to brace them up to get nerve to pull that rope.'" WPA interviews with James V. Parks, Sr., by Kathlyn M. Lathrop, WPA Life Histories Collection, trans. pp. 7–8. Other accounts of Chacón's capture are in Roberta Watt, "History of Morenci, Arizona" (Master's thesis, University of Arizona, 1956), p. 111, quoting from *Copper Era,* November 27, 1902; Frazier Hunt, *Cap Mossman: Last of the Great Cowmen* (New York: Hastings House, 1951), pp. 194–195; Wagoner, *Arizona Territory,* p. 379. On such bandits generally see Paul J. Vanderwood, *Disorder and Progress: Bandits, Police, and Mexican Development* (Lincoln: University of Nebraska, 1981).

25. Quotation from WPA interview with Bates, by Lathrop, trans. pp. 5–6; Patton, *History of Clifton,* p. 102.

26. *Clifton Clarion* October 17, 1883; Dr. John Holt Lacy, "A Good Indian," *Arizona Historical Review,* 3, no. 3 (October 1930), pp. 75–77; Bill O'Neal, *The Arizona Rangers* (Austin: Eakin Press, 1987), p. 36; Justice's Court of No. 3 Precinct, Justice of the Peace B. A. Boyles presiding, Graham County, Docket Book, 1904, Greenlee County Historical Society (hereafter GCHS), Clifton.

27. There is debate among western historians on the question, how violent was the West. Several claim that western violence has been exaggerated: see, for example, Richard White, *"It's Your Misfortune and None of My Own": A New History of the American West* (Norman: University of Oklahoma Press, 1991), pp. 328–332; Frank Prassel, *The Western Peace Officer: A Legacy of Law and Order* (Norman: University of Oklahoma Press, 1972); W. Eugene Hollon, *Frontier Violence: Another Look* (New York: Oxford University Press, 1974); Robert R. Dykstra, *The Cattle Towns* (New York: Knopf, 1968). The study of three counties, including mining camps in Colorado and Arizona, by Clare

V. McKanna, Jr., *Homicide, Race, and Justice in the American West, 1880–1920* (Tucson: University of Arizona Press, 1997), finds, to the contrary, that homicide rates were significantly higher here than further east: 6 per 100,000 in Nebraska, 34 per 100,000 in Las Animas County in Colorado (location of Trinidad and Ludlow mining camps), and 70 per 100,000 in Gila County in Arizona (location of the Globe-Miami mining camps); see p. 157 for a summary of rates. David T. Courtwright in *Violent Land: Single Men and Social Disorder from the Frontier to the Inner City* (Cambridge, Mass.: Harvard University Press, 1996) also found higher rates of violence in the West and in mining camps (105 per 100,000 in Leadville, Colorado, in the 1880s), although his sociobiological causal argument is not convincing. Clifton Catholic church burial records included an average of 1 murder per year in the period 1899–1904, but one would have to assume that not all the dying received proper Catholic interments. Burial records, Sacred Heart Church, Clifton.

28. Despite its roughness, Sacred Heart was already the third Catholic church that had stood in this mining camp. Visiting priests built the first church in 1889, using lumber carted in by burros, but it was destroyed in the flood of January 1891–an event difficult for Mandin to imagine in this arid climate, since he had not lived through a summer yet. Rebuilt immediately, the church was razed by fire just six months later. The twin disasters of 1891 had been so disheartening that until Timmermans rebuilt it in 1895–this time of fire-resistant adobe–the occasional masses were held in various Mexican houses.

29. This and much of the following information comes from *Arizona Bulletin,* 1903, special souvenir edition; interviews with Al Fernandez and Charles A. Spezia, February 15, 1996, and February 9, 1997; and Charlie Spezia's brochure describing a walking tour of Clifton, n.d., GCHS.

30. Al Fernandez, "Rosario (Challo) Olivas"; WPA interview with Charles Ehlig, by Helen M. Smith, WPA Life Histories Collection, trans. p. 3. Sprinkling the streets was not just a matter of cosmetics and convenience: in El Paso around this time, the sanitation department swept the streets of Chihuahuita, the Mexican barrio, without sprinkling, thereby scattering dust and germs and contributing to a tuberculosis epidemic, according to a charity official; see Mario T. García, "The Chicana in American History: The Mexican Women of El Paso, 1880–1920," *Pacific Historical Review,* 49, no. 2 (May 1980), p. 321.

31. Quoted in Mac Millan, "A History of the Struggle," p. 20.

32. *Copper Era,* 1, no. 41 (January 25, 1900).

33. Quotation from Blaine Peterson Lamb, "Jewish Pioneers in Arizona, 1850–1920" (Ph.D. diss., Arizona State University, 1982), p. 255; *Clifton Clarion,* August 1, 1883, and August 29, 1883.

34. Cases of December 23, 1904, and January 13, 1905, from Justice's Court of No.

3 Precinct, Graham County, Docket Book. On opium in another mining town, see Jeremy Mouat, *Roaring Days: Rossland's Mines and the History of British Columbia* (Vancouver: University of British Columbia Press, 1995), pp. 120–121.

35. Mescal is a liquor somewhat similar to tequila, distilled from the juice of the agave plant.

36. *Arizona Bulletin,* 1903, special souvenir edition; Fernandez and Spezia, interviews; Fernandez, "Early Day Entertainment in Our Mining District," "Wild Old Chase Creek," and "The Chicken That Nullified an Agreement"; Spezia walking tour pamphlet; Billy McGinty, *The Old West as Told by Billy McGinty* (n.p.: Ripley Review, 1937), p. 88; Elliott West, "The Saloon in Territorial Arizona," *Journal of the West,* 13, no. 3 (July 1974), pp. 61–73; Elliott West, *The Saloon on the Rocky Mountain Mining Frontier* (Lincoln: University of Nebraska Press, 1979); Ann Burk, "The Mining Camp Saloon as a Social Center," *Red River Valley Historical Review* (Oklahoma), 2, no. 3 (Fall 1975), pp. 381–392; Tom Vaughan, "Everyday Life in a Copper Camp," pp. 57–85 in Carlos A. Schwantes, ed., *Bisbee: Urban Outpost on the Frontier* (Tucson: University of Arizona Press, 1992), p. 65.

37. McGinty, *The Old West,* chap. 9; Chester D. Potter, "Reminiscences of the Socorro Vigilantes," ed. Paige W. Christiansen, *New Mexico Historical Review,* 40, no. 1, (January 1965), pp. 31, 41.

38. Watt, "History of Morenci," p. 96, quoting from *Graham Guardian,* May 29, 1903, and *Morenci Leader,* June 9, 1906. Badger baiting derived from the observation that badgers put up great resistance against dogs that tried to dig them out of their holes. First noticed in California gold-rush mining towns in the 1850s, it was one sport among others including bare knuckle fighting, hunting coyotes on horseback, bearbaiting, and drinking and shooting contests. Cockfighting was popular on the Comstock lode and throughout the Southwest, especially in Tucson. As towns became "civilized," organized groups, notably churches, tried to ban cockfighting. See David Dary, *Seeking Pleasure in the Old West* (New York: Knopf, 1995), pp. 54, 194, 206, 211, 264, 297. Rooster chasing was a Mexican fiesta-day entertainment: a rooster would be buried in the middle of a street, leaving only his head above ground; then men would ride past full speed on horseback, attempting to pull the *gallo* out of the ground. *Arizona Bulletin,* June 23, 1893; this entertainment is also described in Darlis Miller, "The Women of Lincoln County, 1860–1900," in Elizabeth Jameson and Susan Armitage, eds., *Writing the Range: Race, Class, and Culture in the Women's West* (Norman: University of Oklahoma Press, 1997), p. 155.

39. WPA interview with Robert Alexander, by José del Castillo, December 10, 1938, WPA Life Histories Collection, trans. pp. 1–2; Fernandez, "Wild Old Chase Creek"; Watt, "History of Morenci," p. 96; *Morenci Leader,* June 9, 1906.

40. Burk, "The Mining Camp Saloon," p. 384.

41. *Arizona Bulletin,* June 23, 1893, copy at New Mexico State University, Las Cruces.

42. Fernandez interview.

43. Nancy Lee Pritchard, "Paradise Found? Opportunity for Mexican, Irish, Italian, and Chinese born individuals in Jerome Copper Mining District" (Ph.D. diss., University of Colorado, 1992), p. 178; Ronald C. Brown, *Hardrock Miners: The Intermountain West, 1860–1920* (College Station: Texas A & M University Press, 1979), pp. 29–30.

44. A good example is the following letter from a resident of Chloride, Arizona, to the *Miners' Magazine* of March 1903: "Chinese and Japanese are driving the women out of employment, that they have no regard for virtue, and that every Chinese restaurant, laundry or other business house is an opium den and place of assignation, and if a girl should be forced to work for them or in any way come in contact with them and would not submit to them, the best one that ever emigrated to this country would not hesitate to 'dope' her to accomplish his purpose and would not hesitate at murder to appease his carnal infamy."

45. Interview with Carmina García, February 7 and 8, 1997; list of Morenci businesses, 1914, compiled by Al Fernandez, author's possession.

46. Fernandez interview.

47. Fernandez and García interviews.

48. Jeremy Mouat, *Roaring Days,* pp. 120–121; Anne Butler, *Daughters of Joy, Sisters of Misery: Prostitutes in the American West, 1865–1900* (Urbana and Chicago: University of Illinois Press, 1985); Paula Petrik, "Capitalists with Rooms: Prostitution in Helena, Montana, 1865–1900," in *Montana: The Magazine of Western History,* 31 (Spring 1981), pp. 28–41; Elliott West, "Scarlet West: The Oldest Profession in the Trans-Mississippi West," in *Montana: The Magazine of Western History,* 31 (Spring 1981), pp. 16–27.

49. West, "Scarlet West, p. 21.

50. Justice's Court of No. 3 Precinct, Graham County, Criminal Cases, Docket Book. These names, taken from the docket book, could well have been misspelled.

51. Morenci Justice's Court, Criminal, Docket Book, 1901, Greenlee County Courthouse.

52. In every case where a woman lived with a man she was labeled in the census as "wife."

53. In New Mexico in the nineteenth century, 25 to 50 percent of the births were "illegitimate" in Anglo terms; 17 to 18 percent were such in Tucson in the period 1870–1880. Richard Griswold del Castillo, *La Familia: Chicano Families in the Urban Southwest, 1848 to the present* (Notre Dame, Ind.: University of

Notre Dame Press, 1984), pp. 88–91; Rebecca McDowell Craver, *The Impact of Intimacy: Mexican-Anglo Intermarriage in New Mexico, 1821–1846* (El Paso: University of Texas, Southwestern Studies monograph no. 66, 1982), p. 4.

This pattern resulted from several centuries of law as well as practice. Mexico's colonial inheritance included the Spanish *barraganía,* long-term monogamous unofficial relationships, often between rich men and poor women. Mexican men also practiced more casual infidelities, still with respectability and impunity. The New Spain government had encouraged legal marriage, but in the Mexican period anticlericalism inadvertently had the opposite effect. The 1859 Organic Law of Civil Registry required state confirmation of marriage; since most Mexicans associated church ceremonies with marriage, and since these were no longer legally binding, one consequence was to reduce popular commitment to a formal ritual entirely. The 1859 law also granted *patria potestad,* parental rights, over children even to women who were widowed, separated, or unmarried, rights they lost if they remarried–thus further reducing the incentives to marriage. The 1884 code made it easier for men to get legal separations, undermining once more the sacral notion of marriage. At the turn of the century legal marriage continued to decline in Mexico. Carmen Ramos-Escandon, "The Social Construction of Wife and Mother: Women in Porfirian Mexico, 1880–1917," pp. 275–85 in Mary Jo Maynes et al., *Gender, Kinship, Power: A Comparative and Interdisciplinary History* (New York: Routledge, 1996).

54. Susan Johnson, "Sharing Bed and Board: Cohabitation and Cultural Difference in Central Arizona Mining Towns, 1863–73," pp. 77–78 in Susan Armitage and Elizabeth Jameson, ed., *The Women's West* (Norman: University of Oklahoma Press, 1987); and for more examples of this, see also Darlis A. Miller, "Cross-Cultural Marriages in the Southwest: The New Mexico Experience, 1846–1900," pp. 104–105 in Joan M. Jensen and Darlis A. Miller, eds., *New Mexico Women: Intercultural Perspectives* (Albuquerque: University of New Mexico Press, 1986); C. Louise Boehringer, "Mary Elizabeth Post–High Priestess of Americanization (The Story of a Citizen Yet Very Much Alive)," *Arizona Historical Review,* 2, no. 2 (July 1929), pp. 92–100. For an Anglo report on the practice, see Allen H. Rogers, "Character and Habits of the Mexican Miner," *Engineering and Mining Journal,* 85, no. 14 (April 4, 1908), p. 701.

55. "Reminiscence of May C. Doan," *Journal of Arizona History,* Autumn-Winter 1965, p. 195; Rogers, "Character and Habits of the Mexican Miner," p. 701.

56. Craver, *The Impact of Intimacy,* p. 5.

57. Sacred Heart marriage and baptism Records; testimony of Neville Leggatt, trial transcript.

58. Sacred Heart Marriage Register, p. 34, for example.

59. Father Mandin to *Southern Messenger,* October 24, 1904, Clippings Scrapbook, NYFH Archives.

60. Raymond A. Mulligan, "New York Foundlings at Clifton-Morenci: Social Justice in Arizona Territory, 1904–1905," *Arizona and the West: A Quarterly Journal of History,* 6, no. 2 (Summer 1964), p. 106.

61. People began to call themselves *hispanos* in the 1890s, noticeably in New Mexico; but their self-labeling was frequently inconsistent, sometimes *hispano-americano,* sometimes just "Spanish," sometimes "Mexican." Arizona's racial system was not the same as New Mexico's (or California's), and it has been little studied; what follows is my small contribution. On racial categorizations and meanings in the Southwest generally, I am indebted to John R. Chavez, *The Lost Land: The Chicano Image of the Southwest* (Albuquerque: University of New Mexico Press, 1984), pp. 85–86; David G. Gutiérrez, *Walls and Mirrors: Mexican Americans, Mexican Immigrants, and the Politics of Ethnicity* (Berkeley: University of California Press, 1995), p. 33; Tomás Almaguer, *Racial Fault Lines: The Historical Origins of White Supremacy in California* (Berkeley: University of California Press, 1994); John Michael Nieto-Phillips, "'No Other Blood': History, Language, and Spanish American Ethnic Identity in New Mexico, 1880s–1920s" (Ph.D. diss., UCLA, 1997), pp. 96–106. Deena J. González in "Chicana Identity Matters," *Aztlán,* 22, no. 2 (Fall 1997), pp. 123–138, discusses another similar practice, the use of "Spanish-Mexican" in colonial new Mexico, p. 45. On the problems in counting those of Mexican descent in the United States that result from these labeling and conceptualizing shifts, see José Hernández, Leo Estrada, and David Alvírez, "Census Data and the Problem of Conceptually Defining the Mexican American Population," *Social Science Quarterly,* 53 (March 1973), pp. 671–687. Very few scholars have discovered how differently Clifton's Spanish-speaking population describes itself when speaking English or Spanish; several years after I noted it in interviews, I found a reference to the same practice in Arthur L. Campa, *Hispanic Culture in the Southwest* (Norman: University of Oklahoma Press, 1979), p. 5.

62. Al Fernandez, Nellie Marquez, Fermin Palicio, Vicente Aja, and the Esteves, Lavin, and Zorrilla families were all Spaniards. Fernandez, "The Esteves Family from Spain," "Criveiro and the Coronado Incline Tragedy," "A Good Deed by the Morenci Spaniards," "The Manila Soda Works," "The Lavins." The census enumerator may have been as confused as Mandin, because he did not list them or anyone else as Spanish; or he may not have asked.

63. In 1870, 1880, 1890, 1910, and 1920 (but not 1900) the census still offered a "mulatto" category, discontinued afterward. On Louisiana terms, see Joel Williamson, *New People: Miscegenation and Mulattoes in the United States* (New York: Free Press, 1980), p. xii. The U.S. binary system exerted great international influence, in this century particularly, visible in British usage of "black"

to refer to a wide range of darker people; see Victoria C. Hattam, "The Cultural Meaning of Race and Ethnicity in Britain and the United States, 1965–1995," forthcoming. The best introductions to the social construction of "race" in the United States are Michael Omi and Howard Winant, *Racial Formation in the United States* (New York: Routledge, 1986), and Howard Winant, *Racial Conditions: Politics, Theory, Comparisons* (Minneapolis: University of Minnesota Press, 1994). The critical scholarship on race has become voluminous. A few pieces that have influenced my interpretation particularly include Floya Anthias, "Race and Class Revisited–Conceptualising Race and Racisms," *Sociological Review,* 38, no. 1 (February 1990), pp. 19–42; Charles Wagley, "On the Concept of Social Race in the Americas," in Dwight B. Heath and Richard N. Adams, eds., *Contemporary Cultures and Societies of Latin America: A Reader in the Social Anthropology of Middle and South America and the Caribbean* (New York: Random House, 1965), pp. 531–545; Magnus Mörner, *Race Mixture in the History of Latin America* (Boston: Little, Brown, 1967); James F. Davis, *Who Is Black? One Nation's Definition* (University Park: Pennsylvania State University Press, 1991); Lawrence Wright, "One Drop of Blood," *New Yorker,* July 25, 1994, pp. 46–55; David Theo Goldberg, *Racial Subjects: Writing on Race in America* (New York: Routledge, 1997); Ann Laura Stoler, "Racial Histories and Their Regimes of Truth," *Political Power and Social Theory,* 11 (1997), pp. 183–206, and commentaries in the same volume; Loïc J. D. Wacquant, "For an Analytic of Racial Domination," in the same volume, pp. 221–234.

64. The inventor of the term "hypo-descent" was Marvin Harris, *Patterns of Race in the Americas* (New York: Norton, 1964), p. 56.

65. Personal communication, October 1997 (quoted with gratitude).

66. Winant, *Racial Conditions,* p. 23.

67. The list is published in a 1973 Clifton centennial brochure, Special Collections, University of Arizona Library, Tucson. Most of the names are badly misspelled, so separating Spanish from, say, Italian names is often guesswork; hence my figure is an estimate.

68. In figuring counts such as these, it is impossible to distinguish Spaniards from Mexicans. Great Registers of Graham County, 1894, 1902, 1906, and 1910, and Great Register of Greenlee County, 1911, in ADLAPR; Great Register of Greenlee County, 1922, Greenlee County Historical Society.

69. Interview with Carmina García, in Barbara Kingsolver, *Holding the Line: Women in the Great Arizona Mine Strike of 1983* (Ithaca, N.Y.: ILP Press, 1989), 67; interview with Helen Cooper, Morenci, February 9, 1997; Alton Elton Montierth, "A History of Education in Graham County" (Master's thesis, University of Arizona, 1951), passim; Patton, *History of Clifton,* pp. 128–132; Mary Logan Rothschild and Pamela Claire Hronek, *Doing What the Day Brought: An Oral History of Arizona Women* (Tucson: University of Arizona Press,

1992), p. 39; Watt, "History of Morenci," p. 104, quoting from *Morenci Leader,* April 27 and September 28, 1907.

70. Fernandez and Spezia interviews.

71. Quoted in Thomas E. Sheridan, *Arizona: A History* (Tucson: University of Arizona Press, 1995), p. 169. Lawrence Michael Fong, "Sojourners and Settlers: The Chinese Experience in Arizona," pp. 1–30 in *The Chinese Experience in Arizona and Northern Mexico,* pamphlet reprint from *Journal of Arizona History,* 21 (Autumn 1980).

72. Ah Him was chef at the Clifton Hotel, and Ging Sing proprietor of the "American Restaurant" in Chase Creek. *Arizona Business Directory,* 1905–1906.

73. Harold T. Shortridge, *Childhood Memories of a Fabulous Mining Camp, Clifton, Arizona, 1915–1926* (Cottonwood, Ariz.: Harold Shortridge, 1990), p. 25.

74. E.g., *El Obrero,* July 18, 1903, editorial, p. 2: "As a rule a partly educated negro is harder to deal with than any other class of laborer. He feels that he is somewhat better than he really is the very minute he begins to learn anything and trouble we fear would soon come up if his every want was not attended to." The 1905–1906 *Arizona Business Directory* lists two black churches in Clifton–these were almost certainly not separate buildings but congregations meeting in other structures.

75. After writing this I discovered that Robert Orsi described Italians in Harlem after about 1920 in a similar third category; see his "The Religious Boundaries of an Inbetween People: Street *Feste* and the Problem of the Dark-Skinned Other in Italian Harlem, 1920–1990," *American Quarterly,* 44, no. 3 (September 1992), pp. 313–347.

76. Arizona Copper Co. wage ledgers, Special Collections, University of Arizona; Philip J. Mellinger, *Race Labor in Western Copper: The Fight for Equality, 1896–1918* (Tucson: University of Arizona Press, 1995), p. 42. In some Sonoran mining towns, another three-part, multinational "racial" hierarchy prevailed: Americans and Mexican elites at the top; German and Italian foremen and engineers next; Mexican and Yaqui workers at the bottom. Tinker Salas, *In the Shadow,* p. 194.

77. Interview with Elizabeth Jessop Hovde, August 4, 1981, by Mary Logan Rothschild and Pamela Claire Hronek, Arizona State University Archives, Tempe.

78. James H. Bassett, former Arizona Ranger, reminiscence dictated to Law and Legislative Reference Librarian (no name given), 1936, ADLAPR.

79. During the Civil War, Arizona Anglo sentiment was overwhelmingly pro-Confederate; afterward, it turned pro-Democratic. Howard Roberts Lamar, *The Far Southwest, 1846–1912: A Territorial History* (New Haven, Conn.: Yale University Press, 1966), pp. 427–428; idem, "Carpetbaggers Full of Dreams: A Functional View of the Arizona Pioneer Politicians," *Arizona and the West,* 7, no. 3 (Autumn 1965), pp. 187–206; Cecil Robinson, *Mexico and the Hispanic*

Southwest in American Literature (Tucson: University of Arizona Press, 1977, rev. from *With the Ears of Strangers,* 1963), pp. 69–73; Arnoldo de Léon and Kenneth L. Stewart, *Tejanos and the Numbers Game: A Socio-Historical Interpretation from the Federal Censuses, 1850–1900* (Albuquerque: University of New Mexico Press, 1989), chap. 2; *Arizona Bulletin,* 1903, special souvenir edition; Robinson, *Mexico,* pp. 69–73.

80. This pattern was also found by Neil Foley in his study of Texas, *The White Scourge: Mexicans, Blacks, and Poor Whites in Texas Cotton Culture* (Berkeley: University of California Press, 1997), p. 23.

81. Hon. James L. Slayden, "The Mexican Immigrant," *Annals of the American Academy of Political and Social Science,* 93 (January 1921), p. 125.

82. On this point see a similar judgment in Devra Weber, *Dark Sweat, White Gold: California Farm Workers, Cotton, and the New Deal* (Berkeley: University of California Press, 1994), pp. 55–56.

83. Report, n.d., Clifton folder, Diocese of Tucson Archives.

84. Sacred Heart baptism, marriage, and death records, Clifton.

85. A rich new scholarship on whiteness influences this interpretation, notably, David R. Roediger, *The Wages of Whiteness: Race and the Making of the American Working Class* (London, New York: Verso, 1991); idem, *Towards the Abolition of Whiteness: Essays on Race, Politics, and Working Class History* (London, New York: Verso, 1994); Eric Lott, *Love and Theft: Blackface Minstrelsy and the American Working Class* (New York: Oxford University Press, 1993); Theodore W. Allen, *The Invention of the White Race* (London, New York: Verso, 1994); Alexander Saxton, *The Rise and Fall of the White Republic: Class Politics and Mass Culture in Nineteenth-Century America* (London, New York: Verso, 1990); Ruth Frankenberg, *White Women, Race Matters: The Social Construction of Whiteness* (Minneapolis: University of Minnesota Press, 1993).

86. U.S. Immigration Commission, *Dictionary of Races and Peoples* (Washington, D.C.: GPO, 1911).

87. As Hattam argues in "The Cultural Meaning of Race and Ethnicity," the stability of a racial divide depended upon the elaboration of a subcategory, ethnicity, for differences that were not to be considered as fundamental or significant as racial difference.

88. The U.S. census planners, their categories dictated by the eastern black-white binary, classified Mexicans as white. Mexicans were white in 1870, 1880, 1890, 1900, 1920, 1950, and 1960, but not in 1930. In 1910 enumerators had the option to write "other" and "specify" in the margin. In 1930 there was a racial category, "Mexican." In 1940 Mexicans were white "unless they were definitely Indian or some race other than White." U.S. Department of Commerce, Bureau of the Census, *200 Years of Census Taking: Populations and Housing Questions, 1790–1990* (Washington: GPO, 1989). But these categories didn't make sense to Clifton-Morenci census takers. In 1900 enumerator

James Langerman dutifully labeled all the Mexicans "W" for "white" on the form, in keeping with the federal rules, but in 1910 his successor, Claude Hooker, was in unconscious or forgetful resistance: first he labeled them all "M" and then had to write over every entry, adding a darker "W."

89. One historian suggested that in the 1880s, anti-Chinese sentiment was so strong and so unifying to all the non-Chinese that an emerging definition of "white" and "American" seemed headed toward including Mexicans and even blacks. Alexander Saxton, *The Indispensable Enemy: Labor and Anti-Chinese Movements in California* (Berkeley: University of California Press, 1971), pp. 164–165.

90. Yvette Huginnie, "Mexican Labor in a White Man's Town," citing Clarence King, compiler, *The United States Mining Laws and Regulations Thereunder, and State and Territorial Mining Laws to Which Are Appended Local Mining Rules and Regulations* (Washington, D.C.: GPO, 1885).

91. In Bisbee "white" miners protested the employment of Italians and "Slavonic" men. A similar racial line was drawn in Cripple Creek, Colorado. See Elizabeth Jameson, *All That Glitters: Class, Conflict, and Community in Cripple Creek* (Urbana: University of Illinois Press, 1998), chap. 7.

92. J. A. Rockfellow, *Log of an Arizona Trail Blazer* (Tucson: Arizona Silhouettes, 1933), pp. 52–53.

93. Bishop Granjon, "State of the Church in Arizona in November, 1900."

94. Granjon, *Along the Rio Grande*, p. 42. Yet Granjon was at virtually the same time corresponding with a wealthy Anglo Catholic friend who served him informally as a broker, sending him money to invest; letter of February 21, 1904, Granjon-Brophy Correspondence, Diocese of Tucson Archives. Also see Most Rev. John Baptist Salpointe, *Soldier of the Cross: Notes on the Ecclesiastical History of New-Mexico, Arizona, and Colorado,* ed. Odie B. Faulk (Banning, Calif.: St. Boniface's Industrial School, 1898, repr. Tucson: Diocese of Tucson, 1966).

95. Granjon, *Along the Rio Grande*, pp. 9, 42, 58–61, 96, 106, quotations p. 58.

96. Quoted in Arthur J. Rubel, *Across the Tracks: Mexican-Americans in a Texas City* (Austin: University of Texas Press, 1966), p. 37.

97. Ibid, p. 46.

98. William Schaefers, "The Parish Priest and Mexican Settlements," *American Ecclesiastical Review,* 63, no. 4 (October 1920), pp. 391–395.

99. For example, Rev. Vernon M. McCombs, superintendent of the Latin American Mission of the Methodist Episcopal Church, "Rescuing Mexican Children in the Southwest," *Missionary Review of the World,* 46, n.s. (July 1923), pp. 529–532; Robinson, *Mexico,* pp. 44–45, 79.

100. Alan Knight, "The Working Class and the Mexican Revolution, c. 1900–1920," *Journal of Latin American Studies,* 16 (May 1984), p. 56. One Mexican joke goes: "My son, there are three things that pertain to our religion: the Lord, Our

Lady of Guadalupe, and the Church. You can trust in the first two, but not in the third." Quoted in Mosqueda, "Twentieth Century Arizona," p. 90.

101. Granjon to Brophy December 22, 1904, July 19, 1905, and December 21, 1905, in Diocese of Tucson Archives. Copies of most of this correspondence are also in the Brophy Papers, folder 919, Arizona Historical Society, Tucson.

October 2, 1904, Afternoon

1. James B. Allen, *The Company Town in the American West* (Norman: University of Oklahoma Press, 1966), pp. 44–45; Roberta Watt, "History of Morenci, Arizona" (Master's thesis, University of Arizona, 1956), p. 56; Ernest J. Hopkins, *Financing the Frontier* (Phoenix: Valley National Bank, 1950), pp. 8–9, 51. But this position of authority was not peculiar to Mills because of his personality. The Morenci mine superintendent was always the "mayor" of this "unincorporated" town. Jonathan D. Rosenblum, *Copper Crucible: How the Arizona Miners' Strike of 1983 Recast Labor-Management Relations in America* (Ithaca, N.Y.: ILR Press, 1995), p. 5.

2. Allen H. Rogers, "Character and Habits of the Mexican Miner," *Engineering and Mining Journal,* 85, no. 14 (April 4, 1908), p. 702.

3. Here is how I estimated this number: Clifton-Morenci doubled in size, according to the census, between 1900 and 1910. So for 1904 I am estimating 1.4 times the 1900 population. This may be a slight overestimate, because it seems likely that the Anglo population grew less than the Mexican, in which case the proportion of people at the hotel was even greater.

4. *Tucson Citizen,* October 19, 1904.

5. George Whitney Swayne to Hon. M. J. Scanlan, State Board of Charities, Albany, N.Y., n.d., copy in NYFH Archives.

6. *El Paso Herald,* October 8, 1904.

7. *Tucson Citizen,* October 5, 1904.

8. Swayne to Scanlan. Swayne alleged that Charles Bull, editor and publisher of the *Copper Era,* the Clifton newspaper, was among the angry mob.

9. *El Paso Herald,* October 8, 1904.

10. *Ibid.*

11. For more discussion of the vigilantes, see Chapter 7.

12. And how quickly the New York child welfare experts got and accepted this definition of the citizenry. Even the country's leading progressive social-work periodical, *Charities,* justified the "community's" action as a natural response to legitimate indignation; *Charities,* 12, no. 19 (February 4, 1905), p. 407.

13. For example, Hugh Quinn, born in Ireland, registered to vote in 1902, although he does not appear to have been naturalized; 1902 Great Register, of Graham County, ADLAPR.

14. Of course the concept does not do justice to the women in either place, for their power went beyond the formal and the visible. In South Africa, too, the settler women exercised more citizenship than the law would indicate.

15. Leggatt's speech is characterized in the *Arizona Republican,* January 17, 1905, p. 1.

16. Mrs. A. Le. Burge, Morenci, to NYFH Mother Superior, October 6, 1904, in Mount St. Vincent Archives, Riverdale, N.Y.

4. The Mexican Mothers and the Mexican Town

1. Father Mandin to *Southern Messenger,* October 24, 1904, in NYFH Clippings Scrapbook.

2. Carmina García, descendant of the Navarrete family, explained that when she adopted in the 1950s and 1960s in Morenci, it was difficult, the "talk of the town," because hardly anyone had done it before. Personal interview, February 7–8, 1997.

3. On informal adoption among Mexicans, see Mary Logan Rothschild and Pamela Claire Hronek, *Doing What the Day Brought: An Oral History of Arizona Women* (Tucson: University of Arizona Press, 1992), p. 73. On the history of adoption, see Jamil S. Zainaldin, "The Emergence of a Modern American Family Law: Child Custody, Adoption, and the Courts, 1796–1851," *North-western University Law Review,* 73, no. 6 (1979), pp. 1038–1089; Donald E. Chambers, "The Adoption of Strangers," *International Journal of Comparative Sociology,* 16, nos. 1–2 (March–June 1975), pp. 118–125; Julie Berebitsky, "'To Raise as Your Own': The Growth of Legal Adoption in Washington," *Wash-ington History,* 6, no. 1) Spring/Summer 1994), pp. 5–26; Susan Tiffen, *In Whose Best Interest: Child Welfare Reform in the Progressive Era* (Westport, Conn.: Greenwood, 1982); LeRoy Ashby, *Saving the Waifs: Reformers and Dependent Children, 1890–1917* (Philadelphia: Temple University Press, 1984); Linda Gordon, *Heroes of Their Own Lives: The Politics and History of Family Violence* (New York: Viking, 1988); Marilyn Irvin Holt, *The Orphan Trains: Placing Out in America* (Lincoln: University of Nebraska Press, 1992); Margaret Marsh, *The Empty Cradle: Infertility in America from Colonial Times to the Present* (Baltimore: Johns Hopkins University Press, 1996), esp. pp. 17–19, 105–108.

4. Childlessness figured from the manuscript census. Complaint about the air from Mrs. F. H. Kane, of Clifton, to Mother Superior, New York Foundling Asylum, October 6, 1904, in NYFH Archives.

5. It is in examining the death of children that we see vividly the greater poverty and lesser health among the Mexicans than the Anglos. The following figures derive from the 1900 manuscript census.

	WHITE		MEXICAN	
	% losing at least 1 child	*% losing 2+ children*	*% losing at least 1 child*	*% losing 2+ children*
Clifton	24	10.5	48	28.1
Morenci	19	12.5	55	33.3

In other words, the Mexicans lost two to three times as many children as did Anglos. Significant differentials in child mortality were also found in a study of Texas in 1900: here the lifetime number of children who died averaged 1.01 for *Tejanas* (including both the U.S.-born and the Mexican-born) and .53 for Anglos. Arnoldo de Léon and Kenneth L. Stewart, *Tejanos and the Numbers Game: A Socio-Historical Interpretation from the Federal Censuses, 1850–1900* (Albuquerque: University of New Mexico Press, 1989), table 4.3, p. 56.

It is difficult to translate these numbers into an infant mortality rate because the census does not tell us at what ages the children died, but the rate would appear to be significantly higher than the best contemporary estimate: for the United States in 1896, 17.6 percent, or more than one in six, were likely to die before age five; see Samuel H. Preston and Michael R. Haines, *Fatal Years: Child Mortality in Late Nineteenth-century America* (Princeton, N.J.: Princeton University Press, 1991), p. 86. In Los Angeles County in 1916 (the earliest year for which we have a record), the Mexican infant mortality rate was 3.8 times higher than the white: see Richard Griswold del Castillo, *La Familia: Chicano Families in the Urban Southwest, 1848 to the Present* (Notre Dame: University of Notre Dame Press, 1984), p. 101.

6. Personal interview with Ernesto Ochoa, February 13, 1997, and communication from Anna O'Leary, May 10, 1998.

7. By 1882 all the big ranchers of Graham County were Anglo; see the 1882 Land Register, ADLAPR. For an overview of occupational displacement of Mexicans in Texas, see de Léon and Stewart, *Tejanos and the Numbers Game,* chap. 3. Other relevant discussions are in Phillip J. Mellinger, *Race and Labor in Western Copper: The Fight for Equality, 1896–1918* (Tucson: University of Arizona Press, 1995); José Amaro Hernández, *Mutual Aid for Survival: The Case of the Mexican American* (Malabar, Fla.: Krieger, 1983), p. 31; Kaye Lynn Briegel, "Alianza Hispano-Americana, 1894–1965: A Mexican American Fraternal Insurance Society" (Ph.D. diss., University of California, Los Angeles, Department of History, 1974), pp. 20–38; Hubert Howe Bancroft, *Popular Tribunals,* vol. 14 (San Francisco: History Co., 1887), pp. 498, 503, 510.

8. Interview with Carmina García.

9. Al Fernandez, "Horsepower and La Garita" and "The Medinas"; Clifton 1900 census, #1222/1232.

10. Elías's naturalization in June 1894 is listed in the 1894 Great Register of Graham County, p. 7, ADLAPR; Camilio Disa (? name illegible) was listed as "capitalist" in the Clifton 1900 census.

11. This depiction of turn-of-the-century Mexican housing comes from early photographs, Clifton and Morenci files, Arizona Historical Society, Tucson; photo files, Clifton and Morenci, Special Collections, University of Arizona Library, Tucson; personal interviews with Al Fernandez, February 15, 1996, and February 9, 1997, García, and Ochoa; Ramón Eduardo Ruíz, *The People of Sonora and Yankee Capitalists* (Tucson: University of Arizona Press, 1988), p. 89; John Milton Armstrong, "A Mexican Community: A Study of the Cultural Determinants of Migration" (Ph.D. diss., Yale University, Department of Anthropology, 1949), pp. 177–182; Roger C. Owen, *Marobavi: A Study of an Assimilated Group in Northern Sonora* (Tucson: University of Arizona, Anthropological Papers no. 3, 1959), pp. 17–18; WPA interview with Carmen Hillman by Romelia Gómez, WPA Life Histories Collection; James M. Patton, *History of Clifton* (Clifton: Greenlee County Chamber of Commerce, 1977); Nancy Lee Pritchard, "Paradise Found? Opportunity for Mexican, Irish, Italian, and Chinese Born Individuals in Jerome Copper Mining District" (Ph.D. diss., University of Colorado, 1992), chap. 5; Mrs. E. M. Roscoe, unpublished reminiscence letter, n.d., Special Collections, University of Arizona Library; Charles Spezia's brochure for a walking tour of Clifton, Greenlee County Historical Society pamphlet, n.d.; Patricia Preciado Martin, *Songs My Mother Sang to Me: An Oral History of Mexican American Women* (Tucson: University of Arizona Press, 1992), p. 201.

12. On housekeeping, see Josiah McC. Heyman, *Life and Labor on the Border: Working People of Northeastern Sonora, Mexico, 1886–1986* (Tucson: University of Arizona Press, 1991); Julia Yslas Vélez and Socorro Félix Delgado in Martin, *Songs My Mother Sang to Me,* pp. 28–29, 59; Armstrong, "A Mexican Community," p. 193.

13. Interview with García.

14. Rothschild and Hronek, *Doing What the Day Brought,* pp. 22–24; "The Lives of Arizona Women," oral history project, Arizona State University, Tempe, interviews with Ruby Estrada and Lupe Hernández by Maria Hernández.

15. Harold T. Shortridge, *Childhood Memories of a Fabulous Mining Camp, Clifton, Arizona, 1915–1926* (Cottonwood, Ariz.: Harold Shortridge, 1990), p. 53.

16. WPA interviews with Hillman, Isabel Juárez Hernández, Carmen Escoboza Flynn, WPA Life Histories Collection; quotation from Mrs. E. M. Roscoe, unpublished reminiscence letter, n.d.

17. Fernandez, "Four Ninety Pete"–he earned that nickname because he seemed to charge nearly everyone the highest rate, $4.90.

18. On the reputation for immaculate housekeeping, see Douglas E. Foley with Clarice Mota, Donald E. Post, and Ignacio Lozano, *From Peones to Politicos: Class and Ethnicity in a South Texas Town, 1900–1987* (Austin: University of Texas Press, orig. 1977, rev. 1988), p. 55.

19. Jorge Durand and Douglas S. Massey, *Miracles on the Border: Retablos of Mexican Migrants to the United States* (Tucson: University of Arizona Press, 1995).

20. Edith M. Nicholl (Mrs. Bowyer), *Observations of a Ranch Woman in New Mexico* (Cincinnati: Editor Publishing, 1901), p. 10.

21. Griswold del Castillo, *La Familia,* chap. 6; Martin, *Songs My Mother Sang to Me.*

22. Monsignor Henry Granjon, bishop of Tucson, *Along the Rio Grande: A Pastoral Visit to Southwest New Mexico in 1902,* ed. Michael Romero Taylor, trans. Mary W. de López (Albuquerque: University of New Mexico Press, 1986), pp. 64, 109; WPA interview with Juanita Gonzales Fellows, by Roberta F. Clayton, WPA Life Histories Collection; Delgado in Martin, *Songs My Mother Sang to Me,* p. 61; Raquel Rubio-Goldsmith, "Seasons, Seeds, and Souls: Mexican Women Gardening in the American Mesilla, 1900–1940," pp. 140–156 in Heather Fowler-Salamini and Mary Kay Vaughan, eds., *Women of the Mexican Countryside, 1850–1990* (Tucson: University of Arizona Press, 1994), pp. 146–148; Margaret Beeson, Marjorie Adams, and Rosalie King, *Memorias Para Mañana: Nuestra Herencia Mexicana* (Detroit: Blaine Ethridge Books, n.d.), p. 51; Armstrong, "A Mexican Community," pp. 84–85; Margaret Clark, *Health in the Mexican-American Culture* (Berkeley: University of California Press, 1959); John G. Bourke, "Folk-Foods of the Rio Grande Valley," *Journal of American Folk-Lore,* 7, no. 27 (January–March, 1895), pp. 41–71; Fabiola Cabeza de Baca, *We Fed Them Cactus* (Albuquerque: University of New Mexico Press, 1954), pp. 59ff.

23. C. H. Grabill, "Inefficiency and Poor Food of Mexican Miners," *Engineering and Mining Journal,* 109, no. 7, (February 14, 1920), pp. 448–451.

24. From price lists in Tucson around this time we can estimate how much these expenditures would have purchased, but my estimates are probably low since transportation kept Clifton costs high. Some examples: in Tucson beans were 3¢–4¢ per pound, coffee 35¢, lard 8¢–10¢; flour $1.50–$1.90 per 50-pound sack; potatoes $1.35–$2.00 per 100 pounds; onions $2.00–$3.00 per 100 pounds; eggs 20¢–35¢ per dozen. John George Hilzinger, *Treasure Land: A Story* (Tucson: Arizona Advancement Company, 1897), p. 117. Colquhoun reported beef and mutton selling at 12.5¢ per pound; James Colquhoun, *The Early History of the Clifton-Morenci District* (London: William Clowes and Sons, 1924), p. 13. In Jerome, a nearby mining camp, one memoir reports that at the turn of the century, stew meat was 10¢ per pound and Levis were 75¢ each, but such recollections are notoriously inaccurate; Herbert V. Young, *They Came to Jerome, the Billion Dollar Copper Camp* (Jerome, Ariz.: Jerome Historical Society, 1972), p. 51.

25. The records of Vásquez's debt to Arizona Copper are in the files of the Greenlee County Superior Court and Probate Court, in a case in which the company tried to get the money from his estate after he died for the store debt, funeral expenses, and shipping of his five children to Mexico.

26. Arizona Copper company store advertisement, *Copper Era,* February 4, 1904, p. 2.

27. Fernandez, "Watame." On other mining towns, see Ruíz, *The People of Sonora,* p. 89.

28. Fernandez, "Luther Hulsey." The same system is described by Delgado, used in a Tucson Mexican neighborhood, in Martin, *Songs My Mother Sang to Me,* p. 61.

29. WPA interviews with Flynn, Apolonia Mendoza, Hernández, and Eulalia Arana, WPA Life Histories Collection; Fernandez, "One Week in the Life of a Clifton Resident in 1914," "The Wood Gatherers."

30. Figured from the manuscript census. Interestingly, if we can assume that the female-headed households had as many children as the male-headed, then Clifton-Morenci's 9 percent was exactly the national average in 1900; see Linda Gordon and Sara McLanahan, "Single Parenthood in 1900," *Journal of Family History,* 16, no. 2 (1991). This article also reminds us of the importance of counting single mothers who did not head households. On female household headship in Mexico, see Elizabeth Dore, "The Holy Family: Imagined Households in Latin American History," pp. 101–117 in Dore, ed., *Gender Politics in Latin America: Debates in Theory and Practice* (New York: Monthly Review Press, 1997).

31. Elliott West, in "Heathens and Angels: Childhood in the Rocky Mountain Mining Towns," *Western Historical Quarterly,* 14 (1983), pp. 145–164, reports female-headed households made up one out of eight households in some Colorado and Idaho camps in 1870, and 20 percent in Globe and 25 percent in Tombstone in 1880.

32. Because of the way the Clifton census was constructed, without addresses or locations of households, it is impossible to know if some of these female heads were actually living close to kinfolk from which they got help. Ramona Richards, Apolonia Mendoza, and Carmen Hillman are among the female heads of households in the WPA interviews.

33. This discussion of women's earning is based on WPA interviews with Mendoza, Hernández, and Ramona Richards; interviews with L. Hernández and R. Estrada, in Rothschild and Hronek, *Doing What the Day Brought;* interviews with Fernandez and García; Martin, *Songs My Mother Sang to Me;* Laurie Kay Mercier, "Smelter City: Labor, Gender, and Cultural Politics in Anaconda, Montana, 1934–1980" (Ph.D. diss, University of Oregon, Department of History, 1995), pp. 121–127; Elena Díaz Björkquist, *Suffer Smoke* (Houston: Arte Público Press, 1996), p. 79.

34. Interview with L. Hernández, in Rothschild and Hronek, *Doing What the Day Brought,* p. 11. Carmina García remembers her sister earning this way.

35. Paulina Moreno Montoya in Martin, *Songs My Mother Sang to Me,* p. 50.

36. Vélez in Martin, *Songs My Mother Sang to Me,* p. 32.

37. Manuel Gamio, *The Life Story of the Mexican Immigrant: Autobiographic Documents* (Chicago: University of Chicago Press, 1931), pp. 160–161.

38. Interview with Patricia Preciado Martin, February 11, 1997; interview with Helen Cooper, February 9, 1997; Esperanza Montoya Padilla and Carlotta Silvas Martin in Martin, *Songs My Mother Sang to Me,* pp. 97, 101–105, 201; Rothschild and Hronek, *Doing What the Day Brought,* p. 73; Mercier, "Smelter City," pp. 122–124; J. A. Rockfellow, *Log of an Arizona Trail Blazer* (Tucson: Arizona Silhouettes, 1933), p. 122.

39. "The Lives of Arizona Women," interview with Elsie Dunn; interviews with García and Ochoa; WPA interview with Casimira Valenzuela, by Romelia Gómez, WPA Life Histories Collection; Rothschild and Hronek, *Doing What the Day Brought,* pp. 68–69; Griswold del Castillo, *La Familia,* p. 81.

40. The enterprising girl was Apolonia Mendoza, interviewed by Romelia Gómez, WPA Life Histories Collection; Mercier, "Smelter City," p. 127; Rubio-Goldsmith, "Seasons, Seeds, and Soul," p. 149; Padilla in Martin, *Songs My Mother Sang to Me,* pp. 100, 110.

41. Padilla in Martin, *Songs My Mother Sang to Me,* p. 99; Vicki L. Ruiz, *From Out of the Shadows: Mexican Women in Twentieth-Century America* (New York: Oxford University Press, 1998), chap. 3.

42. The same pattern pertained in El Paso; see Mario T. García, "The Chicana in American History: The Mexican Women of El Paso, 1880–1920," *Pacific Historical Review,* 49, no. 2 (May 1980), pp. 315–337.

43. WPA interview with Richards, by Gómez.

44. An extraordinary example can be found in the WPA interview with James Elmo Bartee, who told the story of one "pretty little Mexican gal, almost stole us blind. Louizie [wife] kept complaining about the grocery bill going so high and never being able to keep anything on hand to eat . . . If Louizie hadn't been so mad at that girl, I could have had a big laugh out of it . . . When she caught the girl stuffing something into the front of her dress, she grabbed her and jerked her dress right off her, right in front of me and the children. You could have knocked Louizie over with a feather when she seen little packages go scattering all over the floor. The girl just stood there and stared like a dumb burro; then Louizie began undoing the packages and found bits of sugar, flour, coffee, baking powder, beans, rice, and raisins—not more than a spoonful in each package . . . Of course we got another hired girl, another, another and another, old, young, tall and short, fat and thin, brown, black, and white . . . [they all stole] we hired a white girl; she was a nice girl and a good girl—so my wife said . . . Then all of a sudden the cooked food began to disappear . . . then

one night I made the discovery . . . seen the hired girl dart in [to an old shed] with a package in her hands . . . the hired girl had taken food to an outlaw called Billy Grounds, who had been wounded in gun-battle with another outlaw called Curie Bill . . ." See also Victor S. Clark, "Mexican Labor in the United States," U.S. Bureau of Labor, Bulletin no. 78 (1908), p. 496; García, "The Chicana in American History," p. 326.

45. This description is based on photographs and communication from Yolanda Leyva.

46. *History of the Sacred Heart Parish, Clifton, Arizona,* Golden Jubilee Celebration pamphlet, 1950, Diocese of Tucson Archives; M. Clark, *Health,* pp. 102–108; Montoya and C. S. Martin in Martin, *Songs My Mother Sang to Me,* pp. 46, 210–211.

47. On special occasions there were professional musicians; at least three Mexican men listed "musician" as their occupation in the 1900 census.

48. WPA interviews with Lola Romero, Ilaria Casillas, Hernández, Hillman, WPA Life Histories Collection; Rubio-Goldsmith, "Seasons, Seeds, and Souls," pp. 149–151; *Cuentos y Memorias: Mexican Americans in Miami, Arizona, 1920s–1940s* (Tucson: Committee for Preservation of Mexican American Oral History, 1996), p. 17; interview with Mary Salcido in "Los Mineros," PBS *American Experience* video produced and directed by Hector Galan, 1990.

49. *El Labrador,* March 20, 1904, and July 15, 1904; Briegel, "Alianza Hispano-Americana," p. 65; J. A. Hernández, *Mutual Aid for Survival,* p. 39; Robert J. Rosenbaum, *Mexicano Resistance in the Southwest* (Austin: University of Texas Press, 1981), p. 147; Mellinger, *Race and Labor,* pp. 45, 71–72.

50. This discussion of Mexican mutual benefit societies is informed by Olivia Arrieta, "The Alianza Hispano Americana in Arizona and New Mexico: The Development and Maintenance of a Multifunctional Ethnic Organization," Renato Rosaldo Lecture Series vol. 7, Series 1989–90 (Tucson: Mexican American Studies and Research Center, University of Arizona, 1991); Briegel, "Alianza Hispano-Americana"; Emilio Zamora, Jr., *The World of the Mexican Worker in Texas* (College Station: Texas A & M University Press, 1993), pp. 72–77, 92–109; Juan Gómez-Quiñones, *Roots of Chicano Politics, 1600–1940* (Albuquerque: University of New Mexico Press, 1994), pp. 312–323; Griswold del Castillo, *La Familia,* p. 43; Hernández, *Mutual Aid; El Labrador,* March 20, 1904, and July 15, 1904; interviews with Fernandez; *Cuentos y Memorias,* p. 17.

51. Unfortunately, church-based social activity has not been adequately studied by women's historians; see Fitzgerald, "Brigit's Profession," introduction.

52. The women's culture and resistance that I saw in Clifton resembled surprisingly closely that which I had found among different racial-ethnic groups in my study of domestic violence in Boston during the same period, and that which my colleague Steve Stern found when he examined eighteenth-century Mexico. Linda Gordon, *Heroes of Their Own Lives: The Politics and History of*

Family Violence (New York: Viking/Penguin, 1988); Steve Stern, *The Secret History of Gender: Women, Men, and Power in Late Colonial Mexico* (Chapel Hill: University of North Carolina Press, 1995).

53. Ruíz, *The People of Sonora,* pp. 94ff.; Lin B. Feil, "Helvetia: Boom Town of the Santa Ritas," *Journal of Arizona History,* 9, no. 2 (1968), p. 85. See also the description in Wallace Stegner, *Angle of Repose* (New York: Penguin, 1971), p. 122.

54. *Arizona Bulletin,* July 24, 1903, p. 1.

55. Case of September 17, 1901, from Criminal Docket Books, Morenci, Greenlee County Courthouse. On violence in mining towns, see William E. French, "Prostitutes and Guardian Angels: Women, Work, and the Family in Porfirian Mexico," *Hispanic American Historical Review,* 72, no. 4 (1992), pp. 533–534.

56. August and September cases from Justice's Court of No. 3 Precinct, Graham County, Docket Book, GCHS, pp. 177, 189, 199–200; also reported in *El Labrador,* October 7, 1904, p. 2. On Arizona justices of the peace, see Larry D. Ball, *Desert Lawmen: The High Sheriffs of New Mexico and Arizona, 1846–1912* (Albuquerque: University of New Mexico Press, 1992), chap. 3.

57. Those who discuss it explicitly include Gamio, *The Life Story.* Those who normalize it include Armstrong, "A Mexican Community," p. 397; Paul Ming-chang Lin, "Voluntary Kinship and Voluntary Association in a Mexican-American Community" (Master's thesis, University of Kansas, Department of Sociology and Anthropology, 1963); Erich Fromm and Michael Maccoby, *Social Character in a Mexican Village: A Sociopsychoanalytic Study* (Englewood Cliffs, N.J.: Prentice-Hall, 1970); Arthur J. Rubel, *Across the Tracks: Mexican-Americans in a Texas City* (Austin: University of Texas Press, 1966), p. 61; Lola Romanucci-Ross, *Conflict, Violence, and Morality in a Mexican Village* (Chicago: University of Chicago Press, 1973), pp. 53ff.; Ozzie G. Simmons, "Anglo Americans and Mexican Americans in South Texas" (Ph.D. diss., Harvard University, Department of Sociology, 1952), pp. 60–64; Maxine Baca Zinn, "Chicano Men and Masculinity," *Journal of Ethnic Studies,* 10, no. 2 (Summer 1982).

58. Devra Weber came to the same conclusion about Mexican cotton workers in California's Great Central Valley in her *Dark Sweat, White Gold: California Farm Workers, Cotton, and the New Deal* (Berkeley: University of California Press, 1994), p. 59.

59. George J. Sanchez, *Becoming Mexican American: Ethnicity, Culture, and Identity in Chicano Los Angeles, 1900–1945* (New York: Oxford University Press, 1993); Ruiz, *Out of the Shadows;* Sarah Deutsch, *No Separate Refuge: Culture, Class, and Gender on the Anglo-Hispanic Frontier in the American Southwest, 1880–1940* (New York: Oxford University Press, 1987); Elizabeth Ewen, *Immigrant Women in the Land of Dollars* (New York: Monthly Review Press, 1985).

60. Gamio, *The Life Story,* p. 67.

61. *La Hormiga de Oro,* February 6, 1904, p. 3, March 5, 1904, p. 2; *La Alianza,* October 18, 1900; *La Bandera,* April 11, 1902, p. 3, as well as March 28, 1902, p. 2, April 11, 1902, p. 3, May 2, 1902, p. 3, October 30, 1903, p. 3. For other examples, see Ruiz, *Out of the Shadows.* The Mexican press was entirely in line with the local Anglo press on this; see, for example, *Arizona Bulletin,* September 9, 1904. Anglo observers similarly blamed Mexican women for their pursuit of consumer goods; see Clark, "Mexican Labor in the United States."

62. *La Hormiga de Oro,* August 22, 1903, p. 3.

63. For example, *El Obrero* and *El Labrador.*

64. *El Obrero,* November 21, 1903, p. 1; Ruiz, *Out of the Shadows.*

65. Sara Estela Ramírez, "Surge!" in Magdalena Mora and Adelaida del Castillo, eds., *Mexican Women in the United States: Struggles Past and Present* (Los Angeles: University of California, Chicano Studies Research Center, occasional paper no. 2, 1980), p. 168; also cited, in a slightly different excerpt, by Ruiz, *Out of the Shadows,* p. 99.

66. For example, Magón's "A La Mujer" in the PLM paper *Regeneración,* September 24, 1910, in Mora and del Castillo, Mexican Women in the United States, pp. 159–162; Ruiz, *Out of the Shadows,* p. 99.

67. Gamio, *The Life Story,* pp. 45–46. Gamio wrote that nothing "arouses the distaste and even disgust of the Immigrant as the free-and-easy conduct of the Americanized Mexican girl," in *Mexican Immigrants to the United States: A Study of Human Migration and Adjustment* (Chicago: University of Chicago Press, 1930), p. 89.

68. Gamio, *The Life Story,* p. 189.

69. Ibid., p. 271.

70. Quoted from early-twentieth-century *corridos* collected by Americo Paredes in María Herrera-Sobek, "The Acculturation Process of the Chicana in the Corrido," *Proceedings of the Pacific Coast Council on Latin American Studies,* 9 (1982), pp. 28–29.

71. Gamio, *The Life Story,* p. 258. A sociologist interviewing in the 1940s found definitions of a good wife like these: "My wife will do anything in the world for me. If I ask her to get up in the middle of the night to do something for me, she does, and she never fusses." "My wife does not say anything when I come home drunk." "My present wife is ugly, but she . . . never bothers me, never asks me where I have been when I come in late. Because she acts that way I give her money to send to her mother in Mexico." Simmons, "Anglo Americans and Mexican Americans," pp. 61–62.

72. Gamio, *The Life Story,* p. 252.

73. Ibid., pp. 234–235.

74. Simmons, "Anglo Americans and Mexican Americans," pp. 60–64.

75. Gamio, *The Life Story,* p. 249.

76. Ibid., pp. 237–238. The immigrant women in my *Heroes* articulated similar perspectives.

77. Interview with L. Hernández, in Rothschild and Hronek, *Doing What the Day Brought*, pp. 7, 45–47.

78. Gamio, *The Life Story*, p. 52.

79. Interviews with García and Ochoa; Rothschild and Hronek, *Doing What the Day Brought*, "Growing Up in Arizona"; Fernandez, "Tunnel Smokestack Operation."

80. Gamio, *The Life Story*, pp. 227–228, 274–275; see also Simmons, Anglo Americans and Mexican Americans," pp. 61, 65–74.

81. Alex M. Saragoza, "The Conceptualization of the History of the Chicano Family," in Armando Váldez, Albert Camarillo, and Tomás Almaguer, eds., *The State of Chicano Research on Family, Labor and Migration: Proceedings of the First Stanford Symposium on Chicano Research and Public Policy* (Stanford, Calif.: Stanford Center for Chicano Research, 1983), p. 131.

82. One man, very much the exception, found in studying recent Chicano families that many Chicanas look upon being with a Mexican husband as "a near prison-like atmosphere" and actively work at attracting American husbands. Ibid., pp. 131–132.

83. Richard Griswold del Castillo and Arnoldo De León, *North to Aztlán: A History of Mexican Americans in the United States* (New York: Twayne, 1996), pp. 45, 110; Griswold del Castillo, *La Familia*, pp. 120–121; Darlis Miller, "Cross-Cultural Marriages in the Southwest: The New Mexico Experience, 1846–1900," in Joan M. Jensen and Darlis A. Miller, eds., *New Mexico Women: Intercultural Perspectives* (Albuquerque: University of New Mexico Press, 1986), pp. 95–119; Leonard Pitt, *The Decline of the Californios: A Social History of the Spanish-speaking Californians, 1846–1890* (Berkeley: University of California Press, 1966), pp. 124–125; Sarah Deutsch, *No Separate Refuge: Culture, Class, and Gender on an Anglo-Hispanic Frontier in the American Southwest, 1880–1940* (New York: Oxford Univerity Press, 1987); Rebecca McDowell Craver, *The Impact of Intimacy: Mexican-Anglo Intermarriage in New Mexico, 1821–1846* (El Paso: University of Texas, Southwestern Studies Monograph no. 66, 1982); C. Louise Boehringer, "Mary Elizabeth Post–High Priestess of Americanization (The Story of a Citizen Yet Very Much Alive)," *Arizona Historical Review*, 2, no. 2 (July 1929), pp. 92–100; WPA interview with Fellows.

84. The majority of Anglo men in the New Mexico Territory in 1870 and 1880 were married to Mexican women: Deborah J. Baldwin, "A Successful Search for Security: Arizona Pioneer Society Widows," in Arlene Scadron, ed., *On Their Own: Widows and Widowhood in the American Southwest, 1848–1939* (Chicago: University of Illinois Press, 1988), p. 225; Miller, "Cross-Cultural Marriages," p. 100. James D. Shinkle, *Reminiscences of Roswell Pioneers* (Roswell, N.M.: Hall-Poorbaugh Press, 1966), estimated that 90 percent of Anglo men in nine-

teenth-century New Mexico married Mexican women, p. 92. See also Katherine A. Benton, "Border Jews, Border Marriages, Border Lives: Mexican-Jewish Intermarriage in the Arizona Territory, 1850–1900," 1997 paper, author's possession, pp. 12, 31; Oscar J. Martínez, "Hispanics in Arizona," pp. 87–122 in Beth Luey and Noel J. Stowe, eds., *Arizona at Seventy-five* (Tucson: Arizona State University Public History Program and Arizona Historical Society, 1987), p. 94.

85. On the unusualness of intermarriage in the opposite direction, see Susan L. Johnson, "Sharing Bed and Board: Cohabitation and Cultural Difference in Central Arizona Mining Towns, 1863–1873," in Susan Armitage and Elizabeth Jameson, eds., *The Women's West* (Norman: University of Oklahoma Press, 1987), p. 83; Barbara Kingsolver, *Holding the Line: Women in the Great Arizona Mine Strike of 1983* (Ithaca, N.Y.: ILR Press, 1989), pp. 79–80; Griswold del Castillo and De León, *North to Aztlán*, pp. 35–36; Jane Dysart, "Mexican Women in San Antonio, 1830–1860: The Assimilation Process," *Western Historical Quarterly*, 7, no. 4 (October 1976), p. 370; Edward Murguía, *Chicano Intermarriage: A Theoretical and Empirical Study* (San Antonio: Trinity University Press, 1982).

86. Another reason for neglect of motives is that studies have focused on elites, for whom evidence is easier to get, neglected to offer a class analysis, and failed to consider how intermarriage changed over time.

87. Dysart, "Mexican Women," pp. 365–375; Pitt, *The Decline of the Californios*, pp. 110–125. On theorizing the exchange, see Rosaura Sánchez, *Telling Identities: The California Testimonios* (Minneapolis: University of Minnesota Press, 1995), pp. 215–216; Gayle Rubin, "The Traffic in Women," in Rayna Reiter, ed., *Toward an Anthropology of Women* (New York: Monthly Review Press, 1975).

88. In the late nineteenth century in rural New Mexico intermarried couples usually lived in Anglo neighborhoods. Miller, "Cross-Cultural Marriages," p. 108; Dysart, "Mexican Women," p. 374.

89. Although Clifton-Morenci censuses have no addresses, the census enumerator was instructed to record households in order, so we can judge neighborhoods by looking at the race or nationality of people listed nearby.

90. Alonso, "Work and *Gusto*," p. 179; Alonso, *Thread of Blood*, pp. 84–90, 96; Craver, *The Impact of Intimacy*, pp. 12–13.

91. By contrast, white men marrying Indian women were much derided as "squaw men"; see Cecil Robinson, *Mexico and the Hispanic Southwest in American Literature* (Tucson: University of Arizona Press, 1977, rev. from *With the Ears of Strangers*, 1963), pp. 75, 80ff; Craver, *The Impact of Intimacy*, pp. 23–26; David J. Weber, "'Scarce More than Apes': Historical Roots of Anglo-American Stereotypes of Mexicans," pp. 163–167 in his *Myth and the History of the Hispanic Southwest* (Albuquerque: University of New Mexico Press, 1988);

James M. Lacy, "New Mexicano Women in Early American Writings," *New Mexico Historical Review,* 34, no. 1 (January 1959), pp. 41–51.

92. Foley et. al, *From Peones to Politicos,* p. 55.

93. Miller, "Cross-Cultural Marriages," p. 105; Griswold del Castillo, *La Familia,* p. 74.

94. Ming-chang Lin, "Voluntary Kinship," pp. 70, 80–84.

95. Janet Lecompte, "The Independent Women of Hispanic New Mexico, 1821–1846," *Western Historical Quarterly,* 12 (January 1981), pp. 71–93; Deutsch, *No Separate Refuge,* pp. 44–45; Griswold del Castillo, *The Los Angeles Barrio, 1850–1890: A Social History* (Berkeley: University of California Press, 1979), pp. 69–70, 154; Benton, "Border Jews," p. 36; Donald E. Worcester, "The Significance of the Spanish Borderlands to the United States," *Western Historical Quarterly,* 7, no. 1 (1976), p. 11; James M. Murphy, *The Spanish Legal Heritage in Arizona* (Tucson: Arizona Pioneers' Historical Society, 1966), chap. 3.

October 2, 1904, Evening

1. Colt manufactured the first pistol with revolving bullet chamber, and so the name was often used generically for any revolver or "six-shooter."

2. Americo Paredes, *With a Pistol in His Hand: A Border Ballad and Its Hero* (Austin: University of Texas Press, 1958), p. 16; Cecil Robinson, *Mexico and the Hispanic Southwest in American Literature* (Tucson: University of Arizona Press, 1977), pp. 35–75; Richard H. Peterson, "Anti-Mexican Nativism in California, 1848–1853: A Study of Cultural Conflict," *Southern California Quarterly,* 62 (1980), pp. 309–327; A. Yvette Huginnie, "A New Hero Comes to Town: The Anglo Mining Engineer and 'Mexican Labor' as Contested Terrain in Southeastern Arizona, 1880–1920," *New Mexico Historical Review,* 69 (October 1994), p. 330.

3. Walter Prescott Webb, *The Texas Rangers* (Cambridge, 1935), p. 14, quoted in Paredes, *With a Pistol in His Hand,* p. 17.

4. Explanations for the origin of "greaser" include these: that a Mexican maintained a shop on the Santa Fe trail where ox-cart and wagon wheels were greased; that Mexicans loaded greasy hides for the hide-and-tallow trade onto the clipper ships; that it arose from the work of sheepshearing. It first appeared in an 1884 English dictionary. Carey McWilliams, *North from Mexico: The Spanish-speaking People of the United States* (Philadelphia: J. B. Lippincott, 1949), p. 115.

5. Simpson said explicitly that he had never been in a Mexican household, p. 205; "Report on Families from Whom Children Were Taken," prepared by Thomas D. Bennett for NYFH, n.d., NYFH Archives.

6. "Report on Families," prepared by Bennett.

7. Ibid.; Bennett to Charles E. Miller, "Report on Matters . . .," November 7, 1904, in NYFH Archives.

8. In Spanish, of course.

9. Balles to NYFH, October 7, 1904, and November 3, 1904, NYFH Archives.

10. When a historian writing about Graham County tried to interview Rafael Holguín about these events in 1942, Holguín refused, saying, "No way, I came close to losing my life over the incident, you are now trying to put a feather in your hat with my experience." (I gulped when I heard this.) Interview with Al Fernandez, February 15, 1996, and February 9, 1997; Fernandez, "Foundling Home."

11. El Paso *Herald,* October 8, 1904.

12. *Tucson Citizen,* November 5, 1904, NYFH Archives.

5. The Anglo Mothers and the Company Town

1. Ann Laura Stoler, "Carnal Knowledge and Imperial Power: Gender, Race, and Morality in Colonial Asia," in Micaela di Leonardo, ed., *Gender at the Crossroads of Knowledge: Feminist Anthropology in the Postmodern Era* (Berkeley: University of California Press, 1991), pp. 51–101.

2. Wallace Stegner suggested this point in *Angle of Repose* (New York: Penguin, 1971), pp. 134–135 in particular.

3. Dates are from the manuscript census; testimony of individuals from the trial transcript; interview with Mrs. Louis Abrahams *(sic),* taped 1952, Arizona Historical Society, Tucson; Jennie Parks Ringgold, *Frontier Days in the Southwest* (San Antonio: Naylor Company, 1952).

4. Sarah Butler York, "Experiences of a Pioneer Arizona Woman," written 1921, pub. in *Arizona Historical Review,* 1, no. 2 (July 1928), pp. 69–75; also in Margaret Wheeler Ross, compiler, *History of the Arizona Federation of Women's Clubs and Its Forerunners* (n.d., n.p., privately printed), pp. 331–335, under the spelling Yorke; and in Ruth B. Moynihan, Susan Armitage, and Christiane Fischer Dichamp, eds., *So Much to Be Done: Women Settlers on the Mining and Ranching Frontier* (Lincoln: University of Nebraska Press, 1990), pp. 229–236. See also many memoirs in *So Much to Be Done;* Sue H. Summers memoir in Anne Hodges Morgan and Rennard Strickland, eds., *Arizona Memories* (Tucson: University of Arizona Press, 1984), pp. 68–73; WPA interviews with Mary Langdon Pitt, Mrs. Jacob Scherer, Mary Elizabeth Greenwalt, and May Lee Queen, WPA Life Histories Collection; interviews with Elsie Dunn, Mae Wills, and Elizabeth Jessop Hovde, August 4, 1981, by Mary Logan Rothschild and Pamela Claire Hronek, Arizona State University Archives, Tempe; Cheryl J. Foote, ed., *Women of the New Mexico Frontier, 1846–1912* (Niwot: University Press of Colorado, 1990); Christiane Fischer, ed., *Let Them Speak for Themselves: Women in the American West, 1849–1900* (New York: E. P. Dutton, 1977); C.

Louise Boehringer, "Mary Elizabeth Post–High Priestess of Americanization (The Story of a Citizen Yet Very Much Alive)," *Arizona Historical Review*, 2, no. 2 (July 1929), pp. 92–100; Boehringer, "Josephine Brawley Hughes–Crusader, State Builder," *Arizona Historical Review*, 2, no. 4, (January 1930), pp. 98–107; "Mrs. A. Y. Smith (An Indian Adventure), *Arizona Historical Review*, 7, no. 2 (April 1936), pp. 89–91; "Life Story of Emma Jane Craig Bull," from website www.zekes.com/fimmoody/pioneers/jcraigb.txt; Brigitte Georgi-Findlay, *The Frontiers of Women's Writing: Women's Narratives and the Rhetoric of Westward Expansion* (Tucson: University of Arizona Press, 1996).

5. On men doing women's work see also Mrs. Orsemus Boyd, "Cavalry Life in Tent and Field," orig. 1894, in Fischer, *Let Them Speak,* p. 113; on women doing men's work, see ibid., p. 120; Sarah Bixby Smith, *Adobe Days,* 3d ed. (Los Angeles: Jake Zeitlin, 1931), p. 248–249. Rose Ferber missed spring flowers, blackberries, chestnuts, woolen stockings; Memoir of Rose Stein Ferber, dated August 22, 1959, Rochlin Collection, Bloom Southwest Jewish Archive, University of Arizona, Tucson.

6. The female virtues were not very different from the male, listed in one source as "courage, optimism, self-reliance, aggressiveness, loyalty, and an independent cast of mind and spirit . . . workers and stickers [not] shirkers and quitters . . . natural pioneers, born to conquer the land." Quoted in Catherine McNicol Stock, *Main Street in Crisis: The Great Depression and the Old Middle Class on the Northern Plains* (Chapel Hill: University of North Carolina Press, 1992), p. 41.

7. Population estimates extrapolated from the 1900 and 1910 censuses.

8. *Copper Era,* March 23, 1905, p. 1.

9. *Arizona Bulletin,* September 9, 1904, p. 6.

10. Turner, "The Significance of the Frontier in American History," *Annual Report of the American Historical Assocation for the Year 1893* (Washington: GPO, 1894), pp. 199–217.

11. Geo. H. Kelly, state historian, compiler, *Legislative History of Arizona, 1864–1912* (Phoenix, 1926), p. 228, from a House Resolution of the Twenty-second Territorial Legislature, 1903.

12. Richard White, "Frederick Jackson Turner and Buffalo Bill," in James Grossman, ed., *The Frontier in American Culture* (Berkeley: University of California Press, 1994), pp. 7–65.

13. Al Fernandez, in his columns for the *Copper Era* written mostly in the 1970s, honored several Mexican, Euro-Latin, and even Middle Eastern immigrants as pioneers. His counternarrative stands out precisely for its more democratic racial outlook.

14. The earliest and biggest Jewish contractors were the Zeckendorfs, the Drachmans, and the Goldwaters. Soon Jews were the leading merchants and innkeepers in many cities and mining towns, including Tombstone in its heyday.

In Clifton the Freudenthal-Lesinsky-Solomon clan dominated. Lesinsky was, of course, the father of Clifton-Morenci mining; Samuel Freudenthal was Clifton's first justice of the peace; the three families intermarried and invested in a variety of mines, cattle, and farms until I. E. Solomon of Solomonville became primarily an investment banker at the turn of the century. Lesinsky took David Abraham, father of Sam and Jake (the brothers who ran the Clifton Hotel), into partnership. Jews were numerically second only to Mexicans in Clifton's commerce at the turn of the century, and in wealth the Jews were the equals of any group other than the big copper barons. In addition to the Abrahams, J. Backstein ran Arizona Lumber, a real estate office, and the Gold Belt Mining Company; Louis Ferber owned the Bazaar Store, Clifton's only department store, as well as a haberdashery establishment and a brokerage focused on mining stocks; Morris Friedman, Charlie Burman, and M. Rabenowitz ran other dry-goods shops. Interview with Mrs. Louis Abraham, Arizona Historical Society; Floyd S. Fierman, *Guts and Ruts: The Jewish Pioneer on the Trail in the American Southwest* (New York: Ktav Publishing House, 1985); Fierman, *Roots and Boots: From Crypto-Jew in New Spain to Community Leader in the American Southwest* (Hoboken: Ktav Publishing House, 1987); Fierman, "Samuel J. Freudenthal," in *American Jewish Historical Quarterly*, 57, no. 3 (March 1968), pp. 353–435; Fierman, "Peddlers and Merchants–the Jewish Businessman on the Southwest Frontier: 1850–1880," *Password* (El Paso County Historical Society), 8 (Summer 1963), pp. 43–55; Abraham S. Chanin, *Cholent and Chorizo: Great Adventures of Pioneer Jews on the Arizona Frontier, Sometimes Kosher, Sometimes Not, But Always Fascinating!* (Tucson: Midbar Press, 1995); William J. Parish, "The German Jew and the Commercial Revolution in Territorial New Mexico, 1850–1900," *New Mexico Quarterly*, 29 (Autumn 1959), pp. 307–332; Blaine Peterson Lamb, "Jewish Pioneers in Arizona, 1850–1920" (Ph.D. diss., Arizona State University, Tempe 1982); Fernandez, "Jews of the Southwest." One of the major mercantile capitalists of the area, Harry Drachman, was said to be "the first American child born of American parents in Tucson." John George Hilzinger, *Treasure Land: A Story* (Tucson: Arizona Advancement Company, 1897), p. 78.

15. *Arizona Bulletin,* December 16, 1903, p. 1.
16. Paula Petrik's appraisal in her *No Step Backward: Women and Family on the Rocky Mountain Mining Frontier, Helena, Montana, 1865–1900* (Helena: Montana Historical Society Press, 1987), p. 9, is appropriate: Gentiles responded to the Jews with applause but also "an undercurrent of suspicion and prejudice," recommending "vigilance where credit . . . was concerned," but not allowing "prejudice to interfere with business or fellowship."
17. Quoted in Burl Noggle, "Anglo Observers of the Southwest Borderlands, 1825–1890," in *Arizona and the West*, 2 (1959), p. 123.
18. The George Frazer who was in the posse–his name is spelled variably.

19. James Clifton Colquhoun, *James Colquhoun, 1857–1954: The Man and His Work* (Perth, Scotland: privately printed by D. Leslie, 1970), pp. 16–17.

20. Stock, *Main Street in Crisis,* p. 13.

21. These are also the latest years for which these figures are available, because afterward PD's figures did not report for Detroit Copper separately. Victor A. Ciuccio, "Political Change in a Mexican-American Industrial Community" (Ph.D. diss., Pennsylvania State University, Department of Anthropology, 1975), p. 72.

22. *Phelps Dodge: A Copper Centennial 1881 to 1981,* supplement to *Arizona Pay Dirt* and *New Mexico Pay Dirt* (Bisbee: Copper Queen Pub., 1981), p. 140.

23. *Copper Era,* December 1, 1904, p. 4.

24. J. J. Wagoner, "Development of the Cattle Industry in Southern Arizona, 1870s and 80s," *New Mexico Historical Review,* 26, no. 3 (July 1951), pp. 204–224; Howard Roberts Lamar, *The Far Southwest 1846–1912: A Territorial History* (New Haven, Conn.: Yale University Press, 1966), chap. 19.

25. Wagoner, "Development"; *Clifton Clarion,* August 29, 1883; assessments reported in *Arizona Bulletin,* 1903, special souvenir edition; James M. Patton, *History of Clifton* (Clifton: Greenlee County Chamber of Commerce, 1977), pp. 118–121.

26. I am indebted for this point to Allen Hunter.

27. *El Obrero,* July 4, 1903, p. 2, editorial; *Copper Era,* June 16, 1904, pp. 1, 2; *Arizona Bulletin,* June 5, 1902, p. 2.

28. Editorial, *Arizona Bulletin,* June 5, 1903; Patton, *History of Clifton,* pp. 86–87; Roberta Watt, "History of Morenci, Arizona" (Master's thesis, University of Arizona, 1956), p. 93; *Copper Era,* April 24, 1904, and October 20, 1904.

29. At the turn of the century mines worth an estimated $100 million were officially valued at $2 million. Kelly, *Legislative History of Arizona,* pp. 194–231 passim; Patton, *History of Clifton,* pp. 150–156; Thomas E. Sheridan, *Arizona: A History* (Tucson: University of Arizona Press, 1995), p. 173.

30. Sheridan, *Arizona,* pp. 182–183.

31. Starting in the 1870s numerous relatively small investors competed to mine profitably in Clifton, and many of them operated mercantile businesses simultaneously; when gradually most of their mining failed, they exploited their land and capital in other ways. PD started investing in Morenci in 1881 and took it over in 1897, but Clifton's biggest mine owner was the much smaller Arizona Copper until 1917. Moreover, PD's control in Morenci started early enough that it could soon own all the land, while Clifton's real estate was divided among many different owners. Arizona Copper probably had neither the economic strength nor the legal ability to control Clifton.

32. These necessities do not mean that a company town was inevitable—few things are. In fact, there was no certainty that Morenci's lodes could be profitably developed at all. (No historian dwelling on an incident as contin-

gent as the orphan affair could reasonably be a believer in determinism, after all.) The predilections of individual managers and owners influenced the trajectories of the two towns. Still, the fact that Morenci was so undeveloped just when copper mining was becoming profitable made developing a company town a rational choice. My interpretation on this point largely derives from Josiah McC. Heyman, "In the Shadow of the Smokestacks: Labor and Environmental Conflict in a Company-dominated Town," in Jane Schneider and Rayna Rapp, eds., *Articulating Hidden Histories: Exploring the Influence of Eric R. Wolf* (Berkeley: University of California Press, 1995), pp. 156–174. See also Nancy Lee Pritchard, "Paradise Found? Opportunity for Mexican, Irish, Italian, and Chinese Born Individuals in Jerome Copper Mining District" (Ph.D. diss., University of Colorado, 1992), pp. 227–228.

33. Mrs. E. M. Roscoe, former president, Morenci Women's Club, May 22, 1923, in Special Collections, University of Arizona Library, Tucson.

34. Patton, *History of Clifton;* Watt, "History of Morenci"; Lynn R. Bailey, *Bisbee: Queen of the Copper Camps* (Tucson: Westernlore Press, 1983), pp. 57–59; Ernest J. Hopkins, *Financing the Frontier* (Phoenix: Valley National Bank, 1950), pp. 8–9, 51; *Copper Era,* June 9, 1904; *Morenci Leader,* August 12, 1905.

35. Jonathan D. Rosenblum, *Copper Crucible: How the Arizona Miners' Strike of 1983 Recast Labor-Management Relations in America* (Ithaca, N.Y.: ILR Press, 1995), p. 5.

36. The blueprints are in Leifur Magnusson, "Housing and Welfare Work: A Modern Copper Mining Town," *Monthly Labor Review,* 7, no. 3 (September 1918), pp. 277–284. I could find no blueprints for the PD houses in Morenci. See also Margaret Crawford, *Building the Workingman's Paradise: The Design of American Company Towns* (London: Verso, 1995); James B. Allen, *The Company Town in the American West* (Norman: University of Oklahoma Press, 1966); Keith C. Petersen, *Company Town: Potlatch, Idaho, and the Potlatch Lumber Company* (Pullman: Washington State University Press, 1987); Josiah McC. Heyman, *Life and Labor on the Border: Working People of Northeastern Sonora, Mexico, 1886–1986* (Tucson: University of Arizona Press, 1991).

37. Quotation from *Arizona Bulletin,* special souvenir edition; personal interviews with Helen Cooper, February 9, 1997, and Carmina García, February 7 and 8, 1997; interview with Hovde, by Rothschild and Hronek; Watt, "History of Morenci."

38. Mark C. Vinson, "Vanished Clifton-Morenci: An Architect's Perspective," *Journal of Arizona History,* Summer 1992, pp. 183–206. Information on the facilities and services of these Morenci buildings from *Arizona Bulletin,* 1903, special souvenir edition.

39. Interview with García.

40. The club was used to house scabs in the 1983 strike; Barbara Kingsolver,

Holding the Line: Women in the Great Arizona Mine Strike of 1983 (Ithaca, N.Y.: ILR Press, 1989), p. 51.

41. *El Obrero,* November 21, 1903, p. 4: "USTEDES PUEDEN TRATAR CON SUS LIBROS EN EL HOTEL MORENCI: Si Ud. desea comer en el magnifico y capacioso comedor del Hotel, lleve su libro a la oficina y será tomado la mismo que dinero al contado."

42. *Arizona Bulletin,* 1903, special souvenir edition.

43. Heyman, "Shadow of the Smokestacks," p. 158.

44. Vinson, "Vanished Clifton-Morenci," p. 197.

45. *Arizona Bulletin,* 1903, special souvenir edition.

46. *El Obrero,* passim; list of 1914 Morenci stores prepared by Al Fernandez.

47. García interview.

48. The following discussion of internal colonialism comes primarily from Mario Barrera, *Race and Class in the Southwest* (Notre Dame: University of Notre Dame Press, 1979); Tomás Almaguer, "Toward the Study of Chicano Colonialism," *Aztlán,* 2, no. 1 (Spring 1971), pp. 7–20; Almaguer, "Historical Notes on Chicano Oppression: The Dialectics of Racial and Class Domination in North America," *Aztlán,* 5 nos. 1 and 2 (Spring 1974); and Almaguer, *Racial Fault Lines: The Historical Origins of White Supremacy in California* (Berkeley: University of California Press, 1994); David Montejano, *Anglos and Mexicans in the Making of Modern Texas, 1836–1986* (Austin: University of Texas Press, 1987). Other sources for my comments include Edna Bonacich, "A Theory of Ethnic Antagonism: The Split Labor Market," *American Sociological Review,* 37 (October 1972), pp. 547–559; Robert Blauner, *Racial Oppression in America* (New York: Harper and Row, 1972), chap. 2; Frank Bonilla and Robert Girling, eds., *Structures of Dependency* (Stanford, mimeo, 1973); Guillermo V. Flores and Ronald Bailey, "Internal Colonialism and Racial Minorities in the U.S.: An Overview," pp. 149–160 in Bonilla and Girling, Structures of Dependency; Cardell K. Jacobson, "Internal Colonialism and Native Americans: Indian Labor in the United States from 1871 to World War II," *Social Science Quarterly,* 65, no. 1 (March 1984), pp. 158–171; Edward Murguia, *Assimilation, Colonialism, and the Mexican American People* (Austin: University of Texas Press, 1975); Norma Beatriz Chaloult and Yves Chaloult, "The Internal Colonialism Concept: Methodological Considerations," *Social and Economic Studies,* 28 (December 1979), pp. 85–99; Joseph L. Love, "Modeling Internal Colonialism: History and Prospect," *World Development,* 17 (June 1989), pp. 905–922; Sheridan, *Arizona;* Frank Copper and Ann Laura Stoler, eds., *Tensions of Empire: Colonial Cultures in a Bourgeois World* (Berkeley: University of California Press, 1997).

49. James W. Byrkit, *Forging the Copper Collar: Arizona's Labor-Management War of 1901–21* (Tucson: University of Arizona Press, 1982), p. ix.

50. Interview with Wills, by Rothschild and Hronek, tape 1.

51. Stegner, *Angle of Repose,* pp. 101–102.

52. Moynihan, Armitage, and Dichamp, *So Much to Be Done,* introduction, p. xv.

53. *Copper Era,* January 25, 1900.

54. Shortridge, *Childhood Memories,* p. 23; interview with Mrs. Louis Abraham, "Dutch Lunch Parties," tape 2, p. 31, Arizona Historical Society; Ross, *Arizona Federation of Women's Clubs,* pp. 19–26.

55. Louise Palmer, "How We Live in Nevada," from *Overland Monthly,* May 1869, excerpted in Moynihan, Armitage, and Dichamp, *So Much to Be Done,* p. 115.

56. Fernandez, "One Week in the Life of a Clifton Resident"; Shortridge, *Childhood Memories,* chap. 7; Patton, *History of Clifton,* p. 97, from *Copper Era,* July 25, 1905.

57. Memoir of Rose Stein Ferber, p. 50; interview with Mrs. Louis Abraham, tape 2, pp. 28–29, Arizona Historical Society. On the popularity of dances in mining camps, see Elliott West, "Heathens and Angels: Childhood in the Rocky Mountain Mining Towns," *Western Historical Quarterly,* 14 (1983), pp. 145–164, and Murphy, *Mining Cultures.*

58. Interview with Mrs. Louis Abraham, tape 2, p. 29, Arizona Historical Society; interview with Hovde, by Rothschild and Hronek; *Copper Era,* January 25, 1900; Lin B. Feil, "Helvetia: Boom Town of the Santa Ritas," *Journal of Arizona History,* 9, no. 2 (1968), p. 86.

59. The 1904 smoker is described at length in the *Copper Era,* April 24, 1904. On other mining-camp balls, see Feil, "Helvetia," pp. 77–95.

60. Wagoner, "Development," tells this story, p. 432.

61. The following discussion of fraternal and sororal organizations is derived from Hilzinger, *Treasure Land,* pp. 126–127, 146–147; interview with Jesse Snyder, February 8, 1997, Clifton; Watt, "History of Morenci"; Patton, *History of Clifton;* Shortridge, *Childhood Memories,* chap. 8; Arthur Preuss, compiler, *A Dictionary of Secret and Other Societies* (St. Louis: B. Herder Book Co., 1924); Lynn Dumenil, *Freemasonry and American Culture, 1880–1930* (Princeton, N.J.: Princeton University Press, 1984); Elizabeth Jameson, "High-Grade and Fissures: A Working-class History of the Cripple Creek, Colorado, Gold Mining District, 1890–1905" (Ph.D. diss., University of Michigan, 1987), esp. chap. 6 and appendix; Clifford Putney, "Service over Secrecy: How Lodge-style Fraternalism Yielded Popularity to Men's Service Clubs," *Journal of Popular Culture,* 27 (Summer 1993), pp. 179–190.

62. Watt, "History of Morenci," p. 101, quoting from *Morenci Leader,* November 23, 1907.

63. Unidentified Mandin letter, quoted in several clippings, in NYFH Clippings Scrapbook.

64. Thomas B. Davis, *Aspects of Freemasonry in Modern Mexico: An Example of Social Cleavage* (New York: Vantage Press, 1976), e.g., pp. xxiii and 57.

65. *Copper Era,* March 30, 1905. On admitting all "whites" into the orders, see interview with Mrs. Louis Abraham, tape 2, p. 28, Arizona Historical Society;

Arizona Bulletin, 1903, special souvenir edition, passim. On Catholic attitudes see Preuss, *Dictionary.*

66. Shortridge, *Childhood Memories,* pp. 40–41. Visiting blackface shows are also reported by Fernandez in "Early Day Entertainment in Our Mining District" and "Early Day Fun."

67. His wife recollected, "My husband missed his . . . ah . . . he should have been a minstrel man . . . he was just an artist at it really." Interview tape 1, pp. 9–10, Arizona Historical Society. The whole Abraham family was musical. Jake in particular could also minstrelize and played the banjo in Clifton's Hoorah Orchestra, which consisted of two banjos, two guitars, two mandolins, a clarinet, and a cello.

68. My discussion of minstrelsy relies heavily on Eric Lott, *Love and Theft: Black-face Minstrelsy and the American Working Class* (New York: Oxford University Press, 1993), esp. "Facing West," pp. 201–210.

69. For example, see *By-laws of Coronado Lodge no. 8 of Free and Accepted Masons* (Clifton, 1910).

70. Lamb, "Jewish Pioneers," pp. 257–261; *Arizona Bulletin,* 1903, supplement.

71. The following discussion of white women's organizations comes from these sources: Ross, *Arizona Federation of Women's Clubs,* passim; Boehringer, "Mary Elizabeth Post," p. 9; *CoHoSo,* Clifton High School newspaper, 1, no. 1 (1920–1921), p. 1, from Greenlee County Historical Society, Clifton; Mrs. Jean M'Kee Kenaston, M.E., *History of the Order of the Eastern Star* (Cedar Rapids, Iowa: Torch Press, 1917), pp. 200–203; Summers, memoir in *Arizona Memories,* pp. 72–73.

72. I am indebted primarily to the work of Peggy Pascoe, *Relations of Rescue: The Search for Female Moral Authority in the American West, 1874–1939* (New York: Oxford University Press, 1990), in my interpretation of this women's moral housecleaning.

73. *Bisbee Daily Review,* October 9, 1904, p. 4.

74. Ross, *Arizona Federation of Women's Clubs,* p. 21.

75. Darlis Miller, "Cross-Cultural Marriages in the Southwest: The New Mexico Experience, 1846–1900," in *New Mexico Women: Intercultural Perspectives* (Albuquerque: University of New Mexico Press, 1986), p. 153.

76. Kathleen M. Brown, *Good Wives, Nasty Wenches, and Anxious Patriarchs: Gender, Race, and Power in Colonial Virginia* (Chapel Hill: University of North Carolina Press, 1996), p. 33.

77. Georgellen Burnett, *We Just Toughed It Out: Women in the Llano Estacado* (El Paso: University of Texas at El Paso, Southwestern Studies no. 90, 1990), p. 7; Julie Roy Jeffrey, *Frontier Women: The Trans-Mississippi West, 1840–1880* (New York: Hill and Wang, 1979), pp. 87, 95–105.

78. Back in 1891 there had been a twenty-person Clifton congregation of a New Mexico Presbyterian synod, but it was abandoned due to lack of interest.

79. Margaret H. O'Connell, "History of First Presbyterian Church, Clifton, Arizona," typescript, 1968, GCHS; Patton, *History of Clifton,* pp. 147–149; Summers, memoir in *Arizona Memories,* p. 72; C. Louise Boehringer, "Josephine Brawley Hughes–Crusader, State Builder," *Arizona Historical Review,* 2, no. 4 (January 1930), p. 102.

80. Boehringer, "Mary Elizabeth Post," pp. 92–100.

81. Ringgold, *Frontier Days,* pp. 62–63.

82. Alton Elton Montierth, "A History of Education in Graham County" (Master's thesis, University of Arizona, 1951), p. 68. This salary was lower than elsewhere in Arizona, where female teachers averaged closer to $70 per month and male teachers $80, owing to the greater shortage of women (and of men who would do this job) and the need to offer attractive wages. See Ronald E. Butchart, "The Frontier Teacher: Arizona, 1875–1925," *Journal of the West,* 16, no. 3 (July 1977), pp. 54–67.

83. Montierth, "History of Education"; Watt, "History of Morenci," pp. 104–105; Patton, *History of Clifton,* pp. 127–133.

84. Montierth, "History of Education," p. 67, quoting *Graham County Guardian* November 17, 1905; personal letters from Joe Barriga, January 11, 1996, and August 18, 1996; interviews with García; Cooper; Snyder; Ernesto Ochoa, February 13, 1997; Andrés Padilla, February 15, 1996; and Nellie Marquez, February 15, 1996.

85. As to the reason, my hypothesis is that small merchants, workers, and people of less money and less education retained more power in Clifton in 1904 than in older towns.

86. *Bisbee Daily Review,* October 9, 1904, p. 4.

87. O'Connell, "First Presbyterian Church," p. 3.

88. Edith M. Nicholl, *Observations of a Ranch Woman in New Mexico* (Cincinnati: Editor Publishing, 1901), chap. 2.

89. Ross, *Arizona Federation of Women's Clubs,* p. 25.

90. Donald L. Kinzer, *An Episode in Anti-Catholicism: The American Protective Association* (Seattle: University of Washington Press, 1964), pp. 24–31, 102–111.

91. Maureen Fitzgerald, "Brigit's Profession: Irish-Catholic Nuns, Cultural Resistance, and the Origins of New York City's Welfare System, 1830–1917," forthcoming, typescript, introduction, p. 14.

October 2, 1904, Night

1. There were other hotels, one owned by posseman Mike Riordan, but this was the biggest and Sam Abraham was the biggest businessman after Henry Hill.

2. Annotation on photograph #1279, Arizona Historical Society, Tucson.

3. The child is incorrectly referred to as Joseph Corcoran in the transcript.

4. In 1904 alone the NYFH suffered a smallpox outbreak and a fire that forced

the evacuation of three hundred children. Undated, unidentified clippings in Sisters of Charity Archives, Mount St. Vincent College, Riverdale, NY.

5. At this time in the West, racial definitions could shift from community to community within regions. In Chapell Hill, Texas, for example, Anglos objected to the Foundling Hospital's placement of "white" orphans with Polish farm hands, with complaints very similar to those of the Clifton-Morenci Anglo women: the Poles did not speak English, did not provide adequate health care, fed them poor food. Unidentified clipping (probably reprinted from the *Galveston News*) dated June 20, 1906, in NYFH Archives.

6. The Strike

1. The following description is taken from Ronald C. Brown, *Hard-rock Miners: The Intermountain West, 1860–1920* (College Station: Texas A & M University Press, 1979); Richard Lingenfelter, *The Hardrock Miners: A History of the Mining Labor Movement in the American West, 1863–1893* (Berkeley: University of California Press, 1974); Mark Wyman, "Industrial Revolution in the West: Hard-Rock Miners and the New Technology," *Western Historical Quarterly,* January 1974; Wyman, *Hard Rock Epic: Western Miners and the Industrial Revolution, 1860–1910* (Berkeley: University of California Press, 1979); Al Fernandez interviews, February 15, 1996, and February 7, 1997; James W. Byrkit, *Forging the Copper Collar: Arizona's Labor-Management War of 1901–21* (Tucson: University of Arizona Press, 1982); Alice Hamilton, *Exploring the Dangerous Trades: The Autobiography of Alice Hamilton M.D.* (Boston: Little Brown, 1943); Mary Murphy, *Mining Cultures: Men, Women, and Leisure in Butte, 1914–41* (Urbana: University of Illinois Press, 1997); Ramón Eduardo Ruíz, *The People of Sonora and Yankee Capitalists* (Tucson: University of Arizona Press, 1988), chap. 6; "Los Mineros," PBS *American Experience* video, produced and directed by Hector Galan, 1990.

2. WPA interview with Rafael Ochoa, by José del Castillo, February 1, 1939, WPA Life Histories Collection.

3. Al Fernandez, "The Foreman."

4. Hugh G. Elwes, "Points about Mexican Labor," *Engineering and Mining Journal,* 90, no. 4 (October 1, 1910), p. 662.

5. Evan Fraser-Campbell, "The Management of Mexican Labor," *Engineering and Mining Journal,* 91, no. 22 (June 3, 1911), p. 1104.

6. E.g., from President's Mediation Commission, Sessions at Clifton, Arizona, October 25–30, 1917, p. 105, testimony of Frank McLean of Detroit Copper, making request of Salvador Medina.

7. Fraser-Campbell, "The Management," p. 1104.

8. W. S. Shelby, "Mexican Labor-Contract, Day's Pay, and Task," *Engineering*

and Mining Journal-Press, 114, no. 4 (September 30, 1922), p. 588; Fraser-Campbell, "The Management," p. 1104.

9. President's Mediation Commission, p. 98, testimony of Crespin Medina.

10. Quoted in Lingenfelter, *The Hardrock Miners,* p. 22.

11. Thomas E. Sheridan, *Los Tucsonenses: The Mexican Community in Tucson, 1854–1941* (Tucson: University of Arizona Press, 1986), p. 176; James E. Officer, "Arizona's Hispanic Perspective," Research Report of University of Arizona, May 17–20, 1981 (Phoenix: Arizona Academy, 1981), p. 86.

12. For example, in Bisbee whites were likely to earn twice what Mexicans did; Josiah McC. Heyman, "In the Shadow of the Smokestacks: Labor and Environmental Conflict in a Company-dominated Town," in Jane Schneider and Rayna Rapp, eds., *Articulating Hidden Histories: Exploring the Influence of Eric R. Wolf* (Berkeley: University of California Press, 1995), p. 189; Byrkit, *Forging the Copper Collar,* p. 29; John Rowe, *The Hard-Rock Men: Cornish Immigrants and the North American Mining Frontier* (n.p.: Barnes and Noble Import Division, 1974); Juan Gómez-Quiñones, *Mexican American Labor, 1790–1990* (Albuquerque: University of New Mexico Press, 1994), p. 81.

13. Heyman, "Shadow of the Smokestacks," p. 188.

14. The following description of milling and smelting, from research done by Ellen Baker, comes particularly from Brian Shovers et al., "Butte and Anaconda Revisited: Early-day Mining and Smelting," Montana Bureau of Mines and Geology, *Special Bulletin,* no. 99 (Billings, 1991).

15. Amid the very sparse literature on working conditions in mill and smelter work, I relied particularly on Laurie Kay Mercier, "Smelter City: Labor, Gender, and Cultural Politics in Anaconda, Montana, 1934–1980" (Ph.D. diss., University of Oregon, Department of History, 1995).

16. Arizona Copper Mss., ledgers, vol. 3, and box 11, folder 1, Special Collections, University of Arizona Library, Tucson. Overall in the western mines, rock falls, explosions, and falls down shafts each accounted for about 25 percent of accidents; Alan Derickson, *Workers' Health, Workers' Democracy: The Western Miners' Struggle, 1891–1925* (Ithaca, N.Y.: Cornell University Press, 1988), p. 38. See also Josh DeWind, *Peasants Become Miners: The Evolution of Industrial Mining Systems in Peru, 1902–1974* (New York: Garland, 1987), pp. 170–175.

17. Brown, *Hard-rock Miners,* chap. 5.

18. Ibid.

19. Arizona Copper Mss., ledgers, vol. 3, Special Collections, University of Arizona Library.

20. Derickson, *Workers' Health,* p. 37; see also Frederick L. Hoffman's articles in *Engineering and Mining Journal:* "Fatal Accidents in Metal Mining in the United States," January 14, 1904, and January 21, 1904; "Fatal Accidents in American Metal Mines," March 5, 1910; "Data on Mortality and Morbidity in Miners," June 25, 1910, and July 2, 1910. My calculation of the Clifton-Morenci rate is,

of course, inexact. The three-hundred-day year tried to take account of frequent layoffs, while in Clifton-Morenci workers may have worked on average fewer days; I do not know whether 1912 was a typical year; and I am estimating the miners at about 2,000, although there were probably fewer.

21. Sacred Heart, Record of Interments. The year 1901 was eliminated because, for reason unknown, in this year few causes of death were listed.

22. These accident death rates were not unusual in mines of this period. In nearby Jerome, between 1905 and 1907, three-quarters of all male deaths were due to mine accidents. Nancy Lee Pritchard, "Paradise Found? Opportunity for Mexican, Irish, Italian, and Chinese Born Individuals in Jerome Copper Mining District" (Ph.D. diss., University of Colorado, 1992), pp. 183–184; DeWind, *Peasants Become Miners,* p. 171.

23. Mercier, "Smelter City," pp. 107–114; Fernandez, "The Foreman"; Derickson, *Workers' Health,* pp. 36–37.

24. Derickson, *Workers' Health,* pp. 36–37, 53–54; Mercier, "Smelter City."

25. Frederick L. Hoffman, "Pulmonary Diseases among Miners," *Engineering and Mining Journal,* March 11, 1911; James C. Foster, "The Western Dilemma: Miners, Silicosis, and Compensation," *Labor History,* 26, no. 2 (1985), pp. 268–287; Wyman, "Industrial Revolution," pp. 42–43; Elliott Leyton, *Dying Hard: The Ravages of Industrial Carnage* (Toronto: McClelland and Steward, 1975); Derickson, *Workers' Health,* pp. 30–53; David Rosner and Gerald Markowitz, *Deadly Dust: Silicosis and the Politics of Occupational Disease in Twentieth-century America* (Princeton, N.J.: Princeton University Press, 1991); WPA interview with Ilaria Valenzuela Casillas, by Romelia Gómez, WPA Life Histories Collection; Murphy, *Mining Cultures,* p. 18; Brown, *Hard-rock Miners,* p. 93.

26. The nose hairs and mucus are part of the body's defense against dust, and some miners knew that it was best always to breathe through the nose; at least one miner reported coating the inside of his nose with vaseline to increase its filtering action. Foster, "The Western Dilemma"; Derickson, *Workers' Health,* pp. 41–44.

27. In the Matter of the Estate of Filiberto Vásquez, Final Account and Report, Greenlee County Superior Court, Clifton, various dates 1910 and 1911, Greenlee County Courthouse.

28. Douglas letters of 1905, quoted in Foster, "The Western Dilemma," p. 284.

29. Ruíz, *The People of Sonora,* p. 87.

30. It is possible only to estimate the number of mine, mill, and smelter workers in the Clifton-Morenci camp. Arizona Copper employed about 2,000, approximately half in its Metcalf mines and the rest in its various other plants; Detroit Copper employed somewhat more than 1,000; the other smaller operators, including Shannon Copper, had under 1,000 total. The 3,500 figure, from Rodolfo Acuña, *Occupied America: The Chicano's Struggle toward*

Liberation (San Francisco: Canfield Press, Harper and Row, 1972), p. 96; Phillip J. Mellinger, *Race and Labor in Western Copper: The Fight for Equality, 1896–1918* (Tucson: University of Arizona Press, 1995), pp. 36, 51; and J. J. Wagoner, "Development of the Cattle Industry in Southern Arizona, 1870s and 80s," *New Mexico Historical Review,* 26, no. 3 (July, 1951), p. 384, is probably an exaggeration. But *El Labrador*'s correspondent reported 4,000, June 5, 1903, p. 1. Nevertheless the strike was so large, so disciplined, so complex, and so difficult for the companies to suppress that I find it mysterious that labor historians have not studied it more intensively.

31. *Arizona Bulletin,* June 19, 1903.

32. The eight-hour limit began with a Utah law, upheld by the U.S. Supreme Court in 1898, and Colorado, Montana, and Nevada had passed laws by 1903.

33. Quotation from *Copper Era,* June 18, 1903; see also *Copper Era,* June 13, 1903, editorial; *Bisbee Daily Review,* June 2, 1903; *Arizona Bulletin,* June 5, 1903, for examples.

34. Joseph F. Park, "The 1903 'Mexican Affair' at Clifton," *Journal of Arizona History,* 18, no. 2 (September 1977), pp. 119–148.

35. *Miners' Magazine,* weekly of the WFM, 1903–1905, passim; Sheridan, *Los Tucsonenses,* p. 178; Gómez-Quiñones, *Mexican American Labor,* p. 81; Wyman, *Hard Rock Epic,* p. 39; W. Dirk Raat, *Revoltosos: Mexico's Rebels in the United States, 1903–1923* (College Station: Texas A & M University Press, 1981), pp. 42–44; James C. Foster, ed., *American Labor in the Southwest: The First One Hundred Years* (Tucson: University of Arizona Press, 1982), p. 22; Michael E. Casillas, "Mexicans, Labor, and Strife in Arizona, 1896–1917" (Master's thesis, University of New Mexico, 1979), pp. 6–9; Joseph F. Park, "The History of Mexican Labor in Arizona during the Territorial Period" (Master's. thesis, University of Arizona, 1961), p. 254.

36. Casillas, "Mexicans, Labor, and Strife," pp. 39–40; Casillas, "Mexican Labor Militancy in the United States: 1896–1915," *Southwest Economy and Society,* 4, no. 1 (Fall 1978); Park, "The 1903 'Mexican Affair,'" p. 135.

37. The best discussion of this history is in Yvette Huginnie, "'Strikitos': Race, Class, and Work in the Arizona Copper Industry, 1870–1920" (Ph.D. diss., Yale University, 1991).

38. U.S. Department of the Interior, *Annual Report for Fiscal Year Ended June 10, 1902* (Washington, D.C.: GPO, 1912), pp. 236, 244, reports falling copper prices.

39. This was Arizona Copper's and Detroit Copper's offer; Shannon Copper offered only $2 per day.

40. *El Labrador,* June 5, 1903; *Arizona Bulletin,* June 5, 1903; *Miners' Magazine,* October 1, 1903; *Copper Era,* June 4, 1903, and June 18, 1903; Bill O'Neal, *The Arizona Rangers* (Austin, Tex.: Eakin Press, 1987), p. 49; Park, "The 1903

'Mexican Affair,'" pp. 121, 138; Park, "The History of Mexican Labor," p. 256. *El Labrador* claimed that the Clifton-Morenci workers were receiving a 20 percent pay cut, but according to my calculations it was 10 percent.

41. This priority was characteristic of many Anglo miners' unions as well; see Wyman, "Industrial Revolution," pp. 48–50.

42. Park, "The 1903 'Mexican Affair,'" pp. 138–139; Victor S. Clark, "Mexican Labor in the United States," U.S. Bureau of Labor, *Bulletin,* no. 78, 1908, p. 492.

43. *Copper Era,* June 18, 1903; quotation from Jennie Parks Ringgold, *Frontier Days in the Southwest* (San Antonio: Naylor Company, 1952), p. 165; Captain Thomas H. Rynning, *Gun Notches: The Life Story of a Cowboy-Soldier* (New York: Frederick A. Stokes, 1931), p. 231; see also Wagoner, "Development," p. 386.

44. Quoted in Park, "The 1903 'Mexican Affair,'" pp. 138–139.

45. Perhaps this racist mistake accounts for why we know so little about this organization the Mexican miners were creating. Not even its name has been preserved in any records, so disinterested in Mexican political life were those who created the public record of newspapers and court documents.

46. Cheryl Harris, "Whiteness as Property," *Harvard Law Review,* June 1993, pp. 1709–1791.

47. *Arizona Bulletin,* June 19, 1903, and June 26, 1903, for example. Mellinger, *Race and Labor,* asserts that 20 percent of the Italians were paid at the Mexican rate and none at the Anglo rate, p. 42.

48. Criminal Register of Actions, Territory of Arizona, Graham County Superior Court, Solomonville, Case #965–1/2, ledger book entries June 26–November 4, 1903; *Arizona Bulletin,* June 19, 1903. I have corrected the spellings of names when I knew what was correct; a bewildering variety of spellings appear in the different entries and reports. In addition the number of defendants varies in different references in the court ledger book.

49. James H. Bassett, former Arizona Ranger, reminiscence, dictated to Law and Legislative Reference Librarian (no name given), ADLAPR, Phoenix, 1936.

50. A *corrido* about Salcido appears in the video "Las Mineros" by Hector Galan.

51. Mellinger, *Race and Labor,* gives this number, pp. 50–51. But the disposition of charges against all the different defendants cannot be determined from the fragmentary record I saw at the courthouse.

52. Illustrating the far from sharp distinction between these groups is the story of David Arzate, who joined the posse deputized by Sheriff Parks to hold off the strikers and protect the scabs. The contemporary sources sometimes call Arzate Mexican, sometimes Italian. Whatever his ethnic background, and he might have been both, he became notorious and despised by the strikers for serving the other side. Because "Little Dave" could "talk good Mexican" he was a necessary supplement to John Parks's pidgin Spanish. After the strike

Arzate became an all-around token in the Anglo power structure, serving on juries and as a translator in court. *Arizona Bulletin,* 1903, special souvenir edition; Ringgold, *Frontier Days,* p. 170; Mellinger, *Race and Labor,* p. 43. Two other Latino names appear on the posse list (out of a total of sixty): Jesús Alvarez and Alberto Mungia.

53. Foremen had commonly operated with independent authority throughout the nineteenth century, and they maintained that authority in most industries; the campaign to centralize management was just beginning.

54. *Bisbee Daily Review,* June 12, 1903. Does this sound fanciful? Yet other consuls during this period intervened to try to protect strikers of their countries, and just three years later the Arizona Rangers went into Mexico to suppress a strike at Cananea. Why should these workers have been sure that their country would remain a second-rate power? David Montgomery pointed out to me that the Hungarian consul intervened during the 1909 McKees Rock strike, the Russian consul supported Finnish strikers in Michigan in 1907, Italian consuls in several eastern cities openly fought the power of *padrones* (subcontractors), and British authorities protested the incarceration of British black seamen in South Carolina. "Long before the US championed human rights elsewhere, other governments championed them in the United States." Montgomery, personal letter, May 20, 1998.

55. Ringgold, *Frontier Days,* pp. 165–166; *Arizona Bulletin,* June 12, 1903.

56. Testimony of John Murray, secretary of the Pan-American Federation of Labor Conference Committee, President's Mediation Commission, pp. 189ff. In my discussion of Mexican unionism I am indebted to Rodney D. Anderson, *Outcasts in Their Own Land: Mexican Industrial Workers, 1906–1911* (DeKalb: Northern Illinois University Press, 1976), chap. 2.

57. *Copper Era,* June 5, 1903, p. 3. The association of unions with fraternal organizations was evident not just in mining towns; for example, a railroad workers' union in Laredo, Texas, was connected to Masonic lodges in that city; Emilio Zamora, Jr., "Chicano Socialist Labor Activity in Texas, 1900–1920," *Aztlán,* 6, no. 2 (1975), p. 223.

58. Hernández, *Mutual Aid,* p. 36; Mellinger, *Race and Labor,* pp. 45–47. Mellinger claims that the benefit societies did not play a significant role in the strike, as part of arguing that workers' consciousness and activism derive *only* from their point-of-production experience; he explicitly denounces "gendering" and analyses that focus on communities, pp. 13–14.

59. *Alianza Hispano Americana* (monthly), March 1908, pp. 2–3; Mellinger, *Race and Labor,* p. 45.

60. In this respect the Alianza was similar to the white fraternal organizations and, in fact, it adopted in 1902 the rules and rituals of the Ancient Order of United Workmen, a white group with a chapter in Clifton; the Knights of Pythias had a lodge in Cananea, a nearby mining town in Sonora, which drew

in skilled miners. Emilio Zamora, Jr., *The World of the Mexican Worker in Texas* (College Station: Texas A & M Press, 1993), pp. 72–77, 92–109; Juan Gómez-Quiñones, *Roots of Chicano Politics, 1600–1940* (Albuquerque: University of New Mexico Press, 1994), pp. 312–323; Kaye Lynn Briegel, "Alianza Hispano-Americana, 1894–1965: A Mexican American Fraternal Insurance Society" (Ph.D. diss., University of California, Los Angeles, Department of History, 1974), pp. 53; Ruíz, *The People of Sonora,* p. 195.

61. David Arzate was an officer in 1905, along with former strike leaders. *El Labrador,* January 6, 1905.

62. This does not mean that they could always keep controversy out. In the next Clifton-Morenci strike scabs were kicked out of the Alianza, a severe economic penalty; we do not know if that was happening in 1903. President's Mediation Commission, p. 491, Ainsa testimony.

63. President's Mediation Commission, p. 185, Murray testimony.

64. *Alianza Hispano Americana,* March 1908, p. 3.

65. Quoted in Ruíz, *The People of Sonora,* p. 108.

66. I am grateful to Dick Cluster and Lisandro Perez for help in translating these Resolutions of the Sociedad de Trabajadores Unidos de Nuevo Mexico, in *La Hormiga de Oro,* January 16, 1904, p. 2. I cite this declaration from a New Mexican union because there are no such records from the Clifton-Morenci group. The New Mexican labor newspapers were better established at this time, and they had readers in Clifton-Morenci; see *El Labrador,* June 5, 1903.

67. Alan Knight, "The Working Class and the Mexican Revolution, c. 1900–1920," *Journal of Latin American Studies,* 16 (May 1984), p. 59; A. Yvette Huginnie, "A New Hero Comes to Town: The Anglo Mining Engineer and 'Mexican Labor' as Contested Terrain in Southeastern Arizona, 1880–1920," *New Mexico Historical Review,* 69 (October 1994); Alonzo Crittenden, "Management of Mexican Labor," *Mining and Scientific Press,* August 20, 1921, pp. 267–269; Shelby, "Mexican Labor-Contract"; Clark, "Mexican Labor," pp. 486ff. Quotation from Crittenden, "Management," p. 268.

68. Shelby, "Mexican Labor-Contract," p. 588.

69. Anderson, *Outcasts,* pp. 68–72; Knight, "The Working Class," p. 56.

70. James D. Cockcroft, *Intellectual Precursors of the Mexican Revolution, 1900–1913* (Austin: University of Texas Press, Institute of Latin American Studies monograph no. 14, 1968), pp. 47–48 and passim; Knight, "The Working Class," pp. 51–79; Zamora, "Chicano Socialist," pp. 221–236; Anderson, *Outcasts,* pp. 313–314; Barry Carr, *Marxism and Communism in Twentieth-century Mexico* (Lincoln: University of Nebraska Press, 1992).

71. Zamora, "Chicano Socialist"; Resolutions of the Sociedad de Trabajadores Unidos de Nuevo Mexico, p. 2.

72. Zamora, "Chicano Socialist," p. 228; "Official Election Returns of Graham County," *Copper Era,* December 1, 1904, p. 4.

73. 1902 Graham County Great Register (voting roll), ADLAPR. I figured these proportions crudely, on the basis of Spanish-language surnames.

74. Kenneth L. Steward and Arnoldo De León, "Literacy among *Inmigrantes* in Texas, 1850–1900," *Latin American Research Review,* 20, no. 3 (1985), pp. 180–187.

75. Throughout Mexico industrial workers had higher than average literacy rates; Anderson, *Outcasts,* p. 198.

76. President's Mediation Commission, pp. 11–12, testimony of H. S. McCluskey, miners' representative.

77. *El Labrador,* July 15, 1904.

78. President's Mediation Commission, p. 186, Murray testimony.

79. I am grateful to David Montgomery for reminding me of this practice.

80. Zamora, *The World,* p. 95.

81. Barry Carr, "Labor Internationalism in the Era of Nafta," 1994 unpub. paper; thanks to Allen Hunter for this reference.

82. Raat, *Revoltosos,* pp. 24–29; David M. Pletcher, *Rails, Mines, and Progress: Seven American Promoters in Mexico, 1867–1911* (Ithaca, N.Y.: Cornell University Press, 1958), p. 236; Mellinger, *Race and Labor,* pp. 54–57; Cockcroft, *Intellectual Precursors.*

83. Ruíz, *The People of Sonora,* p. 87.

84. *Arizona Bulletin,* June 19, 1903.

85. Ibid.

86. Alice Hamilton, *Exploring the Dangerous Trades: The Autobiography of Alice Hamilton MD* (Boston: Little Brown, 1943), p. 214.

87. Edwin H. Davison, "Labor in Mexican Mines," Mining and Scientific Press, 92, no. 15 (April 14, 1906), p. 260; Huginnie, "A New Hero"; Elwes, "Points"; Fraser-Campbell, "The Management"; Crittenden, "Management"; Shelby, "Mexican Labor-Contract"; Clark, "Mexican Labor," pp. 486ff.

88. It was alleged, possibly correctly, that Laustaunau was a professional organizer sent from Chicago. *Copper Era* coverage, passim; O'Neal, *Arizona Rangers,* p. 49; Carl M. Rathbun, "Keeping the Peace along the Mexican Border," *Harper's Weekly,* November 17, 1906; Mellinger, *Race and Labor.*

89. Huginnie, "A New Hero," p. 337.

90. President's Mediation Commission, pp. 528, 518, 523, testimony of "citizens" J. C. Gaines and J. F. Nichols.

91. William F. Willoughby, "Employers' Associations for Dealing with Labor in the United States," *Quarterly Journal of Economics,* 20 (November 1905), pp. 110–150; Mellinger, *Race and Labor,* p.

92. The following narrative was compiled from coverage in the *Copper Era, Bisbee Daily Review,* and *Arizona Bulletin;* Ringgold, *Frontier Days,* chap. 5; Rynning, *Gun Notches,* chap. 30; Byrkit, *Forging the Copper Collar;* Bassett, reminiscence.

93. *Bisbee Daily Review,* June 11, 1903, p. 1.

94. Ibid., June 5, 1903, p. 1.

95. Mellinger, *Race and Labor,* pp. 43, 54–55.

96. Bassett, reminiscence.

97. Ibid.

98. O'Neal, *Arizona Rangers,* p. 39, for example.

99. My thanks go to Kerry Woodward for painstaking searches of the census for these men.

100. Bassett, reminiscence.

101. Rathbun, "Keeping the Peace," pp. 1632–1634; Park, "The 1903 'Mexican Affair,'" p. 140; O'Neal, *Arizona Rangers;* Acuña, *Occupied America,* p. 95.

102. Bassett, reminiscence.

103. Graham County Superior Court, Criminal Register of Actions, Case #965–1/2, ledger book entries June 26–November 4, 1903. The record does not indicate whether Relles was convicted.

104. Information on Parks from his sister's memoir, Ringgold, *Frontier Days;* WPA interview with Parks by Kathlyn M. Lathrop, WPA Life Histories Collection; *Arizona Bulletin,* 1903, special souvenir edition. On conflict with the rangers, see *Copper Era,* passim. There was probably already competition about who, the rangers or the sheriff, was to get credit for the recapture of Augustín Chacón. Open conflict broke out following another Clifton flood in January 1905, when the Rangers arrested thirty-six Mexicans wholesale for theft and drunkenness; Deputy Sheriff Hobbs refused to receive them, and most of Clifton denounced the arrests as wholly without foundation; the district attorney then dismissed charges against all but one. The rangers responded with a bizarre harassment arrest of Lee Hobbs for murder, although he was nowhere near the scene of the crime. See *Copper Era,* April 13, 1905, and April 20, 1905; for the rangers' side of the story, see Rynning's version, *Copper Era,* April 27, 1905.

105. O'Neal, *Arizona Rangers,* p. 55.

106. Rynning, *Gun Notches,* p. 232.

107. Rynning, as told to the *Copper Era,* June 13, 1903.

108. Ringgold, *Frontier Days,* p. 167.

109. Contemporaries interpreted Parks's behavior in two ways: either he was trying to practice restraint, or he was stalling until the forces on his side were more numerous.

110. Charles Herner, *The Arizona Rough Riders* (Tucson: University of Arizona Press, 1970), pp. 43, 56, 170–171.

111. Ringgold, *Frontier Days,* p. 174; Bassett, reminiscences; O'Neal, *Arizona Rangers,* p. 51.

112. Larry D. Ball, *Desert Lawmen: The High Sheriffs of New Mexico and Arizona, 1846–1912* (Albuquerque: University of New Mexico Press, 1992), pp. 257, 287; Billy McGinty, *The Old West as Told by Billy McGinty* (n.p.: Ripley Review,

1937), pp. 77–78. Sheriffs in those days were often charged with collecting taxes so they had ample opportunity for corruption and for demanding loyalty.

113. Mellinger, *Race and Labor,* pp. 52–53, quoting *Arizona Republican.*

114. The fact that Governor Brodie had been the first commander of the Arizona National Guard may have inclined him to oblige.

115. *Copper Era,* June 11, 1903; *El Labrador,* June 12, 1903, p. 2.

116. "The sulphur dioxide entered the leaves of plants, combined with the moisture in the plants to form hydrosulphuric acid, and burned up" vegetation; DeWind, *Peasants,* pp. 230–234. See also M. L. Quinn, "Industry and Environment in the Appalachian Copper Basin, 1890–1930," *Technology and Culture,* 34, no. 3 (1993), pp. 575–612; Samuel Truett, e-mail communication, April 11, 1996; Donald Mac Millan, "A History of the Struggle to Abate Air Pollution from Copper Smelters of the Far West, 1885–1933" (Ph.D. diss., University of Montana, 1973).

117. Afterward Arizona Copper and Clifton residents jointly paid for a ten-foot stone wall along Chase Creek. Another flood in 1905 was a repeat: a tailings dam burst, the Chase Creek area was a complete loss, and eighteen people died—two "Americans" and the remainder Mexican. Only one adobe building did not go down in the flooded sections; many Mexicans moved into it and called it "La Arca de Noe." There was talk of abandoning the town. There was much bitterness against the company, and nineteen "citizens" sued for negligence; the company managed to delay until 1912, then settled for a payment of $5,000. This flood also brought big losses to Arizona Copper; afterward it built much better floodwalls of slag mortared together, sixteen inches thick. *Copper Era,* June 25, 1903; James M. Patton, *History of Clifton* (Clifton: Greenlee County Chamber of Commerce, 1977), pp. 80–84.

118. *Miners' Magazine,* August 1903; Graham County Superior Court, Criminal Register of Actions, Territory of Arizona, Case #965–1/2, ledger book entries June 26–November 4, 1903.

119. *Arizona Bulletin,* July 2, 1903.

120. Ibid., June 26, 1903. Tuthill went on to command the Arizona National Guard for years and to serve as a Graham County representative to the Arizona Constitutional Convention of 1910; see Wagoner, "Development," pp. 462, 465.

121. *Bisbee Daily Review,* June 13, 1903.

122. José Amaro Hernández, *Mutual Aid for Survival: The Case of the Mexican American* (Malabar, Fla.: Krieger, 1983), p. 43; David J. Weber, *Myth and the History of the Hispanic Southwest* (Albuquerque: University of New Mexico Press, 1988), p. 218; James R. Kluger, *The Clifton-Morenci Strike: Labor Difficulty in Arizona, 1915–1916* (Tucson: University of Arizona Press, 1970), p. 23.

123. Casillas, "Mexicans, Labor, and Strife," p. 21.

124. *Clifton Clarion,* September 16, 1885, January 11, 1888, and April 19, 1889, quoted in Roberta Watt, "History of Morenci, Arizona" (Master's thesis, University of Arizona, 1956), pp. 29–30.
125. The WFM promoted three further anti-alien bills: prohibiting noncitizens from working on public projects; restricting the importation of contract labor or hiring of aliens; and excluding non-English speakers from hazardous work. The first passed, the others were defeated. In 1914 the unions used the initiative and got an overwhelming popular vote to require that 80 percent of employees of any firm had to be citizens; this Arizona Anti-Alien Law was declared unconstitutional by a U.S. District Court in California and then by the U.S. Supreme Court on November 1, 1915. Discussion in *Survey,* 35 (November 13, 1915), p. 155; *Outlook,* 109 (January 20, 1915), pp. 109–110. Casillas, "Mexicans, Labor, and Strife," pp. 8–9; *Congressional Record,* 61st Cong., 2d sess., 1910, pp. 8321–8332; Sheridan, *Arizona,* pp. 173–179.
126. In the next decades this fearful view of Mexicans would become commonplace where there were large settlements of Mexican workers, in railroads and sharecropping as well as mines. "They are Bolsheviks and want to run every deal they are in on," complained one Anglo in the early 1920s. Douglas E. Foley with Clarice Mota, Donald E. Post, and Ignacio Lozano, *From Peones to Politicos: Class and Ethnicity in a South Texas Town, 1900–1987* (Austin: University of Texas Press, orig. 1977, rev. 1988), p. 49.
127. *Bisbee Daily Review,* June 14, 1903.
128. Byrkit, *Forging the Copper Collar;* Prassel, Frank Prassel, *The Western Peace Officer: A Legacy of Law and Order* (Norman: University of Oklahoma Press, 1972), pp. 116, 163 on Wheeler.
129. *Bisbee Daily Review,* June 13, 1903.
130. *Arizona Bulletin,* June 26, 1903.
131. Ibid., October 16, 1903.
132. Great Registers of Graham and Greenlee Counties, 1894, 1902, and 1922, ADLAPR. The Territorial Legislative Assembly offered the franchise not only to male natural and naturalized citizens but also to those "who shall have declared on oath before a competent court of record his intention to become a citizen." The evidence from the actual voter registers suggests, however, that some men were taken at their word without the requirement that they execute an oath in court. Some of this decline in Mexican voting followed from legal obstacles to voting: a poll tax intermittently in force after 1875, repealed in 1901; differential enforcement of the requirement to prove naturalization; and a literacy requirement passed, along with other burdensome registration requirements, in 1909. Some of the nonvoting resulted from the inability of Mexicans to get candidates and issues representing their interests into the political discourse.
133. It also created the conditions for internationalism in the labor movement, at

a time when the WFM was actively seeking to develop non-U.S. connections, an opportunity the WFM did not seize.

134. Mellinger, *Race and Labor,* p. 56.

October 3–4, 1904

1. George Swayne to Michael J. Scanlan, commissioner, State of New York Board of Charities, n.d., NYFH Archives.
2. *El Paso Herald,* October 8, 1904.
3. Swayne to Scanlan.
4. *El Paso Herald,* October 8, 1904.
5. This is the story from Anthony Blake Brophy, *Foundlings on the Frontier: Racial and Religious Conflict in Arizona Territory, 1904–1905* (Tucson: University of Arizona Press, 1972), p. 60. But the *El Paso Herald* account of October 8, 1904, reports that Dunagan gave the children to Frazer and Archie Morrison.
6. We do not know the name of the child who became a Davis living in Los Angeles.

7. Vigilantism

1. In my interpretation, I am indebted to the work of Richard Maxwell Brown, notably his *Strain of Violence: Historical Studies of American Violence and Vigilantism* (New York: Oxford University Press, 1975); and "The American Vigilante Tradition," in Hugh Davis Graham and Ted Robert Gurr, eds., *The History of Violence in America: Historical and Comparative Perspectives, A Report Submitted to the National Commission on the Causes and Prevention of Violence* (New York: Praeger, 1969), esp. pp. 179–180. I also learned from Samuel Walker, *Popular Justice: A History of American Criminal Justice* (New York: Oxford University Press, 1980), and H. Jon Rosenbaum and Peter C. Sederberg, eds., *Vigilante Politics* (Philadelphia: University of Pennsylvania Press, 1976).
2. Quoted in Paul A. Gilje, *Rioting in America* (Bloomington: Indiana University Press, 1996), p. 80.
3. Christian G. Fritz, "Popular Sovereignty, Vigilantism, and the Constitutional Right of Revolution," *Pacific Historical Review,* 63, no. 1 (1994), pp. 39–66.
4. Stephen Kantrowitz, *Ben Tillman and the Reconstruction of White Supremacy* (Chapel Hill: University of North Carolina Press, forthcoming, 2000).
5. Frank Richard Prassel, *The Western Peace Officer: A Legacy of Law and Order* (Norman: University of Oklahoma Press, 1972). Joe B. Frantz in "The Frontier Tradition: An Invitation to Violence," chap. 4, in Graham and Gurr, *The History of Violence,* cited in n. 1, contradicts himself on this point, alleging that vigilantism arises where regular justice did not reach, p. 138, but also noting how often official lawmen participated in vigilantism, pp. 131–132. For the

myth that vigilantes acted when there was no formal justice, see Hubert Howe
Bancroft, *Popular Tribunals,* vol. 1 (San Francisco: History Co., 1887), p. 10;
Bruce L. Benson, "Reciprocal Exchange as the Basis for Recognition of Law:
Examples from American History," *Journal of Libertarian Studies,* 10, no. 1 (Fall
1991), pp. 53–82.

6. David Grimsted, "Rioting in its Jacksonian Setting," *American Historical Review,* 77, no. 2 (April 1972), pp. 361–397, makes a thoughtful attempt to
distinguish "riot" from revolutionary violence, insurrection, group criminality, civil disobedience, and symbolic violence, p. 365.

7. Philip J. Ethington, *The Public City: The Political Construction of Urban Life in
San Francisco, 1850–1900* (Cambridge: Cambridge University Press, 1994);
Mary P. Ryan, *Civic Wars: Democracy and Public Life in the American City during
the Nineteenth Century* (Berkeley: University of California Press, 1997),
pp. 139–145. Consider also the "squatter governments" in Arizona, Colorado, Nevada, and Dakota as cases of vigilantism. Benson, "Reciprocal Exchange," misses this point. He cites the San Francisco vigilantism episode
as proof that law can exist without a state, failing to grasp that the vigilantes
became the state.

8. William E. Burrows, "The Vigilante Rides Again," *Harvard Magazine,* 75
(December 1975), p. 38, and Burrows, *Vigilante!* (New York: Harcourt Brace
Jovanovich, 1976).

9. In this respect most historical vigilante movements were quite different from
today's militias. The latter consider themselves "sovereign citizens" subordinate to no government (or, sometimes, as in the case of the Posse Comitatus,
only to the county sheriff) and their property as absolutely immune from any
governmental claims. Historical vigilantes did not reject the supremacy of
state and national governments. Mark Pitcavage, "Common Law and Uncommon Courts: An Overview of the Common Law Court Movement,"
available on his website www.militia-watchdog.org/common/htm.

10. Frantz, "The Frontier Tradition," pp. 128–129. See also Grimsted, "Rioting,"
pp. 361–397.

11. David A. Johnson, "Vigilance and the Law: The Moral Authority of Popular
Justice in the Far West," *American Quarterly,* 33, no. 5 (Winter 1981), p. 564.

12. Quoted in Michael James Pfeifer, "Lynching and Criminal Justice in Regional
Context: Iowa, Wyoming, and Louisiana, 1878–1946" (Ph.D. diss., University
of Iowa, 1998), p. 131.

13. Also from Wyoming, 1902, quoted in ibid., p. 89.

14. Johnson, "Vigilance and the Law."

15. John S. Kendall, "'Who Killa De Chief?'" *Louisiana Historical Quarterly,* 22
(1939), p. 492; see also John E. Coxe, "The New Orleans Mafia Incident," in
Louisiana Historical Quarterly, 20 (1937), pp. 1067–1110; Richard Gambino,
*Vendetta: A True Story of the Worst Lynching in America, the Mass Murder of
Italian-Americans in New Orleans in 1891, the Vicious Motivations behind It, and*

the Tragic Repercussions That Linger to This Day (Garden City, N.Y.: Doubleday, 1977).

16. For a related perspective, see Edward Stettner, "Vigilantism and Political Theory," in Rosenbaum and Sederberg, *Vigilante Politics,* pp. 64–75. Brown tries to distinguish objectively between socially constructive and socially destructive vigilantism. The former occurs where the vigilantes represent a community consensus and thus influence the community toward greater coherence and order, the latter where they intensify civil conflict. Unfortunately, as the Clifton-Morenci case illustrates par excellence, no such distinction can be maintained. To say the least, community "consensus" often rests on persecution or exclusion of minority opinion.

17. Frantz, "The Frontier Tradition," pp. 128–129.

18. Quoted in Lynn Perrigo, "Law and Order in Early Colorado Mining Camps," *Mississippi Valley Historical Review,* 28 (June 1941), p. 52.

19. James M. Patton, *History of Clifton* (Clifton: Greenlee County Chamber of Commerce, 1977), pp. 102–104.

20. Robert E. Cunningham, *Trial By Mob* (Stillwater, Okla.: Redland Press, 1957), pp. 23–24.

21. Frantz, "The Frontier Tradition," p. 129.

22. Johnson, "Vigilance and the Law," p. 565; Pfeifer, "Lynching," p. 108.

23. Quoted in Burrows, "The Vigilante Rides Again," p. 38.

24. Richard Maxwell Brown, "Western Violence: Structure, Values, Myth," *Western Historical Quarterly,* 24 (February 1993), pp. 4–20; idem, *Strain of Violence;* idem, "The American Vigilante Tradition." On the question whether Western violence has been exaggerated, see Chapter 3, n. 26.

25. Richard Maxwell Brown has distinguished between old and new vigilantism. A classic case of the "old" anticriminal sort might be that in the Montana mining camps where during the years 1863–1865 a gang of road agents, led by a crooked sheriff, had terrorized the towns; finally abjuring the residents' passivity and intimidation, an anonymous posse captured and hanged thirty men. The San Francisco Vigilance Committee of 1856–the largest such movement in U.S. history–marked a transition, in Brown's terms, to a "new vigilantism," which went after ethnic-religious subordinates (Irish Catholics) in order to unseat a Democratic political machine. But Brown's distinction, between old and new types applies only on average, and it can become difficult to draw the line. Among numerous accounts of these episodes, I have used: Thomas Josiah Dimsdale, *The Vigilantes of Montana, or, Popular Justice in the Rocky Mountains* (Norman: University of Oklahoma Press, 1953; orig. 1866); R. E. Mather and F. E. Boswell, *Vigilante Victims: Montana's 1864 Hanging Spree* (San Jose: History West, 1991); Helen Fitzgerald Sanders, ed., *X. Beidler: Vigilante* (Norman: University of Oklahoma Press, 1957); Burrows, *Vigilante!* Ernest Haycox, *Alder Gulch* (New York: Grosset and Dunlap, 1941); Ethington, *The Public City;* Wayne Gard, *Frontier Justice* (Norman: University of Oklahoma Press, 1949).

26. Bruce E. Boyden, "'The Best Men of the Community': The Social Order of Tombstone, Arizona, and the 'Gunfight at the O.K. Corral,'" ms., November 1996, author's collection.

27. Johnson, "Vigilance and the Law."

28. Duane A. Smith, *Rocky Mountain Mining Camps: The Urban Frontier* (Niwot: University Press of Colorado, 1992, orig. Indiana University Press, 1967), pp. 87–90.

29. Brown, *Strain of Violence,* p. 103.

30. W. Fitzhugh Brundage's taxonomy of types of lynching, in his *Lynching in the New South: Georgia and Virginia, 1880–1930* (Urbana: University of Illinois Press, 1993), does not fit well the varieties of vigilantism.

31. Mather and Boswell, *Vigilante Victims,* pp. 171ff; Burrows, *Vigilante!* p. 157; J. W. Smurr, "Afterthoughts on the Vigilantes," *Montana, The Magazine of History,* 8, no. 2 (April 1958); Brown, *Strain of Violence,* p. 126.

32. Johnson, "Vigilance and the Law," pp. 573–575. I use "Hispanic" because he does.

33. Gerald G. Raun, "Seventeen Days in November: The Lynching of Antonio Rodriguez and American-Mexican Relations, November 3–19, 1910," *Journal of Big Bend Studies,* 7 (January 1995), pp. 157–179; Editorial, "A Mexican Boycott," *The Independent,* 69, no. 3233 (November 17, 1910), pp. 1111–1112.

34. Crystal Feimster has collected scores of cases in which women were active lynchers; see her "Ladies and Lynching: A Gendered Discourse of Mob Violence in the New South," Ph.D. diss., Princeton, forthcoming.

35. A photocopy of the invitation is with the centerfold illustrations in Jennie Parks Ringgold, *Frontier Days in the Southwest* (San Antonio: Naylor, 1952). Other cases I have found in a cursory search include Jean F. Riss, "The Lynching of Francisco Torres," *Journal of Mexican American History,* 2, no. 2 (Spring 1972), pp. 90–121; and a lynching in Globe, Arizona, in 1882 of two Anglo bandits, in Margaret Wheeler Ross, compiler, *History of the Arizona Federation of Women's Clubs and Its Forerunners* (n.p., n.d.), p. 328. Emma Krentz recollects a vigilante hanging of 1888 or 1889 in *Arizona Historical Review,* 6, no. 1 (January 1935), p. 85; Wallace Stegner, in *Angle of Repose* (New York: Penguin, 1971), offers a fictional example of the impact of witnessing a hanging on a woman. Women's attendance at large-audience lynchings can be found in Brundage, *Lynching in the New South,* pp. 37–42, and Arthur Raper, *The Tragedy of Lynching* (Chapel Hill: University of North Carolina Press, 1933).

36. Cunningham, *Trial by Mob,* p. 10.

37. Dimsdale, *Vigilantes of Montana,* p. 80. Dimsdale's story is repeated by Virginia Rowe Towle, *Vigilante Woman* (South Brunswick, N.J.: A. S. Barners, 1966); Sanders, *X. Beidler;* and Haycox, *Alder Gulch,* among others.

38. Frantz, "The Frontier Tradition," pp. 140–141; Oscar O. Mueller, "The Central Montana Vigilante Raids of 1884," *Montana, The Magazine of History,* 1, no. 1 (January 1951), p. 23.

39. Jean Williams, *The Lynching of Elizabeth Taylor,* Western Americana Series no. 11 (Santa Fe: Press of the Territorian, n.d.); Jeff O'Donnell, "Lynching at Spring Ranch," *OldWest,* Summer 1992, pp. 22–27; Harry E. Webb, "With a Noose around Her Neck," *Westerner,* 4, no. 3 (May–June 1972), pp. 14–15, 58; George W. Hufsmith, *The Wyoming Lynching of Cattle Kate, 1889* (Glendo, Wyo.: High Plains Press, 1993).

40. Robyn Wiegman, "The Anatomy of Lynching," *Journal of the History of Sexuality,* 3, no. 3, (January 1993), pp. 445–467.

41. Michael James Pfeifer found sadistic practices in western lynching, however; e-mail communication, August 1998.

42. Fritz, "Popular Sovereignty." For a vivid example, see Christine Granger Klatt, *They Died at Their Posts: A True Historical Account of Murder and Lynching on the Wisconsin Frontier 1881* (Menomonie, Wis.: Dunn County Historical Society, 1976, pamphlet).

43. Ethington, *The Public City,* pp. 145ff.; Burrows, *Vigilante!* pp. 146–147; Augusta B. Warren, "'Judge' Robert Thompson," *California Historical Society Quarterly,* 30, no. 3 (September 1951), pp. 239–241; Mervin B. Hogan, "Freemasonry and the Lynching at Cathage Jail," 1981 typescript, Utah State Library.

44. Smurr, "Afterthoughts," esp. p. 11; Chester D. Potter, "Reminiscences of the Socorro Vigilantes," ed. Paige W. Christiansen, New Mexico Historical Review, 40, no. 1 (January 1965), p. 23–54.

45. Johnson, "Vigilance and the Law."

46. Prassel, *Western Peace Officer,* pp. 105, 114–115, 123.

47. On Mexican folklore regarding the rangers, see Americo Paredes, *With a Pistol in His Hand: A Border Ballad and Its Hero* (Austin: University of Texas Press, 1958), pp. 24–25.

48. Quote from *Report of the Governor of Arizona Made to the Secretary of the Interior for the Year 1884,* p. 10; see also other such reports, passim, Arizona Historical Society, Tucson.

49. Arizona Revised Statutes 11–442 (1901).

50. Prassel, *Western Peace Officer,* p. 131.

51. Isaac Hill Bromley, *The Chinese Massacre at Rock Springs, Wyoming Territory, September 2, 1885* (Boston: Franklin Press, 1886), quoted in Richard Maxwell Brown, ed., *American Violence* (Englewood Cliffs, N.J.: Prentice Hall, 1970), pp. 92–96; Robert Edward Synne, *Reaction to the Chinese in the Pacific Northwest and British Columbia, 1850–1910* (New York: Arno Press, 1978); Michele Shover, "Fighting Back: The Chinese Influence on Chico Law and Politics, 1880–1886," *California History,* 74, no. 4 (Winter 1995–96), pp. 409–421.

52. Richard White, "Outlaw Gangs of the Middle Border: American Social Bandits," *Western Historical Quarterly,* 12 (October 1981), pp. 387–408.

53. Michael J. Pfeifer raised this question in an e-mail contribution to the H-West discussion group, referring to his 1998 dissertation at the University of Iowa,

a comparative study of lynching and criminal justice in Iowa, Wyoming, and Louisiana.

54. Quoted from a newspaper account by Dean Frank C. Lockwood and Captain Donald W. Page, *Tucson: The Old Pueblo* (Phoenix, privately printed, n.d., probably 1933), pp. 68–69.

55. Stewart E. Tolnay and E. M. Beck, *A Festival of Violence: An Analysis of Southern Lynchings, 1882–1930* (Urbana: University of Illinois Press, 1995), p. 86. Charles W. Mills has argued more abstractly and ahistorically for such a contract in *The Racial Contract* (Ithaca, N.Y.: Cornell University Press, 1997).

56. Larry D. Ball, *Desert Lawmen: The High Sheriffs of New Mexico and Arizona, 1846–1912* (Albuquerque: University of New Mexico Press, 1992), appendix B.

57. New Mexican Hispanic ranchers had owned millions of acres of rangeland, granted to them by the king of Spain in the eighteenth century and by the Mexican government after its independence. Held in a complex combination of individual and communal tenure, the land was available to the larger community for grazing and irrigation. After the United States seized the territory in 1848 and railroads made access practical in 1880, Anglo immigrant entrepreneurs, including the railroad developers and corporate ranchers, began buying, leasing, stealing, and swindling the land and scarce water resources away from their Hispanic owners, and then enclosing traditionally open fields with barbed wire. In 1888 José Herrera, a former resident of San Miguel County who had become a Knights of Labor railroad and mine union organizer, returned to his native land and organized Knights there; men recruited from among these members hid themselves under white hoods and began nighttime expeditions to cut and destroy the fences. Numbering in the hundreds, they operated in three large counties. They fought the railroads with both union and sabotage activities, destroying railroad ties and poles at a company storage yard and calling a strike of section hands and teamsters. In 1890 they brought commerce to a halt in the county seat, Las Vegas. The Gorras Blancas succeeded in defending much of the property of the Hispanic landowners.Michael Miller, "Las Gorras Blancas: Night Riders of Las Vegas," *El Palacio,* 91, no. 3 (1986), pp. 16–21; Robert W. Larson, "The White Caps of New Mexico: A Study of Ethnic Militancy in the Southwest," *Pacific Historical Review,* 44, no. 2 (1975), pp. 171–185; Andrew Bancroft Schlesinger, "Las Gorras Blancas, 1889–1891," *Journal of Mexican American History,* 1, no. 2 (1971), pp. 87–143; Jack Kutz, "Las Gorras Blancas: Vigilantes Storm into the Night," *New Mexico Magazine,* 70, no. 3 (March 1992), pp. 58–62.

58. Potter, "Reminiscences."

59. Frantz, "The Frontier Tradition," p. 147.

60. Dimsdale, *Vigilantes of Montana,* p. 104.

61. Ethington, *The Public City,* p. 94; Ryan, *Civic Wars,* p. 142. On this general

point, see White, "Outlaw Gangs," pp. 332–334; Brown, "American Vigilante Tradition," pp. 168, 192; Brown, *Strain of Violence,* passim.

62. Brown, "Western Violence"; Brown, *No Duty to Retreat: Violence and Values in American History and Society* (New York: Oxford University Press, 1991); Pfeifer, "Lynching and Criminal Justice," pp. 111ff; Burrows, *Vigilante!* pp. 146–147; Ethington, *The Public City,* pp. 145ff.; R. E. Mather and F. E. Boswell, *Vigilante Victims: Montana's 1864 Hanging Spree* (San Jose, Calif.: History West Publishing, 1991), p. 162.

63. Brown, *Strain of Violence,* pp. 193–195; Pfeifer, "Lynching and Criminal Justice," pp. 107–108.

64. Quoted in Boyden, "'The Best Men,'" pp. 10–11, 27, 38.

65. Prassel, *Western Peace Officers,* p. 134.

66. John W. Caughey, ed., *Their Majesties the Mob* (Chicago: University of Chicago Press, 1960), pp. 106–109.

67. Quotation from Carroll D. Wright, *Report of the Commissioner of Labor on the Labor Disturbances in Colorado,* Senate Executive Document no. 122, 58th Cong., 3d Sess., 1905, pp. 152–159. See also Elizabeth Jameson, *All That Glitters: Class, Conflict, and Community in Cripple Creek* (Urbana: University of Illinois Press, 1998).

68. Personal letter from Richard Maxwell Brown to author, November 14, 1998.

69. *Graham Guardian,* August 1907, souvenir edition, p. 29.

70. Sherrill Warford, *Verdict, Guilty as Charged: Leadville Justice, 1879–1886* (Leadville, Colo.: Silver City Printing, 1977); Lockwood and Page, *Tucson,* p. 68.

January 1905

1. The New York Foundling Hospital has a large scrapbook of several hundred clippings from all over the country, most of them not properly labeled as to their source and date, and all references to press coverage without citations come from this source.

2. *Phoenix Enterprise,* January 14, 1905.

3. Eugene S. Ives to Charles Miller, NYFH attorney in New York City, February 5, 1905, in NYFH Archives.

4. To my surprise, no Spanish-language newspaper in the United States or Sonora covered this trial. However, the holdings of such newspapers in the U.S. Southwest are incomplete in all the known library archives.

5. Ives to Miller, January 24, 1905; *Copper Era,* October 8, 1904.

6. Un-bylined reportage from the *Arizona Republican,* January 13, 1905, and the *Phoenix Enterprise,* January 12, 1905.

7. *Arizona Republican,* January 17, 1905.

8. *Arizona Republican,* January 14, 1905.

9. *Arizona Republican,* January 17, 1905.

10. Mrs. Samuel Abraham to "Mother," on Clifton Hotel stationery, n.d. but dated October 1904 by the sisters, NYFH Archives.

11. Mrs. F. H. Kane, Clifton, to "Mother Superior," NYFH, October 6, 1904, in NYFH Archives.

12. Mrs. A. Le. Burge, Morenci, to "Mother Superior," October 6, 1904, in Mount St. Vincent Archive.

13. Tuthill and two illegible names to NYFH, October 4, 1904, in NYFH Archives.

14. The author of this letter is unknown because it survives only in the form of a typed excerpt from it, dated November 4, 1904, in NYFH Archives.

15. *New York Daily News,* November 1, 1904; letters and miscellaneous clippings in NYFH Archives.

16. Eugene A. Philbin, attorney, to Sister Teresa Vincent, November 30, 1904, NYFH Archives; Ives to Thomas D. Bennett, December 9, 1904, Ives letterbook, vol. 3, Ives Papers, Special Collection, University of Arizona Library, Tucson; W. H. Brophy to Granjon, November 5, 1904, and again, n.d., Granjon Papers, Diocese of Tucson, Archives. In November Ives also proposed trying the case before a single judge, in which case, he later mused, the U.S. attorney might have had more weight, but Ives's proposal was not accepted; Ives to Miller, January 24, 1905, NYFH Archives.

17. Philbin to Hon. Alexander O. Brodie, January 3, 1905, and Brodie to Philbin, wire and letter, January 4, 1905, in NYFH Archives.

18. E.g., Miller to Sister Teresa, November 14, 1904, in NYFH Archives.

19. Granjon to Father Wynne, November 7, 1904, Granjon Papers; Ives to Miller, December 16, 1904, January 24, 1905, and February 5, 1905, in letterbook, vol. 3, Ives Papers.

20. Timmermans to Granjon, November 5, 1904, and November 6, 1904; Granjon to Father Wynne, November 7, 1904, and November 9, 1904. Granjon Papers.

21. He became president of the Bank of Bisbee in 1900 and was a director of the California Bank and First National Bank. On the Granjon-Brophy friendship, see their correspondence in Granjon Papers, Diocese of Tucson Archives, and Brophy Papers, folder 919, Special Collections, University of Arizona Library, Tucson. Also see Larry Schweikart, "Brophy vs. Douglas: A Case Study in Frontier Corporate Control," *Journal of the West,* 23, no. 1 (January 1984), pp. 49–55; Frank Cullen Brophy, *Though Far Away* (Glendale, Calif.: privately printed, 1940), p. 165. Brophy was the grandfather of Anthony Blake Brophy, one of two people ever to write about the Foundling affair.

22. Granjon-Brophy correspondence, Granjon Papers.

23. Undated report, "Morenci-Clifton Affair," in NYFH Archives. On Brophy's role in the Knights of Columbus, see Brophy, *Though Far Away,* p. 79. Brophy was also an associate and friend of Charles Mills, who, interestingly, traveled East in January and February, missing the whole trial; *Though Far Away,* p. 81.

24. Bennett and Williams, Law Offices in Bisbee, to Miller, November 18, 1904, in NYFH Archives; Brophy to Granjon, November 18, 1904, in Granjon Papers; notarized statement of sureties, November 28, 1904, approved December 5, 1904 by Judge P. C. Little, in Arizona Supreme Court case file, p. 30, ADLAPR.

25. E.g., Brophy to Darlington of New York City, October 31, 1904; E. V. Berrien of El Paso to Brophy, November 3, 1904, in Granjon Papers.

26. *Arizona Bulletin,* June 19, 1903.

27. Granjon to W. H. Brophy, December 22, 1904, in Granjon Papers; Ives to Miller, January 24, 1905, and February 5, 1905, in Ives Papers.

28. For example, clippings from *Houston Chronicle Herald,* October 8, 1904; *Syracuse Herald,* October 8, 1904; *Waco [Texas] Star,* October 9, 1904; *Dallas News,* October 9, 1904; and an unidentified paper in Sacramento, October 8, 1904.

29. Petitions for guardianship for the sixteen orphans then in Clifton are cases numbered 350 through 365, Probate Court 1904, recorded in Min. Book 4, pages 222, 223, 231, 240, 330–332. Copies are in File #19755, p. 49, U.S. Supreme Court, Appellate Case Files Box 3490, National Archives; Supreme Court case file, ADLAPR. The guardianship hearing was originally scheduled for November 2, and Bennett appeared on that date, asking for a two-week continuance, which was granted.

30. Quotation in letter from Bennett to Miller, November 18, 1904, NYFH Archives.

31. Ives to Miller, December 16, 1904, letterbook, p. 264, Ives Papers.

32. On the justices' personal histories, see John S. Goff, *The Supreme Court Justices, 1863–1912,* vol. 1, of *Arizona Territorial Officials* (Cave Creek, Ariz.: Black Mountain Press, 1975), pp. 124–129, 158–165, 170–174; Richard E. Sloan, *Memories of an Arizona Judge* (Stanford, Calif.: Stanford University Press, 1932), esp. chap. 24. See also summaries of their cases from *Arizona Reports,* including 6 Arizona 205 (1899); 8 Arizona 186 (1903); 8 Arizona 221 (1903); 8 Arizona 459 (1904); 9 Arizona 138 (1905); 9 Arizona 405 (1906); 10 Arizona 162 (1906); 12 Arizona 1 (1908); 12 Arizona 124 (1909); 12 Arizona 217 (1909); 13 Arizona 388 (1911). Doan's injunction was printed in the *Arizona Bulletin,* June 19, 1903.

33. Michael Grossberg, *Governing the Hearth: Law and the Family in Nineteenth-century America* (Chapel Hill: University of North Carolina Press, 1985), chap. 7.

34. It appears that the Foundling Hospital and the Sisters of Charity did consider pressing criminal charges; *New York Times,* October 13, 1904.

35. During the two years of litigation there continued to be confusion about how many orphans were in Arizona and in whose hands they were. The various

lists kept by the Foundling Hospital, the lawyers, and the court documents are inconsistent. As Ives sent these writs, he did not know who had Hannah Kane—the writ was made out to "John Doe"—or what exactly had happened to the children given to Dunagan in Morenci. But he had added James Edgerton, who had Ambrose Lamb, not mentioned in the original petitions for guardianship, so there were seventeen writs.

36. Ives to James Parks, January 2, 1905, in letterbook, pp. 318–320, Ives Papers.

37. Arizona Supreme Court case file, Phoenix; *Arizona Reports* Criminal No. 209, 79 Pac. 231.

38. *Copper Era,* December 29, 1904.

39. *New York Journal,* October 6, 1904.

40. Subpoena of Margaret Chacón and letter from Burtch, "To Whom It May Concern," January 6, 1904, in Arizona Supreme Court case file, Phoenix.

41. Some of my interpretation of the legal strategies in the case relies heavily on discussions with Professor Carol Sanger and Jane Larson; I am grateful to them, although they are of course not responsible for any errors I may have made.

42. *Arizona Republican,* January 14, 1905, and January 17, 1905.

43. Clipping from unidentified newspaper, bylined Phoenix, January 10, 1905, in NYFH Archives. Raymond A. Mulligan, "New York Foundlings at Clifton-Morenci: Social Justice in Arizona Territory," *Arizona and the West: A Quarterly Journal of History,* 6, no. 2 (Summer 1964), concurs on the relatively minor importance of religion, p. 117.

44. *Phoenix Enterprise,* January 18, 1905; *Arizona Republican,* January 18, 1905; the lawyers' summations were not taken down by the court recorder, so the newspaper reportage is all we have.

45. *Phoenix Enterprise,* January 18, 1905; *Arizona Republican,* January 18, 1905.

46. Grossberg, *Governing the Hearth,* p. 278; Linda Gordon, "Teenage Pregnancy and Out-of-Wedlock Birth," in Allan M. Brandt and Paul Rozin, eds., *Morality and Health* (Stanford, Calif.: Stanford University Press, 1997).

47. *Arizona Reports,* Criminal no. 209, 79 Pac. 231.

48. *Phoenix Enterprise,* January 21, 1905; *Arizona Republican,* January 22, 1905.

49. *Arizona Republican,* January 22, 1905.

50. Ives to Miller, January 24, 1905 in Ives Papers.

51. Ives to Miller, February 6, 1905; Ives to M. J. Nugent, February 12, 1905, and February 17, 1905, in Ives Papers. On Ives's legislative leadership, see Jay J. Wagoner, *Arizona Territory, 1863–1912: A Political History* (Tucson: University of Arizona Press, 1970), esp. chap. 19.

52. The justices who heard the case were David. J. Brewer, Henry B. Brown, William R. Day, Chief Justice Melville Weston Fuller, John Marshall Harlan, Oliver Wendell Holmes, Jr., Joseph McKenna, Rufus W. Peckham, and Edward Douglass White. Brewer did not participate in the decision.

53. Day wrote that Congress had legislated that the U.S. Supreme Court could accept writs of error and appeals from the territorial and state courts on questions of property worth more than $1,000 and of personal freedom, such as illegal imprisonment or wrongful detention. He cited federal precedents concerning custody fights between father and mother, and father and grandparents, which ruled that child custody was not a matter of forcible imprisonment. Habeas corpus enforcement in respect to "the detention of children by parents" had been based only on courts' opinions of children's best interests, not their legal right to relief from unlawful imprisonment. Avoiding any suggestion that the children were forcibly taken from one guardian by another, Day wrote, "Through imposition the child was placed in custody of those unfit to receive or maintain control over it, and, as above stated, came into the custody and possession of the respondent."

54. New York Foundling Hospital v. Gatti, *US Reports* 203 US 429, October Term, 1906, no. 21.

55. *New York Times,* February 3, 1905.

56. *Los Angeles Examiner,* October 5, 1904; *El Paso Herald,* October 8, 1904; *Sacramento Union,* October 8, 1904; *New York Evening World,* October 13, 1904.

57. *Los Angeles Examiner,* October 5, 1904.

58. Los Angeles, unidentified paper, October 5, 1904.

59. Unsigned letter to Denver Humane Society, June 16, 1904, and Fellows Jenkins of New York Society for the Prevention of Cruelty to Children to Sister Theresa Vincent, July 1, 1904, in NYFH Archives.

60. This letter was published in several papers including the *Arizona Bulletin,* October 21, 1904, and *Copper Era,* October 20, 1904.

61. *Copper Era,* October 8, 1904.

62. Others included "10 Babies Missing" and "Threatened Nurses: Federal Authority to be Invoked in Arizona Matter." *Buffalo Commercial,* October 10, 1904; *St. Paul Globe,* October 13, 1904; *Cincinnati Enquirer,* October 5, 1904.

63. These stories were published in, e.g., *Chattanooga Times; Springfield [Mass.] Union; Atchison [Kan.] Globe; Newark News; Ithaca Journal; Hartford Post; Salt Lake News* and *Tribune; Galveston Tribune; Tacoma News; San Antonio Express; Paterson [N.J.] Call; Chicago New World;* and many other papers. The *New York Daily News* claimed that its petition drive was responsible for this presidential order.

64. Unidentified clipping, October 13, 1904.

65. *Chicago New World,* October 15, 1904.

66. Quoted in *Buffalo Catholic Union and Times,* October 18, 1904.

67. Quoted in *New York Catholic News,* November 12, 1904.

68. *New York Daily News,* October 8, 1904. This failure to recognize the industrial Southwest appeared locally as well. For example, the only Mexican voice in the press coverage of the foundling affair was equally mistaken about Clifton-

Morenci: "The Mexicans . . . own their own farms, ranches, cattle, etc., and are better able financially to take care of themselves than the 'Americans of Arizona.'" *Tucson Citizen,* November 5, 1904.

69. *New Haven Union,* October 9, 1904.

70. *New York Times,* November 6, 1904, p. 6.

71. *Charities,* 12, no. 19 (February 4, 1905), p. 407.

72. Brophy, *Though Far Away,* pp. 135–137; Donald L. Kinzer, *An Episode in Anti-Catholicism: The American Protective Association* (Seattle: University of Washington Press, 1964), pp. 102–111.

73. Brophy, *Though Far Away,* p. 102.

74. Federal Writers Project, "White Slavery Is Attempted in Clifton-Morenci, in 1905," in Archives, ADLAPR. I have corrected spelling errors. Because of the spelling and writing, I believe the original to have been, not a transcribed interview by Kathlyn M. Lathrop, but a piece written by an informant of hers.

75. On Mandin, see *Bisbee Daily Review,* March 3, 1929; unidentified clipping from Tucson paper, March 4, 1929, Mandin file, Diocese of Tucson Archives; Frank Brophy wrote a defense of his father's role in the deportation in the *Arizona Republic,* July 24, 1955, p. 6.

76. Harold T. Shortridge, *Childhood Memories of a Fabulous Mining Camp, Clifton, Arizona, 1915–1926* (Cottonwood, Ariz.: Harold Shortridge, 1990), p. 27; Trace Baker, e-mail communication, July 25, 1998.

77. Members of prominent Morenci families and a renegade priest were arrested, but no one was brought to trial. Roberta Watt, "History of Morenci, Arizona" (Master's thesis, University of Arizona, 1956), pp. 114–115, from newspaper coverage.

78. E. J. Lehmann of Clifton to James H. McClintock, Phoenix, June 5, 1914, in NYFH Archives; *Los Angeles Examiner,* June 2, 1914, and June 3, 1914. This was the coverage of the grocer's original arrest and arraignment; I could not find coverage of the trial.

79. Lehmann to McClintock, June 5, 1914. Having only the name of the man, lacking even a date, I was unable to investigate this allegation further.

8. Family and Race

1. Robert Merton pointed out to me that the orphan story is a "strategic research site." Such a site, in the Merton's words, "exhibits the phenomena to be explained or interpreted to such advantage and in such accessible form that it enables the fruitful investigation of previously stubborn problems and the discovery of new problems for further inquiry." Robert K. Merton, "Multiple Discoveries as Strategic Research Site," pp. 371–382 in Merton, *The Sociology of Science,* ed. N. W. Storer (Chicago: University of Chicago Press, 1973); idem,

"Three Fragments from a Sociologist's Notebooks," *Annual Review of Sociology*, 13 (1987), pp. 10–11. Elsewhere he writes, "problems [can be] brought to life and developed by investigating them in situations that strategically exhibited the nature of the problem." Robert K. Merton, "Notes on Problem-Finding in Sociology," p. xxvii in Robert K. Merton, Leonard Broon, and Leonard Cottrell, Jr., eds., *Sociology Today: Problems and Prospects,* (New York: Basic Books, 1959). I am indebted also to personal communications with Robert Merton at the Russell Sage Foundation. Thanks also to Rosie Hunter for her confidence in the explanatory quality of the orphan story.

2. There would seem to be vast unexplored opportunities for psychological and psychoanalytic interpretations of the intersection of race and family.

3. Linda Gordon, *Heroes of Their Own Lives: The History and Politics of Family Violence* (New York: Viking/Penguin, 1988).

4. Alan Thornhill, Associated Press dispatch, May 28, 1997; Allison Kaplan Sommer in *Jerusalem Post,* August 27, 1997; Nuala O'Faolain in *Irish Times,* June 28, 1997; and many other articles from NEXIS.

5. *Maquiladoras* are export manufacturing plants, typically assembling garments and electronics, situated on the Mexican side of the U.S.-Mexican border, and primarily employing women. Multinational capital is drawn to them because of the low wages, freedom from health and safety regulations, and tax incentives provided by the government.

6. Gloria Anzaldúa, *Borderlands/La Frontera: The New Mestiza* (San Francisco: Aunt Lute Books, 1987), p. 3.

Epilogue

1. Thanks to Ren Farley for computing this for me from the 1990 census.

2. A history of PD labor conflict since 1903 can be found in James W. Byrkit, *Forging the Copper Collar: Arizona's Labor-Management War of 1901–21* (Tucson: University of Arizona Press, 1982); James R. Kluger, *The Clifton/Morenci Strike: Labor Difficulty in Arizona, 1915–16* (Tucson: University of Arizona Press, 1970); D. H. Dinwoodie, "The Rise of the Mine-Mill Union in Southwestern Copper," pp. 46–56 in James C. Foster, ed., *American Labor in the Southwest: The First One Hundred Years* (Tucson: University of Arizona Press, 1982); Mario T. García, "Border Proletarians: Mexican-Americans and the International Union of Mine, Mill, and Smelter Workers, 1939–1946," in Robert Asher and Charles Stephenson, eds. *Labor Divided: Race and Ethnicity in United States Labor Struggles, 1835–1960* (Albany: SUNY Press, 1990), pp. 83–104; "Los Mineros," PBS *American Experience* video, produced and directed by Hector Galan, 1990.

3. The Congress of Industrial Organizations (CIO), inaugurated in 1936, was a federation of industrial trade unions established in response to the failure of

the American Federation of Labor (AFL) to organize workers in mass production industries.

4. Employers are legally permitted to hire permanent replacements when struck by workers over economic issues; they are not permitted to do so when a strike focuses on unfair labor practices. The union's complaints about unfair labor practices—that PD had illegally fired union leaders and was refusing to bargain in good faith—were dismissed by the Phoenix NLRB office, headed by an antiunion Reagan appointee. It was the PD 1983 strike, not the better-known air traffic controllers' strike, that established the precedent for massive permanent replacement of strikers; Reagan could fire the controllers because they were public employees engaging in an illegal strike, but PD's victory suggested that any employer could do it. For recent PD behavior toward labor, see Ruth A. Bandzak, "A Productive Systems Analysis of the 1983 Phelps Dodge Strike," *Journal of Economic Issues,* 25, no. 4 (December 1991), pp. 1105–1125, and idem, "The Strike as Management Strategy," *Journal of Economic Issues,* 36, no. 2 (June 1992), pp. 645–659. On the 1983 strike, the best accounts are Jonathan D. Rosenblum's *Copper Crucible: How the Arizona Miners' Strike of 1983 Recast Labor-Management Relations in America* (Ithaca, N.Y.: ILR Press, 1995), and Barbara Kingsolver's *Holding the Line: Women in the Great Arizona Mine Strike of 1983* (Ithaca, N.Y.: ILR Press, 1989).

5. Rosenblum, *Copper Crucible,* p. 120. The "gamma goats" were six-wheel amphibious carriers (odd, considering how far Clifton-Morenci was from any significant body of water); Hueys are combat helicopters.

6. Ibid., pp. 150, 242–243 n.

Acknowledgments

The help I needed in writing this book was even greater than in my previous work. Entering areas in which I had little expertise when I began—southwestern history, the history of mining, Mexican and Mexican American history—I had to rely on the kindness of friends and strangers.

My gratitude goes above all to current and former residents of Clifton-Morenci. Charlie Spezia, with his passion for history, introduced me to many people and to the materials of the Greenlee County Historical Society. His uncle Al Fernandez has become a living historian of Clifton-Morenci and made me the beneficiary of his compendious memory and writings. As he himself wrote, "Abiding by the consensus, that after a senior citizen has lived most of his life in a community, the people of that community expect that person to serve the role of a historian, regardless. In my case I believe that is the main reason that our people have picked on me to serve in that capacity."

Numerous others from or connected to Clifton-Morenci talked with me, answered my questions, and gave me research tips. For help great and small, I would like to thank Martha Armbrust, Father Joe Baker, Joe C. Barriga, John Chacón, Mary García Chacón, Patricio Chacón, Mike Clover, Helen Cooper, Jackie Cooper, Carmina García, Willie García, Margarita Hinojos, Barbara Kingsolver, Margaret Laren, Patricia Preciado Martin, Nellie Marquez, Father Fred McAninch, Mary Ann McKinney, Mary Milo, Ernesto T. Ochoa, Anna O'Leary, Andrés

Padilla, Elsie R. Patton, Matthew "Pat" Scanlon, Louise Shirley, Jesse Snyder, George Sturges, and Evelyn Vozza.

From the Sisters of Charity of New York, Sister Marilda Joseph Aiello not only guided me through the archives at the Foundling Hospital but also found some valuable material for me through her own archival work, and at the College of Mt. Saint Vincent, Sisters Rita King and Ann Courtenay helped me find what I needed, and I am most appreciative.

I would like to thank archivists Dan Brosnan of the Diocese of Tucson Archives, Rose Byrne and Susan Sheehan of the Arizona Historical Society, Christine Marín of the Chicano Archives at Arizona State University, Peter Steere of the University of Arizona Library Special Collections, and Nancy Sawyer and Melanie Sturgeon of the State of Arizona Department of Library, Archives, and Public Records, who offered assistance of various kinds. Chris Marín then attempted to rescue some invaluable union and Alianza archives that were about to be dumped and, while she did not succeed in bringing them under her protection, at least prevented their immediate destruction.

The University of Wisconsin Graduate School, the Vilas Trust at the University of Wisconsin, and the Russell Sage Foundation offered me research funding and leave from teaching, and this book could not have been written without that help. Russell Sage gave me not just financial support but also a near ideal working environment for ten months; I am particularly grateful to Sara Beckman, Jamie Gray, Auristela Martinez, Madge Spitaleri, Nicole Thompson, and Kerry Woodward for making my time there productive, but a full list of my thanks would have to include the other visiting scholars and the entire staff.

My longest list of thank-yous goes to other scholars who not only allowed me to enter "their" territories but helped me do it. Tom Archdeacon, Ellen Baker, Katie Benton, Laird Boswell, Bruce Boyden, Jeanne Boydston, Anthony Blake Brophy, Richard Maxwell Brown, Caroline Bynum, Suzanne Desan, Colleen Dunlavy, Dionne Espinoza, Richard R. Fernández, Maureen Fitzgerald, Deena González, Ramón Gutiérrez, Vicki Hattam, Josiah Heyman, A. Yvette Huginnie, Betsy Jameson, Steve Kantrowitz, Heinz Klug, Jane Larson, Judith Walzer Leavitt, Yolanda Chávez Leyva, Florencia Mallon, Christine Marín, Ben Marquez, Elaine May, Laurie Mercier, David Montgomery, David Myers, John Michael Nieto-Phillips, Robert Orsi, Peggy Pascoe, Lisandro Perez, Jon Rosenblum, Mary Rothschild, Rubén Rumbaut, Carol Sanger, Francisco Scarano, Gay Seidman, Steve Stern, Teresa T. Thomas, and Sam Truett gave me materials, opinions, time, and expertise with a generosity that made me feel part of a true community of scholars. My gratitude in particular goes to Vicki Ruiz, Raquel Rubio-Goldsmith, and Anna O'Leary who not only shared with me their extensive knowledge but read and gave me comments on the whole manuscript.

Dick Cluster and Nancy Plankey Videla did some translations from the Spanish when I wanted more precision than my own abilities allowed. Ellen Baker, Dorothea Browder, Laura McEnaney, Julianne Unsel, Susan Wirka, and Kerry Woodward provided at various times superb research assistance.

This being an undertaking far different from my previous work, and with much of the work done during periods of stress, I was unusually dependent on the encouragement of friends, family, and colleagues. For this I'd like particularly to thank Rosalyn Fraad Baxandall, Suzanne Desan, Elizabeth Ewen, Stuart Ewen, Barbara Forrest, Ed Friedman, Susan Stanford Friedman, Allen Hunter, Rosie Hunter, Linda Kerber, Heinz Klug, Marion Kozak, Judith Walzer Leavitt, Lewis Leavitt, and Gay Seidman. A special thanks to my agent, Charlotte Sheedy, whose appreciation for this book spurred me on, and to my editor, Joyce Seltzer, who gave me that greatest of gifts, smart, honest, and masterful editing.

Index